Invitation to Critical Thinking

5

FIFTH
EDITION

Invitation to Critical Thinking

5

FIFTH EDITION

JOEL RUDINOW

SANTA ROSA JUNIOR COLLEGE

VINCENT E. BARRY

BAKERSFIELD COLLEGE

THOMSON
™
WADSWORTH

Australia • Canada • Mexico • Singapore • Spain
United Kingdom • United States

THOMSON

WADSWORTH

Publisher: Holly J. Allen
Acquisition Editor: Steve Wainwright
Assistant Editors: Lee McCracken, Anna Lustig
Editorial Assistant: Melanie Cheng
Marketing Manager: Worth Hawes
Marketing Assistant: Kristi Bostock
Print/Media Buyer: Rebecca Cross

Permissions Editor: Bob Kauser
Technical Project Manager: Susan DeVanna
Production Service: Graphic World Publishing Services
Cover Design: Linda Beaupre
Cover Printer: Phoenix Color Corporation
Compositor: Graphic World, Inc.
Printer: Maple-Vail, Binghamton

Printed in the United States of America
1   2   3   4   5   6   05   04   03   02

For more information about our products, contact us at:
Thomson Learning Academic Resource Center
1-800-423-0563

For permission to use material from this text, contact us by:
Phone: 1-800-730-2214   **Fax:** 1-800-730-2215
Web: http://www.thomsonrights.com

Wadsworth/Thomson Learning
10 Davis Drive
Belmont, CA 94002-3098
USA

Library of Congress Control Number: 2003103364

ISBN 0-15-505883-5

Asia
Thomson Learning
5 Shenton Way #01-01
UIC Building
Singapore 068808

Australia
Nelson Thomson Learning
102 Dodds Street
South Melbourne, Victoria 3205
Australia

Canada
Nelson Thomson Learning
1120 Birchmount Road
Toronto, Ontario M1K 5G4
Canada

Europe/Middle East/Africa
Thomson Learning
High Holborn House
50/51 Bedford Row
London WC1R 4LR
United Kingdom

Latin America
Thomson Learning
Seneca, 53
Colonia Polanco
11560 Mexico D.F.
Mexico

Spain
Paraninfo Thomson Learning
Calle/Magallanes, 25
28015 Madrid, Spain

PREFACE

Reflecting on the occasion of this fifth edition of *Invitation to Critical Thinking*, we find it rather sobering to realize that this textbook is as old as many of the students who read it. Much has changed in the world since this book was first published, and so the book itself has had to change to remain in touch with the world inhabited by its students. Many of the examples we used in earlier editions have disappeared from common shared awareness down the memory hole into the dustbin of history. And yet the need in this generation for basic critical thinking skills remains as deep and urgent as ever. And so, although we have had to overhaul the book's contents considerably, the instructional agenda remains the same. We continue to focus on the recognition, analysis, evaluation, and composition of arguments as discursive tools of rational persuasion. New to the fifth edition are:

- A new treatment of the "intellectual virtues" as a basis for understanding the nature and goals of critical thinking in Chapter 1
- A simplified and more "intuitive" argument casting system in Chapter 4
- A new chapter on paraphrasing—including coverage of extended arguments (Chapter 5)
- Expanded coverage of the square of opposition, immediate inferences, mood and figure, and translation into standard form in categorical logic (Chapter 6)
- Streamlined and condensed coverage of the informal fallacies (Chapters 11 and 12)

Meanwhile, the technology of education has been revolutionized in the Information Age. The lecture/discussion approach typical of classroom management a generation ago now seems increasingly quaint and primitive by comparison with the 24-hour global virtual classroom imagined in so many of the educational planning documents we are seeing today. The pace of change is all but overwhelming. One thing it has forced us to do, as authors of a textbook, is to think rather deeply about how we teach critical thinking and about *how* we *might* teach critical thinking. And this has in turn brought two perennial challenges into sharp focus. The first challenge shows up in the observation—confirmed in our classroom experience over and over for years—that the critical thinking course seems generally to work best for those students who already think critically. Such students tend to develop and flourish in the course and seem to get a great deal out of it. Conversely, the students who are most desperately in need of instruction in critical thinking tend to find the text and the course so profoundly baffling and disorienting that they easily give up on it before they show or see any progress. Yet these are the students one most wants to reach. A second, and related, challenge has to do with integrating two essential areas of instructional emphasis that nevertheless seem inevitably at odds with each other. On the one hand, there is a need to break the complexity of critical thinking down into manageable chunks and provide the kind of exercise that moves the student in an orderly way through the material, building skill from the ground up toward greater and more advanced mastery. This is especially important for the student who finds the material most challenging and unfamiliar. On the other hand, there is the need to ground and motivate study by demonstrating the relevance of the material in "real world" applications, where, unfortunately, one never finds it broken down according to the instructional agenda of the course, however that agenda has been laid out.

We've taken several bold and, we hope, effective steps to adapt *Invitation to Critical Thinking* to these challenges in these times. First of all, on the exercise front: When you spot this icon ᴡᴡᴡ in the text, just point your Web browser to http://philosophy.wadsworth.com, and find the companion Web site and appropriate chapter link. There you will find:

- Summaries and study guides—overviews outlining learning objectives for each chapter—are provided online.
- PowerPoint lecture notes are provided for both instructors and students.
- Glossaries are reinforced with online flashcards.
- Short discussion exercises—supported by an electronic bulletin board for discussion online—make the text more interactive, engaging, and Socratic in its presentation of conceptual material.
- An electronic bulletin board also supports critique and peer review of writing assignments.
- Exercises in the text are reinforced with interactive online tutorial support.
- Online quizzes with instant scoring and feedback reinforce student learning.
- An online grade book supports both course management and distance learning.
- Collegial consultation among instructors is supported in an online "staff lounge."

On the real world applications front, we have introduced an integrated series of Term Project assignments, distributed chapter by chapter throughout the text. Each Term Project assignment, indicated by this icon ⚲ᴊ, applies the skill set covered in a particular chapter to a sustained project in which the student applies what she is learning to the study of a real world problem or issue. With the support of InfoTrac College Edition, the series of Term Project exercises walks the student through the steps of selecting, defining, analyzing, and researching an issue; identifying, analyzing, and evaluating arguments; and, finally, designing and composing her own argument in essay form. All the material from the Web site is also available in a course management platform (either WebCT or Blackboard) that can be bundled for free with the textbook.

An integrated instructional support package of this size, complexity, and flexibility owes a great deal to a great many people. We wish to acknowledge especially the contributions of Sean Martin, who wrote the Instructor's Manual for the fifth edition; Michael Donovan, whose work on the fourth edition's prototype of our web tutorial is still visible in our current version; Judith Hawkins, Susan DeVanna, and Stan Loll for all their work in developing the Web ancillary materials for the fifth edition; Carol O'Connell at Graphic World Publishing Services, for her careful and cheerful attention to detail throughout the copyediting and production processes; our new editor, Steve Wainwright, and his staff at Wadsworth for their support and enthusiasm; and the six reviewers of the fifth edition, whose critiques and suggestions were most helpful and illuminating: Hollace Graff, Oakton Community College; Keith Allen Korcz, University of Louisiana at Lafayette; Theodora Lodato, Harris-Stowe State College; Randy Lunsford, Muskegon Community College; Jamie Phillips, Clarion University of Pennsylvania; and Bruce B. Suttle, Parkland College.

Our work as educators would not be possible without the support and encouragement of our colleagues. I would especially like to express my gratitude to the members of the Department of Philosophy, to Bill Stone in the CATE lab, and to the rest of the faculty and staff at Santa Rosa Junior College. What a great place to work! I dedicate this book to my parents, Mattie and Jack, and to my daughter Lindsey.

JOEL RUDINOW

CONTENTS

UNIT TWO: ARGUMENT   71

Chapter 3: Argument Identification   73

Chapter 4: Argument Analysis I: Representing Argument Structure   93

Chapter 5: Argument Analysis II: Paraphrasing Arguments   123

UNIT THREE: DEDUCTIVE REASONING   143

Chapter 6: Evaluating Deductive Arguments I: Categorical Logic   145

Chapter 7: Evaluating Deductive Arguments II: Truth Functional Logic   185

UNIT FOUR: INDUCTIVE REASONING   209

Chapter 8: Evaluating Inductive Arguments I: Generalization and Analogy   211

Chapter 9: Evaluating Inductive Arguments II: Hypothetical Reasoning and Burden of Proof   235

Chapter 12: Informal Fallacies II: Assumptions and Induction   311

Chapter 13: Making Your Case: Argumentative Composition   335

UNIT ONE
The Basics

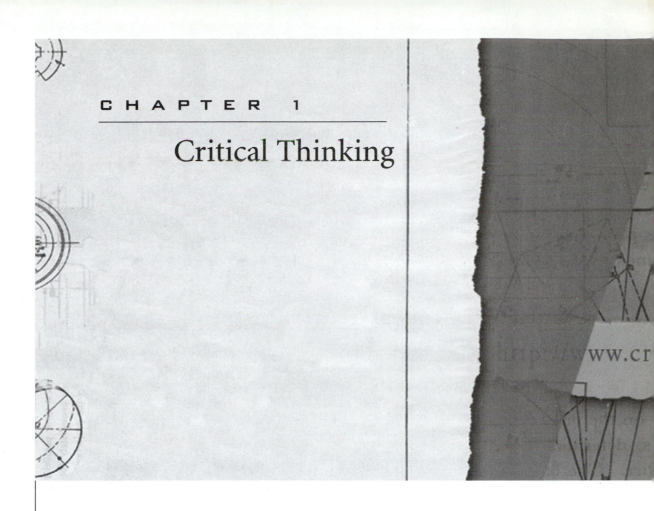

CHAPTER 1

Critical Thinking

In early spring 1997 Marshall Herff Applewhite, leader of the "Heaven's Gate" doomsday cult, led 38 of his followers in a mass suicide. The victims left videotaped statements explaining their actions and beliefs. According to Applewhite and his followers, the appearance of the Hale-Bopp comet was a divine sign of salvation, and a spaceship cruising along in the tail of the comet was waiting to pick them up and take them to the "Next Level" beyond this mortal human world. This story immediately became global front-page news. Here in the United States, the three major news weeklies, *Time, Newsweek,* and *U.S. News & World Report,* all ran extensive cover stories, complete with elaborate sidebars on UFOs, the Internet, comets, and cults. The *Time* and *Newsweek* covers were nearly identical, with captions that read: "Inside the Web of Death" and "'Follow Me': Inside the Heaven's Gate Mass Suicide."

"Believe me, you're just thinking about it too much."

THE IMPORTANCE OF CRITICAL THINKING

These headlines seemed to acknowledge how bizarre the whole episode looked from the outside, while appealing to the morbid curiosity of many readers who wanted a closer look, an inside perspective, a glimpse into what makes such people tick. The *U.S. News & World Report* cover caption, though aimed in the same general direction, had a slightly different spin: "Lost Souls: How Reasonable People Can Hold Unreasonable Beliefs."

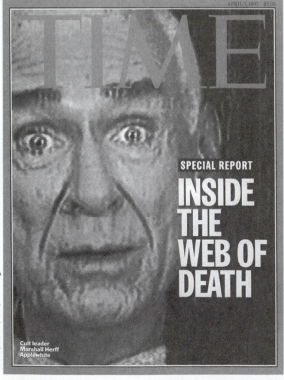

This poses an interesting question: "How is it that reasonable people come to hold unreasonable beliefs?" Notice how this question involves a special kind of *assumption* that in Critical Thinking we call a *presupposition.* In order to entertain this question in the context of this story, you must first assume that at least some of the 39 members of the Heaven's Gate cult were "reasonable people," and you must also assume that at least some of the beliefs that led them to commit mass suicide were "unreasonable beliefs." Do you think these are "reasonable assumptions"? We'll come back to this shortly.

> *Note to the reader:* You may be wondering why we keep italicizing certain words (like *reasonable* and *assumptions*). These are words that we think we should *define* clearly so as to avoid misunderstandings. We'll come back to this shortly.

Whether or not the members of Heaven's Gate were "reasonable people," and however "reasonable" or "unreasonable" their beliefs may have been, it certainly seems reasonable to suppose that from time to time perfectly "reasonable" people come to hold "unreasonable" beliefs about one thing or another. And this is a pretty good point at which to begin talking about Critical Thinking. The Heaven's Gate mass suicide is just an extreme case of a common tendency to be misled against our better judgment. You probably know people you consider "reasonable" who nevertheless hold or have held beliefs that you consider "not entirely reasonable" and maybe even downright "unreasonable," beliefs that maybe got them into all kinds of avoidable trouble. How does this happen? Why

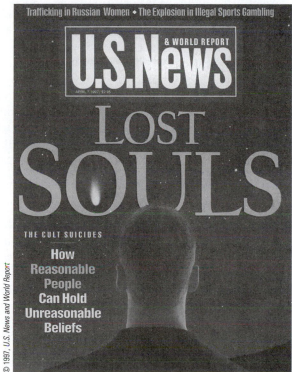

is it that so many otherwise intelligent people get taken in by hucksters and confidence artists when just a little Critical Thinking would protect them from exploitation?

One answer is that there are so many interfering urges, pressures, inducements, and distractions that make it hard, even for reasonable people, to reliably differentiate between reasonable and unreasonable beliefs and courses of action. There are, in other words, many obstacles to Critical Thinking. We'll come back to this topic later in this chapter. But this also shows why Critical Thinking is so important for us each as individuals. Critical Thinking is empowering and can improve a person's chances of success in a career, as a consumer, and so on throughout the wide variety of social roles each of us may be destined to play. This is because Critical Thinking is essential to something even more fundamental and basic: *personal autonomy*. *Autonomy* comes from the Greek words *auto* for "self" and *nomos* for "regulation." An autonomous person is self-regulating or self-directing. Autonomy is empowering because it makes one less dependent upon—and so also less vulnerable to—the dictates, directions, and influence of others. A person who can make up her own mind doesn't *need* others to tell her what to think or do, and so is less likely to be dominated by others. But personal power can easily become perverted. So we should be wary of the similar-*sounding* idea that Critical Thinking might enable us to gain power *over* others. We have seen some actual cases where people have tried to use some of the things they've learned in Critical Thinking to humiliate, control, or otherwise take advantage of people. We would say simply that to apply Critical Thinking toward such goals is to distort, misunderstand, and misuse it. Critical Thinking should be thought of as liberating, not as a "power trip."

As important as Critical Thinking is to our individual well-being, it is equally important to us collectively as a society. As citizens of a democratic republic we enjoy a process of government that is now almost universally recognized as ideal and enlightened in its conception—where political power is held collectively by the entire citizenry and distributed equally among them, according to the "one person/one vote" principle. But Critical Thinking is essential for such a system to function properly, as one of the chief architects of the system, Thomas Jefferson, pointed out when he said,

> In a republican nation, whose citizens are to be led by reason and persuasion and not by force, the art of reasoning becomes of the first importance.[1]

Sadly, Critical Thinking is not as much in evidence in American political life as Jefferson would have hoped. For example, consider California's notorious turn-of-the-millennium energy crisis. Most Californians were cheerfully oblivious to looming problems in the state's electricity industry until the summer of 2000, when the electricity rates in the San Diego area abruptly tripled. All of a sudden, small businesses were being forced into bankruptcy and ratepayers were hysterically calling for boycotts and rate strikes. Elsewhere in the state, business carried on more or less as usual well into the fall, but then in January 2001, again seemingly without warning, the managers of the state's power grid began to announce a series of power shortages and "rolling blackouts" throughout the state. Within weeks, two of the state's largest electric utility companies, Southern California Edison and Pacific Gas and Electric Company, announced that they were on the brink of bankruptcy. We thought these events presented an opportunity to demonstrate the importance as well as some of the difficulty of thinking critically. And so, as this news was breaking, we challenged our students to research the unfolding crisis and invited them to venture opinions about what was going on and what ought to be done about it. We pointed out to our students that each of them was directly affected by the crisis, that there was no shortage of information about it available to them, and that as consumers and citizens they each had both a stake and a voice in the process.

The responses to this challenge, especially in the early stages of the exercise, were telling. Quite a few members of the class were ready to venture opinions right away. Someone would say something like "Well, I think the problem is that we Californians are just wasting a lot of electricity." Or "Well, I think the problem is that the environmentalists have kept any new power plants from being built while the population and the high-tech economy have grown so fast that demand for electricity is through the roof!" Or "Well, I think the problem is that the big energy corporations are manipulating the markets so as to drive up prices and extort rate hikes." Things got interesting when we challenged them—or when they challenged each other—to defend any of these ideas. Where did they get these ideas? How did they know that these things were true? Or if they didn't "know" that these things were true, what reason did they have for thinking these things were true? Were they just speculating? These questions led to general conversational chaos in the class, because for one thing very little actual research had gone into the formation of any of these opinions in the first place. Most of these ideas were in circulation in "the media," but did that make any of them more reasonable than the others? And how reliable were the sources? As Californians, most of us at this stage, students and instructors alike, were caught flat-footed. We were all pretty sadly ignorant of the actual nature and origins of California's energy crisis when it broke into the news, though we might not have wished to admit it.

As we began to look more deeply into the matter, the class soon learned that in 1996 California had enacted legislation that "deregulated" the electric power industry. What did this mean: "deregulate"? Did this mean that there were *no regulations at all* governing the electric power industry anymore? Well, what did it say in the legislation? At this stage, puzzlement and curiosity began to slide down through disappointment toward despair. Members of the class began to throw up their hands and show other signs of being ready to give up, and this *increased* when we placed a copy of the legislation[2] on reserve in the campus library. Some students wondered in exasperation, "Do you really expect us to go and read a 70-page government document, which refers in its opening paragraph to some 20 or so distinct sections of the state Civil Code, the Commercial Code, the Government Code, and the Public Utilities Code, whatever *they* might be?" We suggested that there might perhaps be someone out there who could digest the legislation for us and explain it to us. Let's see what there is on the subject in the library, or on the Internet. After a morning browsing the Internet and peeking into the periodical literature on the crisis, class morale was falling somewhere between cynical apathy and frustration bordering on rage. Here are some typical student reactions,

> "All we're finding here is a lot of controversy among 'the experts' whose theories and analyses conflict."
>
> "And they speak in acronyms and technical terms that no regular person can begin to understand."
>
> "And how can you trust any of these sources anyway?! Everybody's got an axe to grind. They could *all* be lying!"
>
> "If you want us to come up with answers to the energy crisis, maybe you could show us a better way of going about it, because things aren't getting any clearer. They are getting more confusing. This is like thinking in reverse. If we keep up like this, how will we *ever* figure out what is really going on?"

This was an example of what we teachers like to call a "teachable moment" (a moment when there's enough suspense and concentrated frustration built up in the classroom that people are ready to *learn something!*). Here was a room full of typical young adult citizens of the state of California, suddenly realizing that the state's electric energy industry had been operating for almost five years under a new set of complex and mysterious rules enacted by their own elected representatives in state government. And at the same time they were discouraged because they could make neither head nor tail of the public controversy surrounding either the legislation or the energy crisis. Can you see how perfectly this exemplifies Jefferson's point about democracy and the "art of reasoning"?

EXERCISE 1.1 | **Topic for Class Discussion**

Explain how Jefferson's point about democracy and the "art of reasoning" is reflected in the classroom experience reported above.

_____

_____

_____

_____

_____

_____

_____

o

WHAT IS CRITICAL THINKING?

Jefferson spoke of the "art of reasoning." That's what we mean by "Critical Thinking." You're about to embark upon a course of study in Critical Thinking, and you've got a right to know what you're getting into. *We think of Critical Thinking as a set of conceptual tools with associated intellectual skills and strategies useful for making reasonable decisions about what to do or believe.* That fancy-sounding formulation can be condensed to this: Critical Thinking is using reason to make up your mind. There are those words *reason* and *reasonable* again. Maybe now would be a good time for us to define them.

The word *reasonable* derives from the word *reason*. So let's start there. *Reason* comes from the Latin word *ratio* for "calculation" or "computation," a highly disciplined use of intelligence for problem solving. *We think of reason as the capacity to use disciplined intelligence to solve problems.* On this basis it is fairly easy to explain the meaning of other words in the same family. For example, "reasoning" can be understood as using disciplined intelligence to solve a problem or determine a course of action. A "reasonable decision" can be understood as one arrived at through the use of reason. A "reasonable person" can be understood as one who (at least ordinarily) uses reason to decide what to do or believe. An "unreasonable person" can be understood as one who is failing or refusing to use reason in deciding what to do or believe. And so on.

IS CRITICAL THINKING NEGATIVE? Lots of people seem to think that the word *critical* involves negativity almost by definition; criticism is fault-finding, a critic is a fault-finder, and so anything with the word *critical* in its name must be similarly concerned with finding faults and weaknesses and other negative things. This myth comes primarily, we think, out of a misunderstanding of the word *critical*. The word *critical* and its cognates, *criticism, critic, critique,* and so on, all derive from the Greek word *kritikos* for "discernment" or "the ability to judge," which in turn derives from the Greek word *krinein* for "decision making." This is the way we prefer to understand Critical Thinking. It is concerned with decision making—period. So, yes, it is interested in finding faults and in negative considerations, but not *only* in finding faults and other negatives. It is equally concerned with recognizing strengths and other positives. Critical Thinking is interested in the "pros" as well as the "cons."

EXERCISE 1.2 | **Topic for Class Discussion**

Remember that question we started out with about the members of Heaven's Gate: "How is it that reasonable people come to hold unreasonable beliefs?" Now how would you answer the question we posed in response to it: "Is it reasonable to assume that at least some members of the Heaven's Gate cult were reasonable people and also that at least some of their beliefs were unreasonable beliefs?" We'll come back to this shortly.

Reason is a pretty special and important capacity. Some have held that it is a distinctively human capacity. An old tradition defines humans as the "rational animals," the *only* species with the capacity to reason. Other animals have intelligence. But, according to this particular tradition, *only humans cultivate and develop their intelligence through discipline so as to solve problems.* On the other hand, there are others who disagree with this and think that there is evidence of reason and reasoning in the behavior of at least some *non*human animals, too.

EXERCISE 1.3 | **Topic for Class Discussion**

What do you think about this? Do you think reason is a distinctively human capacity or not? Why? Or why not?

But whether reason is a distinctively human characteristic or not, whether it is *confined to* the human species or not, it has certainly proven to be an important species survival trait in humans. Without it we humans would be severely handicapped in the struggle for survival. It is therefore easy to see how we come to recognize reason as an *essentially human* trait, one that pertains to human beings *as* human beings. This does not mean that all members of the species are equally reasonable, or equally reasonable at all times. What it does mean is that we *presume* that all members of the human species have reason—in other words, that they all have the capacity to cultivate and develop their intelligence through discipline so as to solve problems. We do not restrict this presumption to exclude any category of human beings. This presumption is not gender specific. It is not restricted by age, race, or ethnicity. It applies to all human beings as human beings.

EXERCISE 1.4 | **Topic for Class Discussion**

What do you think about this? Do you think reason is an "essentially human" trait or not? Why? Or why not?

DISCIPLINE In our definition of *reason,* the word *disciplined* is very important. So let us take a moment to reflect on the meaning of *discipline.* There are two things we think we should point out about this crucial concept right at the start. First, any discipline will have rules, or at least regularities of some kind. To master any discipline you need to learn the rules and regularities. And so secondly, discipline takes practice. Music is a good example of a "discipline." To become a musician you need to learn some rules and regularities by practicing. The same is true of Critical Thinking. Some people worry that entering into a "discipline" with all its "rules and regularities" means submitting to some form of enforced conformity to some rigid orthodoxy—in other words, that all "critical thinkers" must come out thinking in exactly the same way. This is worrisome because thinking is one way we become and manifest and express ourselves as individuals. But if we think for a minute about the comparison to music as a discipline, this worry can be dismissed. All the great musicians throughout history have been highly distinctive individuals. The same is true of writing as a discipline. Practice leads to greater mastery, which opens up many avenues for individual self-expression. And so too with thinking.

IS THERE ROOM FOR CREATIVITY?   When we said that Critical Thinking involves discipline, we meant that it involves mastering rules and regularities and requires practice. Sometimes people jump from this to the conclusion that Critical Thinking does not involve or encourage creativity. We think this stems in part from the (mistaken) idea that creativity is essentially a matter of *breaking* the rules. On the contrary, it often turns out that creativity is very much involved in *following* the rules. Sometimes it takes an original creative insight to know just how to interpret and apply the rules in a given situation. Such situations are often described as calling for "judgment" or "discretion." We hope and anticipate that you'll recognize examples of this sort of situation from time to time as you work your way through this book.

EXERCISE 1.5 | **Freewrite**

Freewriting, like brainstorming, is a technique for liberating creative mental energy. When you freewrite, you don't worry about parallel sentence structure, split infinitives, sentence fragments, or any of the other editorial problems your instructors will nag you about when you're working on an essay. When you freewrite you don't worry about anything—even spelling—that might interfere with simply getting your ideas flowing and on paper.

OK. So here's the exercise: Now that you've learned how we define Critical Thinking, what do you think you can gain from studying it? Take out a fresh sheet of paper and freewrite for 15 minutes on the topic of what you hope and expect to get out of a course in Critical Thinking. Don't plan what you're going to write. Just start writing. And don't stop to reconsider, refine, edit, or correct what you've written. Just keep writing. If you can't think of a good way to begin, just complete this sentence: "What I hope and expect to get out of a course in Critical Thinking is . . . "

When you have written for 15 minutes, finish your thought and save what you've written. We'll be coming back to this. Ready? Go.

OBSTACLES TO CRITICAL THINKING

Naturally, what people actually gain from the study of Critical Thinking varies widely, depending on many variable factors. What we *hope* our students will come away with in the end boils down to this: Critical Thinking is a natural development of your reasoning capacity with many useful applications in your daily life. We *hope* that everyone who studies the concepts, skills, and strategies that we cover in this book will come to understand them as natural refinements of "common sense." And we expect that anyone who arrives at this understanding will find many occasions to apply Critical Thinking in his or her daily life.

Now this may sound very nice, but it does give rise to a bit of a puzzle: We are saying that Critical Thinking is natural for us as human beings. However, when

we pay attention to the way people actually think and behave, the impression we get is that a lot of pretty "normal" people don't think critically very much at all, ever. Or they think critically only about certain things on certain occasions, but not at all about other things (sometimes the things that matter most). And this makes us wonder: Why isn't something as important and natural as Critical Thinking more common? Why is it that so many people seem not to be able to tell the difference between thinking critically and thinking in completely *un*critical ways? Why is it that so many people find Critical Thinking so *un*natural—not only so difficult, but so difficult to *understand*—when they first begin to study it? As we said earlier in this chapter, we think the answer is that there are many *obstacles* to Critical Thinking—urges, pressures, inducements, and distractions that make it hard, even for reasonable people, to think critically. In addition we are taught to believe things and understand things in ways that confuse and mislead and otherwise interfere with the natural refinement of common sense. And so, as it unfortunately turns out, many of us need to *unlearn* a fair amount before we begin to appreciate how "natural" Critical Thinking can be for us. Many people find that they need to radically reorient themselves and their thinking processes and change some deeply engrained thinking habits as they learn what it is like to think critically.

For example, let's go back and review that class discussion of California's energy crisis. It seems that people are often ready to "make up their minds" to one degree or another on the basis of . . . what? Well, often on the basis of little or no particular information, from sources whose *identity* is vague and indeterminate, and whose credibility and reliability are simply assumed. Common sense tells us

that in a general discussion, where conflicting ideas are being advanced in competition against each other, the question must arise of whether one's ideas have enough of a basis to stand up and hold their own. And so we find that we really *must* look more deeply into the sources of our information and the assumptions underlying our beliefs in order to think critically about what is at issue. Now, if people have not learned how to do this sort of thing, it can seem like "thinking in reverse," probably because, at least for a while, it seems to take us *further away* from "making up our minds." The search for truth seems long and hard. This can be discouraging—raising "obstacles" to Critical Thinking. Let's start with a common "myth":

RELATIVISM/SUBJECTIVISM

Sometimes people get so discouraged, they seem to "give up" searching for the truth altogether. They even say things like "There's really no such thing as the 'truth,' at least not 'Truth' with a capital *T*."

EXERCISE 1.6 | Agenda for Class Discussion

What do you think about this? First, what do you think the statement "There's really no such thing as the 'truth,' at least not 'Truth' with a capital *T*" *means*? Second, do you think it's true? Or not? Third, does it make sense to ask whether it's true?

No doubt there are quite a few things that *might be* meant by this statement. But they all probably boil down to some version or variation of this: *The so-called "truth" is always "relative" to some particular "point of view"; in other words, what's "true-for-me" may not be "true-for-you."* This position is often referred to as "Relativism" or "Subjectivism." It is a big obstacle to Critical Thinking. We say it is a "myth," and we propose to refute it with an argument. Here is the argument: It is impossible to say or believe that "Relativism" or "Subjectivism" is true without contradicting yourself. (Try it.) Therefore, it is unreasonable to say or believe that "Relativism" or "Subjectivism" is true.

EXERCISE 1.7 | **Topic for Class Discussion**

What do you think about this? Do you find this argument convincing? Explain. Why? Or why not?

It would not be at all surprising if the question were to arise in this discussion of what exactly we mean by "truth." This turns out to be a surprisingly deep philosophical question because there are a number of competing "philosophical theories of truth." If you are interested in learning about and considering these theories in detail, we recommend taking a course in metaphysics and/or epistemology.* For our purposes here in overcoming the obstacle to Critical Thinking posed by "Relativism/Subjectivism," we are going to assume a "commonsense understanding" of the nature of "truth." We are going to assume that truth is a relationship between a belief or a statement on the one hand and reality or the world on the other. A belief or statement is true if (and only if) it corresponds to something real. For example, if you believe or say that there is a growing hole in the earth's ozone layer, your belief or statement is true if (and only if) there *really is* a growing hole in the earth's ozone layer. Now, on the basis of this conception of truth, what can we say about the search for truth? Well, the search for truth can be long and hard. Scientists have had to work long and hard to find out about the earth's ozone layer. And to the extent that disagreement persists among scientists who have studied the earth's ozone layer, we should recognize that the search for truth may still be ongoing. But in many instances the search for truth is neither very long nor very hard at all. For example, it's not all that difficult to find out how much you weigh, is it?

"LIMITED" RELATIVISM/SUBJECTIVISM

Often people will cling to some limited version of "Relativism/Subjectivism," even after granting that "Relativism/Subjectivism" can't *generally* be true. A popular version of "Limited Relativism/Subjectivism" is based on a distinction between "matters of fact" and "matters of opinion" that goes something like this: "Factual matters" are matters that pertain to the "facts." The "facts," in turn, are those things that are provable or knowable beyond doubt or question. Everything else is a "matter of opinion." And, when it comes to matters of opinion, there's really no such thing as the "truth," at least not "Truth" with a capital *T*.

---

* Metaphysics is the branch of philosophy concerned with the nature of reality; epistemology is the branch of philosophy concerned with belief and knowledge.

EXERCISE 1.8 | **Topic for Class Discussion**

What do you think about this? Does this view seem any more reasonable than "General Relativism/Subjectivism"? Explain. Why? Or why not?

One way in which this sort of limited version of "Relativism/Subjectivism" may be stronger and more defensible than the general across-the-board version is that it cannot so easily be refuted by instantly deriving a self-contradiction from it. But it is still a major obstacle to Critical Thinking. One big problem with it is that almost everything, even science, turns out to be a "matter of opinion," simply because it is so hard to prove or know *anything* "beyond doubt or question." The problem arises when we give up the search for truth just because we recognize room for doubt and disagreement. Critical Thinking doesn't give up the search for truth so easily. To overcome the obstacles to Critical Thinking posed by "Relativism/Subjectivism," whether limited or not, we must cultivate an attitude of *patience and tenacity in pursuit of the truth*. We will be coming back to this shortly.

EGOCENTRISM

Another big obstacle to Critical Thinking—a kind of opposite to "Relativism/Subjectivism"—arises out of the tendency to cherish and defend those beliefs most closely associated with one's identity. Even in science one can find examples of egocentrism standing in the way of Critical Thinking. Galileo's astronomical treatise, *Dialogue on the Two Chief Systems of the World* (1632), was a thoughtful and devastating attack on the traditional geocentric view of the universe proposed by the ancient Greek Ptolemy (second century A.D.) and accepted by most scholars and scientists of Galileo's time. Galileo's treatise was therefore an attack not only on the views these authorities held but also on the authoritative status that they were privileged to enjoy, and so also on their self-images. Their reaction was to censor Galileo. Pope Urban, who was persuaded that Simplicio, the butt of the whole dialogue, was intended to represent himself, ordered Galileo to appear before the Inquisition. Although never formally imprisoned, Galileo was threatened with torture and ordered to renounce what he had written. In 1633 he was banished to his country estate. His *Dialogue,* together with the works of Kepler and Copernicus, were placed on the Index of Forbidden Books, from which they were not withdrawn until 1835. This tendency to cherish and defend those beliefs most closely associated with one's identity is not *unnatural*. We're each naturally inclined to favor and defend ourselves and so also anything with which we identify ourselves. We are naturally "egocentric," in our thinking as well as in our interests and concerns. But this natural and understandable tendency, if left unchecked, can, as in the case of Galileo and his contemporaries, close one's mind to the possibility that one is mistaken. And that would surely stand in the way of thinking critically. In order to understand how to keep this natural inclination in healthy check, let's start with a series of "thought experiments":[3]

EXERCISE 1.9 | Thought Experiment

Try saying, "Some of my beliefs are not true." Do you notice a problem with this? If so, explain. Do you nevertheless find it a reasonable thing to say about yourself? If so, explain.

Some people notice a problem when they say "Some of my beliefs are not true" because they recognize that part of believing something is believing that it *is* true. Some people find this problem manifesting itself at the level of their own particular beliefs: "If I were to do an inventory of my beliefs, wouldn't they *all* strike me as true?"

EXERCISE 1.10 | Thought Experiment

What do you think about this? Try the above thought experiment using some of your own beliefs. Identify 5–10 beliefs that you have. Do they all strike you as true? Or does it occur to you to wonder whether any of them might not be true? What more general conclusion, if any, do you draw from these results?

What *is* a belief, anyway? Think of a belief as a kind of "investment of trust or confidence." A belief, like any other investment, can be very difficult to abandon, even when evidence begins to show that it was a bad investment. Realizing and writing off a loss can be so painful that many a person will hang on to a bad investment in the hope that it will eventually turn around to be a good one. "Is this evidence really conclusive? Maybe there's something wrong with this evidence." Questioning the evidence against one of your beliefs is one thing, but when this reluctance to admit that one has made a bad investment in a belief rises to the level of *denying* or *refusing to heed* the evidence, then what we have is not Critical Thinking but wishful thinking.

EXERCISE 1.11 | Thought Experiment

What do you think you would do if you became aware of evidence indicating that one or more of your beliefs is not true?

Some people say, "If I found out that something was not true, I would just stop believing it." It would be nice if things were this simple, but we frequently do engage in wishful thinking and we are capable even of profound self-deception. "How can this be?" you might wonder. "How can a person know that something is not true and continue to believe it? How can a person be both the successful deceiver and the victim of the deception at the same time?" These are good questions. There is something deeply puzzling about the phenomenon of self-deception. But self-deception is a fact of human life, and we're sure that if you think for a minute or so you'll be able to come up with an example or two from your own experience of the sort of thing we're talking about. You probably know people who have on occasion talked themselves into believing things that they knew weren't true: for example, that they were ready for the midterm exam when in fact they knew at some level that they weren't really prepared. If we were *perfectly* rational creatures we would no doubt recognize the inconsistency involved in self-deception, and so self-deception probably would never occur. But there is no doubt that it does occur. We are rational creatures, but not perfectly so. We are also (in some ways and at some times) irrational creatures, and our wishes and desires often overwhelm our good sense. So we often persist in believing what we want to believe or what we wish were true in spite of what we know or have every good reason to believe.

EXERCISE 1.12 | Thought Experiment

A moment ago we imagined someone saying, "If I were to do an inventory of my beliefs, wouldn't they all strike me as true?" Try now to describe what it would actually be like to complete an inventory of your beliefs. How long would it take? How would you start? What kind of procedure would you use? How would you keep track? . . . After you've struggled with this for a while, go ahead and begin an inventory of your beliefs, on paper. Give yourself a measured five minutes and see what you come up with.

Most people are immediately struck by the realization that they have many more beliefs to keep track of than they ever would have imagined had they not been prompted to consider enumerating them. If one tried to organize an inventory of one's beliefs by sorting them into categories, a very similar realization occurs: beliefs of so many different *kinds*!

EXERCISE 1.13 | Thought Experiment

Do you have any beliefs about how many beliefs you have? For example, do you believe that you have more beliefs than you can count? If so, what category would such a belief fall into? When did you realize that you had beliefs of this sort? For example, were you aware that you had beliefs of this sort before you tried this thought experiment?

By this point, most people are struck by what might be described as a "Major Inventory Control Problem." This problem arises out of two conditions. First, there is uncertainty about the current inventory of beliefs. How many of these beliefs that I've just noticed have been here with me all along? And how many more beliefs do I have yet to notice? Second, there is the dynamic condition of our belief systems. In other words, our belief systems are not static. They are constantly undergoing change and revision as we deal with incoming information. Let's consider how this process normally works. We live in what has come to be known as the "information age," a label that derives from the awesome volume of information bombarding us constantly on a daily basis. Just think of the amount of material contained in the average metropolitan daily newspaper. Now multiply that by seven days a week, and then again by the number of metropolitan population centers you can think of in a few short minutes. Now add to this weekly, monthly, quarterly, and annual publications, books, radio, television—literally hundreds of separate stations, channels, and cable services, many of them broadcasting round the clock. And now add the Internet! This should be enough to make the point that there's far too much information to pay attention to, let alone absorb. Consequently, each of us has to be very selective about where we direct our attention in this overwhelming flow of information. Actually, this is nothing new or peculiar to our age. In fact, it's part of the human condition. There's always more to pay attention to than any of us has attention. And if you're like most people, even within the narrow range of information you do become aware of, you continue to be selective. Some incoming information will be actively incorporated into your belief system, while other information is rejected. What do you suppose are the main factors that govern this process? What do you suppose determines these selections? Among the most important and influential of these factors are the existing contents of our belief systems. The way we deal with incoming information is determined in large part by what we already believe. Our belief systems are "self-editing."

EXERCISE 1.14 | Topic for Class Discussion

So, what do you suppose common sense would suggest at this stage?

Each of us has a large and constantly evolving belief system comprising a huge number of beliefs—so many that trying to count them seems crazy. Most of these beliefs we routinely just *assume*. In other words, we take them for granted. We regard them as true without questioning them, or determining the adequacy of whatever evidence there may be to support them, or wondering where they came from and whether those sources are reliable or not. So, if you're like most people, a large part of your belief system is probably "subterranean" and functions in a largely unexamined way, as a set of assumptions of which you are probably not even fully aware and which influences its own ongoing evolution. Based on the sheer *size* of a normal person's belief system, common sense surely suggests the strong probability that some of those beliefs are not true, especially as long as they remain unexamined.

EXERCISE 1.15 | Thought Experiment

Suppose that you were actually able to complete a thorough inventory of each and every one of your beliefs. And suppose that you had been able to weed out each and every false or dubious item from that inventory, and now here you are at the end, considering the very last item in the inventory: Belief #457,986,312 "Some of my beliefs are not true." What do you think you should do with this belief? Would you weed it out or not? Explain.

To overcome the obstacles to Critical Thinking posed by the pitfalls of "Ego-centrism," we must cultivate an attitude of *intellectual humility*, in other words, a recognition of our fallibility or liability to error, while at the same time maintaining a patient and tenacious commitment to the pursuit of truth. But, as we shall see, even such a healthy attitude as intellectual humility can give rise to another kind of obstacle to Critical Thinking.

INTIMIDATION BY AUTHORITY

An authority is an expert source of information outside ourselves. The source can be a single individual (a parent, a teacher, a celebrity, a clergy member, the president), a group of individuals (doctors, educators, a peer group, a national consensus), or even an institution (a religion, a government agency, an educational establishment). Whatever its form, authority can exert considerable influence on our belief systems. And it's easy to see why. Consider how difficult it is to become an expert about *anything*. Nobody can ever hope to become an expert about *everything*. There's almost always going to be someone around who knows more about whatever we're interested in than we do ourselves. And so a person with a healthy attitude of intellectual humility is likely to find it helpful to consult authorities for their expert opinions.

EXERCISE 1.16 | **Thought Experiment**

Now go back and reconsider your belief inventory with regard to sources. How many of the things that you believe can you trace back to your own direct experience? Take as an example some area of interest or concern that is of intimate personal importance to you (like your own physical health). How many of the things that you believe about your own physical health have you derived from sources other than your own direct experience? In such cases can you identify the precise source of the belief? Explain.

If you're like most of the rest of us, chances are that a lot of the things you believe you've gotten from other sources. Beliefs about world history, the direction of the economy, the events of the day, the existence of God and an afterlife, the state of your health—what are the sources of all of these beliefs? Chances are that you got many of them by relying on the words of others, sources you are in effect trusting as authorities. Again, all of this is perfectly normal and natural. But common sense should warn us that there is a risk inherent in trusting someone other than ourselves when we make up our minds. How do we know that the authority we trust is in fact reliable?

Beyond this inherent risk (a risk that can at least be managed) there is a deeper danger. We can so rely on authority that we stop thinking for ourselves. For a vivid and extreme example, look at what happened to the members of the Heaven's Gate cult. Inside the cult a rigid authoritarian regime trained members to "purify" their "vehicles" (bodies) through systematic self-denial and unquestioning obedience to authority. Punishable offenses included: "*knowingly breaking any instruction or procedure; trusting one's own judgment or using one's own mind; having private thoughts; curiosity; criticizing or finding fault with one's teacher or classmates."* Such blind acceptance of and obedience to authority is of course incompatible with intellectual autonomy and Critical Thinking.

But just how likely is it that a normal intelligent person would be susceptible to such a debilitating abuse of trust? How vulnerable are we really to the dictates of authority? How subtle might its negative influence be? Consider a series of experiments conducted by psychologist Stanley Milgram in the 1960s.[4] Milgram's famous experiment consisted of asking subjects to administer strong electrical shocks to people the subjects couldn't see. The subjects were told that they could control the shock's intensity by means of a shock generator with 30 clearly marked voltages, ranging from 15 to 450 volts and labeled from "Slight Shock (15)" to "XXX—Danger! Severe Shock (450)." We should point out that the entire experiment was a setup: No one was actually administering or receiving shocks. The subjects were led to believe that the "victims" were being shocked as part of an experiment to determine the effects of punishment on memory. The "victims," who were in fact confederates of the experimenters, were strapped in their seats with electrodes attached to their wrists "to avoid blistering and burning." They were told to make no noise until a "300-volt shock" was administered, at which point they were to make noise loud enough for the subjects to hear (for example, pounding on the walls as if in pain). The subjects were reassured that the shocks, though extremely painful, would cause no permanent tissue injury. When asked, a number of psychologists predicted that no more than 10 percent of the subjects would follow the instruction to administer a 450-volt shock. In fact well over half did (26 out of 40). Even after hearing the "victims" pounding, 87.5 percent of the subjects (35 out of 40) followed instructions to increase the voltage. It seems clear that many normal intelligent people, when instructed by an authority, will act against their better judgment. To overcome the obstacles to Critical Thinking posed by the intimidating influence of authority, what we need is simply to maintain our *intellectual independence.*

CONFORMISM

Further experiments seem to show that not only are people's actions susceptible to external influence, but their judgment itself is as well. For example: look at the line segments in the accompanying figure:

Which of the three lines below matches the one on the right?

A _____

B _____   _____

C _____

Do your trust your own perceptual judgment here? It is pretty obvious that line segment B is the one matching the line segment on the right. Do you think you could ever be persuaded to doubt your own perceptions and choose A or C? Maybe not, but experiments indicate that many normal intelligent people *can be* persuaded to alter their perceptual judgments, even when their judgments are obviously correct. These experiments involved several hundred individuals who were asked to match lines just as you did. In each group, however, one and only one subject was naive, that is, unaware of the nature of the experiment. The others were instructed to make incorrect judgments in some cases and to exert "peer pressure" on the naive subject to change his or her correct judgment. The results: When subjects were not exposed to peer pressure, they inevitably judged correctly. But peer pressure produces a measurable and significant tendency toward conformity, the tendency increasing as the majority increased toward unanimity.[5] What is most interesting about these results is what they show about the power of "peer pressure." Psychologically we are all, at some level, aware of our liability to error, even in our perceptual judgments. But it is still remarkable that peer pressure is powerful enough to erode people's confidence in their own perceptual experience and judgment. Consider how much *more* intimidating peer pressure must be when applied to anything more remote from you than your very own perceptual experience and judgment!

What accounts for such intimidating power? Like many other creatures, we human beings are social animals. Our chances of survival and of flourishing are greatly enhanced by association with others of our kind. We do much better in groups than as individuals. So we are naturally fearful of isolation. At the same time, cooperation among individual members and group loyalty are both essential to the successful organization of any group, to the coordination of any group project, and to the maintenance of the group as a stable entity. So there is a natural tendency in any group toward conformity and orthodoxy. And there arises within any group a hierarchy of authority through which orthodoxy is established and conformity to it is reinforced. All of this is perfectly natural and makes sense in terms of its survival value for the individual, for the group, and for the species. However, if this natural and functional tendency is not kept within healthy limits, the fear of isolation can overcome our basic common sense, increasing rather than minimizing our liability to error. To overcome the obstacles to Critical Thinking posed by the intimidating influence of authority, peer pressure, and orthodoxy, what we need is to cultivate and maintain *intellectual courage*.

ETHNOCENTRISM

Another major obstacle to Critical Thinking—a close relative of "Egocentrism"—also arises out of our natural tendency as social animals to gather together in groups and to identify ourselves with and in terms of our social groupings. To see how this happens, try the following little thought experiment:

EXERCISE 1.17 | **Thought Experiment**

Cultural "Categories": How many distinct cultural groups can you identify in five minutes by simply describing yourself? "I am a(n) _____." [You could even start with your name (which identifies your family).]

However narrowly or broadly these groupings are defined—from kinship groupings (families) out to something as broad as a gender—cultural categories play an important role in the formation of our individual personal identities because we identify ourselves to a large extent in terms of them. Ethnic consciousness, like self-awareness, and ethnic pride, like self-esteem, are important ingredients in a healthy personality and society. But they each have corresponding perversions that, when they arise, stand as obstacles to Critical Thinking (and cause lots of other sorts of serious grief as well). The natural human tendency to be egocentric also can affect our attitudes regarding groups with which we identify. And so there arises a tendency to believe in the superiority of our family, our circle of friends, our age group, our religion, our nation, our race, our ethnicity, our gender, our sexual orientation, our culture. Thus egocentricity, the view that mine is better—my ideas, my experience, my values, my agenda—becomes ethnocentricity, the view that ours is better—our ideas, our values, our ways. In recent years cultural identity has gained recognition as a matter of political importance. Multiculturalism is high on the agenda of most educational institutions now sensitive to the importance of cultural diversity in the community and the curriculum. Instructors now strive to reflect multiple cultural perspectives in their courses (and authors in their textbooks). In Critical Thinking cultural diversity and an awareness of alternative cultural perspectives are especially useful because of the limitations inherent in *any* given cultural perspective. An appreciation of cultural diversity contributes to open-mindedness, an essential ingredient of Critical Thinking. To overcome the obstacles to Critical Thinking posed by ethnocentrism, we must cultivate an attitude of *respectful intellectual tolerance* and maintain and strengthen our *intellectual humility*.

UNEXAMINED ASSUMPTIONS

As we write these words, the whole world is still reeling in shock over the spectacular multiple airliner hijackings and attack on the World Trade Center Towers in New York City and the Pentagon in Washington, D.C. We have no doubt that when you read these words, these stunning events will still be remembered. We can't be certain at this moment as we write precisely how they will be remembered or precisely what will have happened since, though it does seem clear at this moment (September 13, 2001, two days later) that many things will be changing in their wake. But now, as you read these words, we'd like you to try to imaginatively move yourself back in time to September 11, 2001. Perhaps you remember where you were and what you were doing when you first learned that two airliners, apparently hijacked, had flown directly into the two World Trade Center Towers in New York City—causing the eruption of massive fires that eventually resulted in the collapse of both buildings—while a third airliner had crashed directly into the Pentagon in Washington, D.C. In particular, we'd like you to try to recover a sense of the confusion, and of the urgency we all felt to know what was happening and to figure out what to do about it.

To help you conjure up the mood, let us remind you that as we write these words, thousands of people remain missing and unaccounted for, rescue workers are digging through rubble searching for survivors, the New York Stock Exchange is completely shut down, as is all commercial air travel to and from and within the United States. There is considerable speculation about the identities and affiliations of the perpetrators of these attacks. But, as of this moment, only a handful of fragments from the beginnings of the investigation have been made public. The FBI has obtained the passenger lists and boarding passes from the flights. Cell phone calls from passengers aboard one of the hijacked airliners report that hijackers with knives have taken control of the flight. A car has been impounded at Boston's Logan Airport. A few individuals have been "detained for questioning." There is, again, considerable speculation about the identities and affiliations of the perpetrators of the attacks. But it is already pretty well focused on a particular terrorist organization led by one Osama bin Laden, whose base of operations is reported to be in Afghanistan. President Bush, Vice President Cheney, Secretary of State Colin Powell, and other government officials, as well as the television journalists covering the story, have been careful to refer to bin Laden so far only as the "prime suspect." Meanwhile, however, the Bush administration is mobilizing an international coalition, as well as domestic public support, for a "War Against Terrorism."

EXERCISE 1.18 | Thought Experiment

Now see if you can feel how difficult it is to "suspend judgment." If someone asks you, "What do you think is happening?" or "What do you think we should do about it?" you are "suspending your judgment" when you sincerely say "I don't know."

There comes a point for most people where it is no longer possible to suspend judgment. The urgency of the need we feel to initiate *some* plan of action makes the suspense unbearable. Though we may not *know* what has happened to any degree of certainty, we nevertheless feel we must do *something*. So, we begin to make "assumptions." Do you remember that "assumption" was the first of those words we said we needed to define clearly in order to avoid misunderstanding? So here is what we mean by "assumption." *An assumption is a "claim" which is taken to be true without "argument."* In this definition we use two terms, "claim" and "argument," which also need to be explained. A claim is a statement that "claims for itself (whether rightly or wrongly) the value of being true." If someone says, "Hi. How are you?" this would not be a claim—the language is not being used to make a statement that claims to be true. If someone asks you "What time is it?" this would not be a claim. But if someone says something like "The attack on the World Trade Center Towers in New York City was the work of the bin Laden terrorist organization al-Qaeda," a claim is being made. Argument is a concept that we will define and develop in detail in Chapters 3, 4, and 5 of this book. For the time being just think of an argument as support for a claim. So an assumption is a statement that claims to be true and is taken to be true without support.

EXERCISE 1.19 | Find the Argument

Argument is a concept that we will define and develop in detail in Chapters 3, 4, and 5 of this book, but it is a concept we have already put to use. *Where?*

Perhaps you have heard the cliché *Beware of assumptions; to "assume" makes an "ass" out of "u" and "me."* This is part of a widespread myth according to which *all* assumptions are suspect or dangerous and so we should try to avoid making *any assumptions at all.*

EXERCISE 1.20 | Thought Experiment

Pick any topic or subject you like, and try thinking about it without making any assumptions.

The main problem with this widespread myth is that it is *practically impossible* to follow as a recommendation for how to conduct one's reasoning. The more seriously you take it, the more paralyzed you get. All reasoning must start somewhere. When Thomas Jefferson wrote in the Declaration of Independence,

> We hold these truths to be self-evident, that all men are created equal, that they are endowed by their Creator with certain unalienable Rights, that among these are Life, Liberty and the pursuit of Happiness,

these were the "starting points" of the reasoning. When he said "We hold these truths to be *self-evident*," he was saying that he thought it reasonable to assert these claims without support, that is, as assumptions.

Of course there is *risk* involved in making *any* assumption: namely, the risk that what you are assuming is not true. No doubt we're making some assumptions when we say this, but it seems clear that in practice it is *impossible* to reason about *anything* without making at least *some* assumption(s). And so, *some* such risk is inherent and inevitable in reasoning as such. In other words, there is no way to eliminate this risk entirely. But this risk increases—in other words, assumptions are more "dangerous"—to the extent that they remain *hidden*. As long as assumptions are hidden they are not open to discussion, to challenge, to debate, to deliberate consideration (as any serious claim to the truth should be). So the obvious way to keep the risk down would be to *be aware of the assumptions we're making*. Notice that Jefferson's assumptions in the Declaration of Independence are *not* hidden. Thus, we would replace the cliché "Beware of Assumptions" with the maxim "Be Aware of Assumptions" and posit this as a Critical Thinking "Rule of Thumb."

CRITICAL THINKING TIP 1.1

~~BEWARE of Assumptions~~   BE AWARE of Assumptions

There is also a very important corollary to this rule of thumb: *Don't forget the assumptions you are making (don't forget that they ARE assumptions)*. This is essential to avoiding one of those pitfalls that lead otherwise reasonable people into unreasonable beliefs and ill-advised courses of action. Assumptions in their essential nature—*by definition*—are "taken to be true without support." So, as we just explained above, the risk of error increases as soon as we forget about the need to discuss, challenge, debate, and deliberately consider whether what we are assuming is really true. And don't forget the point we made earlier about the difficulty this poses for many people. Seriously examining assumptions, on the basis of which you thought you were going to make up your mind, can easily seem like "thinking in reverse."

INFERENTIAL ASSUMPTIONS

Where should we look for assumptions? Common sense would suggest that we be especially vigilant in two particular directions. Where people are making "inferences," or "drawing conclusions"—by which we mean reasoning from one claim to another—we should look for assumptions in between the claims in the inference.

EXERCISE 1.21 | **Identifying Hidden Assumptions ("Between the Lines")**

Suppose a fellow student says to you, "As a society we really shouldn't be relying on computers as much as we do." And you wonder why, and she says, "Well, don't forget, computers are designed and built by human beings." What is she assuming?

Notice how the reasoning here goes from her *answer* back up to the claim you challenged. But how does the reasoning get from the claim "computers are designed and built by human beings" to the claim you originally challenged "that we shouldn't rely on computers as much as we do"? There is an assumption being made that serves as a "missing link in the chain of reasoning." Can you figure out what this assumption is? Assumptions that play this sort of linking role are often called "Inferential Assumptions." We'll return to this concept in Chapters 3 and 4.

PRESUPPOSITIONS

Another important place to look for assumptions is "underneath" the claims being made. Sometimes in order to make any sense of what *is* stated or expressed explicitly, we are required to assume additional claims that are not stated explicitly.

EXERCISE 1.22 | **Identifying Hidden Assumptions ("Beneath the Surface")**

Go back and look at the *U.S. News & World Report* cover reproduced on page 5 in this chapter. Read the caption under the main headline. What two assumptions do you have to make in order to make sense of this caption?

This is the way the *U.S. News & World Report* cover works. The caption under the main headline "Lost Souls" reads: "How Reasonable People Can Hold Unreasonable Beliefs." In order to make sense of this caption you need to assume that the 39 members of the Heaven's Gate cult (or at least *some* of them) were "reasonable people," and you also need to assume that the beliefs that led them to commit mass suicide (or at least *some* of those beliefs) were "unreasonable beliefs." Assumptions of this kind—the kind that must be made in order for what *is* explicitly said to make sense—are often called "*pre*-suppositions." We'll be developing this concept also in Chapters 3 and 4.

EXERCISE 1.23 | **Topic for Class Discussion**

On June 24, 1997, the United States Air Force issued its official explanation of the Roswell Incident. The Roswell Incident is probably the most famous incident of an alleged Earth landing of extraterrestrials, long thought by many UFO believers to involve a government cover-up, because the sightings occurred and the debris was collected on and around a government military reservation (Roswell Air Force Base in New Mexico), and because the government maintained an "official silence" about the incident for 50 years. The official explanation: An experimental high-altitude weather balloon and several humanoid "crash test dummies" fell to Earth from very high altitudes. "Conspiracy theorists" were not convinced. There was much debate. Here is an opinion we heard on the radio. How many assumptions can you identify? "There's no government cover-up, and there were no aliens. Look, if you were an alien and you were scoping out the Earthly terrain, the last place you'd go would be to one of the most highly fortified and tightly secured military installations in the United States."

_____

_____

_____

_____

_____

From this discussion of obstacles to Critical Thinking, a sort of "portrait of the critical thinker" begins to emerge. A critical thinker is a person who combines an array of "intellectual virtues" and displays these virtues in his or her intellectual life. A critical thinker is patient, tenacious, humble, courageous, tolerant, and respectful of diversity of opinion in pursuit of the truth. The critical thinker sticks with the search for truth. The critical thinker is not in too big a hurry to have done with the search for truth, although it may be long and arduous. The critical thinker is humble in recognizing his or her own limitations and liability to error. But the critical thinker is not easily intimidated by authority or by popular opinion or peer pressure. The critical thinker recognizes the value of diverse perspectives and viewpoints and is respectful of the views of others with whom he or she may disagree. With this portrait of the critical thinker in mind, let us now return to a question we raised earlier in this chapter: How is it that reasonable people come to hold unreasonable beliefs? Chances are that this is because people have given up the search for truth, or lost their patience and jumped to a hasty conclusion of the search for truth, or become intimidated (lost their courage and independence), or become arrogant (lost their humility) in pursuit of the truth.

EXERCISE 1.24 | Critical Thinking Self-Assessment

Part 1, A Critical Thinking "Role Model": Based on your understanding of Critical Thinking as defined and explained so far in Chapter 1, identify the person(s) you think best exemplify it. Explain your selection.

Part 2, A Critical Thinking "Self-Assessment": Assess your own habits of mind in terms of the "intellectual virtues" found in the above portrait of the critical thinker.

In the search for truth I am,

Extremely patient, relatively patient, about average, somewhat impatient, very impatient.

Very tenacious, relatively tenacious, about average, will give up, will give up easily.

Etc.

LOOKING AHEAD: ISSUES AND DISPUTES

You may have heard the expression "Reasonable people may differ . . ." An *issue* is what we call a topic about which reasonable people may differ. Should there be a law against abortion? Should animals be used in medical experimentation? Does intelligent extraterrestrial life exist? What is the average temperature of the water in Lake Tahoe? Is there a global environmental crisis? What drives people to commit acts of terrorism? Does the Federal Reserve Board's raising interest rates indicate that they think the recession is over? These are all questions to which a number of significant and conflicting alternative responses are both genuinely open and defensible. These are all good examples of our concept of an issue.

Sometimes it seems as though reasonable people may differ about anything, everything, even nothing at all. It would help if we could dispense with disputes over nothing at all. So before we begin to discuss issues, let us explain more deeply what we mean by "*genuinely* disputable" by pointing out and setting aside another kind of thing that frequently *passes for* an issue.

MERE VERBAL DISPUTES

Philosopher William James tells the story about how on a camping trip everyone got into a dispute over the following puzzle:

> The corpus of the dispute was a squirrel—a live squirrel supposed to be clinging to one side of a tree-trunk; while over against the tree's opposite side a human being was imagined to stand. This human witness tries to get sight of the squirrel by moving rapidly round the tree, but no matter how fast he goes, the squirrel moves just as fast in the opposite direction, and always keeps the tree between himself and the man, so that never a glimpse of him is caught.

The resultant problem now is this: *Does the man go round the squirrel or not?* He goes round the tree, sure enough, and the squirrel is on the tree; but does he go round the squirrel?[6]

James's idea was that although you can easily imagine people going round and round in an endless dispute over such a puzzle, you can just as easily dissolve the puzzle by drawing a simple terminological distinction: It all depends upon what you mean by "going round" the squirrel.

> If you mean passing from the north of him to the east, then to the south, then to the west, then to the north again, obviously the man does go round him, for he occupies these successive positions. But if on the contrary you mean being first in front of him, then on the right of him, then behind him, then on the left, and finally in front again, it is quite as obvious that the man fails to go round him, for by the compensating movements the squirrel makes, he keeps his belly turned towards the man all the time, and his back turned away.[7]

Since it hardly matters which meaning of "going round" the squirrel applies, this could be called a "merely verbal" dispute. To put it another way, there's no *real* issue here; the dispute arises out of a simple "ambiguity" (for an explanation of this concept, see the section "Ambiguity and Vagueness" in Chapter 2) in the way the puzzle is worded. A similar example is the old dispute "If a tree falls in the forest and nobody is there to hear it, is there a sound?" Clarifying the meaning of "sound" dissolves the dispute. If you're talking about sound *waves*, then presumably there are sounds whether or not anyone is there to hear the tree fall. But if you mean sound *sensations*—the experience of sound—then the falling tree makes no sound, for no one is there to experience the sound sensations.

Perhaps it would be nice if all issues were as trivial as these. Perhaps it would be nice if all disputes arose out of simple ambiguities and could be dismissed as mere "matters of semantics." On the other hand, perhaps it would be boring if all disputes were idle and there were no real, serious, and urgent issues to argue about. Reasonable people may differ about this, possibly leading to another kind of idle dispute. But in any case, most genuinely important disputes are concerned with genuine issues of one sort or another. The rest of this book will be devoted to developing and refining strategies and procedures for resolving serious disputes about real and important issues, which comprise a variety as wide as all of human interest and concern.

ISSUE ANALYSIS

CRITICAL THINKING TIP 1.2

"If we want to understand something very complex, we must approach it very simply, and therein lies our difficulty—because we always approach our problems with assertions, with assumptions or conclusions, and so we are never free to approach them with the humility they demand."

—Krishnamurti

Because they inherently involve conflict, all issues present a certain amount of psychological discomfort. They all seem to "cry out" for resolution. But a critical thinker must discipline herself to be patient in pursuit of the truth. Thus, another aspect of thinking critically that often gives the impression of "thinking in reverse" has to do with issues and their analysis. Before we begin to "make up our minds" about how to resolve a given issue, it is useful to do some analysis of the issue.

Among the immediate challenges that most issues present is their inherent complexity. Take the first of the issues we mentioned above as an example. The question whether there should be a law against abortion, even though it is worded as a simple "yes-or-no" question, is hardly a simple issue. The minute you look at it closely and begin to confront it seriously, what you will see is that what you have in front of you is not just one issue but more like a whole nest of them, resembling a can of worms. This is because there are *so many different things* under the umbrella heading of "abortion" that reasonable people can disagree about. For example, reasonable people will disagree over whether abortion belongs in the same moral category as murder, or homicide, or elective surgery, or birth control. Reasonable people will disagree over whether a woman's reproductive processes are private, and so also over whether the government may legitimately interfere with her choices. Reasonable people will disagree over whether the fetus is a person or only a potential person. Reasonable people will disagree over whether potential persons have rights. Reasonable people will disagree over whether the right to life overrides other rights that may come into conflict with it, and over whether the right to life includes the right to use another person's body as a life-support system. Even among those who agree that the law *should* restrict abortion, reasonable people will disagree, for example, over whether the restriction should be total or partial, rigid or flexible, and if partial and flexible, over what the exceptions should be, and so on. So much complexity! It seems even that there might be too many dimensions of complexity to count. The challenge this poses for human intelligence is confusion: another one of those things that make it difficult—even for reasonable people, and even when they're not distracted by external pressures or internal longings and fears—to discriminate between reasonable and unreasonable beliefs. Most interesting issues are deep and complex enough to present this sort of challenge. So the first step of issue analysis is to take the issue apart and see what subsidiary issues are contained within it.

EXERCISE 1.25 | Issue Analysis I

Set the egg timer for three minutes. Then brainstorm for subsidiary issues. See how many distinct issues you can see arising out of any single one of the following issues:

- Should animals be used in medical experimentation?
- Does intelligent extraterrestrial life exist?
- What is the average temperature of the water in Lake Tahoe?
- Is there a global environmental crisis?
- What drives people to commit acts of terrorism?
- Does the Federal Reserve Board's raising interest rates indicate that they think the recession is over?

The next step is to find an approach to the issue that will help us to bring its complexity under intellectual control rather than allowing its complexity to confuse and overwhelm us. One approach that immediately occurs to many people is to narrow the focus of the inquiry. For example, rather than try to resolve the whole nest of issues we can see arising out of the abortion debate, we might confine ourselves to the issue over whether the fetus is a person or only a potential person. This approach is a reasonable one, and is often very useful. But it never completely disposes of the problem. Suppose we do narrow our focus down to the issue over the status of the fetus. Is the fetus a person or just a potential person? But here again, the minute you look closely at this issue and begin to confront it seriously, what you will see is not just one issue but a whole nest of them, resembling a can of worms. What are the biological changes that take place during fetal development? How do the criteria for personhood relate to the biology of fetal development? Is personhood simply a biological matter? Or is it an essentially political matter? Or a spiritual matter? What precisely is meant by this word *person*? What are the criteria for being a "person"?

LOGICAL PRIORITY

With any such complex inquiry what we really need is to be able to develop an *orderly agenda of inquiry*. An "agenda" is a list of things to do. The function of an agenda is to monitor progress, especially when there are a lot of things to keep track of. An agenda of inquiry would be a list of issues to resolve. Its function would be so that you can know whether you are making progress toward resolving the main issue (the issue you started with) in which the others are embedded rather than going round and round in circles or wandering aimlessly and getting lost in it all. To develop an agenda, we must "prioritize," which simply means putting things into some kind of serial order. In any agenda, something has to come first, something has to come next, and so on. There may well often be several reasonable orders to follow in an agenda of inquiry. And an agenda of inquiry probably ought to be always open to revision. Nevertheless, some ways of ordering an agenda of inquiry are more "logical" than others. Suppose we start out trying to resolve the issue of what to do about California's energy crisis. Very shortly we should notice that any resolution to this issue we might consider presupposes some resolution to the subsidiary issue of what the *causes* of the crisis are. This would indicate that the issue as to the causes of the crisis is "logically prior" to the issue as to the remedies. Similarly, any resolution to the issue of whether the fetus is a person will presuppose some resolution to the issue of what the criteria for personhood are. In other words, the issue as to the criteria for personhood is logically prior to the issue of whether the fetus is a person. Whenever we notice this sort of relationship, it makes sense to address issues in order of their logical priority.

EXERCISE 1.26 | **Issue Analysis II**

Now take the list of subsidiary issues you brainstormed in Exercise 1.25 and prioritize it.

ISSUE CLASSIFICATION

The next step of issue analysis comes from recognizing that there are different "types" of issues and that strategies and procedures appropriate for issues of one type may not be very appropriate for issues of other types. For example, the procedures for determining the average temperature of the water in Lake Tahoe will not be much use in resolving the question of whether animals should be used in medical experimentation. We propose to sort issues into the following three categories: Factual Issues, Evaluative Issues, and Interpretive Issues.

In this connection we are going to be using the terms "factual," "evaluative," and "interpretive" in a way that departs slightly but significantly from what we believe is current popular usage. Our impression is that people generally draw a very sharp distinction between "factual" matters on the one hand and "evaluative and interpretive" matters on the other, but also that people generally do not draw any very sharp and clear distinction at all between "evaluative" and "interpretive" matters. Popular usage seems to go something like this: "Factual matters" are matters that pertain to the "facts." The "facts" are everything that is proven or known beyond doubt or question. Everything else (values, interpretations, whatever) is a "matter of opinion" and as such can never be proven or established as true.[8]

If you agree with any of this, now we're going to try to talk you out of it. First of all, this way of talking and thinking fails to recognize the need for strategies and procedures to resolve issues about what the facts actually are. Secondly, it doesn't open up any useful strategic or procedural options for resolving evaluative or interpretive issues. We are therefore going to stipulate meanings with somewhat greater precision and utility than popular conventional usage has for the words *factual, evaluative,* and *interpretive.* We will use *factual* to refer to "matters that can be investigated by the methods either of *empirical science* or of *documentary research.*" We will use *evaluative* to refer to "matters that concern the *merits* of things." And we will use *interpretive* to refer to "matters that concern the *meanings* of things."

These categories are neither mutually exclusive nor exhaustive. This means that a given issue may have aspects that belong to more than one of these categories or fall outside all of them. Bear in mind that the purpose of this categorical scheme has little to do with labeling issues or sorting them "correctly." It's more about clarifying the agenda of inquiry. Recognizing a given issue as belonging to a particular type is potentially valuable in determining what strategies and procedures will be most likely to lead to a resolution of the issue. To approach an issue as a factual issue is to raise questions of evidence. What sort of evidence would be relevant and decisive? What evidence is there already available which bears on the issue? What additional evidence is required? What sorts of experiment or research would be needed in order to obtain that additional evidence? To approach an issue as an evaluative issue is to raise questions of standards. To approach an issue as an interpretive issue is to raise the question of interpretive hypotheses.

FACTUAL ISSUES

In modern Olympic history which nation has won the most medals in weight lifting? What city is the world's coldest national capital? What is the average temperature of the water in Lake Tahoe? All of these are factual questions. They illustrate what we mean by saying that factual matters can be investigated by doing empirical science or documentary research. If a dispute were to arise about any of these questions—say, for example, during a game of Jeopardy or Trivial Pursuit—there are already well-established procedures available for settling it. We might look the information up in a reliable source (documentary research). Or if the information is not already recorded, we could easily imagine the sort of scientific investigation by which the information could be gathered.

Having said that, we should also note right away that things are not always so simple with factual issues. Suppose that for some reason we needed to figure out how many feral cats are living in the city of San Francisco? In this case the question is not "theoretically" difficult to answer. It's a simple factual matter of counting the cats. But in practice how in the world is anyone ever going to count all the feral (wild) cats in the city of San Francisco?! They run away. They hide. They breed like, uh, feral cats. So we would need to "estimate" the number in some way. In fact, things might not be very simple even with the simple (or simple-sounding) examples we mentioned above. Suppose we were asked to determine the average temperature of the water in the Pacific Ocean. You can begin to appreciate the difficulty of determining matters of fact.

Doing good science involves both evaluation and interpretation, as does doing good documentary research. The question of whether or not there is a global environmental crisis is a good example. Suppose we approach it initially as a factual question. What sort of evidence would be relevant? Well, suppose there were hard empirical evidence of significant changes in weather patterns on a global scale. That would be relevant evidence. Notice that evaluation (of the evidence) is already involved. "Hard" evidence *has merit,* "significant" changes *merit attention.* And supposing for the moment that we do have "hard" evidence of significant global weather anomalies, we would still need some understanding of their causes in order to answer our original question. And this will involve interpreting the evidence we already have as well as additional evidence we may seek concerning, for example, extraordinary fluctuations in the average temperature in the Pacific Ocean and so on. We will discuss all of this further in Chapters 8 and 9.

EVALUATIVE ISSUES

Now let's reconsider the first two issues we mentioned above. Should there be a law against abortion? Should animals be used in medical experimentation? One thing should be clear right away: Neither of these issues can be resolved *simply* as a matter of fact. We could not possibly hope to settle a dispute over the right and proper legal status of abortion by doing documentary research alone. Nor could we hope to settle a dispute over the use of animals in experimental medicine on the basis of empirical science alone. Not that documentation and empirical evidence are irrelevant to these issues. Just as evaluation and interpretation are important parts of any good factual inquiry, so good science and good documentary research often play a crucial role in evaluation and interpretation. But no amount of empirical evidence and/or documentation could possibly be *by itself decisive* in either of these issues. So it would make sense to approach them initially not as factual issues, and the word *should* is a clue that they are each fundamentally evaluative issues, which raises the question of standards. What standards of evaluation are we concerned with? In each of these issues it is apparent that moral or ethical standards are central. So they will need to be clarified in the course of the inquiry. Interpretive and factual questions will take their place in the agenda of inquiry as they arise in the process of clarifying and applying these moral or ethical standards. We will discuss this further in Chapter 10.

INTERPRETIVE ISSUES

Suppose that in her first speech before the United Nations General Assembly the newly appointed U.S. ambassador makes five explicit references to human rights, free trade, opium, democracy, and Hong Kong. Is the United States "sending a message" to Beijing? And if so, what is the message? Or take this example from our earlier list of issues: Does the Federal Reserve Board's raising interest rates indicate that they think the recession is over? These questions indicate issues concerning what things mean, or how they should be understood. Such issues frequently arise in our attempts to understand things whose meanings may be flexible, complicated, multilayered, obscure, or even deliberately veiled. Issues of this sort are probably the most complex and difficult issues procedurally that we are likely to encounter in everyday discourse. Yet they are also absolutely fundamental to the process of communication, since they have to do with the discernment of meaning. Indeed, many, perhaps most, of the activities you will be performing throughout this book involve interpretation. Deciding whether a particular passage is an argument or not involves interpretation. Deciding whether a passage is intended to serve an expressive or persuasive or informative function involves interpretation. There is no single simple procedure for resolving interpretive issues or settling interpretive disputes. Rather, a number of kinds of information are relevant to interpretation, some of which have already been mentioned and some of which we will discuss further in Chapters 2, 9, and 10.

For example, the conventions governing the use of a term or expression are relevant to its interpretation. Similarly, there are what are known as "diplomatic conventions," which would be relevant to the interpretation of communications between one government—for example, through its U.N. ambassador—and another. In addition to conventions, information about the context surrounding a passage is relevant to its interpretation. Knowing that a particular speech was delivered before the U.N. General Assembly rather than, for example, by confidential communiqué to the Chinese ambassador, is an important piece of information that can guide us closer to an accurate understanding of what was meant. Contextual information in the case of oral communication, as well as in film and video, includes facial expression, vocal inflection, bodily posture, timing, and so on.

It should be apparent already that gathering and sifting evidence of such a wide variety, especially in living contexts, where time is of the essence, is a process of considerable complexity and subtlety. And there is a good deal of disagreement among theorists about what the proper procedures are for doing interpretive work and how they should be applied in different sorts of interpretive controversy. Nevertheless, interpretation is something you are probably pretty good at by now. So you no doubt already recognize that some interpretive issues can be resolved relatively firmly and easily, whereas others are more difficult and may be quite resistant to resolution. In disputed cases, perhaps the most useful procedural strategy is the use of hypothetical reasoning. This involves formulating and testing interpretive hypotheses. A hypothesis is a particular sort of conscious assumption. It is an idea we *assume* to be true for the purpose of exploring or testing it. This procedure also has important applications in dealing with factual issues. We will be discussing it in greater detail in Chapter 9.

EXERCISE 1.27 | **Issue Analysis III**

Number each of the following sets of questions or issues in ascending order of logical priority, first to last. Then classify each question or issue as to type. Explain your rankings and classifications.

- [ ] Should there be a law against "hate speech" on the Internet?
- [ ] What is "hate speech"?
- [ ] Should the service provider or the government be responsible for the enforcement of regulations prohibiting "hate speech" over the Internet?
- [ ] What kinds of penalties should be imposed on people who post "hate speech" on the Internet?

- [ ] Is time travel possible?
- [ ] Is time travel technically feasible?
- [ ] Is the technical feasibility of time travel worth investigating?
- [ ] What is meant by "time travel"?

- [ ] What are the defining criteria for being a person?
- [ ] Should abortion be prohibited under criminal law as a form of homicide?
- [ ] Is abortion a form of homicide?
- [ ] Is the human fetus a person?

- [ ] Should same-sex couples be allowed to join in legally sanctioned marriages?
- [ ] Will the recognition of same-sex marriages undermine the purposes of legally sanctioned marriage?
- [ ] What purpose(s) is (are) served by the institution of legally sanctioned marriage?
- [ ] Could civilization survive the collapse of an institution as important as legally sanctioned marriage as a result of the recognition of same-sex marriages?

COMPOSING AN "ISSUE STATEMENT"

An "issue statement" is a composition whose purpose is to clearly communicate an interest in a topic, a topic about which we anticipate disagreement among reasonable people. An issue statement can be composed very briefly—for example, as a single short sentence—or at greater length—for example, as the opening chapter of a book. The ability to compose issue statements is essential both to successfully communicating our own opinions and to understanding the viewpoints of others (as we will explain in Chapter 5). Either way, composing an issue statement can and should involve careful and appropriate use of the techniques of issue analysis discussed above in this chapter. Eventually, when you compose a complete argumentative essay, a well-crafted issue statement will be an important part of your essay's introduction. We will work on this in greater detail in Chapter 13.

EXERCISE 1.28 | Term Project: Issue Statement I

Compose a 250-word Issue Statement (one page standard double-spaced) incorporating your results from Exercises 1.25 and 1.26. In your Issue Statement, try not to "take sides."

EXERCISE 1.29 | Issue Statement II

Compose a 250-word Issue Statement (one page standard double-spaced) presenting an issue of your choice. In your Issue Statement, try not to "take sides."

ADDITIONAL EXERCISES

As you work through the exercises throughout this book, keep in mind what we said earlier about relativism and the search for truth. There are some questions for which there's no such thing as the correct answer, and yet even in such cases, most likely some answers will be better than others. What matters most of all is how you reason your way to your answer, and whether your reasoning holds up under scrutiny. When you discuss these exercises, don't be afraid to challenge answers that may be offered by your instructors, but you should also try to understand and appreciate the reasoning your instructors may have to offer in support of their preferred answers.

■ **EXERCISE 1.30**   Let us use the term "world-view" to refer to the self-regulating system of assumptions and other beliefs according to which a person views the world or deals with incoming information. One of the most valuable things about the diversity of cultures you will find on most contemporary college campuses is what one can learn from cultures other than one's own about the limitations of one's own world-view. Here is a little exercise in self-awareness and appreciation of cultural diversity: Try to identify three items in your own world-view that are not shared by or which conflict with the world-view of a typical member of some identifiable culture other than your own. You may find it useful, perhaps even necessary, to approach one or more of your fellow students whose cultural heritage(s) differs from your own, and learn a bit from them about the distinctive characteristics of their culture(s).

■ **EXERCISE 1.31**   Another of the valuable things about cultural diversity is what one can learn about common or shared humanity. Here is a follow-up exercise in cultural awareness: Try to identify three items in your own world-view that are or would be shared by a typical member of some identifiable culture other than your own.

■ **EXERCISE 1.32**   From your own experience, give an example of "self-deception" in which you or someone you know well persisted in maintaining a belief in the face of powerful contradictory evidence. As best you can, explain how this was possible for the person.

■ **EXERCISE 1.33**   Identify 10 beliefs that you hold on the basis of some external authority. As best you can, identify the authoritative source of the belief in each case. Then evaluate the authority. Is the authority generally reliable? Is the authority an appropriate one for the belief in question?

■ **EXERCISE 1.34**   Do you have access to the Internet? If so this exercise won't need much in the way of explanation. (If you don't have access to the Internet, ask your instructors where you can get access to the Internet on your campus.) Search the Internet under "Critical Thinking," and log what you find on the chart below.

Internet Address	Site Name	Brief Description

■ **EXERCISE 1.35**   *"Freewrite Rewrite":* Now, with this introductory chapter under your belt, review what you wrote earlier in Exercise 1.5, your freewrite on what you hope and expect to get out of a course in Critical Thinking. Have your hopes and expectations changed in any way as a result of your reading and experiences in the course so far? With the benefit of these experiences, now edit your earlier thoughts into a short essay of one or two pages on the topic of what you hope and expect to get out of a course in Critical Thinking.

GLOSSARY

assumption   an unsupported claim

assumption, hidden   an unstated or implied assumption

assumption, inferential   hidden assumption that functions as added support linking a stated premise with a conclusion

authority   an expert or source of information outside ourselves

claim   a statement which is either true or false

egocentrism   favoritism for oneself and the beliefs, values, traditions, and groups with which one identifies

ethnocentrism   favoritism for the beliefs, values, and traditions of one's ethnic group

issue   a topic about which reasonable people may disagree

issue, factual   an issue to be resolved by either the methods of empirical science or documentary research

issue, evaluative   an issue concerning the merits of things

issue, interpretive   an issue concerning the meanings of things

logical priority   a kind of order among issues where one issue presupposes a resolution of a second issue, the second is logically prior to the first

presupposition   assumption required in order to make sense of what is explicitly stated

reason   1. the human capacity to use disciplined intelligence to solve problems
2. a claim used as a premise
3. a claim used as an explanation

relativism   the view that the truth is "relative" and varies

subjectivism   the view that the truth is "relative" or varies from individual to individual

truth   the agreement of an idea with reality

world-view   the self-regulating system of assumptions and other beliefs through which a person receives and interprets new information

ENDNOTES

[1] Thomas Jefferson, "The Declaration of Independence."

[2] California State Assembly Bill #1890.

[3] This series of thought experiments is derived from Jonathan Bennett's unpublished lectures on Descartes, given at the University of British Columbia, 1970–1972.

[4] Stanley Milgram, *Obedience to Authority: An Experimental View* (New York: Harper & Row, 1974).

[5] See S. E. Asch, "Effects of Group Pressure Upon the Modification and Distortion of Judgment," in M. H. Guetskow (ed.), *Groups, Leadership and Men* (Pittsburgh: Carnegie Press, 1951); S. E. Asch, "Opinions and Social Pressure," *Scientific American* (September 1955): 31–35; S. E. Asch, "Studies of Individual and Conformity: A Minority of One Against a Unanimous Majority," *Psychological Monographs* 70 (1956): 9.

[6] William James, *Pragmatism*, Lecture II (Cambridge, Mass.: Harvard Univ. Press, 1975).

[7] Ibid.

[8] This is a version of "relativism."

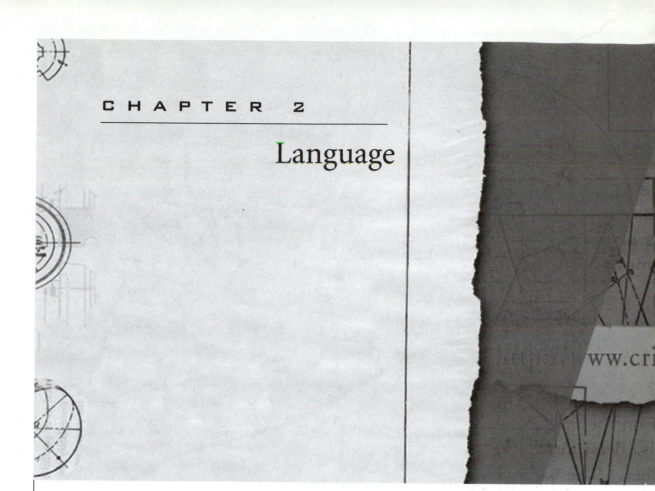

CHAPTER 2

Language

"Some people have a way with words.
Some no have way." STEVE MARTIN

Sometimes people wonder why there is a chapter on language in a book about thinking. Try to imagine what thinking would be like without language. Hard to imagine, isn't it? In fact, the harder you try, the more you notice language creeping into the effort. The more you notice yourself trying to "put the ideas into words," so to speak, the more it seems clear that thinking, as we know it, can't be separated from language. Language is a fundamental medium of our thinking—a basic environment and material within which our thoughts take form and gain expression. There are other ways, too, perhaps, in which our thinking takes shape and comes out. Language (narrowly conceived, as words) is not the *only* thing you pay attention to in finding out what and how people think. Posture, gesture, vocal inflection, timing, context, and so on are all meaningful dimensions of human communication, and they frequently guide our interpretations of people's words. But none is

more important than language itself. It is language itself that is most central and basic. Indeed, to say that posture, gesture, vocal inflection, timing, context, and so on are meaningful dimensions of human communication is almost as good as saying that they are linguistic dimensions of human communication—either part of language (more broadly conceived) or at least language-like. In any case, when you boil it all down, the most important and best way of finding out what and how people think is by attending to what they *say*.

WHAT IS LANGUAGE?

This is one of those questions you hope your children don't ask you when they're little and persistent in their curiosity. But here is a powerful way to approach a question like this: think in terms of *function*.[1] For example, if we were trying to figure out or explain what a telephone is, a good place to begin would be to ask what a telephone is *for* and why it has the peculiar features it has—or what its peculiar features contribute to that purpose or goal. For example, it has a handset with that distinctive peculiar shape. And why does it have that shape? Well, the shape functions so that you can easily hold the thing in one hand while you both talk into one end of it and listen at the other. And that's a pretty useful combination of features to have in a device designed to enable people to have a conversation outside each other's physical presence. Thus, the essential function, as well as the functional essence, of a telephone is a technological means of remote conversation. So now let's think about language in the same way.

EXERCISE 2.1 | Uses of Language

Use your imagination. How many distinct uses of language can you think of in five minutes?

Use or Function	Example

We imagine that you will have noticed that language has a large and wide variety of actual and potential uses. Let us all marvel for just a moment at the flexibility, utility, and power of language as a set of tools. Language can be used to describe the world or some part of it, to pose problems, to suggest solutions, to issue orders, make agreements, tell stories, tell jokes, sing songs, exchange greetings, buy things, sell things, make friends, insult enemies, and so on and on. Can language be said to serve any specific *single essential* function amidst all this variety? Well, first remember these points from Chapter 1: Human beings are social animals. Our chances of survival and of flourishing are greatly enhanced by association with others of our kind. We do much better in groups than as individuals. This places a high premium on *cooperation* and *coordination with others*. Thus, the essential function, as well as the functional essence, of language would seem to be *communication*. What exactly is "communication"? Communication is what we do to achieve "common understanding"—essential to cooperation and coordination—among two or more sentient beings.

FUNCTIONS OF LANGUAGE

Let us now consider the wide variety of actual and possible uses of language from the point of view of Critical Thinking. Given our understanding of Critical Thinking as a discipline for making reasonable decisions about what to do or believe, it makes sense to single out several general uses or functions of language for special attention.

THE INFORMATIVE FUNCTION OF LANGUAGE

Let us begin with a concept we introduced in Chapter 1: *A "claim" is a statement that claims for itself (whether rightly or wrongly) the value of being true.* Writing in 370 B.C. Hippocrates, the father of Western medicine, wrote,

> Speaking generally, all parts of the body which have a function, if used in moderation and exercised in labors to which each is accustomed, become healthy and age slowly. But if unused and left idle, they become liable to disease, defective in growth, and age quickly.

Here Hippocrates was reporting the results of empirical observation and making general claims about how physical exercise and health are related, claims he clearly thought to be true and wanted others to accept as true. *When we use language in this way for making claims, language is performing its "informative" function.* A few more typical examples:

Washington, D.C., is the capital of the United States of America.
Laetrile is (or is not) an effective treatment for cancer.
U.S. presidential elections are held every four years.
Business Administration is currently the most popular college major.
One out of 10 Americans has herpes.
The Democrats have never controlled the U.S. House of Representatives.

Notice that the last statement is false. "Informative," as we are using it here, includes *misinformation.* Not just true statements, but false statements, statements whose truth is not yet determined, statements whose truth may be in doubt, such as "Extraterrestrial life exists" and "The next U.S. president will be a Republican," all count as examples of the informative function of language.

THE EXPRESSIVE FUNCTION OF LANGUAGE

In addition to its utility for making claims and conveying information, language has important and powerful capacities to express and arouse emotion. A bumper sticker we used to see quite a lot reads:

> Mean people suck!

Quite possibly the authors of this statement, as well as some of those who drive around with it on their cars, are making a claim they think is true. But the main thing that such a bumper sticker accomplishes is to express an "attitude"—

to vent and to arouse emotional energy. *Whenever language is used to vent or arouse feelings, it is said to perform its expressive function.* Poetry furnishes some of the best examples of the expressive function of language:

So fair, so sweet, withal so sensitive,
Would that the Little Flowers were to live,
Conscious of half the pleasures which they give . . .
—William Wordsworth

Here again, though the poet *may* be making a claim he thinks is true and worth communicating about the aesthetic value of flowers, the poetry functions even more powerfully as an expression of emotion and to evoke an emotional mood in the reader. The importance of the expressive function of language for Critical Thinking has to do with the role of emotion in decision making. Emotional energy is very powerful, easily capable of overwhelming common sense. This is not to say that emotion should play *no role at all* in decision making. Emotional energy can and sometimes does reinforce and enhance a process of rational deliberation. But again, given our understanding of Critical Thinking as a discipline for making reasonable decisions about what to do or believe, it is generally advisable to *be aware* of the expressive function and use of language insofar as it may interfere with rational decision making.

CRITICAL THINKING TIP 2.1

~~BEWARE of Emotion~~   BE AWARE of Emotional Language

THE DIRECTIVE FUNCTION OF LANGUAGE

Let us refocus once again on the functional essence of language and the survival value of coordination and cooperation for us all as human beings. Any interest in coordination or cooperation quickly translates into an interest in other people's behavior and ways of influencing it. How do we get other people to cooperate with us? How do we get them to do what we want? We say things like,

"Please pass the butter."

"Caution: Keep hands and feet away while machine is in use."

Language serves a directive function when it is used in an attempt to influence the behavior of another person. If someone is fortunate (?) enough to be in a position of power or authority, then perhaps they can issue commands and give orders, but ordinarily when we are with our peers our directive uses of the language take the form of requests and suggestions. When we make requests and offer suggestions, we generally are counting on at least a willingness to cooperate in the other party. But what do we do when we can neither command nor presuppose a willingness to cooperate? Generally speaking, what we need to do under these circumstances is *be persuasive*. We try to influence the beliefs and motivations be-hind the behavior we want. Now of course language is flexible and powerful enough to lend itself well to this purpose. Critical Thinking is especially inter-ested in this particular kind of directive use of language—what we will call *per-suasive* language. This is where the directive function of the language comes to incorporate the informative and expressive functions of language, because in or-der to influence people's beliefs and motivations, it is often necessary to convince people to accept certain claims as true, and it often proves useful to arouse emo-tional energy. For example, remember the quotation from Hippocrates we used above to illustrate the informative function of language:

> Speaking generally, all parts of the body which have a function, if used in moderation and exercised in labors to which each is accustomed, become healthy and age slowly. But if un-used and left idle, they come liable to disease, defective in growth, and age quickly.

We encountered this quotation posted on the wall of our health club in the gymnasium near the mirror wall that you face when you are on the exercise ma-chinery. Next to the quotation is a life-sized photo-poster showing a young woman athlete in peak physical condition about to serve a volleyball. She looks GREAT! In this context the quotation is clearly being used persuasively as a motivator.

EXERCISE 2.2 | Functions of Language

For each of the following examples, determine the primary language function. (Occasionally there is more than one primary language function.) Be prepared to explain the reasoning behind your answer.

	Informative	"The suspect left the scene driving a green convertible with out-of-state plates."	Explain your answer:
	Expressive		
	Directive		
	Persuasive		

	Informative	"Follow highway 12 west to Madrone Road, take Madrone to Arnold Drive, then turn left and drive two miles till you see the golf course."	Explain your answer:
	Expressive		
	Directive		
	Persuasive		

	Informative	"We must all hang together or assuredly we shall all hang separately." —Ben Franklin (to other signers of the Declaration of Independence)	Explain your answer:
	Expressive		
	Directive		
	Persuasive		

	Informative	Teenage moviegoer after seeing *Spiderman:* "Awesome!"	Explain your answer:
	Expressive		
	Directive		
	Persuasive		

	Informative	"Combine 2 cups water and 1 tablespoon butter and bring to a boil. Stir in rice and spice mix, reduce heat and simmer for 10 minutes."	Explain your answer:
	Expressive		
	Directive		
	Persuasive		

	Informative	"How 'bout those Dallas Cowboys cheerleaders, ya know what I'm sayin'?!"	Explain your answer:
	Expressive		
	Directive		
	Persuasive		

	Informative	Noticing that it was five minutes past bedtime, Mrs. Cleaver said, "Okay Beaver, let's close the book now and go to bed."	Explain your answer:
	Expressive		
	Directive		
	Persuasive		

MEANING IN LANGUAGE

How do words get to mean what they mean? (Another one of those questions you hope your children don't ask you when they're little and persistent in their curiosity.) Let's start by briefly examining a primitive theory: that words are essentially labels for things. For example, the word *cat* functions as a label. It "stands for" and "points to" the animal. We can use it not only to identify an in-

dividual animal, distinguishing it from other things, but also for the purpose of categorization (grouping things together—in this case to refer to feline creatures). A moment's reflection and you can readily see how useful labels are. Just imagine how hard it would be to talk about people, in general as a group, if we didn't have labels like *humanity* or *people*. Imagine how hard it would be to talk about something like the functions of language if we didn't have the word "function"—or some other word with the same function. Labels also help us to point things out, or refer specifically to some particular part of a complex situation, as in "Please pass the *butter*." Labels help us orient ourselves in new and unfamiliar surroundings, as in "Where's the *restroom*?" Labels are like "verbal handles" enabling us to mentally "come to grips with" our world and our experience. In Arabic there are more than five thousand words that pinpoint differences of age, sex, and bodily structure among camels. Consider how much more it must be possible to say—and to think—about camels in Arabic than in English. From this we can appreciate how tempting it may be to generalize from labels to the whole of language.

Next, how do labels come to mean what they mean? How does the word *cat* come to stand for the animal and the category? Speakers of English use "cat," while speakers of French use *chat*, speakers of Spanish use *gato*, and speakers of German use *Katze*. These are similar enough to make one wonder if there isn't some "natural" connection between the label and what it is a label for. Some labels, like "hiccup" and "splash," do seem to have some sort of identifiable natural connection to the things they stand for. A label that *sounds like* what it is a label for is called an "onomatopoeia." But not all labels have this sort of obvious and straightforward connection with their jobs. In fact, most don't. For example, "onomatopoeia"—or for that matter, look at *any* of the words in this sentence. Some of them—"for," "at," "any," "the," "in"—don't even seem to function as labels at all.

For a more comprehensive and deeply explanatory theory of meaning, we might do well to return to the notion of language's essential function, or functional essence, as a set of tools for achieving common understanding, and look at things like this: Words are noises that human beings have assigned "meanings" to. Speakers of English use *cat* to refer to feline creatures, while speakers of French use *chat*, speakers of Spanish use *gato*, and speakers of German use *Katze*. There is nothing "required" or "natural" about such assignments of meaning to noises. Any other sound *could* have been made to stand for what *cat* stands for in English, and likewise in the other language communities. These assignments of meaning are merely "conventional"; that is to say, they are based on human conventions. Other words, like *the*, and *and*, and *so*, and *on*, and so on have meanings in accordance with their conventional uses, with the roles they conventionally play in putting words together into meaningful sentences. Much the same can be said of syntax as of word meaning. "Syntax" refers to the structural regularities in the ways words are put together to communicate thoughts and ideas. In English we put adjectives before nouns, as in "white house." In Spanish the adjective typically follows the noun: "casa blanca." The difference is a matter of convention.

So, what is a "convention"? *A convention is simply a behavioral regularity that we maintain and follow in order to solve problems of coordination.* Suppose that you and your friend are cut off in the middle of a cell phone conversation. Here you have what we might call a "coordination problem." What each of you should do depends on what the other person does. If you both dial each other's cell phone number, you both get a busy signal. If you both hang up and wait, well, . . . you wait. You get back in contact if, and only if, one of you dials while the other waits. What should you do? Well, suppose that in the past when this sort of thing has happened, you have always been the one to dial, and that has worked, and you know it has worked, and your friend knows it has worked, and you know that your friend knows it has worked, and you know that your friend knows that you know this, and so on. So, if you now pick up the phone and dial while your friend waits, and you do these things because you are both thinking that this will solve the coordination problem, because both of you know that it has worked in the past, etc., you are following a "convention."[2] The basic problems of communication, understanding one another and making oneself understood, are coordination problems. Language can usefully be understood as a vast system of conventions we learn to follow in order to solve such problems.

A number of interesting and important consequences follow from this way of viewing language. First of all, linguistic conventions are, in one sense, arbitrary. This means that they could have been other than they are. And indeed, linguistic conventions evolve, sometimes quite rapidly and dramatically. But though linguistic conventions could have been other than they are and may well change over time, they nevertheless do regulate meaningful discourse. Linguistic conventions are thus a lot like the rules in a game.

Think of the rules governing organized sports like American football or basketball and you'll see what we mean. One rule in American football states that the dimensions of the playing field between the end zones is 100 yards; another prescribes exactly 11 players per team. These rules are arbitrary; they could be other than what they are. For example, Canadian football is played on a 110-yard field with 12 players on each side. And the rules of a game can be changed by common consent. Thus, for example, the three-point field goal in professional and collegiate basketball is a relatively late addition to the game. But the rules, whatever they are, do regulate the game. If you choose to play American football, then you must play by its rules. If you play Canadian football, you must observe its rules.

Similarly, in playing the language game, we must generally abide by the conventions of the particular language in which we are attempting to communicate. And we can rightly expect others to do the same. Conventions in language are somewhat more flexible and informal than rules are in games. For one thing, you don't get thrown out of the game for committing five unconventional speech acts. Furthermore, sometimes violating a linguistic convention can be a very creative and effective way of communicating something unique and special. Nevertheless, meaningful departures from the conventions of our language presuppose those conventions as generally binding. If this were not the case, departing from our language's conventions would lead to hopeless confusion.

In *Through the Looking Glass,* Alice and Humpty Dumpty have the following conversation:

> ". . . there are 364 days when you might get un-birthday presents."
>
> "Certainly," said Alice.
>
> "And only *one* for birthday presents, you know. There's glory for you!"
>
> "I don't know what you mean by 'glory'," Alice said.
>
> Humpty Dumpty smiled contemptuously. "Of course you don't—till I tell you. I meant, 'there's a nice knock-down argument for you!'"
>
> "But 'glory' doesn't mean 'a nice knock-down argument'," Alice objected.
>
> "When I use a word," Humpty Dumpty said, in a rather scornful tone, "it means just what I choose it to mean—neither more nor less."[3]

Just imagine the confusion that would reign if, like Humpty Dumpty, each of us used words to mean exactly what we wanted them to mean, "neither more nor less." To avoid such chaos and inconvenience, we generally presuppose a conventional interpretation of what someone says. If a writer or speaker doesn't indicate a departure from conventional usage, we normally assume that the person is following conventional usage. Of course, this works both ways, which is why generally speaking it's best to *follow conventional usage* when we try to communicate. When we do use a word in an unconventional way, we need to give our audience extra guidance to our meaning. If we don't, we're likely to lose them. It should be obvious what happens when you and your audience are not coordinated regarding what you mean: Communication breaks down.

EXERCISE 2.3 | "Communication Breakdown"

Topic for Class Discussion: Here is an actual example of communication breakdown. Read the following newspaper story[4] and then see if you can identify the factors that account for the breakdown in communication.

Neighbors Chop Down Redwood: Claim to Have Had Permission

An East Napa Street front yard is now barren, following a misunderstanding between neighbors.

When Rene Alonzo returned to Sonoma in early December, he drove straight past his East Napa Street home. Realizing his mistake, he backed up, parked and slowly got out of his car. Seeing his lawn, he gasped and fell back against the vehicle. The house was the same as always, but his prized old-growth trees were gone.

Alonzo had been away for six weeks. Caring for his wife who is in the hospital. He hoped to bring her back to the Sonoma house that she has owned for 35 years since before their marriage. But after seeing the property, Alonzo wanted to spare her the shock.

Three trees had been removed, along with hedges on the side of the house. Alonzo couldn't believe what he was seeing. "These trees are 150 years old," he said.

Alonzo said that a caretaker at the house had contacted him while he was away and said that the new neighbors had asked permission to remove a single overhanging branch from one of the trees. Alonzo agreed but said that he had no idea they were going to take out the entire trees. "We don't even know the neighbors. We've never even met them," Alonzo said.

Mona Couchman has lived at 351 East Napa Street with her husband and 3-year old daughter since September. She said that her family decided to have the trees removed on the Monday after Thanksgiving because they were top heavy and could possibly fall and hurt people. "Our neighbors are very upset about it, but it seems that this is an issue of dangerous trees," Couchman said.

Couchman said that she wanted to contact Alonzo, but the caretaker would not give her his number. She said that the caretaker understood that they were going to remove the trees and was surprised when Alonzo was shocked. "We're very reasonable people. We wouldn't do it if we knew how irate he would be," Couchman said. According to Couchman there was no mention of only removing one branch. "We never, ever said that," she said.

Alonzo claims that his property is worth half a million dollars less now that the trees are gone. "It would have been better if they knocked down part of the house. At least you could rebuild it," he said.

The incident was reported to the Sonoma Police Department, but Capt. Robert Wedell said that it is no longer being investigated as a crime because "there was no intent to do harm. It's now up to the parties to resolve it," Wedell said.

DIMENSIONS OF MEANING: PRECISION AND CLARITY

In the story you just read we have a pair of next-door neighbors who have never spoken to each other face-to-face, and probably never will. Their only communications so far have been through intermediaries, first the caretaker, and now lawyers. No doubt there are several important lessons to be drawn from this unfortunate tale. You can see, for instance, what people mean when they say "Get it in writing." And you can see the importance of two dimensions of communication in particular, precision and clarity.

AMBIGUITY AND VAGUENESS

Let us now distinguish and define two important concepts having to do with precision and clarity in communication and that will prove increasingly useful as we proceed: ambiguity and vagueness. Each of these can be a source of confusion in communication (which may help explain why they so often get confused with each other). *To say that a term or expression is "ambiguous" is to say that it has more than one conventional meaning.* In other words, it can be conventionally understood in more than one way. For example, the word "bank" can mean:

1. any piled up mass, such as snow or clouds
2. the slope of land adjoining a body of water
3. the cushion of a billiard or pool table
4. to strike a billiard shot off the cushion
5. to tilt an aircraft in flight
6. a business establishment authorized to receive and safeguard money, lend money at interest, etc.

By permission of Johnny Hart and Creators Syndicate, Inc.

Saying that a term is "vague" means that it is not entirely clear what it does and doesn't apply to. In technical terms, *a vague term or expression is one that has an indefinite "extension"* (see the section on denotation and connotation below). For example, the term "bald" clearly applies to actor Jason Alexander or basketball commentator Dick Vitale. It clearly does not apply to Bill Clinton or Brad Pitt. But there is an indefinite area in between where it isn't clear whether a person is bald or not. Vagueness itself admits of degrees according to how big the "gray area" is. Thus "bald" is less vague than "happy," and "vague" is itself pretty vague (which is a pretty vague thing to say). Vagueness and ambiguity are both singled out as the focus of criticism in, for example, the margins of student essays. But it is important to be aware that both vagueness and ambiguity are *useful* features of the language. They each contribute to language's inherent *flexibility*. Ambiguity gives language the flexibility to handle multiple meanings at once. Without ambiguity many jokes, plays on words, puns, and much of the richness of poetry and literature in general would be impossible. Vagueness gives language the flexibility it needs to adapt to unforeseen and unforeseeable situations, by leaving questions of definition and judgment open to deliberation in context.

EXERCISE 2.4 | Ambiguity and Vagueness

In each of the following examples highlight any terms or expressions that are used in an ambiguous way, and highlight any terms or expressions that are vague. Explain your answers.

	Explain your answers:
Rappers continue to get a bad rap in the press.	
How do reasonable people come to hold unreasonable beliefs?	
Headline: "Drunk Gets Nine Months in Violin Case"	
The streets are perfectly safe here in New York City. It's the muggers you have to watch out for.	
Random urinalysis for drugs in safety-sensitive job categories does not constitute an unreasonable search.	
A man walks up to the Zen Buddhist hot dog vendor and says, "Make me one with everything."	
Nuclear energy is just as natural as any other fuel, and cleaner than many already in use.	
Let me reassure the public that your government is doing everything within its power to make sure that the traveling public is as secure against the threat of terrorism as it can possibly be.	
According to the Supreme Court, flag burning is protected under the First Amendment as an instance of political speech.	

DENOTATION AND CONNOTATION

Let us now look more closely at word meaning and develop an important distinction between two of its dimensions, denotation and connotation, starting once again with labels. Consider the word *bridge*. What does the word *bridge* mean? In one sense, as a label, the word means what it serves to refer or point to. It points to a group of objects: bridges. This pointing-to relationship between a label and the things it is a label for is called *denotation*. The set of things denoted by a term is called the term's *extension*. For example, the extension of the word *bridge* includes the Golden Gate Bridge; the extension of the word *building* includes the Empire State Building. And so we could also say that at least part of what the word *bridge* means is the whole set of things it denotes (in other words its extension) including the Golden Gate Bridge; and part of what the word *building* means is its extension, including the Empire State Building. The word *building* has a very large and relatively diverse extension that includes the Empire State Building, the Sydney Opera House, the Pentagon, the lighthouse at Point Reyes, and the outhouse behind the barn. They're all buildings. But not everything is a building. This book is not a building. Nor is every structure a building; nor even everything built; the Golden Gate Bridge is a structure, but not a building. Why is this and how do we know? In many cases this is so and we know it to be so because there are *criteria* that determine the extension of the term. Bridges and buildings are bridges or buildings because they satisfy criteria that make them bridges or buildings rather than, say, tunnels or microchips. These criteria, which define the extension of the term, are called the term's *intension*. And so we could also say that part of what the word *bridge* means is its intension, this set of criteria that define its extension. If the intension of a term is part of its meaning, we don't want to confuse it with what the term denotes. So we'll say that it is part of the term's *connotation*.

In addition to the extension and the intension of a word—we'll say these comprise the word's *literal* meaning—most words also come with a penumbra of additional dimensions of meaning that arise out of their conventionally implied associations. For example, *prima donna* literally means "the principal female singer in an opera company." But the term has come by conventional association to carry the added meaning of "a vain, temperamental person." Consequently, using the term *prima donna,* especially outside of the specialized context of opera, is an effective way of putting someone down. These additional dimensions of meaning are included among the word's "connotations." So, similarly, the word *tabloid* literally means a newspaper formatted at about half the size of a standard-size newspaper page and with no horizontal fold. But because many newspapers in tabloid format have tended toward journalistic sensationalism, the word *tabloid* conventionally carries an additional negative or pejorative connotation of "disreputable journalism." Of course, such connotations need not be derogatory. Many are complimentary. "Diplomat" sounds so much more respectable to many an ear than "politician." "Moderate" sounds so much more thoughtful than "wishy-washy." Here we can see the importance of language's expressive function to what we might call the "artistry" of persuasion. It becomes possible, through the careful selection of terminology (choosing a word such as "artistry," for example) to color a statement emotionally.

EXERCISE 2.5 | Labels/Denotation/Connotation

Agenda for Class Discussion: One of the most astute observers of language these days is linguist Geoffrey Nunberg. He is a regular contributor to the National Public Radio program *Fresh Air,* whose hostess, Terry Gross, describes him as having "the best ear in America for listening to how the English language is changing, the best mind for interpreting those changes, and the most amusing way of explaining it all." Read the following selection, in which Nunberg comments on labels, changing conventions, denotations, and connotations. Here is an agenda of questions for class discussion (or an essay assignment).

1. What are the labels Nunberg is commenting on? (Note: There are more than two.)
2. Carefully describe the connotations of each of these labels.
3. What are Nunberg's explanation and assessment of these connotative developments?
4. Do you agree or disagree?

100% Solution

I got a mail-order catalog the other day from a company that specializes in home and health-care products—at least they used to call them products, but now that word's been entirely eliminated from their catalog in favor of the word 'solutions.' You can find seat cushions in the section on stress relief solutions, bathrobes in spa care solutions, and support bras in intimate apparel solutions.

The solutions game began in the early 1980s when companies like IBM started using the word to describe the packages of hardware, software and services they were selling to corporate customers. In a sense, it's just a new way of pitching your offerings as answers to customers' needs and anxieties, in the time honored tradition of ring around the collar and the heartbreak of psoriasis, except that the word 'solutions' makes its point in a proactive way. In the old days, when people said, 'I've got a solution for you,' you assumed that somebody had mentioned a problem somewhere along the line. Now the two have come unhitched.

Solutions aren't solutions for anything anymore. When you do a search on 'solutions' at the Web site of Compaq or Apple Computer you find that it's anywhere from two to three times as frequent as the word 'problems.' Business people don't like to hear talk about problems; it seems to betray a negative mind-set. If there are difficulties you absolutely have to mention, you try to find another name for them, as in, 'We had a number of challenges this quarter,' or, 'There are several known issues installing the beta release of the printer driver.'

By now there are hundreds of firms that have incorporated that word 'solutions' into their company names, and by no means all of them are high-tech. There's the beachwear-maker Sun Solutions, which is not to be confused with Solar Solutions, which sells propane ranges and composting toilets. And then there's Bright Horizons Family Solutions, an outfit that manages corporate daycare centers, whose portfolio presumably includes story hour solutions and snack solutions, not to mention nap solutions for clients with crankiness issues.

It's hard to think of a company that couldn't say it was in the solutions business now. Smuckers, your toast coating solutions provider. And in fact, one reason why so many companies are sticking the word into their names is that they don't have to let on as to what they're actually selling, particularly if they're still in the embarrassing position of making things. Things have low margins and high capital costs; they're expensive to ship; they lead to liability lawsuits. They get you in trouble with the EPA. If you make them domestically, you have to deal with unions. If you make them overseas, people get on your back for running sweatshops.

It's no wonder the manufacturing sector is a diminishing part of the American economy. In 1950, material goods made up more than half the GDP. Now they account for less than a quarter of it. And companies that aren't in the position to stop making things altogether, can at least relabel them as solutions. It suggests that their products are just an ancillary sideline of their real business, like the terry cloth slippers they throw in when you go for a massage. That's the beauty of solutions, nobody has to tip their hands.

It's a perfect complement for those empty corporate names that marketing consultants paste together out of strings of chopped up syllables. Take the Ohio outfit called Amnova Solutions. What line of work would you say they're in? Client-server applications, health-care benefits administration, fabric transfers and decorative wall coverings? As it happens it's the last of those, but the others are just as plausible. These aren't like those old-fashioned corporate names that were designed to conjure up an image of a particular product made by a real company. You feel sorry for the members of a softball team who have to take the field with Amnova Solutions written on their uniforms.

Names like these are attempts to create pure brands; free signifiers that float in the ether, ready to light on anything that somebody's willing to pay for. That's what the new economy comes down to in the end: Just one big intersection with people at every corner holding signs that say, 'Will solve for cash.'[5]

EXERCISE 2.6 | Labels/Denotation/Connotation

For each of the following labels, give an example from its extension and two substitute labels, one with positive connotations and one with negative connotations.

Label	Example	Positive	Negative
Environmental Activist	Julia Butterfly Hill	Defenders of the earth	Tree huggers
Spectator Sports			
Occupations			
Corporations			
Animals			

DEFINITIONS

A definition is an explanation *of the meaning of a term.* The word *definition* and its close relatives *define, definite, definitive,* and so on all come from the Latin *definire* for "setting boundaries or limits." The most basic use we have for definitions is in teaching people the language. One simple sort of definition often used for the purpose of teaching the language consists in pointing out *examples* of the term being defined. For example, if someone didn't know what *reptile* meant, you could help that person by pointing out snakes, lizards,

turtles, crocodiles and so on. This kind of definition is called *ostensive definition*—from the Latin word for "show," as in "*show* me what it means." Another basic strategy of definition, also useful for the purpose of teaching new or unfamiliar vocabulary, is through "synonyms." From the Greek for "same name," *synonyms* are words or expressions that have the same meaning. For example, suppose we run across the word *poltroon* in a line of verse about pirates (rhymes with "doubloon"). If we didn't know that *poltroon* is a synonym for "coward," we might easily wind up thinking that the line was about a parrot or a drunken sailor or something. Knowing where a word comes from can tell you a lot about what it means, and many words have fascinating histories—or *etymologies.* For example, the word *etymology* comes through Middle English and Old French from Medieval Latin *ethimologia,* which is derived from Latin *etymologia,* which came from the Greek *etumologia,* which is based on the Greek word *etumon,* which means "true sense of the word." Help in understanding a new or unfamiliar term (like "burqa" or "gigabyte") is something even fluent speakers of any language need regularly, because language is dynamic and evolving constantly. This is why we have dictionaries—and why they need to be updated periodically.

WHAT DICTIONARIES DON'T DO

In a good dictionary, in addition to the spelling and the pronunciation key, we are likely to find examples, synonyms, etymologies, and other information helpful in understanding the conventional meanings of words. But a dictionary generally won't tell you the meaning of a word that is being used in an unconventional way—although knowing what the word conventionally means is often very helpful and maybe even essential for figuring out the unconventional meaning.

Suppose a writer or speaker wants to communicate an idea for which no conventionally understood term is exactly right. This could happen when there's some new invention or category to deal with (like "gigabyte"). But it can also happen with well-established vocabulary that we need to depart from conventional usage and use words in unconventional ways in order to get our meanings across. Typically, this will be in order to achieve *greater precision* than is generally needed for conventional purposes of communication. In specialized or technical disciplines like geometry, for example, words like *point, line,* and *plane* are given quite specific meanings much more precise than their conventional ones. In legal and other policy contexts it is often necessary to make distinctions and classifications more precisely than conventional vocabulary will express. For example, "In this contract, for purposes of determining benefit eligibility a 'full-time employee' shall be defined as an 'employee working 25 hours or more per week.'" For these purposes definitions are often "stipulated." The word *stipulate,* which comes from the Latin word for "bargaining," means "to specify as in an agreement." In effect what we're doing when we stipulate a definition is "laying down the terms of an agreement" about how a word is to be used and understood in the context of some discourse, where conventional usage and understanding are inadequate or un-suitable in some way.

EXERCISE 2.7 | **Definition Scavenger Hunt**

- Make up one example of definition by synonymy.
- Find an example of definition by synonymy in a dictionary.
- Find one example of stipulated definition in this book.

Something else dictionaries don't generally do, or at least don't generally do very well or very reliably:

EXERCISE 2.8 | **Essential Definitions I**

Read the following list of words and check the ones you're confident that you know and understand.

- art
- beauty
- communication
- drugs
- entertainment
- freedom
- information
- jazz

- love
- music
- news
- obscenity
- pornography
- religion
- sign
- terrorism

We'd be willing to bet that you know and understand every word on this list. We'd be willing to bet that if you ran across any of these words in a sentence, you wouldn't need to go look it up in a dictionary. And you'd be able to use any of these words quite comfortably and correctly in your own conversation and writing because you are already quite familiar with the conventional meanings of all of these words. Right?

EXERCISE 2.9 | **Essential Definitions II**

Now, go through the list and see how many of these words you think you'd be able to teach to another person ostensively. Remember this means being able to point out examples in order to indicate what the word means.

Still no problem, right? Well, maybe a little problem here and there with one or two of the more "abstract" ones. But in general, pretty manageable, yes?

EXERCISE 2.10 | Essential Definitions III

OK. So now here's a real challenge: Take any of the words on this list and explain its intension. Remember what "intension" means. The intension of a word is the set of criteria that define the word's extension, which is the set of examples it conventionally applies to.

Criteria, the plural form of *criterion,* derives from the same Greek root as "critical," which you remember from Chapter 1 is about "decision making." *Criteria are rules or standards for decision making.* So the criteria that define a word's extension would be the rules or standards according to which we decide whether the word applies or not. We expect that you will find this surprisingly hard. Take *music* for example. Remember, this is a word you know well. It's in your working vocabulary. You don't need a dictionary to help you understand a question like, "Do you want to listen to some music?" And you can easily identify examples of music. Now try to state the criteria according to which you decide whether something is music or not. This is not as easy as one might think. What you're trying to state here is a kind of definition that we're going to refer to as an "essential definition." People have often described what we're challenging you to try to do here as "stating the *essence—*or *essential nature—*of" (in this case) music. Another way to describe what you're trying to do is this: Think of the extension of the word *music* as though it were a bounded territory. The things that the word *music* conventionally applies to, all the things in its extension, are "inside the boundaries of the territory"; things to which the word *music* does *not* apply are "outside the boundaries." And so what you're trying to do is produce a verbal map of the territory, or describe its boundaries in words. (Remember, the word *definition* comes from the Latin for "setting boundaries or limits.")

Now you might wonder what essential definitions are good for. What special purpose or purposes do they serve? Assuming that people are familiar with the word we're defining, there's no need to teach it as a new vocabulary item. And in that case why would we need *any* sort of definition? Well, sometimes the way things are classified is a matter of great importance. Suppose the local city government has just passed a new city ordinance regulating the sale and distribution of "obscene" and "pornographic" materials to minors. Now suppose the local purveyor of recorded entertainment (CDs, tapes, videos) is brought up on charges of violating the ordinance in connection with the sale of a Britney Spears music video to a 16-year-old. The case turns partly on whether or not the Britney Spears video is "obscene" and/or "pornographic," and that turns on the criteria for "obscenity" and "pornography." Now these would presumably be stipulated in the city ordinance. But suppose you are on the city council and you have to *draft* the ordinance. So you have the challenge of coming up with the wording of the criteria according to which it will be decided whether something is "obscene" or "pornographic." So, there we are back at the challenge of formulating the essential definitions. But couldn't we just look these up in a dictionary?

EXERCISE 2.11 | Essential Definitions IV

OK. Go ahead and try it. Go through the list and see how many satisfactory essential definitions you can find in a good dictionary. Try *terrorism*.

Occasionally you may find a satisfactory essential definition in a dictionary. But it is better to approach this as a "figure it out" kind of a challenge rather than a "look it up" kind of a challenge. Why is that so? Well, let's take the last word on the list as our example. Here is the definition of *terrorism* supplied by the *American Heritage Dictionary of the English Language:* "The use of terror, violence, and intimidation to achieve an end."[6] According to this definition, any act of war, indeed any deliberate use of violence or intimidation, down to the actions of a schoolyard bully or the enforcer on a hockey team, would qualify as terrorism. Do we really want to define this category so broadly? Or do we want a definition that makes finer distinctions possible? Conventional usage of the term *terrorism* is, we think, slightly more selective—something like this: "Terrorism is when 'the bad guys' (the enemy) use terror, violence, and intimidation to achieve an end." But this is of course a "double standard" and therefore clearly useless for any serious discussion of international political conflict. Sometimes, as in connection with international politics, we are not in a position of authority so as to be able to just stipulate a meaning that departs from general conventional usage. Such definitions truly need to be "negotiated."

In the "obscenity/pornography" example we need a ruling as to whether the Britney Spears video is "obscene" or not. An essential definition of "obscenity" should tell us what to look for in the video to see if it satisfies or fails to satisfy the criteria for "obscenity." In the case of "terrorism" what we need is a set of criteria that will help us distinguish acts of terrorism from other kinds of behavior that may or may not involve the use or threat of violence. We are now going to present some concepts and strategies for figuring out this sort of definition when just looking it up isn't a satisfactory option.

NECESSARY AND SUFFICIENT CONDITIONS

First, let us stipulate the definitions of two important ingredients of essential definitions: "necessary conditions" and "sufficient conditions." In order to fulfill its function, an essential definition must allow you to do two things: rule things in and rule things out. Necessary and sufficient conditions are the parts of an essential definition that enable you to rule things in and rule things out.

A necessary condition is a characteristic or set of characteristics required *for membership in the word's extension.* To illustrate we will use an example that's quite a bit easier to define essentially than any of the words on the above list. Let us define the word *square* as used in plane geometry. The essential definition can be stated in two words: "equilateral rectangle." A square is defined essentially as an equilateral rectangle. In this definition both "equilateral" and "rectangle" indicate necessary conditions. In other words it is required that something be both equilateral and rectangular in order to be included in the extension of the word *square*.

If you find out that something is not equilateral or not rectangular, you don't need to know anything more about it. You already know enough to rule it out.

A sufficient condition is a characteristic or set of characteristics that is by itself adequate *for membership in the word's extension.* Again, in the essential definition of *square* as an equilateral rectangle, the set of characteristics, equilateral and rectangle, together constitute a sufficient condition. In other words, if you find out that something is both equilateral and rectangular, you don't need to know anything more about it. You don't have to know its size, its age, its color, its value, or molecular structure. You already know enough to rule it in.

A "DIALOGICAL" APPROACH TO ESSENTIAL DEFINITIONS

As we said, providing an essential definition of a word like "square" is relatively simple and straightforward. "Obscenity" is harder to define. "Music" is *much* harder to define. In fact, words like *music,* and *art,* and *information,* and *jazz,* and *love,* and others like *justice, liberty, equality, racism, terrorism,* and so on are so hard to define in this way that many people give up the attempt. People who persist in the attempt to formulate essential definitions of words like these are often called "philosophers," and their attempted essential definitions are often called "philosophies" or "theories" and take a whole book to present and explain, as in "Kant's philosophy of art" or John Rawls's *A Theory of Justice.* This involves thinking in a careful and disciplined way about examples and the precise wording of the definition. We call the following approach "dialogical" because it goes back and forth in dialogue form. To illustrate it we'll continue with the simple example we used above to explain what necessary and sufficient conditions are.

STEP #1   Formulate a definition. Just go for it. Write it down (so that it stays put and doesn't start changing and evolving before you get to Step #2). When we gave the essential definition of square above, we were able to do it in two words, and we got to it in one step, without any of this back-and-forth business. Squareness is a pretty simple essence to capture in words, but that's pretty rare. We can't expect to get to the essence in one step of two words very often. In most of the interesting cases we're more likely going to need to try something and then tinker with it, refine it, and adjust it. This dialogical approach is designed to help the tinkering process stay on a productive track. So for purposes of illustration let's imagine that we had initially defined the word *square* as an "equilateral shape."

CRITICAL THINKING TIP 2.2: Three Things to Avoid in Step #1

Circularity: A definition is circular if it defines a word in terms of itself. The problem with circularity is that it defeats the purposes of definitions. Once when we were learning Spanish we ran across a conjugated form of the verb *fructificar.* Having no idea what this meant, we referred to the Spanish/English dictionary in the back of the book, where we learned that *fructificar* is Spanish for "to fructify." What we really needed to know was what "to fructify" means ("to fructify" is "to bear fruit"). The rest we had already figured out. The purposes of the definition will be defeated by circularity whether what you are trying to do is teach the conventional meaning of a new or unfamiliar word, stipulate an unconventional meaning, or give an essential definition.

Obscurity: A similar problem results from obscurity. If the terminology in which the definition is formulated is even less familiar than the word being defined, or more difficult to grasp and understand, then the definition will be harder to understand than the word whose meaning it is supposed to explain. Now it's not always possible to avoid obscurity, especially in formulating an essential definition, because people are not all familiar with the same words. What is obscure to one reader may be quite familiar to another. Even more important, sometimes the ideas you will need to capture in words are themselves out of the ordinary and only relatively obscure words will do the trick. Basically you should try to keep the words as simple and familiar as the ideas you're working with will permit.

Negativity: A definition should explain what a word means, not what it doesn't mean. Of course, some words defy affirmative definition. "Orphan" means a child whose parents are not living; "bald" means the state of not having hair on one's head. Unless negativity is an essential element in the meaning of the word, try to formulate the definition in the affirmative.

STEP #2   Critique Step #1 by example. Using what you know about shapes you can see that something's not entirely right about the definition of *square* as an "equilateral shape." And you can demonstrate this by means of an example:

The example does two important things. First, it exposes a flaw in the definition as formulated in Step #1, because the example fits all the criteria specified in the definition but it's not a legitimate member of the extension of the word *square*. In other words the example *refutes* the definition. *An example used for this purpose, or which accomplishes this purpose, we will call a "counterexample."* There are two kinds of counterexample: counterexamples that show that the definition is "too broad" or "overly inclusive" or "lets in too much" (this is how the triangle example above works); and counterexamples that show that the definition is "too narrow" or "overly restrictive" or "leaves out too much." An example that *is* a legitimate member of the extension of a word but does not satisfy all of the criteria specified in a proposed definition would show that definition to be too narrow. The second thing the counterexample does is point the way in Step #3.

STEP #3   Revise the original definition. What was wrong with the definition of "square" as an "equilateral shape"? Our first definition was too broad, as demonstrated by our counterexample in Step #2, so we know we need to make the definition more restrictive. That means adding another necessary condition. How shall we formulate it? The counterexample in Step #2 gives us good guidance here: not enough sides. So that's what we want to add to our definition in Step #3. So let's revise our definition to say that "square" means "equilateral quadrilateral." ("Quadrilateral," of course, means "four-sided figure.")

STEP #4   Repeat Step #2 (critique Step #3 by example). Once again, using what you know about shapes you can see that something's still not entirely right about the definition of "square" as an "equilateral quadrilateral." And you can demonstrate this by example:

STEP #5   Repeat Step #3 (revise the revised definition). What was wrong with the definition of *square* as an "equilateral quadrilateral"? Once again our definition was too broad, as demonstrated by our counterexample in Step #4, so we know we need to make the definition even more restrictive. That means adding another necessary condition. How shall we formulate it? The counterexample in Step #4 again gives us good guidance: The angles are not 90-degree angles. So that's what we want to add to our definition at this point. And so we arrive at "square" means "equilateral rectangle." ("Rectangle" of course means "four-sided figure with 90-degree angles.")

STEP #6   Keep going as needed. At this point the process is complete for the essential definition of the word *square* because it isn't possible to refute our current definition by example. Anything that fits all the criteria specified in our current definition will turn out to be a legitimate member of the extension of the word, and vice versa: Any member of the extension will turn out to satisfy all the criteria in our definition. The word and our definition are *co-extensive,* which means they have the same extension. That's how we know we're done.

EXERCISE 2.12 | **Essential Definitions V**

Critique the following formulations as though they were intended to function as essential definitions. Explain your criticisms. Use examples where appropriate.

	Too Broad	A "dinosaur" is an extinct animal.	Explain your answer:
	Too Narrow		
	Circular		
	Unclear or Figurative		

	Too Broad	"Rape" is forcing a woman to have sex against her will.	Explain your answer:
	Too Narrow		
	Circular		
	Unclear or Figurative		

	Too Broad	"Faith" is the substance of things hoped for, the evidence of things not seen. —Hebrews 11:1	Explain your answer:
	Too Narrow		
	Circular		
	Unclear or Figurative		

	Too Broad	"Economics" is the science that treats of the phenomena arising out of the economic activities of men in society. — J. M. Keynes	Explain your answer:
	Too Narrow		
	Circular		
	Unclear or Figurative		

	Too Broad	A "circle" is a closed plane curve.	Explain your answer:
	Too Narrow		
	Circular		
	Unclear or Figurative		

	Too Broad	"Circular": of or pertaining to a circle; the property of circularity.	Explain your answer:
	Too Narrow		
	Circular		
	Unclear or Figurative		

	Too Broad	"Pornography" is any pictorial display of human sexuality or nudity.	Explain your answer:
	Too Narrow		
	Circular		
	Unclear or Figurative		

	Too Broad	A "definition" is an explanation of the meaning of a term.	Explain your answer:
	Too Narrow		
	Circular		
	Unclear or Figurative		

	Too Broad	"Alimony": that's when two people make a mistake and one of them continues to pay for it.	Explain your answer:
	Too Narrow		
	Circular		
	Unclear or Figurative		

GENUS AND DIFFERENTIA

A related strategic approach involves a two-step procedure and the concept of categories:

STEP #1 Locate the extension of the term you are defining within some larger category (called the "genus"). So, for example, squares are part of the larger category of plane geometric figures.

STEP #2 Now specify the feature or set of features (called the "differentia") that distinguishes the extension you are defining from the rest of the larger category. In this case you want to specify the feature or set of features that distinguishes squares from the rest of the plane geometric figures.

Term	Larger Category	Distinguishing Characteristics
square	plane geometric figure	with 4 equal sides and 90 degree angles

Similarly:

Term	Larger Category	Distinguishing Characteristics
spoon	utensil	consisting of a small, shallow bowl with a handle, used in eating or stirring
watch	machine	portable or wearable for telling time
ethics	branch of philosophy	concerned with morality

Notice that the definition of *square* we arrived at by using the dialectical approach is worded differently than the one we arrived at by genus and differentia. But the two definitions, "equilateral rectangle" and "plane geometric figure with four equal sides and 90-degree angles" are synonymous. They express the same criteria. The necessary and sufficient conditions for being in the extension of "square" are the same in either case. These two strategic approaches can also be effectively combined. If you're stuck, you can use the genus/differentia approach to formulate an initial definition, and you can use the dialectical approach to critique and refine a definition by genus and differentia.

Let us reflect for a moment on the importance of the material we've just covered. Think about why words are important. Think about all the things you do with words. Think about what obstacles you would face if all of a sudden you found yourself in a community or a part of the world where no one speaks your language. Think about what your life would be like if all of a sudden you were deprived of the ability to speak or write or make yourself understood with words. Think about how important mutual understanding is—to you personally, to the maintenance of any sort of interpersonal relationship, to world affairs. Think about how misunderstanding arises. Keep these thoughts in mind as you study further in this book.

ADDITIONAL EXERCISES

■ **EXERCISE 2.13** Spend a few (5–10) minutes observing what happens in some open public area, like a busy intersection, or the campus quadrangle, or a shopping mall. Write a paragraph that contains a strictly factual descriptive account of what you observed. Next write a paragraph that, besides being informative, is also entertaining. Next write a paragraph that uses the information in a persuasive way.

Informative

_____

_____

_____

_____

_____

_____

_____

Entertaining

_____

_____

_____

_____

_____

_____

_____

_____

_____

Persuasive

_____

_____

_____

_____

_____

_____

_____

_____

_____

■ **EXERCISE 2.14**　Explain both the conventional meaning and the current emotional connotations of the following terms:

- "New Democrat"
- "New Right"
- "liberal"
- "welfare queen"
- "Barbie"
- "high technology"
- "higher learning"
- "ivory tower"
- "free trade"
- "free market"
- "free world"

- "fundamentalist"
- "extremist"
- "hard-liner"
- "drug-free zone"
- "gay"
- "big government"
- "big business"
- "family entertainment"
- "adult entertainment"
- "urban"
- "inner city"

■ **EXERCISE 2.15**　In traffic, have you ever noticed how anyone going slower than you are is an "idiot," while anyone going faster than you are is a "maniac"? The same thing can be called by different names, depending on whether one is for it or against it. For example, if you're for a proposal to outlaw retail discounts on certain merchandise, you might call it the "fair trade practices act"; if you're against it you might call it a "price-fixing law." Take a current issue or piece of legislation and give it a favorable and an unfavorable name by which it could be designated.

■ **EXERCISE 2.16**　Imagine yourself as the creator of a successful national consulting firm specializing in political slogans. Your clients cover the spectrum of issues and interest groups. This month the following groups have scheduled rallies in major cities for the causes listed below. Your job is to come up with a set of five catchy slogans to successfully communicate each group's message. You're also scheduled to address a national radio audience at the end of the month on the topic of "Successful Strategies for Political Communication." You plan to use your work for your current roster of clients to explain the secrets of your success.

- MADD (Mothers Against Drunk Driving)—demanding tougher penalties for drunk driving
- PETA (People for the Ethical Treatment of Animals)—opposing the use of animal subjects in AIDS research at the State University Medical Center
- ACT-UP—counter-demonstration in support of accelerating the pace of AIDS research
- NORML (National Organization for the Reform of Marijuana Laws)—supporting national legislation to permit medical use of marijuana
- DARE—counterdemonstration to keep marijuana classified as an illegal substance
- EarthFirst—supporting a moratorium on logging in old-growth redwood forests
- National Wise Use Coalition—counterdemonstration supporting the rights of private interests to harvest timber resources on private lands
- American Family Association—opposing a permit for an Eminem concert
- American Civil Liberties Union—counterdemonstration against censorship

- San Francisco Historical Preservation Society—supporting a citywide ordinance banning skateboarding on all sidewalks and public spaces
- Thrasher Magazine—counterdemonstration in support of skateboard right-of-way

■ **EXERCISE 2.17**   In each of the following examples highlight any terms or expressions that are used in an ambiguous way, and highlight any terms or expressions that are vague. Explain your answers.

	Explain your answers:
Asked why he robbed banks, notorious bank robber Willy Sutton replied, "That's where the money is."	
He was thrown from the car as it left the road. Later he was found in the ditch by some stray cows.	
As the great escape artist Harry Houdini drove south along Jefferson Boulevard, he suddenly turned into a side street.	
Baseball pitcher Tug McGraw, asked if he preferred Astroturf to grass, said, "I don't know. I never smoked Astroturf."	
Sexual harassment is defined as unwelcome sexual advances, requests for sexual favors and other verbal or physical conduct of a sexual nature when: • submission to such conduct is made either explicitly or implicitly a term or condition of an individual's employment, admission, or academic evaluation; • submission to such conduct is used as a basis for evaluation in personnel decisions or academic evaluations affecting an individual; • such conduct has the purpose or effect of unreasonably interfering with an individual's performance or of creating an intimidating, hostile, offensive, or otherwise adverse working or educational environment; • or the conduct has the purpose or effect of interfering with a student's academic performance, creating an intimidating, hostile, offensive, or otherwise adverse learning environment or adversely affecting any student.	

■ **EXERCISE 2.18**   How many definitions can you find in the first two chapters of this book? List them in the chart below.

Page #	Term defined	Definition

■ **EXERCISE 2.19**   In the following examples highlight any terms or expressions that are either undefined and should be defined, or are defined in some incorrect or inadequate way and should be redefined. Explain your answers.

	Explain your answers:
I don't know why some people get so mad about companies like Enron that deceive, or even victimize, the public. Such practices are part of the meaning of free enterprise, which everyone knows is the foundation of our political, social, and economic institutions. Free enterprise means that all of us should do what we think is best for ourselves. That's all business is doing—looking out for itself. If consumers are deceived or damaged, then that's their fault. Let them take a page from the book of free enterprise and look out for themselves. Rather than condemning business for being ambitious, aggressive, shrewd, and resourceful, we should praise it for acting in accordance with the doctrine of free enterprise, which is the American way.	

Murder is whatever prevents a life from coming into existence. By this account, abortion is murder. All societies have proscriptions against murder, and rightly so. There is no more heinous act than to take the innocent life of another. A society that does not stand up to murderers cannot call itself truly civilized. It's obvious, then, that if the United States is worthy of the term "civilized," it must prohibit abortion and deal harshly with those who have committed or commit abortions, since these people are murderers.	Explain your answers:

■ **EXERCISE 2.20**   At the end of Chapter 1 (Exercise 1.28) the instructions were to compose a one-page Issue Statement. Now let's review and revise that composition. Identify any key terms or concepts in your first draft relevant to understanding the issue. Make sure that these terms are clearly defined. Check to see that you are using terminology in ways that are consistent with conventional usage, or that where you depart from conventional usage, your intended meaning is clear. Check your draft for emotionally loaded descriptions or labels. Where there is a detectable bias, try to reformulate the wording to eliminate it. Remember the distinction between the Informative and the Persuasive uses of language. An "Issue Statement" should not be a persuasive composition.

GLOSSARY

ambiguous   a term or expression has more than one conventional meaning

analysis   the process of breaking things down into their constituent elements

connotation   the intension plus the emotional impact of a term

convention   a behavioral regularity followed in order to solve interpersonal coordination problems

counterexample   example used to refute a general claim, as for example in a definition

definition   an explanation of the meaning of a term or expression

definition, essential   definition that gives a term's intension

definition, ostensive   definition by example

definition, stipulative   definition that specifies an unconventional meaning of a term for use in a specific context of discourse

denotation   the relationship between a word and the objects it "points to"

differentia   characteristics that distinguish the extension of a term from the genus

etymology   the history of a word

extension   the set of objects denoted by a term

explanation   language used to facilitate understanding

genus   larger category within which the extension of a term is located

intension   the criteria that define the extension of a term

necessary condition   a characteristic or set of characteristics required for membership in the word's extension

sufficient condition   a characteristic or set of characteristics that is by itself adequate qualification for membership in the word's extension

synonymy   sameness of meaning

vague   a term or expression with an indefinite extension

verbal dispute   a dispute arising out of overlooked verbal ambiguity

ENDNOTES

[1] The Greek philosopher Aristotle was an early developer of this approach. For a more recent treatment of this concept as a general strategy, see David N. Perkins, *Knowledge as Design* (Hillsdale, N.J.: Erlbaum, 1986).

[2] This account of linguistic convention is derived from Jonathan Bennett, *Linguistic Behavior* (London: Cambridge Univ. Press, 1976) and David Lewis, *Convention* (Cambridge, MA: Harvard Univ. Press, 1969).

[3] Lewis Carroll, *Through the Looking Glass,* in *The Complete Works of Lewis Carroll* (New York: Random House, 1936), p. 214.

[4] William Wetmore, "Neighbors Chop Down Redwood, Claim to Have Had Permission," *Sonoma Index-Tribune,* Tuesday, December 25, 2001, p. 1. Reprinted with permission of the *Sonoma Index-Tribune.*

[5] "100% Solution," from *Fresh Air,* July 18, 2001, NPR. For more see, Geoffrey Nunberg, *The Way We Talk Now* (New York: Houghton Mifflin, 2001). Reprinted by permission of the author.

[6] *American Heritage Dictionary of the English Language* (New York: Houghton Mifflin, 1979), p. 1330.

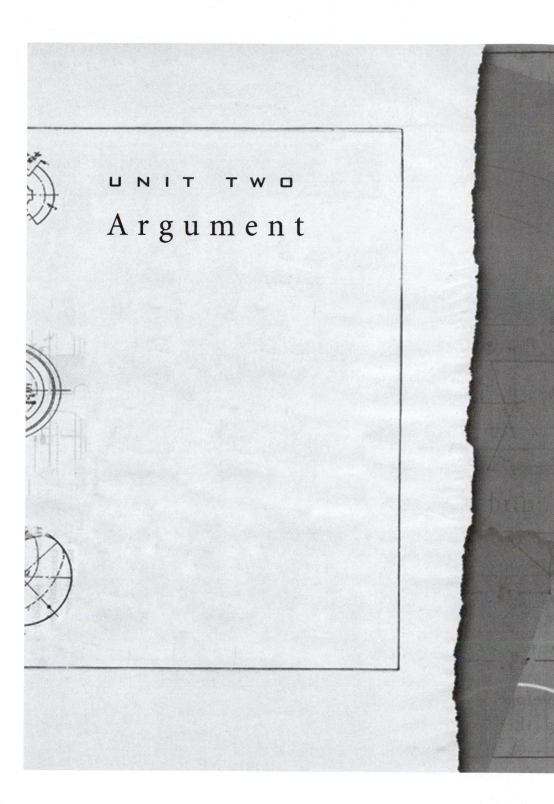

UNIT TWO
Argument

C H A P T E R   3

Argument
Identification

L̲et us now suppose that you and some
other reasonable person find yourselves divided over an issue—say, for example,
what rules should apply to trials of people accused of international terrorism.
One of you is of the opinion that such cases should be tried under international
law, while the other thinks that such cases should be tried under the laws of the
nation that has suffered a terrorist attack. What do reasonable people do when
they recognize they are divided over an issue? They argue. In this chapter we will
introduce and develop the concept of an "argument" as at once a product of critical thinking and an object to which critical thinking is applied.

The word *argument* is ambiguous. For clarity let us center on one of its conventional meanings and set aside the other as outside our focus of primary concern. In this book we are primarily concerned with the sense of the word *argument* in which an individual person *makes* or *offers* an argument, not the sense in
which two people *have* an argument. In the sense of the word with which we're

"This is where your mother and I had our first argument."

primarily concerned, an "argument" can be defined as *a composition whose primary purpose is to persuade a person by appealing to the person's reasoning capacity.* To reinforce this distinction, consider the following portion of the Monty Python's Flying Circus "Argument Clinic" sketch. A "customer," played by Michael Palin, enters the reception area requesting an argument and is sent down the hall to room 12A, where he finds an attendant, played by John Cleese.

Monty Python's "Argument Clinic"

Customer: Is this the right room for an argument?

Attendant: I told you once.

C: No you haven't.

A: Yes I have.

C: When?

A: Just now.

C: No you didn't.

A: I did.

C: Didn't!

A: Did!

C: Didn't!

A: I'm telling you I did.

C: You did not!

A: Oh, I'm sorry. Just one moment. Is this the five-minute argument or the full half hour?

C: Oh, just the five minutes.

A: Ah, thank you. Anyway, I did.

C: You most certainly did not.

A: Look, let's get this thing clear. I quite definitely told you.

C: No, you did not.

A: Yes I did.

C: No you didn't.

A: Yes I did!

C: No you didn't!

A: Yes I *did!*

C: No you *didn't!*

A: Yes I *DID!*

C: No you *DIDN'T!*

A: *DID!*

C: Oh now look. This isn't an argument.

A: Yes it is.

C: No it isn't. It's just contradiction.

A: No it isn't.

C: It IS!

A: It is NOT!

C: Look. You just contradicted me.

A: I did not.

C: Oh, you did.

A: No, No, No.

C: You did just then!

A: Nonsense.

C: Oh, this is futile . . .

A: No it isn't.

C: I came here for a good argument.

A: No, you didn't. No, you came here for an *argument.*

C: Well, an argument isn't just contradiction.

A: Can be.

C: No it can't. An argument is a connected series of statements intended to establish a proposition.

A: No it isn't.

C: Yes it is. It's not just contradiction.

A: Look if I'm going to argue with you I must take up a contrary position.

C: Yes, but that's not just saying "No it isn't."

A: Yes it is.

C: No it *ISN'T!*[1]

The humor here depends on both senses of the term *argument*. What the attendant is offering is a perverse trivialization of the kind of argument that two people *"have."* In this sense *argument* is synonymous with *dispute*—a kind of verbal conflict, which Cleese's character has reduced in this scene to mere mechanical contradiction of whatever Palin's character says. Again, this is not the sense of the word *argument* with which we are primarily concerned in this book.

Palin's character is interested in something more substantial, and he gives a definition:

> An argument is a connected series of statements intended to establish a proposition.

This is an alternative to the functional definition given previously. It also gives the intention of the word *argument* in the sense with which we are primarily concerned, but it does so by reference to structural features rather than function. In other words, *an argument is a composition consisting of a set of claims one of which, called the "thesis" or "conclusion," is understood or intended to be supported by the other(s), called the "premise(s)."* The two definitions, functional and structural, are closely linked (because the structure suits the function) and can be combined as follows. *An argument is a composition—whose primary purpose is to persuade a person by appealing to the person's reasoning capacity—consisting of a set of claims, one of which, called the "thesis" or "conclusion," is understood or intended to be supported by the other(s), called the "premise(s)."* To persuade someone by appeal to her reasoning capacity, typically one presents a composition consisting of a series of claims, some of which support others. In what follows we will be using both parts of this definition. The functional part of the definition will serve as a basis for argument identification. The structural part of the definition will serve as a basis for argument analysis.

DEFINITION

An argument is a composition—whose primary purpose is to persuade a person by appealing to the person's reasoning capacity—consisting of a set of claims, one of which, called the "thesis" or "conclusion," is understood or intended to be supported by the other(s), called the "premise(s)."

Our study of argument can be divided into four main skill areas: argument identification, argument analysis, argument evaluation, and argument design and construction. Argument identification is about recognizing arguments and telling them apart from other sorts of material. Argument analysis is about taking arguments apart and understanding how they are put together and designed to work. Argument evaluation involves appraising their strengths and weaknesses. And argument design and construction is about generating original arguments of our own.

Here is a simple example of an argument: "International legal institutions cannot be relied upon to bring international terrorists to justice. And international terrorists are not entitled to the protection of the U.S. Constitution or Bill of Rights. Therefore, international terrorists should be tried in secret by U.S. military tribunals." "International terrorists should be tried in secret U.S. military tribunals" is the claim the others are intended to support and establish. For the purposes of our study of Critical Thinking, the relationships of support are the ones that matter here. We want to focus our attention on the "argumentative structure" of the composition—rather than, for example, its grammatical structure. If we wanted we could combine all three claims in the above argument into a single sentence. "Since we can't rely on international legal institutions to bring international terrorists to justice and the U.S. Constitution and Bill of Rights don't apply to terrorists, they should be tried in secret by U.S. military tribunals." So, a point to bear in mind as you proceed: Although the grammatical structure of a passage is *sometimes* a good guide to its "argumentative structure," it's the "argumentative structure" (*regardless of* its grammatical structure) that we want to get at.

ARGUMENT IDENTIFICATION

Arguments are compositions in language, which as you know is an immensely flexible medium of expression. Open any magazine or daily newspaper and you will find a wide variety of material composed in language, including some arguments. Listen in on any conversation and you will hear many things going on, quite possibly including argumentation. It is not so difficult to identify cases of verbal conflict, especially when one is involved. But identifying arguments, in the sense relevant to our purposes, can be much more difficult, especially when they are embedded in larger, more complex contexts. This is in part because recognizing arguments involves recognizing the speaker's or the writer's intentions and because speakers and writers can have complex intentions and do not always make their intentions perfectly clear in what they write and say.

Distinguishing arguments from explanations, or jokes, or greetings, or narratives, or instructions is a matter of discerning the author's intentions to persuade by appeal to reason. Sometimes it is clear that what the author is trying to do is to persuade by appeal to reason. In that case what the author has put forward is clearly an argument. Sometimes it is clear that the author is trying to do something other than persuade by appeal to reason. In that case what the author has put forward is clearly not an argument. Sometimes an author may be trying to do two or more things at once: say, persuade by appeal to reason and amuse the reader. Sometimes it's just not clear what the author is trying to do.

We often make claims without arguing for them: "Baseball is a popular sport in the United States. Football is generally played in the winter. Hockey is a popular sport in Canada. Basketball can be played inside or outside. Soccer is played throughout the world." These claims are nonargumentative. None of them is intended to support or establish any of the others; so, taken as a group, they do not constitute an argument.

We also make claims when we are trying to explain things: "The class on the history of music has been canceled for lack of enrollment"; "The horse was frightened by a snake in the grass"; "Last night's rain made the streets wet." These are explanatory claims. They help explain something: the cancellation of the class, the spooking of the horse, the wet pavement. They are, in other words, presumably intended to help someone understand something better.

The basic difference between such nonargumentative passages and arguments is one of intent or purpose. If people are interested in establishing the truth of a claim and offer evidence intended to do that, then they are making an argument. But if they regard the truth of a claim as nonproblematic, or as already having been established, and are trying to help us understand *why* it is the case (rather than *establish that it is* the case), then they are explaining. Thus, when we say, "The streets are wet because it rained last night," ordinarily we would not be trying to establish that the streets are wet. Presumably that fact is already apparent to any observer, and so we would more likely be offering an explanation of how they got that way. But if we say, "You should take your umbrella today because the forecast calls for rain," ordinarily we would not understand the statement that you should take your umbrella as an established truth, because advice like this ordinarily isn't offered to people we think are already convinced. Thus, in this case we are more likely setting forth an argument.

EXERCISE 3.1 | Argument Identification

Which of the following passages express or contain arguments? You can use either the functional or the structural parts of the definition of "argument" or both to make your determination.

Argument Explanation (Other)	"A principle I established for myself early in the game: I wanted to get paid for my work, but I didn't want to work for pay." —poet Leonard Cohen	Explain your answer:
Argument (Explanation) Other	"I object to lotteries because they're biased in favor of lucky people."	Explain your answer:
Argument Explanation (Other)	"The most serious issue facing journalism education today is the blurring of the distinctions between advertising, public relations, and journalism itself."	Explain your answer:

	Argument	"Even the most productive writers are expert dawdlers, doers of unnecessary errands, seekers of interruptions—trials to their wives and husbands, associates, and themselves. They sharpen well-pointed pencils and go out to buy more blank paper, rearrange their office, wander through libraries and bookstores, change words, walk, drive, make unnecessary calls, nap, day dream, and try not 'consciously' to think about what they are going to write so they can think subconsciously about it." —Donald M. Murray, *Write before Writing*	Explain your answer:
4)	Explanation		
	(Other)		

	(Argument)	"Gentlemen of the jury, surely you will not send to his death a decent, hard-working young man, because for one tragic moment he lost his self-control? Is he not sufficiently punished by the life-long remorse that is to be his lot? I confidently await your verdict, the only verdict possible: that of homicide with extenuating circumstances." —Albert Camus, *The Stranger*	Explain your answer:
5)	Explanation		
	Other		

conclusion (handwritten) *premise*, *premise* × twice in (handwritten) *conclusion* (handwritten)

conclusion stated twice in different words. (handwritten)

	Argument	"It seems that mercy cannot be attributed to God. For mercy is a kind of sorrow, as Damascene says. But there is no sorrow in God; and therefore there is no mercy in him." —Thomas Aquinas	Explain your answer:
6)	Explanation		
	Other		

	Argument	"I knew a guy once who was so influenced by statistics, numbers ruled his entire life! One time he found out that over 80 percent of all automobile accidents happen within five miles of the driver's home. So he moved!"	Explain your answer:
7)	Explanation		
	(Other) *narrative*		

	Argument	"Willy Loman never made a lot of money. His name was never in the paper. He's not the finest character that ever lived. But he's a human being, and a terrible thing is happening to him. So attention must be paid. He's not to be allowed to fall into his grave like an old dog. Attention, attention must be paid to such a person." —Arthur Miller, *Death of a Salesman*	Explain your answer:
8)	Explanation		
	Other		

ARGUMENT ANALYSIS

As we indicated earlier, argument analysis involves taking arguments apart into their structural elements so as to better understand how they are designed and intended to work. Argument analysis is a natural extension of argument identification, because argument identification already involves recognizing a set of claims as composed for a certain intended purpose.

PREMISES AND CONCLUSIONS

If an argument is a set of claims some of which are understood or intended to support the other(s), then we may proceed to define two important basic concepts for both argument identification and argument analysis: the concepts of premise and conclusion. *The **premises** of arguments are the claims offered in support of the **conclusion**. The **conclusion** is the claim that the **premises** are offered to support.*

Thus far we have considered two simple arguments:

(1) We can't rely on international legal institutions to bring international terrorists to justice. The U.S. Constitution and Bill of Rights don't apply to terrorists.

They should be tried in secret by U.S. military tribunals.

(2) The weather forecast calls for rain.

You should take your umbrella today.

The solid line indicates the transition from supporting material to what the material supports, or from premise(s) to conclusion. Statements above the line are the premises; statements below the line are conclusions. We will call this line the *inference line*. The word "inference" refers to the step we take in our minds from the premise(s) to the conclusion. As soon as you recognize something as an argument, you are in position to take a positive first step in argument analysis: identify the conclusion. Let's make this a "Rule of Thumb" for argument analysis.

CRITICAL THINKING TIP 3.1

First Find the Conclusion

SIGNAL WORDS

As we mentioned earlier, identifying arguments can be difficult, especially when they are embedded in larger contexts, because recognizing arguments involves recognizing the author's intentions. Similarly, identifying the premises and conclusion of an argument can be difficult, especially when we find them embedded in longer passages. If you read and listen carefully, however, you can pick up clues to the presence of arguments and to the identity of premises and conclusions in

written or spoken discourse. One of the most important clues is the *signal* ·
or *signal expression*. Speakers and writers can and often do signal their inte
by using a word or expression to indicate the presence of a premise or concl.
or relationship of support. Here are some of the words and phrases that conventionally indicate conclusions:

TABLE 3.1   Conclusion Signals

- so
- therefore
- thus
- consequently
- it follows that
- as a result
- hence
- in conclusion
- shows that

On first reading a passage, it is often useful to circle such signals when you run
across them, especially if the passage you are reading is long and complex. Doing
so alerts you to the crucial relationships of support within the passage, and thus
gives you "landmarks" to its argumentative structure.

International legal institutions cannot be relied upon to bring international terrorists to
justice. And international terrorists are not entitled to the protection of the U.S. Constitution or Bill of Rights. (Therefore,) international terrorists should be tried in secret by U.S.
military tribunals.

Noticing the word "therefore" in the last sentence helps us locate the argument's conclusion, "International terrorists should be tried in secret by U.S. military tribunals." It also helps us recognize that the first two claims are offered as
reasons or premises in support of that conclusion.

Just as "therefore" is conventionally used to signal a conclusion, there are several conventional ways to signal a premise or premises. Here are some of the
words and phrases that conventionally indicate premises:

TABLE 3.2   Premise Signals

- since
- because
- for
- follows from
- after all
- due to
- inasmuch as
- insofar as

Again, in reading a passage, it can be quite useful to circle such expressions so
as to locate and keep track of premises.

(Since) we can't rely on international legal institutions to bring international terrorists to justice and the U.S. Constitution and Bill of Rights don't apply to terrorists, they should be tried in secret by U.S. military tribunals.

In this passage the word *since* introduces the premises that support the arguer's position in favor of secret military trials in cases of terrorism.

Now having said this, we need to add two words of caution: first, a reminder about ambiguity. Many of the words that are conventionally used to signal arguments also have other conventional applications. So, you can't simply rely on the presence of the signal words listed above as an absolutely foolproof indication of the presence of an argument. For example if we compare:

"You should take your umbrella (because) the forecast calls for rain."

with

"The streets are wet <u>because</u> it rained last night."

we see that the first is an argument in which the word *because* introduces a premise, but the second is an explanation. In the second, the word *because* introduces a claim whose intended function is not to *prove* or *establish* but rather to *explain* the wetness of the streets. *Because* and other such terms (like *since* and *for*) are ambiguous in this way. Sometimes they function to indicate the presence of an argument, and sometimes not. Like most interpretive work, identifying arguments—and even recognizing an expression as an argument signal—is in large measure context dependent.

Secondly, many of the arguments you will encounter contain no signals. Sometimes you're just supposed to "get" that an argument is what is being presented.

"Look, if we can't trust international law to convict terrorists, who don't deserve the protection of our Constitution or Bill of Rights anyway, why *shouldn't* they be tried in secret by the U.S. military?"

This passage, in one sentence, still makes three claims. And evidently the passage is an argument, because one of the claims made in it is evidently supported by the others. How can we tell this? Well, start by taking the sentence as a whole and ask yourself, what is its *point*?

EXERCISE 3.2 | Find the Conclusion

Highlight the point of the passage:

"Look, if we can't trust international law to convict terrorists, who don't deserve the protection of our Constitution or Bill of Rights anyway, why shouldn't they be tried in secret by the U.S. military?"

We expect that you will have zeroed in on the question at the end, "why shouldn't they [the terrorists] be tried in secret by the U.S. military?" Even though it is expressed in the grammatical form of a question, there is a claim being made here: "The terrorists *might as well* be tried in secret by the U.S. military." Now ask the natural next question, "*Why* should we accept this claim?" As soon as you ask this "Why?" question, you can see that the rest of the sentence is responding to your question with two additional claims: "We can't trust international law to convict terrorists" and "terrorists don't deserve the protections of our Constitution or Bill of Rights." In effect, the author has anticipated a challenge—naturally arising in the mind of any reasoning being, that a controversial claim be given some rational support—and has tried to meet this challenge. These two additional supporting claims are therefore the argument's premises. Notice once again that it is the argumentative structure, not the grammatical structure, that matters for our purposes in Critical Thinking. Notice also that in any passage of argumentative material, argument analysis boils down very simply to figuring out what supports what.

EXERCISE 3.3 | Argument Signals

Circle the signals, then highlight the conclusions in the following passages:

- Our whole class has to stay after school for an hour. So I'm going to need a ride home, because the bus leaves right after school.

- Humans and many higher animals have very similar neurophysiological structures. Humans and animals exhibit many of the same behavioral responses to stimuli. It is reasonable to suppose that animals feel pain and pleasure as we humans do.

- "And he went from there, and entered their synagogue. And behold, there was a man with a withered hand. And they asked him, 'Is it lawful to heal on the Sabbath?' so that they might accuse him. He said to them, 'What man of you, if he has one sheep, and it falls into a pit on the Sabbath, will not lay hold of it and lift it out? Of how much more value is a man than a sheep? So it is lawful to do good on the Sabbath'." (Matthew 12:9–12)

- Two out of three people interviewed preferred Zest to another soap. Therefore, Zest is the best soap available.

- In the next century more and more people will turn to solar energy to heat their homes because the price of gas and oil will become prohibitive for most consumers and the price of installing solar panels will decline.

- People who smoke cigarettes should be forced to pay for their own health insurance since they know smoking is bad for their health, and they have no right to expect others to pay for their addictions.

- It's no wonder that government aid to the poor fails. Poor people can't manage their money.

- Even though spanking has immediate punitive and (for the parent) anger-releasing effects, parents should not spank their children, because spanking gives children the message that inflicting pain on others is an appropriate means of changing their behavior. Furthermore, spanking trains children to submit to the arbitrary rules of authority figures who have the power to harm them. We ought not to give our children those messages. Rather, we should train them to either make appropriate behavioral choices or to expect to deal with the related natural and logical consequences of their behavior.

- Public schools generally avoid investigation of debatable issues and instead stress rote recall of isolated facts, which teaches students to unquestioningly absorb given information on demand so that they can regurgitate it in its entirety during testing situations. Although students are generally not allowed to question it, much of what is presented as accurate information is indeed controversial. But citizens need to develop decision-making skills regarding debatable issues in order to truly participate in a democracy. It follows then that public schools ought to change their educational priorities in order to better prepare students to become informed, responsible members of our democracy.

- Ever since the injury to Jerry Rice, the Raider running game has been under pressure to produce. But since their won/lost record is best in the AFC West, we must conclude that the loss of Rice, while damaging to their overall offense, has not been devastating.

- Late Night Radio Talk Show Host: "I've heard more heart attacks happen on Monday than on any other day of the week, probably because Mondays mark a return to those stressful work situations for so many of you. So let's all call in sick this Monday, ok, folks, because we don't want any of you to check out on us."

- Since capital punishment is a form of homicide, it requires a strong justification. Simple vengeance is not an adequate justification for homicide. Therefore, since there is no conclusive evidence that capital punishment deters violent crime, capital punishment is not justified.

DEEPER ANALYSIS

Recognizing that people generally require reasons to persuade them to accept a controversial claim, we set forth an argument. In the argument additional claims are made in support of the claim we are trying to persuade people to accept. But these additional claims may be challenged as well. Recognizing this, authors frequently anticipate the need to supply further support for the premises of their arguments—in other words, to build in arguments for the premises of their arguments. For this reason arguments often call for analysis in depth, as layer upon layer of support may require.

> International legal institutions, (because) they are fragile and not well established, cannot be relied upon to bring international terrorists to justice. And international terrorists are not entitled to the protection of the U.S. Constitution or Bill of Rights, (because) these documents pertain only to U.S. citizens. (Therefore,) international terrorists should be tried in secret by U.S. military tribunals.

Circling the signal words in the above passage helps us to recognize several important features of this argument's structure. It enables us to notice first that the premise "international legal institutions cannot be relied upon to bring international terrorists to justice" has embedded in it an additional claim, "they [international legal institutions] are fragile and not well established." Once we see this we can also recognize that this embedded claim is intended to support the one it is embedded in. Similarly, we notice that the premise "international terrorists are not entitled to the protection of the U.S. Constitution or Bill of Rights" is now followed by a further supporting claim: "these documents [the U.S. Constitution and Bill of Rights] pertain only to U.S. citizens."

From this relatively brief example, you can already see that a great deal of complexity can be packed into a few words. So you can also easily imagine what a challenge might be involved in taking apart a large and complex argument and keeping track of all of the relationships of support between its many claims. In Chapter 4 we will give you a few tools for coping with this kind of challenge.

EXERCISE 3.4 | **Argument Analysis/Layers of Support**

Circle the signals, and then highlight the conclusions in the following passages. Next highlight the premises. Use a second color for premises that support the conclusion *directly,* and a third color for premises that support other premises.

- The mother-in-law can't be the murderer. The victim, a vigorous 200-pound athlete, was strangled by the murderer's bare hands. The murderer must have very well developed upper-body strength. The mother-in-law is a frail 80-year-old woman.

- Part of believing something is believing that it's true. So if I were to do an inventory of my beliefs, they'd all seem true to me. Or, to put it another way, if I knew something was false, I wouldn't believe it. So it doesn't really make sense for me to say that some of my own beliefs are false.

- I've been mistaken in the past. I've learned on numerous occasions, and pretty much throughout my life, that things that I believed to be true were really false. Why should it be any different now? So if I were to do an inventory of my beliefs, I probably wouldn't notice the false ones, but I'd still bet there are some in there somewhere.

- "Nor is there anything smart about smoking. A woman who smokes is far more likely than her nonsmoking counterpart to suffer from a host of disabling conditions, any of which can interfere with her ability to perform at home or on the job. . . . Women who smoke have more spontaneous abortions, stillbirths, and premature babies than do nonsmokers, and their children's later health may be affected."[2]

- "Since the mid '50's, for example, scientists have observed the same characteristics in what they thought were different cancer cells and concluded that these traits must be common to all cancers. All cancer cells had certain nutritional needs, all could grow in soft agar cultures, all could seed new solid tumors when transplanted into experimental animals, and all contained drastically abnormal chromosomes—the 'mark cancer'."[3]

HIDDEN DEPTHS

In Chapter 1 we explained how important it is to be aware of the assumptions that may be involved in the reasoning under analysis, and that one of the important places to look for hidden assumptions is "underneath" the claims being made in the argument. We defined *presuppositions* as the kind of assumption that must be made in order for what is explicitly said to make sense. In this example, from one of the exercises at the end of Chapter 1, an argument is being made against the claim that extraterrestrial aliens crash-landed at the U.S. Air Force Base at Roswell, New Mexico.

> If you were an alien trying to scope out earthly terrain, the last place you'd go would be to one of the most highly fortified and tightly secured military installations in the United States.

Notice that this argument presupposes alien reasoning as essentially similar to our own human reasoning, in particular that aliens would be able to recognize a military installation as such if they saw one and that they would recognize such a place as dangerous and to be avoided.

EXERCISE 3.5 | Argument Analysis/Hidden Presuppositions

What presuppositions can you identify in the argument in Exercise 3.2 above:

"Look, if we can't trust international law to convict terrorists, who don't deserve the protection of our Constitution or Bill of Rights anyway, why shouldn't they be tried in secret by the U.S. military?"

Presuppositions:

_____

_____

_____

Just as people sometimes put forward arguments without signals, leaving it up to the listener or reader to recognize the argument as such, so people frequently put forward arguments that aren't completely stated. Sometimes what's hidden is the part of the argument we want to find first. Sometimes it's the argument's point, or conclusion, that you're just supposed to "get." Suppose that you are standing in line at the polling place on election day, waiting to have your registration verified and receive your official ballot, and you overhear the official say to the person in front of you:

> I'm sorry, sir, but only those citizens whose names appear on my roster are eligible to vote, and your name does not appear.

Clearly there is something further implied here. The implied conclusion, which is evidently intended to follow from the two claims explicitly made, is that the person in front of you is not eligible to vote. This example, then, does express an argument. And recognizing it as such depends upon recognizing that the two explicitly stated claims "point to" the unstated conclusion.

EXERCISE 3.6 | Argument Analysis/Unstated Conclusions

Each of the following arguments has an unstated conclusion. Formulate the conclusion.

1. I'm sorry, but you may stay in the country only if you have a current visa, and your visa has expired. Therefore,

   You cannot stay in the country.

2. God has all the virtues, and benevolence is certainly a virtue.

   Therefore,

   └ *God is benevolent.*

3. Either the battery in the remote control is dead or the set's unplugged, but the set is plugged in.

   Therefore,

   └ *The battery in the remote control is dead.*

4. All mammals suckle their young, and all primates are mammals, and orangutans are primates.

   Therefore,

   └ *Orangutans suckle their young.*

5. Software is written by humans, and humans make mistakes.

   Therefore,

   └ *Software will make mistakes.*

6. Legislation that can't be enforced is useless, and there's no way to enforce censorship over the Internet.

   Therefore,

   └ └ *Censorship over the internet is useless.*

In Chapter 1 we explained that another one of the important places to look for hidden assumptions is "between" the claims being made in the argument. We defined *inferential assumptions* as the kind of assumptions that play the role of "missing link in a chain of reasoning." Suppose once more that you are standing in line at the polling place on election day, and you overhear the official say to the person in front of you:

> I'm sorry, sir, but only those citizens whose names appear on my roster are eligible to vote.

Here again the context makes clear that the official is offering support for the claim that the person in front of you is not eligible to vote. But in addition to the unstated conclusion, there is an unstated premise:

> Your name does not appear on my roster.

Implied conclusions and premises are important parts of the logical structure of the arguments in which they occur, and they need to be taken into account in our analyses and evaluations of such arguments. How do we tell that there is an unstated claim ("that the person's name does not appear on the roster of eligible voters") in the last example? So now let us look between the premise and conclusion:

> Only those citizens whose names appear on my roster are eligible to vote.
> _____
> Therefore you are not eligible to vote.

The missing premise "Your name does not appear on my roster" is clearly implied, because it would seem to be the only way to get from the explicitly stated premise to the conclusion.

EXERCISE 3.7 | Argument Analysis/Hidden Inferential Assumptions

Each of the following arguments has an unstated premise. Formulate the missing premise.

1. "International terrorists are not entitled to the protection of the U.S. Constitution or Bill of Rights, because these documents pertain only to U.S. citizens."

   International terrorists are not us citizens.

2. All propaganda is dangerous. Therefore, network news is dangerous

   Because

   Network news is propaganda.

3. UCLA will play in the Rose Bowl, because the Pac 10 champion always plays in the Rose Bowl,

   And

   UCLA is the Pac 10 champion

4. Everything with any commercial potential eventually gets absorbed into the corporate world, so the Internet will eventually get absorbed into the corporate world

   Because

   the internet has commerical potential

5. Hip-hop is a fad, so it will surely fade,

   Because

   Fads fade.

This is the most challenging kind of argument analysis, for the obvious reason that some of the things we are trying to account for are hidden. In Chapter 5 we will give you a few additional tools for coping with this kind of challenge.

We'll close this introduction to argument analysis with a few more exercises and examples to practice on.

ADDITIONAL EXERCISES

The following additional exercises should help you determine your readiness to move on to Chapters 4 and 5.

■ **EXERCISE 3.8**   In each of the following examples, check all issue categories that apply. Most important, explain each classification you make.

	Argument	The game has been delayed because of rain.	Explain your answer:
	(Explanation)		
	Other		

	Argument	"While taking my noon walk today, I had more morbid thoughts. What is it about death that bothers me so much? Probably the hours. Melnick says the soul is immortal and lives on after the body drops away, but if my soul exists without my body I am convinced all my clothes will be loose fitting." —Woody Allen	Explain your answer:
	Explanation		
	(Other)		

not percusion

	Argument	I've heard more heart attacks happen on Monday than on any other day of the week, probably because Mondays mark a return to stressful work situations for so many.	Explain your answer:
	(Explanation)		
	Other		

	(Argument)	"Gentlemen of the jury, surely you will not send to his death a decent, hard-working young man, because for one tragic moment he lost his self-control? Is he not sufficiently punished by the lifelong remorse that is to be his lot? I confidently await your verdict, the only verdict possible: that of homicide with extenuating circumstances." —Albert Camus, *The Stranger*	Explain your answer:
	Explanation		
	Other		

	Argument	"One woman told me that brown spots, a bugaboo to older women, were twice as numerous on the left side of her face and arm due to daily use of her car. The right, or interior, side of her face and right arm showed far fewer brown spots. Since these unattractive marks seem to be promoted by exposure to the sun, either cover up or use a good sunscreen."[4]	Explain your answer:
	Explanation		
	(Both)		
	Other		

	Argument	"In bureaucratic logic, bad	Explain your answer:
	(Explanation)	judgment is any decision that can	
	Both	lead to embarrassing questions,	
	Other	even if the decision was itself right.	
		Therefore no man with an eye on a	
		career can afford to be right when	
		he can manage to be safe."[5]	

■ **EXERCISE 3.9** Using the punctuation and signals as clues to missing elements, fill in the blanks of the following "argument skeletons" with the letter **P** (for premise), **PS** (for premise support), or **C** (for conclusion).

- _____P_____ and _____P_____. So, _____C_____.
- _____C_____, because _____P_____, since _____PS_____.
- Inasmuch as _____P_____, _____P_____, for _____C_____.
- (1) _PS_. Therefore, since _____P_____, _____C P_____.
- (2) _PS_. Therefore, _____C_____, since _____P_____.
- _____C_____. This follows from _____P_____, and _____P_____.

■ **EXERCISE 3.10** Construct an argument based on each of the argument skeletons in Exercise 3.9.

■ **EXERCISE 3.11** Assume that each of the following passages is an argument. Fit the claims in each passage into the argument skeleton provided.

- College education affects one's earning potential. Research shows that college graduates make more money over a lifetime than non–college graduates do.
  _____ for, _____.
- This new diet won't help me lose weight. No diet I've ever tried has worked.
  _____. So, _____.
- Bill must be a poor student. Bill spends most of his time watching ESPN.
  _____ since _____.
- Students come to school to learn. Students should have no say in curriculum decisions. Because _____, _____.

■ **EXERCISE 3.12** For each of the following passages either highlight or state the conclusion:

- "Yond Cassius has a lean and hungry look. . . . Such men are dangerous."[6]
- "Only demonstrative proof should be able to make you abandon the theory of Creation; but such a proof does not exist in nature."[7]

- "When we regard a man as morally responsible for an act, we regard him as a legitimate object of moral praise or blame in respect of it. But it seems plain that a man cannot be a legitimate object of moral praise or blame for an act unless in willing the act he is in some important sense a 'free' agent."[8] *Conclusion.*

■ **EXERCISE 3.13**   Arrange the following eight sentences to produce a logically coherent argument.

- If a broadcaster won't provide public service aimed at improving the lot of children and the democratic process, Congress and the FCC should find someone who will—or make the broadcaster pay for using the channel.

- Second, the democratic process is what enables us to choose our leaders.

- Beyond this, we are one of the only three countries that do not provide public-service time to political candidates; the others are Sri Lanka and Taiwan.

- Dinner-hour sitcoms and teen-oriented dramas show indiscriminate and consequenceless sex, and cable and video make available to children in their own homes movies they would not be permitted to see in a theater.

- An estimated $1 billion went to TV stations last year to buy campaign commercials, while TV news about campaigns dramatically declined.

- Quality TV for children will never be lucrative enough to earn its way onto the schedule.

- As former Democratic senator and presidential candidate Bill Bradley summarized it, "Today political campaigns function as collection agencies for broadcasters. You simply transfer money from contributors to television stations."

- So it must be the price of admission to the airwaves.[9]

■ **EXERCISE 3.14**   At the end of Chapter 1 (Exercise 1.28) the instructions were to draft a one-page Issue Statement, which you revised at the end of Chapter 2 (Exercise 2.20). Now let's try a little research. Research essentially means finding out something we don't already know. In researching an issue we need to gain access to reliable information relevant to our topic, and most important, since our topic is the subject of debate and disagreement among reasonable people, we need to gain access to arguments of a reasonably high standard representing the diversity of opinion on our topic. Go to InfoTrac College Edition and research the issue articulated in your Issue Statement. Your goal is to identify at least three extended arguments representing at least two distinct positions on your issue. We recommend looking ahead to the section in Chapter 13 on "Research and the Media," pp. 339–344.

GLOSSARY

analysis   the process of breaking complex things down into their constituent elements
argument   (defined functionally): a composition whose primary function is to persuade a person by appealing to the person's reasoning capacity; (defined

structurally) a composition consisting of a set of claims one of which, called the "thesis" or "conclusion," is supported by the other(s), called the "premise(s)"

conclusion   the claim in an argument supported by the premise(s)

premise(s)   the claim(s) in an argument that support the conclusion

signal word   word indicating the presence of an argument or argument part

thesis   conclusion, especially in an extended argument

ENDNOTES

[1] "The Argument Clinic," *Monty Python's Flying Circus—Just the Words,* Roger Wilmut, ed. (New York: Random House, 1989), Vol. 2, p. 86.

[2] Jane E. Brody and Richard Engquist, "Women and Smoking," Public Affairs Pamphlet 475 (New York: Public Affairs Committee, 1972), p. 2.

[3] Michael Gold, "The Cells That Would Not Die," in "This World," *San Francisco Chronicle,* May 17, 1981, p. 9.

[4] Virginia Castleton, "Bring Out Your Beauty," *Prevention,* September 1981, p. 108.

[5] John Ciardi, "Bureaucracy and Frank Ellis," in *Manner of Speaking* (New Brunswick, N.J.: Rutgers University Press, 1972), p. 250.

[6] Wm. Shakespeare, *Julius Caesar.*

[7] Moses Maimonides, *The Guide for the Perplexed.*

[8] C. Arthur Campbell, "Is 'Freewill' a Pseudo-Problem?" *Mind,* 60, no. 240 (1951), p. 447.

[9] Adapted from Newton N. Minow, "Television, More Vast Than Ever, Turns Toxic," *USA Today,* May 9, 2001, p. 15A.

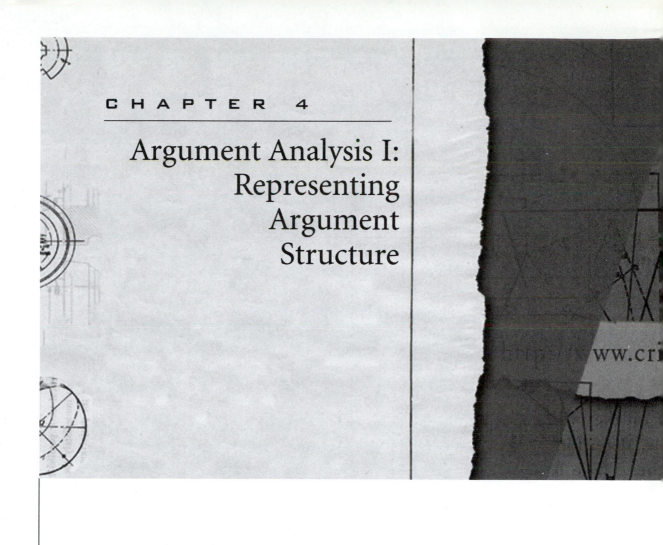

CHAPTER 4

Argument Analysis I: Representing Argument Structure

THE GOAL OF ARGUMENT ANALYSIS

The basic purpose of analysis—the intellectual process of taking complex things apart into their more basic elements—is to help us understand complex things. In Chapter 1 we applied analysis to issues. Here we will apply analysis to arguments. Argument analysis is important in Critical Thinking as a crucial first step toward argument evaluation. In this connection, it is worth bearing in mind what we said in Chapter 1 about being patient in pursuit of the truth. When we're "involved" in an issue, and especially in the heat of discussion, as soon as we recognize that an argument is being presented we may feel ready to endorse

"But I see you're having difficulty following my argument."

or reject it, often simply on the basis of whether we agree with its point or not. However, before we pass judgment as to the merits of an argument, we need to make sure that we have understood the argument accurately, fairly, and in detail. That is the goal of argument analysis, and the main reason it comes *before* argument evaluation is that it makes no sense to pass judgment on something we don't adequately understand.

In Chapter 3 we defined an "argument" as *(a) a composition, whose primary purpose is to persuade a person by appealing to the person's reasoning capacity,* and *(b) a composition consisting of a set of claims one of which, called the "thesis" or "conclusion," is understood or intended to be supported by the other(s), called the "premise(s)."* Just as the functional part of the definition (a) is a good basis for argument identification, the structural part of the definition (b) will now serve as a basis for argument analysis. Breaking an argument down into its constituent elements is a matter of taking it apart structurally. The crucial structural relationships in arguments, as you can see clearly in the structural definition, are relationships of support. So argument analysis really boils down to figuring out what supports what. With short and simple arguments, this can be a relatively easy thing to do, especially if the argument is fully expressed, with signal words clearly indicating which claim is the conclusion and which claim(s) support it. But many of the arguments you will encounter in real life are more challenging and difficult to deal with. An argument may be long and complex. It may be less than fully expressed. Parts of the argument may be veiled or implied, or perhaps just not worded clearly. Material extraneous to the argument may surround or be mixed in with the claims that make up the argument. In this chapter we offer you strategies and suggestions for analyzing arguments that present these challenges.

A good place to begin would be with the goal of argument analysis: a fair and accurate understanding of the argument in detail. How could we know if we had achieved this goal? How could we tell whether our understanding of someone else's argument is fair and accurate? Well, one obvious way to proceed would be to compare our understanding of the argument to the author's understanding of it. If we could talk directly to the author of the argument, we might say something like:

> If I understand your argument correctly, your point is . . .

> or

> Are you saying . . . ?

and then we would restate the argument to the author in our own words. The author could then tell us whether we got it right or whether our understanding is mistaken in any way.

Obviously we can't *always do* this. We can't expect to be able to check the accuracy of our grasp of *every* argument directly with its author. Nevertheless, this is a pretty good way to understand the goal of argument analysis. *Can we take the argument apart and reassemble it in our own words without changing what it means or how it is designed to work as a tool of rational persuasion? In a word, can we "paraphrase" the argument?* This is a very good test, indeed probably the best test, of the adequacy of our grasp of another person's argument. In the end it's the paraphrase that matters. The paraphrase is the measure of the degree to which we have succeeded in achieving the goal of argument analysis. We will return to paraphrasing in Chapter 5.

ELEMENTARY PROCEDURES

People who have a great deal of practice and experience with arguments and argumentation can often go straight to paraphrasing, and can do so accurately and "intuitively"—that is, without resort to any other procedures. But when we are just beginning the study of arguments and our intuitions are not grounded in extensive experience and practice, additional techniques and procedures may be not only useful but essential in establishing a firm footing in argument analysis.

CIRCLING AND HIGHLIGHTING

Let us begin with two simple procedures introduced in Chapter 3. When we recognize that an argument is being presented, a very useful first step would be to scan the passage for signal words and circle any that we find, as, for example, in the following passage:

> International legal institutions, (because) they are fragile and not well established, cannot be relied upon to bring international terrorists to justice. And international terrorists are not entitled to the protection of the U.S. Constitution or Bill of Rights, (because) these documents pertain only to U.S. citizens. (Therefore,) international terrorists should be tried in secret by U.S. military tribunals.

A second step would then be to identify the argument's conclusion and highlight it, thus:

EXERCISE 4.1 | Highlighting

You do the highlighting. We'll show you WHERE.

International legal institutions, (because) they are fragile and not well established, cannot be relied upon to bring international terrorists to justice. And international terrorists are not entitled to the protection of the U.S. Constitution or Bill of Rights, (because) these documents pertain only to U.S. citizens. (Therefore,) INTERNATIONAL TERRORISTS SHOULD BE TRIED IN SECRET BY U.S. MILITARY TRIBUNALS.

A third step would then be to challenge the argument's conclusion, in effect asking *why* we should accept it as true. We will then find that wherever the passage is responding directly to this question, there are premises, which we could highlight in a new color so as to distinguish these premises clearly from the argument's conclusion, thus:

EXERCISE 4.2 | Highlighting

You do the highlighting. We'll show you **where**.

International legal institutions, (because) they are fragile and not well established, **cannot be relied upon to bring international terrorists to justice.** And **international terrorists are not entitled to the protection of the U.S. Constitution or Bill of Rights,** (because) these documents pertain only to U.S. citizens. (Therefore,) INTERNATIONAL TERRORISTS SHOULD BE TRIED IN SECRET BY U.S. MILITARY TRIBUNALS.

Deeper layers of support may be discovered by repeating the third step. ==We now challenge the argument's premises highlighted above, in effect asking why we should accept *them* as true.== We will then find that wherever the passage is responding directly to *this* question, there are further premises, which we could highlight in a new color so as to distinguish them clearly from the claims that they support, thus:

EXERCISE 4.3 | **Highlighting**

You do the highlighting. We'll show you *where*.

International legal institutions, (because) *they are fragile and not well established,* **cannot be relied upon to bring international terrorists to justice. And international terrorists are not entitled to the protection of the U.S. Constitution or Bill of Rights,** (because) *these documents pertain only to United States citizens.* (Therefore,) INTERNATIONAL TERRORISTS SHOULD BE TRIED IN SECRET BY U.S. MILITARY TRIBUNALS.

EXERCISE 4.4 | **Circling and Highlighting**

Circle and highlight the following examples:

Since it is only a matter of time before space-based missile defense technology becomes obsolete, and since the funds that would be used to develop this technology are sorely needed to rebuild the economy, now is not the time to invest in a missile-defense shield. *conclusion*

The history of technology shows that all technology eventually becomes surpassed and outmoded. Therefore, it is only a matter of time before space-based missile defense technology becomes obsolete, and since the funds that would be used to develop this technology are sorely needed to rebuild the economy, now is not the time to invest in a missile-defense shield. *conclusion*

A space-based missile defense shield is our only realistic option for national defense in the nuclear age. After all, any defense program that relies on nuclear deterrence raises the risk of nuclear war, and that is not a realistic option for national defense. The Star Wars program is the only option yet proposed that does not rely on nuclear deterrence. *conclusion*

MAPPING

Many people find it helpful to visualize argument structure. One of the simplest ways of ==visualizing argument structure would be in terms of spatial relationships.== So, using only two dimensions (easiest to handle on a sheet of paper), and using the above example, we can arrange the claims in the argument to reflect the hierarchy and structure of the relationships of support thus:

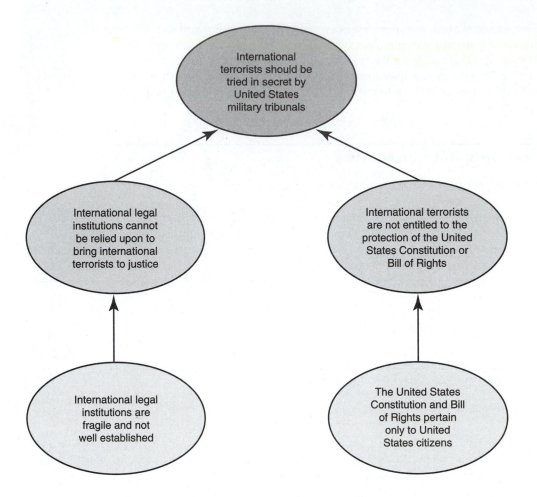

The conclusion appears at the top of the diagram, supported by two premises, each of which is supported in turn by a further premise.

A system like this could be easily expanded to represent deeper and more elaborate argument analysis. In this same example in Chapter 3 we noted that additional claims were presupposed and implied within the argument. The claim that international terrorists are not entitled to the protection of the U.S. Constitution and Bill of Rights presupposes that we already know who the terrorists are prior to trial. And the inference from the claim that the U.S. Constitution and Bill of Rights pertain only to U.S. citizens to the claim that international terrorists are not entitled to the protection of the Constitution and Bill of Rights depends on the additional assumption that the terrorists are not U.S. citizens. These hidden elements might be represented in the diagram as follows:

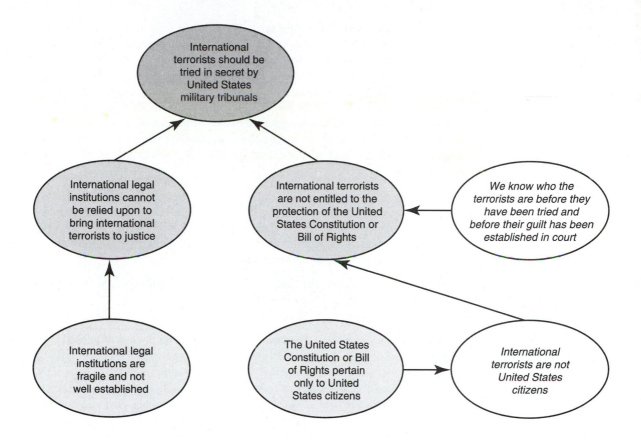

 The use of *italics* sets these new elements apart as implied or hidden in the original passage. Also, notice that the inference from the claim that the U.S. Constitution and Bill of Rights pertain only to U.S. citizens to the claim that international terrorists are not entitled to the protection of the Constitution and Bill of Rights now goes *through* the additional assumption that the terrorists are not U.S. citizens. Looking ahead to the evaluation of arguments, we can see from the diagram already that attention is drawn to the second of the two main premises as a possibly vulnerable point in the argument.

CASTING

A graphic system for representing argument structure should do what an organizational "flow chart" does for understanding any complex system. Ideally, it should be capable of representing an indefinitely large number of elements (in the case of arguments, claims) and an indefinitely large number of relevant relationships between them. Notice in the two diagrams above how the complexity of the graphic system of representation grows with the complexity of the analysis. A great deal can be done with colors and shapes and typefaces and symbols and arrows and two spatial dimensions. But we also want a system that is simple enough to learn and remember and apply to the kind of material we're likely to encounter in our everyday lives—material like newspaper stories and magazine articles. To that end we now present a simplified variation on the above mapping system—a system we will call "casting." The casting system follows essentially the same steps as used earlier in mapping the argument (see the accompanying figure). The claims that constitute the argument are isolated and marked for identification and then arranged in two-dimensional space so as to reflect the relationships of support among them.

1. Put brackets at the beginning and end of each claim.
2. Number the claims consecutively in their order of appearance in the passage.
3. Arrange the numbers spatially on the page according to relationships of support among the claims they stand for.

Using the above example, the casting system works as follows (see the accompanying figure and compare the earlier figure on page 98):

[International legal institutions, (because) {they are fragile and not well established, (1)} cannot be relied upon to bring international terrorists to justice. (2)] And [international terrorists are not entitled to the protection of the U.S. Constitution or Bill of Rights, (3)] (because) [these documents pertain only to U.S. citizens. (4)] (Therefore,) [international terrorists should be tried in secret by U.S. military tribunals. (5)]

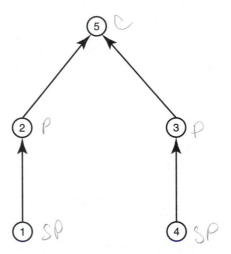

Notice in the above that special brackets {} were useful in isolating claim #1 as support for claim #2 in which it is embedded.

The system can be extended to represent hidden or unstated elements within the argument. To keep this distinction clear (the one between explicit and implicit claims of the argument), we might use letters instead of numbers to represent hidden or unstated elements. Using the same example, the casting would look like this (see the accompanying figure and compare the figure on page 99):

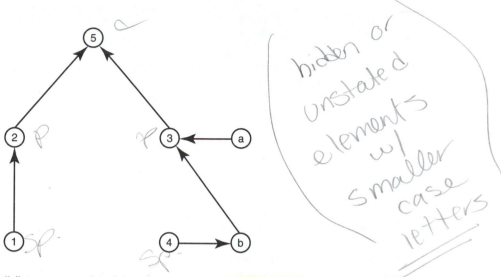

Here the letter "a" represents the claim that we know already who the terrorists are and the letter "b" represents the claim that the terrorists are not U.S. citizens, as explained above. Implied but unstated conclusions can be handled in a similar way. For example, this argument from *Julius Caesar:*

["Yond Cassius has a lean and hungry look . . . ①] [Such men are dangerous." ②]

leads, obviously, to the unstated conclusion: "Cassius is dangerous." We may represent it as a crucial element in the argument by assigning it the letter "a":

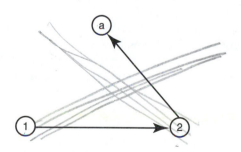

EXERCISE 4.5 | Basic Casting

Complete the castings of the following arguments.

Since [it is only a matter of time before space-based missile defense technology becomes obsolete, (1)] and since [the funds that would be used to develop this technology are sorely needed to rebuild the economy, (2)] [now is not the time to invest in a missile-defense shield. (3)]

[The history of technology shows that all technology eventually becomes surpassed and outmoded. (1)] Therefore, [it is only a matter of time before space-based missile defense technology becomes obsolete, (2)] and since the funds that would be used to develop this technology are sorely needed to rebuild the economy, (3)] [now is not the time to invest in a missile-defense shield. (4)]

[A space-based missile defense shield is our only realistic option for national defense in the nuclear age. (1)] After all, [any defense program that relies on nuclear deterrence raises the risk of nuclear war, (2)] and [that is not a realistic option for national defense. (3)] [The Star Wars program is the only option yet proposed which does not rely on nuclear deterrence. (4)]

Although the complexity and variety of arguments you may chance to encounter is practically endless, you can do quite a bit to orient yourself to the argument using just the few simple tools outlined above (see the accompanying figure). It is important not to confuse the grammatical structure of a passage in a composition with the structure of the argument it conveys. In some cases, with very carefully and clearly written passages of argumentation, the grammar and the structure of the argument may coincide. The author may construct the passage so that the grammar can be used as a guide to the argument. But in many cases not. What matters most for argument analysis is not the grammar of the composition but what supports what. A general rule of thumb is: Break a grammatical unit down when and only when different parts of the grammatical unit play separate and distinct roles in the argument in terms of support relationships. And, by the same token, disregard grammatically distinct repetitions of the same claim. Finally, remember to stay focused on the argument. In many cases the composition you're analyzing will contain material that is extraneous to the argument: tangential asides, background information, entertaining embellishments, rhetorical flourishes, and so on. Occasionally we encounter passages in which the author draws and defends a conclusion while at the same time conceding a point to the opposition. Such "concession claims" may be germane to the discussion, and they may make a "diplomatic" contribution to the reception of the author's thesis, though they do not by themselves lend support to it. A general rule of thumb is: Be thorough but stay relevant. If you think you understand and can explain the distinct contribution a given claim makes to the argument, include it in your analysis. Otherwise leave it out.

1. Circle signals.

2. Use highlighters to identify conclusion, main premises, and further supporting premises.

3. Put brackets at the beginning and end of each claim.

4. Number the claims consecutively in their order of appearance in the passage.

5. Arrange the numbers spatially on the page according to relationships of support among the claims they stand for.

EXERCISE 4.6 | Circling and Basic Casting

There is no better way to build and hone skills in this area than practice. Use the circling, highlighting, and casting system outlined above on the following examples.

1. That cell phone we looked at yesterday stores a half-hour's worth of messages, as opposed to this one's 20 minutes. It also has better automated dialing features than this one; and this one's $30 more expensive. I think we should get that other one.

2. A college education makes you aware of interests you didn't know you had. This helps you choose a satisfying job. Job satisfaction is itself your best assurance of personal well-being. Certainly personal well-being is a goal worth pursuing. Therefore a college education is a worthy goal.

3. Capital punishment should not be permitted because it in fact consists of killing human beings, and killing human beings should never be permitted by society.

4. Because killing human beings should never be permitted by society, capital punishment should not be permitted; for it in fact consists of killing human beings.

5. Most marriages between people under 20 end in divorce. This should be enough to discourage teenage marriages. But there is also the fact that marrying young reduces one's life options. Married teenagers must forget about adventure and play. They can't afford to spend time "finding themselves." They must concentrate almost exclusively on earning a living. What's more, early marriages can make parents out of young people, who can hardly take care of themselves, let alone an infant.

6. Suicide no longer repels us. The suicide rate is climbing, especially among blacks and young people. What's more, suicide has been appearing in an increasingly favorable light in the nation's press. When we surveyed all articles on suicide indexed over the past 50 years in the Reader's Guide to Periodical Literature, we found that voluntary deaths . . . generally appear in a neutral light. Some recent articles even present suicide as a good thing to do. . . . They are written in a manner that might encourage the reader to take his own life under certain circumstances. . . ."[1]

7. We must stop treating juveniles differently from adult offenders. Justice demands it. Justice implies that people should be treated equally. Besides, the social effects of pampering juvenile offenders have

sinister social consequences. The record shows that juveniles who have been treated leniently for offenses have subsequently committed serious crimes.

8. More and more silent evidence is being turned into loudly damning testimony. Over the past ten years, no area has developed faster than the examination of blood stains. Before we used to be satisfied with identifying a blood sample as type A, B, AB, or O. Now we have three or more different antigen and enzyme systems. The probability that any two people will share the same assessment of their blood variables is .1% or less. The size, shape, and distribution of blood spatters tell much about the location and position of a person involved in a crime. The use of bite-mark evidence has skyrocketed. Even anthropology is making a courtroom contribution. Some anthropologists can identify barefoot prints as well as match a shoe to its wearer.²

9. Capital punishment does ensure that a killer can never strike again. But it consists of killing human beings, and killing human beings should never be allowed. Therefore capital punishment should not be permitted.

10. A college education increases your earning potential. In addition, it makes you aware of interests you didn't know you had. Most important, it teaches one the inherent value of knowledge. It is true, of course, that a college education is very expensive. Nevertheless, a college education will be worth every penny it costs.

INTERMEDIATE CHALLENGES

Ever since the beginning of this book we have noticed that there are often hidden claims to account for in argument analysis. Critical Thinking Tip 1.1 was to Be Aware of Assumptions, especially "between" and "underneath" claims presented persuasively in arguments. And we have used several examples involving hidden claims in illustrating the tools of argument analysis presented earlier. In dealing with such hidden elements, the hard part is not the diagramming. It is not at all difficult to handle hidden claims in the mapping or casting systems presented above (just use letters instead of numbers). The hard part is figuring out *where* and *what* the hidden elements are.

Not that this is *always* hard. It's not. Sometimes it's quite obvious. Suppose someone says, "Do you trust your textbooks? I don't. I'm convinced they contain mistakes because they're written by humans." Now look at the argument in the last sentence.*

[I'm convinced they (textbooks) contain mistakes ①] (because) [they're written by humans. ②]

It's obvious (isn't it?) that there's a hidden premise in here, namely, "Humans make mistakes," or something like that, represented by the letter "a" in the accompanying figure:

---

* When I first began teaching Critical Thinking in 1984, I adopted Howard Kahane's *Logic and Contemporary Rhetoric* as the textbook for my course. I found this and another related example I use later in this chapter at the end of the first exercise in his Chapter 1. I still find these examples useful. This is my humble tribute to the late Howard Kahane, whose textbook is widely adopted to this day.

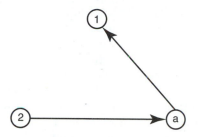

In an obvious case like this one, the question of *just how* we figure this out doesn't arise, any more than the questions of where and what the hidden premise is. All of this is just "obvious." The problem is that it's not *always* "obvious." In fact, as one would expect, typically it's not at all "obvious" where or what the hidden claims in an argument might be, for the simple—and obvious—reason that they're hidden.

Suppose you and a friend are solving a puzzle in which you are supposed to match the names and brief biographies of 20 people from a set of clues, and your friend says, "Pat must be a man because here in the fifth clue it says that Pat is Jason's *father*." You can see right away from the claim that Pat is Jason's father that Pat must be a man. But this conclusion does not follow from the claim that Pat is Jason's father *alone*. It also depends on the fact that (by definition) a father is a male parent, and the claim that a parent is presumably an adult, and the fact that (again by definition) a man is an adult human male. Ordinarily it would not be necessary to spell these three claims out explicitly as premises in order to fully appreciate the reasoning, any more than it was necessary to spell them out in the original presentation of the reasoning. In general, we go to the trouble of spelling out these hidden elements in the reasoning where the hidden or missing elements are both crucial *and controversial* and where they *bear on the evaluation of the argument*. It is important to go to this sort of trouble especially where there seems to be something *wrong* with a particular argument, for example: "You say textbooks don't contain mistakes? Here, I'll prove it to you that they do. My science book says that whales are mammals. But everybody knows that whales live in the sea, which is what a fish is, an animal that lives in the sea."[3] We will reconstruct this argument fragment shortly. For now, it will be sufficient to note that the reasoning evidently has *some* weaknesses in it *somewhere*. Spelling out all of its elements, even the ones that are obvious, becomes useful when we attempt to pinpoint those weaknesses.

In the "Real World of Public Discourse" arguments are often presented as sketches or fragments—what logicians traditionally refer to as "enthymemes." This means that parts of the reasoning are left for readers or members of the audience to recognize on their own, guided by context and the logic of the argument. And this is something that happens with great frequency in the media and in everyday conversation. Why is this? This happens for several reasons, some good, some not so good. Here is a good reason. Sometimes, as in the "humans make mistakes" example, things are *so* obvious that spelling them out completely and explicitly would be unnecessary, needlessly time-consuming, or even insulting to the intelligence of one's audience. So we often leave things out of our presentation of the argument as a matter of economy or common courtesy. On the other hand, sometimes people leave things out because they aren't completely aware of all of the assumptions that their reasoning depends on. And sometimes there is even an attempt to gloss over elements in an argument whose maker would just as soon we not notice or consider carefully. In any case, since this is something that happens with great frequency in the real world of public discourse, it will be well worth focusing on the question of just how we figure out where and what the hidden claims in an argument may be.

It is worth reminding ourselves what we are up to in all of this. When we reconstruct argument fragments, we are trying to make sense of what people say (and *don't* say). Imagine that you are waiting to be seated at a busy beachfront restaurant immediately behind an attractive couple who happen to be barefoot. The hostess looks at the barefoot couple, says not one word, but points to a sign that reads "No shirt, no shoes, no service." In this context it is reasonable to understand the hostess's gesture as a justification for refusing to seat the couple; in other words, it functions as an argument in support of her refusal to seat them. So, if we were casting the argument, we might represent her refusal to seat the barefoot couple by assigning it the letter "a." So far, the argument looks like this:

where "1" stands for "If you are not wearing a shirt and shoes, you will be refused service" (what the sign means); and where "a" stands for "you are being refused service" (addressed to the barefoot couple). There is also an unstated premise, namely that the couple are not wearing shoes. And you can easily understand why it's not stated: Again, this is because it's obvious—especially, we may presume, to the couple. If we want our casting to reflect this as a part of the justification for the refusal of service (which it obviously is), we assign it the letter "b." So the fully analyzed argument looks like this:

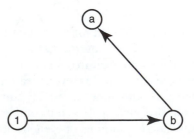

where "b" stands for "you are not wearing shoes" (addressed to the barefoot couple). The hostess says not one word, but the *context and the inner logic of the argument itself help us to make sense* of her gesture as a meaningful one and grasp its meaning as an argument. So now let us return to our obvious example. How do we know that the hidden claim is "Humans make mistakes" and not something different, like "Elephants make mistakes," or something completely different, like "Cycling is a great way to meet other single people"? Well, you could say, "We know that 'Humans make mistakes' is the hidden claim because it's the one that makes the most sense of what the arguer *did* say."

EXERCISE 4.7 | Casting Hidden Claims

Formulate the missing elements and complete the casting for each of the following arguments. Pay close attention to your own reasoning as you work each of these examples out. See if you can feel the "force of logic" at work.

I'm sorry, but [you may stay in the country only if you have a current visa; (1)] [your visa has expired. (2)]	**Casting**
Hidden Claim(s)	
[God has all the virtues, (1)] (so) [God must have benevolence. (2)]	**Casting**
Hidden Claim(s)	
[Either the battery in the remote control is dead or the set's unplugged, (1)] but [the set is plugged in. (1)]	**Casting**
Hidden Claim(s)	
[All species of mammal suckle their young, (1)] and [all primates are mammals, (2)] and [orangutans are primates. (3)]	**Casting**
Hidden Claim(s)	

So far the examples are all relatively "obvious." But many cases are much more difficult. Frequently there are *several different ways* of "making sense" of what someone says. Then, too, sometimes what people say just doesn't make very much sense. It won't always be possible to know, with certainty, which of several different statements should be cast in the role of missing premise, or whether one should be bothering to look for missing premises at all. The "bad news" is that there is no simple algorithm for making sense of what people say. Rather, it involves the application of multiple criteria that sometimes conflict with one another. Hence, it tends to yield multiple solutions, each with advantages and liabilities. The most one can expect by way of systematic guidance to this sort of process is a set of guidelines—"rules of thumb," as we will continue to present here. The "good news" is that you already know how to do this sort of interpretive work, at least in obvious cases like those discussed already. And as you work with these guidelines, building experience and cultivating sensitivity and judgment, keeping in mind that you may expect to find exceptions to any "rule of thumb," you will get even better at it.

Our interest in making sense of what people say by reconstructing their arguments from fragments has ultimately to do with assessing the merits of these arguments as reasoning. Ultimately what we want to know is how good or bad the argument is, and this is because we are trying to determine how much sway to give the argument in our own deliberations and decision making. What this means in commonsense terms is that we want as complete and as fair a rendition of the argument as we can arrive at.

COMPLETENESS

Back we go once again to our obvious example (see the figure on page 105). The argument as originally stated was, "I'm convinced textbooks contain mistakes because they're written by humans." Now let us consider how we know that there is an unstated premise in it in the first place. In other words, how do we know that the original statement of the argument is not complete? Well, just focus on the premise for a moment: "Textbooks are written by humans." True enough. But *from this claim alone* the conclusion "Textbooks contain mistakes" doesn't follow. If it is clear that the conclusion doesn't follow from the premise (or more precisely from the totality of the premises) explicitly presented in the argument, then we should be on the lookout for hidden premises. When we say "doesn't follow," we are using an important and fundamental concept of logic—the concept of deductive validity (which we will discuss more thoroughly in Chapter 6). For the time being, let's understand this concept to mean simply that even if the premise is true the conclusion could still be false.

EXERCISE 4.8 | **Does It Follow?**

For each pair of claims, suppose that the first claim is true, then determine whether the second one "follows."

Follows		Prisons do not rehabilitate anyone.
	Does not follow	Prisons are ineffective as punishment for criminal behavior.

Follows		The United States must become energy-independent.
	Does not follow	The United States should develop solar energy on a widespread basis.

Follows		Abortion involves the taking of a human life.
	Does not follow	Abortion should not ever be encouraged.

Follows		There are 35 students registered in this class.
	Does not follow	There are at least 30 students registered in this class.

Follows		God is perfect.
	Does not follow	Therefore, God is good.

Follows		Everything with any commercial potential eventually gets absorbed into the corporate
	Does not follow	world, so the Internet will eventually get absorbed into the corporate world.

Follows		People who were born at exactly the same time often have vastly different life
	Does not follow	histories and personalities. Therefore, astrology is not a reliable predictive system.

When we identify an argument as an enthymeme—when we determine, in other words, that its conclusion doesn't follow from its explicitly stated premises alone—we in effect sense a gap or hole in it. But we can be more specific than this. The hole has a more or less definite shape that we can discern, to some extent at least, by paying close attention to what surrounds it—to the argument's conclusion and explicit premise(s). Think of this as similar to searching for a missing piece in a jigsaw puzzle. You study closely the shapes and colors of the pieces that surround the one you're searching for. This helps you find the missing piece. When the puzzle is an incompletely stated argument and what we're searching for is a missing premise, we can guide ourselves by close attention to what the conclusion and explicit premise(s) of the argument are "about." This helps us get a better sense of the "shape" of the hole or gap we're trying to fill, and so also of the missing premise that can fill it. So, in the example we've been discussing, the conclusion is about textbooks and things that contain mistakes, while the premise is about textbooks and things written by humans. What we are looking for is something that will "complete this circle of relationships," as it were. What we should be looking for, then, is a claim that makes some sort of connection between things written by humans and things that contain mistakes.

EXERCISE 4.9 | Completing the Argument

Complete the following arguments, using all and only the words from the following list:
benevolence, depends, develop, effective, fails, homicide, never, unless, virtues, why

1. God has all the virtues. And ___benevolence___ is one of the ___virtues___ So God must have benevolence.

2. Abortion involves the taking of a human life. And that's ___homicide___, and you would ___never___ encourage homicide, would you? So, abortion should not ever be encouraged.

3. Prisons do not rehabilitate anyone. No criminal penalty that ___fails___ to rehabilitate can be ___effective___. That's ___why___ prisons are ineffective as punishment for criminal behavior.

4. The United States must become energy-independent. ___Unless___ we develop solar energy on a widespread basis, our survival ___depends___ on increasingly scarce petrochemical energy. That's why the United States should ___develop___ solar energy on a widespread basis.

FAIRNESS

We assume that anyone reading this book has a "sense of fairness." However, if we all have an intuitive sense of fairness, we also all know how easy it is to fall into dispute over—and how difficult it can be to resolve—*issues* of fairness. A commonsense rule of thumb in applying the concept of fairness in pursuit of the truth would be "when in doubt, don't be *unfair*."

CRITICAL THINKING TIP 4.1

When in doubt, don't be Unfair.

What does this rule of thumb mean in practice? Well, remember that argument analysis is a means to the end of determining how good or bad the argument is. In practice, then, the general rule of thumb, "When in doubt, don't be unfair," means that in analyzing a given argument, we should *try to avoid discrediting* the argument. Of two otherwise equally reasonable competing interpretations, we should subscribe to the one that does the argument the most credit. In other words, as indicated above, we should favor the interpretation that *makes the most sense of* what the arguer did say.

As applied to argument analysis, the first consideration regarding fairness would be *accuracy*. Analysis is a form of interpretation. Whenever we "complete" an argument by attributing an unstated claim to it, we are interpreting the "text" of the argument and in so doing going beyond what the "text" of the argument actually says. "Text" means the retrievable record of what was said. With written arguments we don't *generally* have the convenient opportunity to question a person if we think there are hidden elements in her argument. We have only—or primarily—the text of the argument to consult. In oral contexts, when we are listening to someone present an argument, the opportunity for questioning a person is often available. But even so, as we already pointed out, people are not always fully aware of all the assumptions they are making, and there may on occasion even be an unwillingness to learn or to admit that some particular claim is assumed or implied within a given argument or position. So again, we fall back on the text. In assessing the accuracy of the analysis of an argument, remember from Chapter 2 that we are entitled to assume a conventional understanding of the words in the text of an argument. We may also use logic (as we will explain further in Chapter 6) as a guide to our analysis. And of course, all of this is governed by the general rule of thumb: "When in doubt, don't be *unfair.*"

PLAUSIBILITY

For example, when formulating a hidden claim, we should favor the most "plausible" of the available alternative formulations. "Plausibility" is a concept we will develop and apply more deeply and extensively in Chapter 7. The word *plausibility* literally means "deserving of applause." But it has a more precise technical meaning relating to credibility or believability. In technical terms plausibility is an estimate of a claim's capacity to survive close critical examination. If we were to devise strenuous tests designed to *falsify* a claim, how well would the claim survive such tests? A claim is "plausible" to the extent that we think it likely the claim would survive such tests. A claim is "implausible" to the extent that we think it unlikely the claim would survive such tests. Plausibility, in other words, is a *preliminary estimate* of a claim's truth value. Consider this example:

> Since Smith is a police officer, he's probably in favor of gun-control legislation.

Here the conclusion, "Smith is probably in favor of gun-control legislation," does not follow from the premise "Smith is a police officer" alone. And to complete the inference, we are looking for a claim that makes some sort of connection between being a police officer and favoring gun-control legislation. There are a number of distinct alternatives we might consider casting in the role of missing premise. Take, for example, these two:

1. All police officers favor gun-control legislation.
2. Most police officers favor gun-control legislation.

The first formulation is less plausible than the second one. This is because the first formulation makes a stronger claim than the second one. The stronger a claim is, the harder it is to prove (and the more vulnerable it is to refutation). So we should favor the second alternative in reconstructing this argument.

EXERCISE 4.10 | **Plausibility**

Rank the following sets of claims in terms of plausibility. Compare your rankings with those of someone else in the class. Wherever your rankings conflict, explain your initial ranking. Compare notes and see whether your ranking is affected.

1. a. Some of the produce sold in the major supermarkets is irradiated.
   b. A lot of the produce sold in the major supermarkets is irradiated.
   c. Most of the produce sold in the major supermarkets is irradiated.

2. a. Tax evasion is a common practice.
   b. Everybody cheats on their taxes.

3. a. Cell phone usage is on the rise.
   b. The cell phone industry is growing at the rate of 65.89% a month.

4. a. It is probable that the al-Qaeda terrorist network is still actively planning further attacks.
   b. It is possible that the al-Qaeda terrorist network is still actively planning further attacks.
   c. It is certain that the al-Qaeda terrorist network is still actively planning further attacks.

5. a. There is intelligent life in outer space.
   b. Some nonhuman animals have the capacity for language.

6. a. The use of computer technology in weapons systems increases the risk of a nuclear accident.
   b. The perfection of a space-based missile defense system is feasible.

7. a. Some of the assassins of President Kennedy are still alive.
   b. Some of the assassins of President Kennedy presently hold high office in Washington.

8. a. Human adults generally use less than 10% of the capacity of their minds.
   b. The universe is finite.

Now let's put this all together and apply it to the following example mentioned above:

You say textbooks don't contain mistakes? Here, I'll prove it to you that they do. My science book says that whales are mammals. But everybody knows that whales live in the sea, which is what a fish is, an animal that lives in the sea.

Let's begin by numbering the claims, for our casting:

[You say textbooks don't contain mistakes? Here, I'll prove it to you that they do. (1)] [My science book says that whales are mammals. (2)] But everybody knows that [whales live in the sea, (3)] which is what [a fish is, an animal that lives in the sea. (4)]

Notice that we have bracketed the first two sentences as claim #1. This is an example of grammatical structure and logical structure diverging from each other. Claim #1 is evidently the conclusion, and we can easily capture it in a single sentence: "Textbooks contain mistakes." You may also have noticed that we ignored the (bad) grammar of the sentence in bracketing claim #4. But claim #4 really needs to be reworded in order to accurately reflect the argument. What the arguer is evidently trying to say is "Any animal that lives in the sea is a fish." This at any rate is how we would paraphrase claim #4. Claim #2 is offered as direct support for the conclusion. But what about claims #3 and #4? They both seem intended to contribute support for the conclusion, but the support is not direct. And there do seem to be some missing links involved. Nevertheless, a preliminary casting of these relationships might be helpful at this stage.

Suppose it's true that the arguer's science book says that whales are mammals (claim #2). The conclusion that textbooks contain mistakes would not follow from that alone. What claim would complete the inference from this premise to the conclusion? One additional implied claim is that the arguer's science book is a textbook. A second additional implied claim is that the statement that whales are mammals is mistaken, or simply "Whales aren't mammals." The first of these claims is pretty obvious and also pretty obviously part of the arguer's position. The second is implausible—indeed false—but it *must be* part of the arguer's position, as we can see quite clearly from claims #3 and #4, which are offered in support of it. So, in spite of the falsity of the claim that whales are not mammals, it is not *un*fair to attribute it to the argument. So let us assign the letter "a" to the first and the letter "b" to the second of these hidden claims.

"a" = "My science book is a textbook."
"b" = "Whales aren't mammals."

And cast the result as follows:

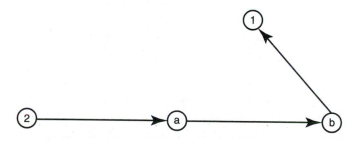

Now let us consider the relationship between claims #3 and #4 and "b." Suppose it is true that whales live in the sea (claim #3) and that any animal that lives in the sea is a fish (claim #4). It would not follow from these two claims alone that whales are not mammals. But what would follow from these two claims alone is the claim that whales are fish. But from this claim alone, the claim that whales are not mammals still would not follow. But if we add the claim that no fish are mammals, which is highly plausible—indeed true by definition—and again obviously part of the arguer's position, then the argument is complete. So let us assign the letter "c" to the claim that whales are fish and the letter "d" to the claim that no fish are mammals.

"c" = "Whales are fish."
"d" = "No fish are mammals."

And now we can complete the casting:

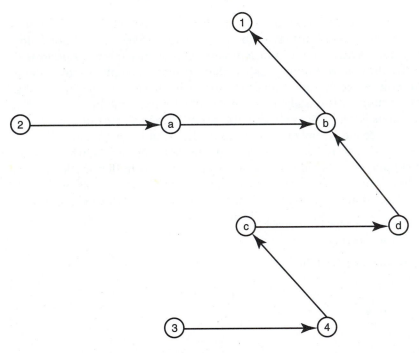

In this case, the analysis of the argument enables us to precisely pinpoint the argument's weakness: claim #4. Everything else in the argument is either true, presumably true, or logically derived from what is offered in its support.

EXERCISE 4.11 | **Reconstructing Missing Premises**

Select the best reconstruction of the missing premise from the alternatives offered for each of the following enthymemes:

Everything with any commercial potential eventually gets absorbed into the corporate world, so the Internet will eventually get absorbed into the corporate world.		Corporations have the power to absorb any business assets they want to.
		Corporations are inherently profit oriented, and so are naturally drawn to anything with commercial potential.
	✓	The Internet has commercial potential.

Some of these people can't be golfers. They're not carrying clubs.		Some golfers are carrying clubs.
		Everyone carrying clubs is a golfer.
	✓	All golfers carry clubs.

Constitutionally only the House of Representatives may initiate a money-raising bill. Thus when the Senate drafted the recent tax bill, it acted unconstitutionally. Therefore, the proposed tax bill should not be made law.	✓	Any bill the Senate drafts should not be made law.
		Any bill that originates unconstitutionally should not be made law.
		Any tax bill originating in the Senate should not be made law.

If capital punishment isn't a deterrent to crime, then why has the rate of violent crime increased since capital punishment was outlawed?		Because the rate of violent crime has increased since capital punishment was outlawed, it must be a deterrent.
		An increase in the rate of crime following the abolition of a punishment proves that the punishment is a deterrent.
	✓	An increase in the rate of crime following the abolition of a punishment is evidence that the punishment is a deterrent.

"I feel that since we are doing a science fiction show, morals don't enter into it—because none of it is true." —X-Files director Kim Manners	✓	All science fiction is immoral.
		All science fiction is false.
		Morals do not enter into fictional worlds.

Add naught to MacNaughton—because you don't dilute a great Canadian Whisky.	✓	MacNaughton is a great Canadian Whisky.
		Adding something to a great Canadian Whisky would dilute it.
		MacNaughton is a great Canadian Whisky, and adding something would dilute it.

"Murphy's law of [computer] programming states that no nontrivial program is free of bugs. A corollary states that any program with more than 10 lines is by definition nontrivial. The bottom line—your program will have bugs."[4]		Any computer program with 10 lines or less is trivial.
		Your computer program is nontrivial.
	✓	Your computer program has more than 10 lines.

People who were born at exactly the same time often have vastly different life histories and personalities. Therefore, astrology is not a reliable predictive system.	People who believe in astrology are superstitious.
	√ Astrology predicts that people born at exactly the same time would not have vastly different life histories and personalities.
	No two people are born at exactly the same time.

Since no human system of justice is infallible and capital punishment imposes an irreversible penalty, capital punishment is an unacceptable form of punishment.	If we could perfect our system of justice so that all and only guilty people got convicted, then capital punishment would be acceptable.
	√ No irreversible penalty is acceptable as a form of punishment in a fallible system of justice.
	You can let a person out of prison if they turn out to be innocent, but you can't bring a person back to life.

Just as we did with Chapter 3, we'll close this chapter on basic tools and techniques of argument analysis with a few more examples to practice on. Do your best to analyze the arguments contained in the passages assembled below, using any and all of the techniques of argument analysis presented in Chapters 3 and 4. As you work especially with the more lengthy and complex passages, do not be surprised or discouraged if you find that the casting becomes as hard to construct and grasp as the passage itself. Keep the goal of argument analysis in mind—a fair and accurate understanding of the argument in detail. Also bear in mind that the best measure of success in achieving this goal is what we will be working on in the next chapter—the paraphrase of the argument.

EXERCISE 4.12 | **Term Project: Argument Analysis**

At the end of Chapter 3 (Exercise 3.14) the instructions were to research the issue articulated in your Issue Statement and to identify at least three extended arguments representing at least two distinct positions on that issue. Now in one of these three extended arguments locate and highlight the thesis (or conclusion). Then locate and highlight the premises that support the thesis directly. Then locate and highlight the premises that support these main premises. Construct a casting of these elements of the argument.

ADDITIONAL EXERCISES

Do your best to analyze the arguments contained in the following passages, using any and all of the techniques of argument analysis presented in Chapters 3 and 4. Take note of any areas of difficulty you encounter. Then go on to Chapter 5.

EXERCISE 4.13 "Evolution is a scientific fairy-tale just as the 'flat earth theory' was in the 12th century. Evolution directly contradicts the Second Law of Thermodynamics, which states that unless an intelligent planner is directing a system, it will always go in the direction of disorder and deterioration. Evolution requires a faith that is incomprehensible!"[5]

EXERCISE 4.14 " 'We shall make no distinction,' the President proclaimed, 'between terrorists and countries that harbor terrorists.' So now we are bombing Afghanistan and inevitably killing innocent people because it is in the nature of bombing (and I say this as a former Air Force bombardier) to be indiscriminate, to 'make no distinction.' We are committing terrorism in order to 'send a message' to terrorists. . . . War is terrorism, magnified a hundred times. Yes, let's find the perpetrators of the awful acts of September 11. We must find the guilty parties and prosecute them. But we shouldn't engage in indiscriminate retaliation. When a crime is committed by someone in a certain neighborhood, you don't destroy the neighborhood."[6]

EXERCISE 4.15 "A scientific colleague of mine, who holds a professorial post in the department of sociology and anthropology at one of our leading universities, recently asked me about my stand on the question of human beings having sex relations without love. Although I have taken something of a position on this issue in my book, *The American Sexual Tragedy,* I have never quite considered the problem in sufficient detail. So here goes. In general, I feel that affectional, as against non-affectional, sex relations are desirable. It is usually desirable that an association between coitus and affection exist—particularly in marriage, because it is often difficult for two individuals to keep finely tuned to each other over a period of years."[7]

EXERCISE 4.16 "It isn't likely that managed competition [the Clinton health care reform concept] can be counted on to save money. For one thing, at least two managed-care setups must be present in a community if there is to be competition, and each of them needs a potential market of roughly 250,000 people to achieve economies of scale. Only about half of all Americans, it turns out, live in places densely populated enough to support two or more such programs. What's more, insurers would constantly hustle to win and retain business, because employers would constantly be shopping for better deals, just as they do now. The sales staff, recruiters, advertising personnel, and clerical staff that such 'marketing' entails contribute nothing to the provision of health care. And the physicians, nurses, and others whom insurers and HMOs [Health Maintenance Organizations] hire to oversee—that is, second-guess—the decisions individual doctors make with individual patients—an essential feature of managed care—have to be paid too, adding to the overhead cost. Administrative costs already soak up about $225 billion a year—25 cents of every dollar spent on health care in this country. Under managed competition, such costs would, at best, stay the same. More probably, they would increase."[8]

■ **EXERCISE 4.17**   "To the extent that it is working at all, the press is always a participant in, rather than a pure observer of, the events it reports. Our decisions on where (and where not) to be and what (and what not) to report have enormous impact on the political and governmental life we cover. We are obliged to be selective. We cannot publish the Daily Everything. And so long as this is true—so long as we are making choices that 1) affect what people see concerning their leaders and 2) inevitably cause those leaders to behave in particular ways—we cannot pretend we are not participants."[9]

■ **EXERCISE 4.18**   "Scientists are human beings with their full complement of emotions and prejudices, and their emotions and prejudices often influence the way they do their science. This was first clearly brought out in a study by Professor Nicholas Pastore in 1949. In this study Professor Pastore showed that the scientist's political beliefs were highly correlated with what he believed about the roles played by nature and nurture in the development of the person. Those holding conservative political views strongly tended to believe in the power of genes over environment. Those subscribing to more liberal views tended to believe in the power of environment over genes. One distinguished scientist (who happened to be a teacher of mine) when young was a socialist and environmentalist, but toward middle age he became politically conservative and a firm believer in the supremacy of genes!"[10]

■ **EXERCISE 4.19**   "Many a reader will raise the question whether findings won by the observation of individuals can be applied to the psychological understanding of groups. Our answer to this question is an emphatic affirmation. Any group consists of individuals and nothing but individuals, and psychological mechanisms which we find operating in a group can therefore only be mechanisms that operate in individuals. In studying individual psychology as a basis for the understanding of social psychology, we do something which might be compared with studying an object under the microscope. This enables us to discover the very details of psychological mechanisms which we find operating on a large scale in the social process. If our analysis of socio-psychological phenomena is not based on the detailed study of human behavior, it lacks empirical character and, therefore, validity."[11]

■ **EXERCISE 4.20**   "Flextime (Flexible Working Hours) often makes workers more productive because being treated as responsible adults gives them greater commitment to their jobs. As a result it decreases absenteeism, sick leave, tardiness and overtime, and generally produces significant increases in productivity for the work group as a whole. For example, in trial periods in three different departments, the U.S. Social Security Administration measured productivity increases averaging about 20%. None has reported a decline."[12]

■ **EXERCISE 4.21**   "Government control of ideas or personal preferences is alien to a democracy. And the yearning to use governmental censorship of any kind is infectious. It may spread insidiously. Commencing with suppression of books as obscene, it is not unlikely to develop into official lust for the power of thought-control in the areas of religion, politics, and elsewhere. Milton observed that 'licensing of books . . . necessarily pulls along with it so many other kinds of licensing.' Mill notes that the 'bounds of what may be called moral police' may easily extend 'until it encroaches on the most unquestionably legitimate liberty of the individual.' We should beware of a recrudescence of the undemocratic doctrine uttered in the seventeenth century by Berkeley, Governor of Virginia: "Thank God there are no free schools or preaching, for learning has brought disobedience into the world, and printing has divulged them. God keep us from both'."[13]

■ **EXERCISE 4.22**   "What, after all, is the foundation of the nurse's obligation to follow the physician's orders? Presumably, the nurse's obligation is to act in the medical interest of the patient. The point is that the nurse has an obligation to follow physician's orders because, ordinarily, patient welfare (interest) thereby is ensured. Thus when a nurse's obligation to follow a physician's order comes into direct conflict with the nurse's obligation to act in the medical interest of the patient, it would seem to follow that the patient's interests should always take precedence."[14]

■ **EXERCISE 4.23**   "American institutions were fashioned in an era of vast unoccupied spaces and pre-industrial technology. In those days, collisions between public needs and individual rights may have been minimal. But increased density, scarcity of resources, and interlocking technologies have now heightened the concern for 'public goods,' which belong to no one in particular but to all of us jointly. Polluting a lake or river or the air may not directly damage any one person's private property or living space. But it destroys a good that all of us—including future generations—benefit from and have a title to. Our public goods are entitled to a measure of protection."[15]

■ **EXERCISE 4.24**   "These days music is truly global in sweep. The genie's out of the bottle, never to return, with MP3, Napster/Scour, and Freenet and Gnutella rendering all previous lines of demarcation meaningless. There's a revolution in progress, leveling everything in its path. Copyrights, masters, negatives, books, records, and films; it's all the same to a binary number, or a carbon atom and hydrogen qubit. Legislation, global police monitoring by knocking on two million doors—I don't think so. All I know is, you can't afford to make the customer your enemy. They no longer want to purchase a CD with ten or twelve songs on it to get the two they really want. They are also hip enough to know about artists' earnings and no longer want to pay the price for all the people in the middle of the distribution chain. These technological changes have provided an unexpected and highly efficient platform for rebellion for the current generation. We better get together and figure it out—and quickly!"[16]

■ **EXERCISE 4.25**   "In policy debates one party sometimes charges that his or her opponents are embracing a Nazi-like position. . . . Meanwhile, sympathizers nod in agreement with the charge, seeing it as the ultimate blow to their opponents. . . . The problem with using the Nazi analogy in public policy debates is that in the Western world there is a form of anti-Nazi 'bigotry' that sees Nazis as almost mythically evil beings. . . . Firsthand knowledge of our own culture makes it virtually impossible to equate Nazi society with our own. The official racism of Germany, its military mentality, the stresses of war, and the presence of a dictator instead of a democratic system make Nazi Germany in the 1940s obviously different from America in the 1980s."[17]

GLOSSARY

casting   a graphic system for representing the structural relationships within an argument; or a graphic representation of a particular argument

enthymeme   an argument containing an inferential assumption

main premises   the premises offered as direct support for the thesis

paraphrase   a reformulation intended to capture the same meaning

plausibility   the credibility or believability of an idea that we estimate as likely to survive critical scrutiny

relevant   related to the topic under discussion

thesis   conclusion, especially of an extended argument

ENDNOTES

[1] Elizabeth Hall and Paul Cameron, "Our Failing Reverence for Life," *Psychology Today,* April 1976, p. 108.

[2] Bennett H. Beach, "Mr. Wizard Comes to Court," *Time,* March 1, 1982, p. 90.

[3] Howard Kahane, *Logic and Contemporary Rhetoric*, 5th ed. (Belmont, CA: Wadsworth, 1997).

[4] Daniel Appleman, *How Computer Programming Works* (Emeryville, CA: Ziff-Davis Press, 1994).

[5] Dr. Edward Blic, *21 Scientists Who Believe in Creation* (Harrisonburg, VA: Christian Light Publications, 1977).

[6] Howard Zinn, "It Seems to Me," *The Progressive* (November 2001), p. 8.

[7] Albert Ellis, *Sex Without Guilt* (New York: Lyle Stuart, Inc., 1966).

[8] Judith Randal, "Wrong Prescription: Why Managed Competition Is No Cure," *The Progressive* (May 1993), pp. 23–24.

[9] Meg Greenfield, "When the Press Becomes a Participant," *The Washington Post Company, Annual Report*, 1984, p. 21.

[10] Ashley Montagu, *Sociobiology Examined* (Oxford: Oxford University Press, 1980), p. 4.

[11] Eric Fromm, *Escape From Freedom* (New York: Avon Books, 1965), p. 158.

[12] Barry Stein et al., "Flextime," *Psychology Today,* June 1976, p. 43.

[13] Jerome Frank, dissenting opinion in *United States v. Roth,* 354 U.S. 476, 1957.

[14] E. Joy Kroeger Mappes, "Ethical Dilemmas for Nurses: Physicians' Orders versus Patients' Rights," in T. A. Mappes and J. S. Zembatty, eds., *Biomedical Ethics* (New York: McGraw-Hill, 1981), p. 100.

[15] Amitai Etzioni, "When Rights Collide," *Psychology Today,* October 1977.

[16] Quincy Jones, *Q: The Autobiography of Quincy Jones* (New York: Doubleday, 2000) p. 299.

[17] Gary E. Crum, "Disputed Territory," *Hastings Center Report,* August/September 1988, p. 31.

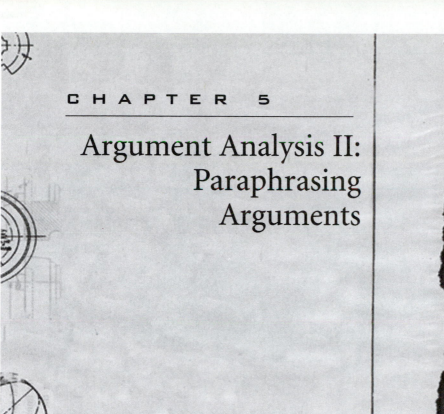

CHAPTER 5

Argument Analysis II: Paraphrasing Arguments

If you want to complain about Marilyn Manson, start from the beginning. Start with Shakespeare. What was *Romeo and Juliet* about? Suicide! OZZY OSBOURNE

In Chapter 4 we introduced the concept of *paraphrasing* as the best test of one's understanding of an argument. Paraphrasing means taking apart and then re-assembling a text in your own words. This is both easier and harder than it sounds. We hope and expect that the simple tools, procedures, and guidance presented in Chapter 4 will prove to be useful in paraphrasing arguments, but you will soon see that paraphrasing arguments takes us way "beyond" the simple and mechanical application of Chapter 4's tools and procedures. Let us begin by looking at paraphrasing in general and trying to explain that mysterious remark we just made about its being both easier and harder than it sounds. Try the following as an exercise:

*"To paraphrase the great Vince Lombardi, packaging
isn't everything, it's the only thing."*

EXERCISE 5.1

Look at the text below. Imagine that it's a newspaper headline—the "joke" kind that Jay Leno sometimes
uses on the *Tonight Show*. Write out in a grammatically correct sentence what you think the "actual"
(imaginary) news story might be.

IRAQI HEAD SEEKS ARMS

Complete this sentence: The "real story" is that . . .

We imagine that most of you will have come up with something like this: The "real story" is that the leader of Iraq is trying to get weapons. See how easy this is? That's paraphrasing. The hard part is explaining how you did it.

Jokes of this type depend on ambiguity. There are two meanings here: the one about the leader of Iraq and one about body parts. "Getting" the joke depends on recognizing both. In effect, getting a joke of this type depends on paraphrasing the same text twice. And again, this is both easy (to do) and hard (to explain). We know this is easy to do because people "get" jokes like this pretty routinely. Whole batches of these "Believe It or Not . . . Real Headlines from Actual Newspapers" jokes circulate widely on the Internet. In fact, here is a short list of them.

EXERCISE 5.2 | Topic for Class Discussion

Pay close attention to your own reasoning processes as you read these. See if you can figure out precisely how you "get" these jokes. Are you following any "rules"?

"Believe It or Not . . . Real Headlines from Actual Newspapers"

Police Campaign to Run Down Jaywalkers

Safety Experts Say School Bus Passengers Should Be Belted

Drunk Gets Nine Months in Violin Case

Survivor of Siamese Twins Joins Parents

Farmer Bill Dies in House

Stud Tires Out

Prostitutes Appeal to Pope

Panda Mating Fails; Veterinarian Takes Over

Soviet Virgin Lands Short of Goal Again

British Left Waffles on Falkland Islands

Eye Drops off Shelf

Teacher Strikes Idle Kids

Bush Wins on Budget, But More Lies Ahead

K9 Squad Helps Dog Bite Victim

Stolen Painting Found by Tree

Two Soviet Ships Collide, One Dies

Red Tape Holds Up New Bridge

Typhoon Rips Through Cemetery; Hundreds Dead

Astronaut Takes Blame for Gas in Spacecraft

Kids Make Nutritious Snacks

Air Head Fired

We think that the truth of the matter is that you're following lots of rules. For example paraphrasing the "real story" meaning of "Teacher Strikes Idle Kids" seems to depend on figuring out that "idle" is the verb and "strikes" is a noun. Here you are applying a rule of *syntax,* or grammar. But distinguishing the "parts of speech" isn't much help when you get to "Stolen Painting Found by Tree." In this case, distinguishing the "real story" meaning from the "joke" meaning depends on making a *semantic* distinction. In the "real story" the preposition "by" means "next to"; in the joke it means "through the action or agency of." There are more rules than you can shake a stick at. How do you know when to apply which rule?

Now here is something even more fascinating. We would not be at all surprised if many of our readers were baffled to one degree or another by what we have just said about syntax and semantics—and maybe even by our explanations of the two jokes—but still you get the jokes. The point here is that getting the joke, which involves paraphrasing the text twice, *does not seem to depend on being able to explain—or even being able to state—the rules you are following* as a speaker of the language when you paraphrase. Easy to do—hard to explain.

This is an example of a larger phenomenon: the awesome complexity of human intelligence. What we each do routinely as fluent speakers of a language—and getting jokes is a good measure of one's fluency—is *so* complex and subtle that to reduce it to a set of calculations and mechanical procedures is a huge undertaking (called *linguistics*). So, the reason this process is so hard to explain is not that there are no rules involved or calculations being made, and it's not that the calculations made in a given case can't be traced or that the general rules and procedures being followed can't be spelled out. But it *would take a very large book* to account for it within a comprehensive system. And it would take a huge amount of computer power even to *approximate* it mechanically in practice. This, by the way, pretty much captures the challenge of "artificial intelligence" as applied to conversation. The moral of this story is that following the steps and procedures presented in Chapter 4, especially in a "mechanical" way, will not *by itself* do the trick of argument analysis, if we understand argument analysis as a particular variety or application of paraphrasing. At the start of Chapter 4 we indicated that in the end it's your paraphrase of the argument—*your grasp of the meaning of the text, expressed in your own words*—that counts. Underlining, highlighting, mapping, casting—these are all merely means to that end. As useful as these tools may be in many cases, they are to full-fledged argument analysis like training wheels are to riding a bike.

For example, now look at the quotation from rock musician Ozzy Osbourne used as the opening epigram for this chapter:

> If you want to complain about Marilyn Manson, start from the beginning. Start with Shakespeare. What was *Romeo and Juliet* about? Suicide![1]

There is clearly an argument being presented here. But unless you can paraphrase it, you won't get anywhere trying to cast it. So, how *do* we go about paraphrasing an argument like this?

EXERCISE 5.3 | Paraphrasing an Argument I

Thought experiment/Topic for class discussion: Start with this question: What do we need to *know* in order to *understand* the argument? Go through the argument and list the things that a person would need to know or be familiar with in order to understand what Ozzy Osbourne is saying.

What do you need to know or be familiar with in order to understand what Osbourne is saying? Here's our list: You need to know who Marilyn Manson is. You need to know what the complaints about Marilyn Manson were. You need to know who Shakespeare was. It helps to know the plot of *Romeo and Juliet.* It also helps to know who Ozzy Osbourne is. Just for fun (and it's good exercise too), *before* you read any further, continue this exercise as a research assignment. Find this stuff out. Look it up.

EXERCISE 5.4 | Paraphrasing an Argument II

Research assignment: Who is Marilyn Manson? What were the complaints made about him? Who was Shakespeare? What is the plot of *Romeo and Juliet*? Who is Ozzy Osbourne? When you have all of this information, see if you can paraphrase the argument.

_____

_____

_____

_____

_____

_____

_____

Marilyn Manson is the stage name of a 1990s gothic rock act whose lead singer took on the persona "Anti-Christ Superstar." Once you know who Marilyn Manson is, it's easy to figure out what the complaints have been. His work of course was controversial. Concerts were banned, boycotts were organized against the sale of merchandise, and so on, because of concern that Marilyn Manson's music, music videos, and stage show might exert a Satanic influence on teenagers and lead them into depravity. Shakespeare is of course the great Elizabethan playwright, whose most famous tragedy, *Romeo and Juliet,* tells the story of the double suicide of two young lovers kept apart by their feuding families.

Ozzy Osbourne rose to prominence in the 1970s as lead singer of the British heavy metal band Black Sabbath. He, too, was the subject of much controversy like that provoked by Marilyn Manson, including a landmark legal battle over the 1981 song "Suicide Solution," allegedly the cause of a teenage gunshot suicide. Now, with this information, go back to paraphrasing Osbourne's argument, starting with the conclusion.

EXERCISE 5.5 | Paraphrasing an Argument III

What is Osbourne's main point?

_____

_____

What is Osbourne's basis of support for this main point?

_____

_____

With the above information, it's not at all difficult to see that Osbourne's point is to defend Manson (as well as Osbourne's own work) against censorship, based on a comparison with Shakespeare. There you have it: a paraphrase of Osbourne's argument. This was accomplished essentially by *situating the text we're trying to paraphrase in a meaningful context.* This is important enough to qualify as a rule of thumb: Whenever we undertake to paraphrase an argument, we should pause to orient ourselves to the context in which the argument appears. We should begin with the question: What does a person need to know in order to understand this argument? And, of course, we should therefore make sure that we *do* know whatever a person needs to know in order to understand the argument.

CRITICAL THINKING TIP 5.1

When paraphrasing, orient yourself to the context.

It is time to apply what we've learned to some more advanced examples. Let us briefly review. Here are the important guidelines to argument analysis.

TABLE 5.1 Guidelines for Paraphrasing

- *The Goal:* To establish a fair, accurate, and detailed understanding of the argument—as a preliminary to rendering a judgment of its quality.
- *The Measure:* The paraphrase of the argument—your grasp of the meaning of the text, expressed in your own words—is what counts most.

- *Rule of Thumb:* Orient yourself to the argument's context.
- *Rule of Thumb:* Find the conclusion first.
- *Rule of Thumb:* When in doubt, don't be unfair—make the argument out to be as reasonable as possible.

ADVANCED APPLICATIONS

So far, the arguments we have used for purposes of illustration have all been quite short. Many of the arguments you will encounter are much longer. Arguments are often presented in the form of letters, speeches, essays, even whole books. Analyzing short arguments is, as you already know, challenging in several ways. The results of the analysis of short arguments, or more precisely short presentations of arguments, can easily be longer and more complex than the texts analyzed. This was the case, for example, with the argument analyzed at the end of Chapter 4 about textbooks, mistakes, whales, mammals, and fish. Longer arguments present an additional and "opposite" challenge: the challenge of compressing, or distilling a lengthy presentation into something that can be grasped more quickly than the original. Fortunately, however, this challenge can also be met by approaching it with the guidelines discussed above. The goal and the measure of success remain the same. And the rules of thumb still apply. We propose now to illustrate all of this with an example. We suggest that you try your hand at paraphrasing it *before* you read what we have to say about it. So try the following exercise *before reading the rest of this chapter.*

EXERCISE 5.6 | Paraphrasing an Argument

The following is an excerpt of an essay published in the aftermath of the September 11 terrorist attacks. The essay, which appeared in the Ft. Worth *Star Telegram* on December 6, 2001, is by syndicated columnist Molly Ivins. After reading the passage, follow the above guidelines and *paraphrase the argument in 50 words or less*.

Destroying Freedoms in Order to Save Them

With all due respect, of course, and God Bless America too, has anyone considered the possibility that the attorney general is becoming unhinged?

Poor John Ashcroft is under a lot of strain here. Is it possible that his mind has started to give under the weight of responsibility, what with having to stop terrorism between innings against doctors trying to help the dying in Oregon and California? Why not take a Valium, sir, and go track down some nice domestic nut with access to anthrax, OK?

Not content with the noxious USA PATRIOT bill (for "Uniting and Strengthening America by Providing Appropriate Tools Required to Intercept and Obstruct Terrorism" Act—urp), which was bad enough, Ashcroft has steadily moved from bad to worse. Now he wants to bring back FBI surveillance of domestic religious and political groups.

For those who remember COINTELPRO, this is glorious news. Back in the day, Fearless Fibbies, cleverly disguised in their wingtips and burr haircuts, used to infiltrate such dangerous groups as the Southern Christian Leadership Conference and Business Executives Against the War in Vietnam. This had the usual comedic fallout and was so berserk that there was a standing rule on the left: Anyone who proposed breaking any law was automatically assumed to be an FBI agent.

Let's see, who might the Federal Fosdicks spy upon today? Columnist Tom Friedman of The New York Times recently reported from Pakistan that hateful Taliban types are teaching in the religious schools, "The faithful shall enter paradise, and the unbelievers shall be condemned to eternal hellfire." Frightful! Put the Baptists on the list. Those who agitate against the government, constantly denigrating and opposing it? Add Tom DeLay, Dick Armey and Rush Limbaugh to the list. . . .

© Molly Ivins. Reprinted by permission of POM, Inc.

Paraphrase

_____

_____

_____

_____

Now that you have paraphrased Ivins's argument, it will be instructive to compare both your process and your results to our own. We'll take you through it step by step. We begin with an orientation to the context of the argument. One of the most important contextual dimensions where arguments are concerned is the *issue* to which the argument is addressed. In fact, the issue is probably the single most important contextual landmark you will be able to find in most cases. Having a clear and solid grasp of the issue will make identifying and formulating the thesis of the argument much easier than it would otherwise be. So the very first thing we would do is to formulate a brief issue statement.

EXERCISE 5.7 | **Issue Statement**

We highly recommend reviewing the section of Chapter 1 on Issues, Issue Analysis, and Composing "Issue Statements." When you have done that, answer the following question: What is the issue Molly Ivins is addressing in her argument? Try to compose your answer in one sentence.

_____

_____

Ivins's argument is addressed to the issue of the U.S. government's official response to the September 11 terrorist attacks. This is, of course, a very complex issue. So it might be well advised to do a little issue analysis and focus a little more precisely: We could start by making a distinction between U.S. *domestic* and *foreign* policy. Ivins's argument is concerned particularly with the government's response in the area of *domestic security and law enforcement*. In general terms this issue might be expressed in the form of the question, "Is the U.S. government doing what it should be doing with regard to domestic security and law enforcement in response to the September 11 terrorist attacks?"

Besides the issue, what else does a person need to know to understand Ivins's argument? As in the case of the shorter argument discussed above, this "research agenda" can be derived by carefully scanning or reading through the argument. Go ahead and try it. Then carry out the research. Look the information up (see Exercises 5.3 and 5.4).

EXERCISE 5.8

Develop and carry out a contextual research agenda for Molly Ivins's argument. Follow the instructions given in Exercises 5.3 and 5.4.

Here are our results: In this case, you need to know that John Ashcroft is the U.S. attorney general in the George W. Bush administration. You need to know that serious acts of terrorism involving the distribution of deadly anthrax through the mail remained unsolved at the time the column was written. You need to know at least a little bit about the "USA PATRIOT Act"—an antiterrorism measure rushed through Congress and signed into law in October 2001, just six weeks after September 11. It gives sweeping new surveillance powers to U.S. international intelligence and domestic law enforcement agencies and it eliminates checks and balances that were put into place after previous misuse of surveillance authority by these agencies. You need to know that COINTELPRO is an acronym for covert domestic "counterintelligence programs" run by the FBI from 1956 to 1971, in which FBI agents infiltrated domestic political organizations in an attempt to neutralize domestic political dissent and combat the "threat of communism." You need to know that the Southern Christian Leadership Conference was the civil rights organization founded in 1957 by Dr. Martin Luther King. You need to know that revelations of COINTELPRO covert surveillance on law-abiding U.S. citizens, including Dr. King, were what led to the checks and balances now eliminated under the USA PATRIOT Act. You need to know that the Taliban was the repressive theocratic regime that ruled most of Afghanistan and gave safe haven to Osama bin Laden since 1996, and that the events of September 11 turned the Taliban into an "official enemy" of the United States. You need to know that Tom DeLay and Dick Armey are both Texas Republicans and that, as majority whip and majority leader in the House of Representatives, they are two of the most powerful politicians in the United States. And of course, everybody presumably recognizes Rush Limbaugh as the host of a right-wing radio talk show.

We could go further than this. The more you know about the context, the more deeply you can appreciate the details and nuances of the argument. For example, it also helps to know that Fearless Fosdick was a cartoon character created by cartoonist Al Capp (in the comic strip *Li'l Abner*) as a parody of *Dick Tracy* (Dick Tracy did endless battle with horrible villains and, though occasionally wounded in battle, always got his man). Fosdick is a farce. Gullible and in awe of corrupt authority, he is forever getting shot full of bullet holes like Swiss cheese. It helps to know that COINTELPRO operations often weren't as "covert" as the operatives seemed to think they were. It also helps to recognize the reference in Ivins's title to a notorious Vietnam-era piece of Orwellian doublespeak by which Pentagon officials explained that it was necessary to "destroy certain villages in order to save them."

But we have enough of a context already to enable us to take the next step and identify Ivins's main point, or "thesis." Remember, Ivins's thesis will be her answer to the question in which we formulated the issue in our one-sentence issue statement above:

> Is the U.S. government doing what it should be doing with regard to domestic security and law enforcement in response to the September 11 terrorist attacks?

Ivins's answer to this question is evident. She does *not* think that the U.S. government (personified here by Attorney General Ashcroft) is doing what it should be doing in terms of domestic security and law enforcement in response to the terrorist attacks. In particular, Ivins is arguing that the USA PATRIOT Act and

Ashcroft's call to reauthorize FBI surveillance of domestic religious and political groups are not what the U.S. government should be doing. Why not?

Asking the question "Why not?" at this point directs attention to the support Ivins offers for her thesis. Rereading the text of her argument against the backdrop of the contextual information assembled above, we can now boil that support down to this. The measures Ashcroft has taken and called for will not enhance security against terrorist attacks but they *will* destroy our freedoms. And if they are applied consistently to those on the domestic scene whose political actions and agendas are like those of our "official enemies," the results will be a farce. While serious acts of terrorism, quite possibly of domestic origin, remain to be solved, we'll wind up spying on Baptists, the Republican congressional leadership, and right-wing radio talk show hosts.

So, our paraphrase: Ivins is arguing that the USA PATRIOT Act and reauthorizing FBI surveillance of domestic religious and political groups are not what our government should be doing, because these things will result only in the farcical destruction of our own freedoms (40 words).

Using Chapter 4 tools, we might now underline, highlight, and cast our paraphrase as follows:

[THE USA PATRIOT ACT AND REAUTHORIZING FBI SURVEILLANCE OF DOMESTIC RELIGIOUS AND POLITICAL GROUPS ARE NOT WHAT WE SHOULD BE DOING, (1)] (because) [**these things will result only in the farcical destruction of our own freedoms. (2)**]

The conclusion (claim #1) does not follow from the premise (claim #2) alone. There is an additional implied premise—a claim so obvious that it "goes without saying": "Engaging in the farcical destruction of our own freedoms is not what our government should be doing." Thus, assigning it the letter "a," we might add to the casting as follows:

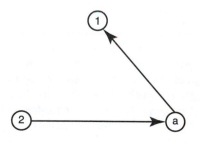

So far, we have arrived at a very short paraphrase of a much longer text. In effect, our paraphrase compresses Ivins's entire argument into a single sentence of 40 words, consisting of just two claims: her thesis and one supporting premise. In addition, and more important, as a result of the process we used to get this far, we are in a very good position to explain the argument in greater depth and detail should that be necessary or desirable. The support for the main premise (claim #2) may be found in the two paragraphs of contextual information we assembled above. Indeed, you might have noticed, along the way to our 40-word paraphrase we passed through an intermediate-length paraphrase of Ivins's premises.

PRACTICE, PRACTICE, AND MORE PRACTICE

That's the only way to get good at this. And the good news is, the better *you* get, the easier *it* gets. So we conclude this chapter with a pair of relatively long arguments for you to practice on.

EXERCISE 5.9

The two compositions below present opposing positions on another part of the September 11 debate. Paraphrase each of the two arguments using the procedures illustrated above. Target length for each paraphrase: 250 words (the rough equivalent of one standard page of double-space text).

An Open Letter to President Bush and the U.S. Congress

October 2001

The events of the past few days have made everyone understand how vulnerable a free and open society is to mass destruction and terror. But this terrible vulnerability is part of the strength of such a society, not a hallmark of its weakness. It takes courage to allow the free movement of people and ideas. That courage is predicated on voluntary acceptance of great risk, and not upon ignorance of its likelihood. The immediate response to such a catastrophe is anger and hatred. But the system of laws that supports the U.S. and its allies has been designed by generations of great people to ensure that anger and hatred are never given the final word. Justice, truth, and respect for individual differences are principles whose power far outweighs the thoughtless desire for revenge. More importantly, revenge breeds revenge. It seems terribly dangerous to provide individuals motivated precisely by the desire to increase pain and suffering the luxury of the war they so much desire. Such a war turns them from rigid, totalitarian cowards to soldiers; from failures who are willing to prey upon the innocent to heroic exemplars of the fight against overwhelming external oppression. The craven acts of terrorism perpetrated in New York and Washington are dignified intolerably by their classification as acts of war. The individuals who perpetrated these appalling events must be regarded and treated as criminals, as international pariahs, who have committed crimes against humanity, and who must be brought publicly and rationally to justice. Our great technological power makes us increasingly vulnerable to the rigid madness of the ideologically committed and resentful. To turn against such madness with indiscriminate revenge seeking is merely to react in the same primitive and deadly manner. To risk the slaughter of innocent people in the hunt for such revenge is to absolutely ensure that constant episodes of international terror will come to be the hallmark of 21st-century existence. The entire world stands behind the U.S., in the hope that the commission of crimes against civilization can be exterminated. Such solidarity was absolutely unthinkable even fifteen years ago. The U.S. therefore has an unparalleled opportunity to demonstrate its unshakeable commitment to its own principles, particularly under such conditions of extreme duress, and to provide the world with the hope that democracy and freedom can truly rise above the parochial ideological madness of the past. Such a demonstration would truly lift the American state above all past national institutions, and would continue the tradition of great spirit that allowed for the rehabilitation of Germany and Japan after the Second World War. Perhaps the events of September 11 might therefore be regarded as the last war of the second Christian millennium, instead of the first war of the third. In consequence, we implore you to react with discrimination, to target only those truly responsible, and to avoid the cruel and thoughtless errors characterizing humanity's blind and ethnocentric past. Please punish only the guilty, and not the innocent. Otherwise the cycle of terror that seems an ineradicable part of human existence will never come to an end.

Sincerely,

1. Jordan B. Peterson, Professor, Department of Psychology, University of Toronto, *peterson@psych.utoronto.ca*
2. Daniel C. Dennett, University Professor, Director, Center for Cognitive Studies, Tufts University, *ddennett@tufts.edu*
3. Steven Pinker, Professor, Department of Brain and Cognitive Sciences, Massachusetts Institute of Technology (MIT), *spinker@mediaone.net*
4. Hilary Putnam, Professor Emeritus, Department of Philosophy, Harvard University, Cambridge, MA, USA, *hputnam@fas.harvard.edu*

Et al.

War, Not "Crimes":
Time for a Paradigm Shift

October 1, 2001

"Make no mistake: The United States will hunt down and punish those responsible for these cowardly acts." So spoke President Bush in his address to the nation soon after the catastrophic events of September 11.

I agree with the president's sentiments but disagree with two specifics in this statement. First, there was nothing cowardly about the attacks, which were deeds of incredible—albeit perverted—bravery. Second, to "hunt down and punish" the perpetrators is deeply to misunderstand the problem. It implies that we view the plane crashes as criminal deeds rather than what they truly are—acts of war. They are part of a campaign of terrorism that began in a sustained way with the bombing of the U.S. embassy in Beirut in 1983, a campaign that has never since relented. Occurring with almost predictable regularity a few times a year, assaults on Americans have included explosions on airliners, at commercial buildings, and at a variety of U.S. governmental installations. Before last week, the total death toll was about 600 American lives.

To me, this sustained record of violence looks awfully much like war, but Washington in its wisdom has insisted otherwise. Official policy has viewed the attacks as a sequence of discrete criminal incidents. Seeing terrorism primarily as a problem of law enforcement is a mistake, because it means:

- Focusing on the arrest and trial of the dispensable characters who actually carry out violent acts, leaving the funders, planners, organizers, and commanders of terrorism to continue their work unscathed, prepared to carry out more attacks.

- Relying primarily on such defensive measures as metal detectors, security guards, bunkers, police arrests, and prosecutorial eloquence—rather than on such offensive tools as soldiers, aircraft, and ships.

- Misunderstanding the terrorist's motivations as criminal, whereas they are usually based on extremist ideologies.

- Missing the fact that terrorist groups (and the states that support them) have declared war on the United States (sometimes publicly).

- Requiring that the U.S. government have unrealistically high levels of proof before deploying military force. If it lacks evidence that can stand up in a U.S. court of justice, as is usually the case, no action is taken. The legalistic mindset thus ensures that, in the vast majority of cases, the U.S. government does not respond, and killers of Americans pay little or no price.

The time has come for a paradigm shift, toward viewing terrorism as a form of warfare. Such a change will have many implications. It means targeting not just those foot soldiers who actually carry out the violence but the organizations and governments that stand behind them. It means relying on the armed forces, not policemen, to protect Americans. It means defense overseas rather than in American courtrooms. It means that organizations and governments that sponsor terrorism—not just the foot soldiers who carry it out—will pay the price.

It means dispensing with the unrealistically high expectations of proof so that when reasonable evidence points to a regime's or an organization's having harmed Americans, U.S. military force can be deployed. It means that, as in conventional war, Washington need not know the names and specific actions of enemy soldiers before fighting them.

It means retaliating every single time terrorism harms an American. There is no need to know the precise identity of a perpetrator; in war, there are times when one strikes first and asks questions later. When an attack takes place, it could be reason to target any of those known to harbor terrorists. If the perpetrator is not precisely known, then punish those who are known to harbor terrorists. Go after the governments and organizations that support terrorism.

It means using force so that the punishment is disproportionately greater than the attack. The U.S. has a military force far more powerful than any other in the world: Why spend hundreds of billions of dollars a year on it and not deploy it to defend Americans?

I give fair warning: The military approach demands more from Americans than does the legal one. It requires a readiness to spend money and to lose lives. Force works only if it is part of a sustained policy, not a one-time event. Throwing a few bombs (as was done against the Libyan regime in 1986, and against sites in Afghanistan and Sudan in 1998) does not amount to a serious policy. Going the military route requires a long-term commitment that will demand much from Americans over many years.

But it will be worth it, for the safety of Americans depends ultimately not on defense but on offense; on victories not in the courtroom but on the battlefield. The U.S. government needs to establish a newly fearsome reputation, so that anyone who harms Americans knows that retribution will be certain and nasty. Nothing can replace the destruction of any organization or government that harms so much as a single American citizen.

To those who say this approach would start a cycle of violence, the answer is obvious: That cycle already exists, as Americans are constantly murdered in acts of terrorism. Further, by baring their teeth, Americans are far more likely to intimidate their enemies than to instigate further violence. Retaliation will reduce violence, not further increase it, providing Americans with a safety they presently do not enjoy.

Reprinted by permission of Daniel Pipes. From *The National Review*, October 1, 2001.

ADDITIONAL EXERCISES

At the end of Chapter 4, we supplied a baker's dozen of examples of argumentation taken from a variety of sources in public discourse for analysis using basic tools and techniques covered in Chapters 3 and 4. Now try these examples again, with the additional tools and techniques of paraphrasing covered in this chapter. See if these don't help you over the rough spots. Keep the goal of argument analysis in mind—a fair and accurate understanding of the argument in detail, expressed in your own words.

■ **EXERCISE 5.10**   "Evolution is a scientific fairy-tale just as the 'flat earth theory' was in the 12th century. Evolution directly contradicts the Second Law of Thermodynamics, which states that unless an intelligent planner is directing a system, it will always go in the direction of disorder and deterioration. Evolution requires a faith that is incomprehensible!"[2]

■ **EXERCISE 5.11**   " 'We shall make no distinction,' the President proclaimed, 'between terrorists and countries that harbor terrorists.' So now we are bombing Afghanistan and inevitably killing innocent people because it is in the nature of bombing (and I say this as a former Air force bombardier) to be indiscriminate, to 'make no distinction'. We are committing terrorism in order to 'send a message' to terrorists. . . . War is terrorism, magnified a hundred times. Yes, let's find the perpetrators of the awful acts of September 11. We must find the guilty parties and prosecute them. But we shouldn't engage in indiscriminate retaliation. When a crime is committed by someone in a certain neighborhood, you don't destroy the neighborhood."[3]

■ **EXERCISE 5.12**   "A scientific colleague of mine, who holds a professorial post in the department of sociology and anthropology at one of our leading universities, recently asked me about my stand on the question of human beings having sex relations without love. Although I have taken something of a position on this issue in my book, *The American Sexual Tragedy*, I have never quite considered the problem in sufficient detail. So here goes. In general, I feel that affectional, as against non-affectional, sex relations are desirable. It is usually desirable that an association between coitus and affection exist—particularly in marriage, because it is often difficult for two individuals to keep finely tuned to each other over a period of years."[4]

EXERCISE 5.13   "It isn't likely that managed competition [the Clinton health care reform concept] can be counted on to save money. For one thing, at least two managed-care setups must be present in a community if there is to be competition, and each of them needs a potential market of roughly 250,000 people to achieve economies of scale. Only about half of all Americans, it turns out, live in places densely populated enough to support two or more such programs. What's more, insurers would constantly hustle to win and retain business, because employers would constantly be shopping for better deals, just as they do now. The sales staff, recruiters, advertising personnel, and clerical staff that such 'marketing' entails contribute nothing to the provision of health care. And the physicians, nurses, and others whom insurers and HMOs [Health Maintenance Organizations] hire to oversee—that is, second-guess—the decisions individual doctors make with individual patients—an essential feature of managed care—have to be paid too, adding to the overhead cost. Administrative costs already soak up about $225 billion a year—25 cents of every dollar spent on health care in this country. Under managed competition, such costs would, at best, stay the same. More probably, they would increase."[5]

EXERCISE 5.14   "To the extent that it is working at all, the press is always a participant in, rather than a pure observer of, the events it reports. Our decisions on where (and where not) to be and what (and what not) to report have enormous impact on the political and governmental life we cover. We are obliged to be selective. We cannot publish the Daily Everything. And so long as this is true—so long as we are making choices that 1) affect what people see concerning their leaders and 2) inevitably cause those leaders to behave in particular ways—we cannot pretend we are not participants."[6]

EXERCISE 5.15   "Scientists are human beings with their full complement of emotions and prejudices, and their emotions and prejudices often influence the way they do their science. This was first clearly brought out in a study by Professor Nicholas Pastore in 1949. In this study Professor Pastore showed that the scientist's political beliefs were highly correlated with what he believed about the roles played by nature and nurture in the development of the person. Those holding conservative political views strongly tended to believe in the power of genes over environment. Those subscribing to more liberal views tended to believe in the power of environment over genes. One distinguished scientist (who happened to be a teacher of mine) when young was a socialist and environmentalist, but toward middle age he became politically conservative and a firm believer in the supremacy of genes!"[7]

EXERCISE 5.16   "Many a reader will raise the question whether findings won by the observation of individuals can be applied to the psychological understanding of groups. Our answer to this question is an emphatic affirmation. Any group consists of individuals and nothing but individuals, and psychological mechanisms which we find operating in a group can therefore only be mechanisms that operate in individuals. In studying individual psychology as a basis for the understanding of social psychology, we do something which might be compared with studying an object under the microscope. This enables us to discover the very details of psychological mechanisms which we find operating on a large scale in the social process. If our analysis of socio-psychological phenomena is not based on the detailed study of human behavior, it lacks empirical character and, therefore, validity."[8]

EXERCISE 5.17   "Flextime (Flexible Working Hours) often makes workers more productive because being treated as responsible adults gives them greater commitment to their jobs. As a result it decreases absenteeism, sick leave, tardiness and overtime, and generally produces significant increases in productivity for the work group as a whole. For example, in trial periods in three different departments, the U.S. Social Security Administration measured productivity increases averaging about 20%. None has reported a decline."[9]

EXERCISE 5.18   "Government control of ideas or personal preferences is alien to a democracy. And the yearning to use governmental censorship of any kind is infectious. It may spread insidiously. Commencing with suppression of books as obscene, it is not unlikely to develop into official lust for the power of thought-control in the areas of religion, politics, and elsewhere. Milton observed that 'licensing of books . . . necessarily pulls along with it so many other kinds of licensing.' Mill notes that the 'bounds of what may be called moral police' may easily extend 'until it encroaches on the most unquestionably legitimate liberty of the individual.' We should beware of a recrudescence of the undemocratic doctrine uttered in the seventeenth century by Berkeley, Governor of Virginia: "Thank God there are no free schools or preaching, for learning has brought disobedience into the world, and printing has divulged them. God keep us from both'."[10]

EXERCISE 5.19   "What, after all, is the foundation of the nurse's obligation to follow the physician's orders? Presumably, the nurse's obligation to act in the medical interest of the patient. The point is that the nurse has an obligation to follow physician's orders because, ordinarily, patient welfare (interest) thereby is ensured. Thus when a nurse's obligation to follow a physician's order comes into direct conflict with the nurse's obligation to act in the medical interest of the patient, it would seem to follow that the patient's interests should always take precedence."[11]

■ **EXERCISE 5.20**   "American institutions were fashioned in an era of vast unoccupied spaces and pre-industrial technology. In those days, collisions between public needs and individual rights may have been minimal. But increased density, scarcity of resources, and interlocking technologies have now heightened the concern for 'public goods,' which belong to no one in particular but to all of us jointly. Polluting a lake or river or the air may not directly damage any one person's private property or living space. But it destroys a good that all of us—including future generations—benefit from and have a title to. Our public goods are entitled to a measure of protection."[12]

■ **EXERCISE 5.21**   "These days music is truly global in sweep. The genie's out of the bottle, never to return, with MP3, Napster/Scour, and Freenet and Gnutella rendering all previous lines of demarcation meaningless. There's a revolution in progress, leveling everything in its path. Copyrights, masters, negatives, books, records, and films; it's all the same to a binary number, or a carbon atom and hydrogen qubit. Legislation, global police monitoring by knocking on two million doors—I don't think so. All I know is, you can't afford to make the customer your enemy. They no longer want to purchase a CD with ten or twelve songs on it to get the two they really want. They are also hip enough to know about artists' earnings and no longer want to pay the price for all the people in the middle of the distribution chain. These technological changes have provided an unexpected and highly efficient platform for rebellion for the current generation. We better get together and figure it out—and quickly!"[13]

■ **EXERCISE 5.22**   "In policy debates one party sometimes charges that his or her opponents are embracing a Nazi-like position. . . . Meanwhile, sympathizers nod in agreement with the charge, seeing it as the ultimate blow to their opponents. . . . The problem with using the Nazi analogy in public policy debates is that in the Western world there is a form of anti-Nazi 'bigotry' that sees Nazis as almost mythically evil beings. . . . Firsthand knowledge of our own culture makes it virtually impossible to equate Nazi society with our own. The official racism of Germany, its military mentality, the stresses of war, and the presence of a dictator instead of a democratic system make Nazi Germany in the 1940s obviously different from America in the 1980s."[14]

■ **EXERCISE 5.23**   At the end of Chapter 3 (Exercise 3.14) the instructions were to research the issue articulated in your Issue Statement, and to identify at least three extended arguments representing at least two distinct positions on that issue. Now apply all that you have learned about argument analysis to the results of your research. Try to paraphrase the arguments you found in your research in 100 words or less each.

ENDNOTES

[1] Ozzy Osbourne, *Rolling Stone,* #736, p. 28.

[2] Dr. Edward Blic, *21 Scientists Who Believe in Creation* (Harrisonburg, VA: Christian Light Publications, 1977).

[3] Howard Zinn, "It Seems to Me," *The Progressive* (November 2001), p. 8.

[4] Albert Ellis, *Sex Without Guilt* (New York: Lyle Stuart, Inc., 1966).

[5] Judith Randal, "Wrong Prescription: Why Managed Competition Is No Cure," *The Progressive* (May 1993), pp. 23–24.

[6] Meg Greenfield, "When the Press Becomes a Participant," *The Washington Post Company, Annual Report,* 1984, p. 21.

[7] Ashley Montagu, *Sociobiology Examined* (Oxford: Oxford University Press, 1980), p. 4.

[8] Eric Fromm, *Escape from Freedom* (New York: Avon Books, 1965), p. 158.

[9] Barry Stein et al., "Flextime," *Psychology Today,* June 1976, p. 43.

[10] Jerome Frank, dissenting opinion in *United States v. Roth,* 354 U.S. 476, 1957.

[11] E. Joy Kroeger Mappes, "Ethical Dilemmas for Nurses: Physicians' Orders versus Patients' Rights," in T. A. Mappes and J. S. Zembatty, eds., *Biomedical Ethics* (New York: McGraw-Hill, 1981), p. 100.

[12] Amitai Etzioni, "When Rights Collide," *Psychology Today,* October 1977.

[13] Quincy Jones, *Q: The Autobiography of Quincy Jones* (New York: Doubleday, 2000), p. 299.

[14] Gary E. Crum, "Disputed Territory," *Hastings Center Report,* August/September 1988, p. 31.

UNIT THREE

Deductive
Reasoning

CHAPTER 6

Evaluating Deductive Arguments I: Categorical Logic

Now that we have covered argument identification and analysis, we are ready to address the evaluation of arguments. Most of us intuitively recognize qualitative differences between arguments, especially where the differences are relatively great. That is to say, we have little difficulty in intuitively recognizing the superiority of an excellent argument to one that is extremely weak.

But our intuitions may fail to guide us where competing arguments are more closely matched. Different people often have conflicting intuitions about which of two closely matched competing arguments is superior, and we may even experience conflicting intuitions ourselves individually. Nor do our intuitions help us explain our evaluative judgments. So, we need a bit of theory to support, guide, and explain our evaluative intuitions. For theoretical purposes we'll make a basic distinction between the structural features of an argument and the materials used in its construction. One way to understand this distinction is to think of an argu-

"I shall now punch a huge hole in your argument."

ment as a building. Now suppose we are evaluating buildings, for example, while buying a house. Some houses are obviously and intuitively better built than others. We can tell "intuitively" that the White House is a stronger building than the outhouse. But we need a more systematic set of criteria to make reasonable decisions where houses are more closely matched. Buildings are complicated, so there are many criteria relevant to evaluating buildings. That's why we would want to make the set of criteria "systematic." The system gives us organization.

One way to organize is to divide. And with buildings, a reasonable and powerful first distinction for purposes of evaluation would be between the materials used and the how those materials are put together—the design and the execution of the design. So also in evaluating arguments we could look at "design factors" and "materials factors." In this comparison (or "analogy") the "materials" are the premises of the argument, the "design" is the plan according to which the premises are assembled in support of the conclusion. We will begin in this chapter with "design factors," returning to "materials factors" in Chapter 10.

DEDUCTIVE AND INDUCTIVE REASONING

The first consideration in design is always function. In reasoning and its evaluation, an important functional design consideration is "inferential security." In Chapter 3 we introduced the term "inference" as the mental step we take in reasoning from premise(s) to conclusion. In taking this step, we want to know how secure we are against falling into error. Thus, "inferential security" refers to the degree to which an inference is safe. In terms of function we can sort arguments into two design categories: deductive and inductive. Deductive inferences are designed to achieve "absolute security" in the inference. Inductive inferences are designed to manage risk of error where absolute security is unattainable.

Consider the following two examples:

1. Your neighbor, Jones, is a member of the American Association of University Professors. Only members of the faculties of accredited colleges and universities are eligible for membership in the American Association of University Professors. Therefore your neighbor, Jones, is a college professor.

2. Your neighbor, Jones, wears a tweed sport coat with patches on the elbows, he carries a battered briefcase, and he rides his bicycle to the college campus every day. Therefore, your neighbor, Jones, is a college professor.

Notice how much stronger the connection is between the premises and conclusion in the first example as compared with the second example. In the first example we could say that anyone who fully understands what the sentences in the argument mean must recognize that the premises cannot both be true without the conclusion also being true. But that is not the case with the second argument. In the second example we could say at most that the premises, if true, make the conclusion reasonable or likely. As we'll go on to explain more fully in the next two chapters, deductive reasoning, when it is well designed and constructed ("valid"), completely eliminates all risk of error in the inferential move from the premises to the conclusion. In inductive reasoning, the truth of the premises makes the conclusion reasonable, probable, or likely, but not certain. This difference between deduction and induction will be reflected in different sets of evaluative criteria. Accordingly, an early step in the process of evaluating arguments is deciding which set of criteria should be applied, or in other words, whether the argument should be evaluated as a deduction or as an induction.

Before we address this question, we'd better clear up an old and widespread misunderstanding about the essential difference between induction and deduction. It is often said that deduction moves from general premises to particular conclusions, while induction moves in the opposite direction from particular premises to general conclusions. It is true of *some* deductive inferences that they move from general premises to particular conclusions. But it's not an essential distinguishing feature of all deductions. For example:

Ford Motor Company has reported record profits for last year. General Motors has reported record profits for last year. And Chrysler has reported record profits for last year. Therefore, all of the major U.S. auto manufacturers made money last year.

is a deductive argument with particular premises and a general conclusion. Similarly, it is true of *some* inductive inferences that they move from particular premises to general conclusions. But it's not an essential distinguishing feature of all inductive inferences. For example:

> All U.S. presidents have so far been men. Therefore, it is likely that the next U.S. president will be a man.

is an inductive argument with a general premise and a particular conclusion.

DEDUCTIVE AND INDUCTIVE SIGNALS

Just as the presence of arguments, premises, and conclusions is frequently indicated by means of signal words, so the *modality* of the inference—that is, whether it should be evaluated as a deductive or an inductive one—is often indicated by signal words. Deductive signals include:

certainly

necessarily

must

For example:

> Your neighbor, Jones, is a member of the American Association of University Professors. Only members of the faculties of accredited colleges and universities are eligible for membership in the American Association of University Professors. Therefore, your neighbor, Jones, (must be) a college professor.

Inductive signals include:

probably

in all likelihood

chances are

it is reasonable to suppose that

it's a good bet that

For example:

> Your neighbor, Jones, wears a tweed sport coat with patches on the elbows, he carries a battered briefcase, and he rides his bicycle to the college campus every day. (I'd be willing to bet) your neighbor, Jones, is a college professor.

But just as with argument indicator words discussed so far, we need to be aware of the ambiguities and other nuances of meaning in context in order to avoid overly mechanical readings of things. And, as in all instances of argument analysis, we are guided by the rules of thumb that we should try to make the argument out to be as reasonable as possible. For example, even if someone said,

> Your neighbor, Jones, wears a tweed sport coat with patches on the elbows, he carries a battered briefcase, and he rides his bicycle to the college campus every day. Therefore, your neighbor, Jones, *must be* a college professor.

it would still be appropriate to evaluate the argument as an induction. A reasonable and charitable reading would interpret the speaker as having "overstated" the certainty of the conclusion relative to the premises. And similarly, if someone were to say,

> Your neighbor, Jones, is a member of the American Association of University Professors. Only members of the faculties of accredited colleges and universities are eligible for membership in the American Association of University Professors. *I'd be willing to bet* your neighbor, Jones, is a college professor.

it would be appropriate to evaluate the argument as a deduction. A reasonable and charitable reading would interpret the speaker as having "understated" the certainty of the conclusion relative to the premises.

EXERCISE 6.1 | Deductive/Inductive

For each of the following passages, indicate whether the argument presented should be considered a deductive argument or an inductive argument.

	Deductive	Since tests proved that it took at least 2.3 seconds to operate the bolt of the rifle, Oswald obviously could not have fired three times—hitting Kennedy twice and Connally once—in 5.6 seconds or less.
	Inductive	

	Deductive	At bottom I did not believe I had touched that man. The law of probabilities decreed me guiltless of his blood. For in all my small experience with guns I had never hit anything I had tried to hit, and I knew I had done my best to hit him.
	Inductive	
		— Mark Twain

	Deductive	All of the leading economic indicators point toward further improvement in the economy. You can count on an improved third quarter.
	Inductive	

	Deductive	During an interview with the school paper, Coach Danforth was quoted as saying, "I think it's safe to assume that Jason Israel will be our starting point guard next year. Both of our starting guards are graduating this spring and no one else on the team has Jason's speed and ball handling skills."
	Inductive	

ARGUMENT FORM

For the rest of this chapter we will concentrate on the first of these two argument design categories, deductive inferences. In Chapter 7 we will focus on inductive inferences. As a first step we must introduce the important notion of argument form. Consider the following argument:

Because [all humans are mortal (1)] (and) [all Americans are human, (2)] (it follows that) [all Americans are mortal. (3)]

Casting the argument shows that premises 1 and 2 together support conclusion 3. But now we want to look more closely at the *way* in which the premises relate to the conclusion. Let us first represent the argument according to a conventional format:

(1)   All humans are mortal.

(2)   All Americans are humans.

∴(3)   All Americans are mortal.

In this format the premises are listed in order of their appearance above the solid line and the conclusion is listed below it. The symbol (∴) can be read as shorthand for "therefore." Notice that in this particular argument there appears to be a very strong connection between the conclusion and the premises: It is impossible to deny the conclusion without also denying at least one of the premises (or contradicting yourself). Try it. Now consider a second example:

[All corundum has a high refractive index. (1)] And [all rubies are corundum. (2)] (So) [all rubies have a high refractive index. (3)]

Represented in the same conventional format, the argument looks like this:

(1)   All corundum has a high refractive index.

(2)   All rubies are corundum.

∴(3)   All rubies have a high refractive index.

Notice that here too the same very strong connection appears to exist between the conclusion and the premises. You might be less well acquainted with the optical properties and gemological classification of precious stones, but if you found out that all corundum has a high refractive index and all rubies are corundum, you would then *know* that all rubies have a high refractive index. (So if a particular stone has a low refractive index it *can't* be a ruby.) It would be impossible to deny this conclusion without also denying at least one of the premises (or contradicting yourself). Try it. Now consider the following two claims:

(1)   All mammals suckle their young.

(2)   All primates are mammals.

Suppose these two claims are true. What conclusion could you draw from these two claims as premises?

(1)   All mammals suckle their young.

(2)   All primates are mammals.

∴(a)   ?

If you said, "All primates suckle their young," then notice once again that the same very strong connection appears to exist between your conclusion and the two premises. Finally, suppose someone argues as follows:

[All propaganda is dangerous. (1)] (That's why) [all network news is dangerous. (2)]

From what you learned in previous chapters you can see that this argument depends on a missing premise *a*.

(1) All propaganda is dangerous.

(a) ?
_____
∴(2) All network news is dangerous.

What is the missing premise *a*? No doubt you can see that the missing premise is "All network news is propaganda." Notice once again the very strong connection between the conclusion and the two premises. If you suppose that both premises are true, you cannot deny the conclusion without contradicting yourself. Try it. You may have some doubt about the conclusion in this case. But if you doubt the truth of the conclusion, you must also doubt the truth of at least one of the premises. Now let's reconsider the four examples we have just examined:

(1) All humans are mortal.	(1) All corundum has a high refractive index.
(2) All Americans are humans.	(2) All rubies are corundum.
∴(3) All Americans are mortal.	∴(3) All rubies have a high refractive index.
(1) All mammals suckle their young.	(1) All propaganda is dangerous.
(2) All primates are mammals.	(a) ?
∴(a) ?	∴(2) All network news is dangerous.

These four examples have something important in common. It is a single and simple common feature that explains not only how we can arrive at the conclusion in the third example that "All primates suckle their young" and how we can fill in the missing premise in the fourth example that "All network news is propaganda"; but most important it explains the very strong connection that holds between the conclusion of each of the four arguments and its premises. All four arguments follow the same pattern or form. Here is what the form looks like schematically:

(1) All A's are B's	(1) All _____ are _____.	
(2) All B's are C's	or	(2) All _____ are _____.
∴ (3) All A's are C's	∴ (3) All _____ are _____.	

DEDUCTIVE VALIDITY

Deductive validity is another name for the kind of connection that holds between the conclusion and premises of arguments that follow this (or any other deductively valid) form. The essential property of a deductively valid argument form is this: If the premises of an argument that follows the form are taken to be true, then the conclusion of the argument (no matter what it is) must also be true. Because this is a feature of the *form* (or *pattern*) an argument follows rather than of the argument's specific content, deductive validity is sometimes referred to as "formal validity."

Of course, there are very many forms that arguments can follow. Some of them are so commonly used and well known that they have been given names. You just met a variation of Barbara. Barbara is a deductively valid form. This means that for any argument whatsoever, as long as it follows the form, accepting the premises forces you to accept the conclusion. Try it. Make some up. Even something as absurd as this:

(1)   All fish can fly.

(2)   All snakes are fish.

∴ (3)   All snakes can fly.

EXERCISE 6.2 | **Deductive Validity**

True *False*	A deductively valid argument can have a false conclusion.	Explain or give example.
True *False*	A deductively valid argument can have false premises.	Explain or give example.
True *False*	One cannot tell whether a deductive argument is valid without knowing whether its premises are actually true.	Explain or give example.
True *False*	A deductively valid argument can have false premises and a true conclusion.	Explain or give example.
True *False*	A deductively valid argument can have true premises and a false conclusion.	Explain or give example.

INVALIDITY

Deductively valid argument forms are important because they provide a guarantee that if the premises of the argument are true, the conclusion must be as well. But not every form or pattern is deductively valid. Consider the following example:

(1)   All Americans are human.

(2)   All Californians are human.

∴(3)   All Californians are Americans.

Many people initially see nothing deficient in this as a piece of reasoning. This is probably because (1) they can see that the claims are in some way related to each other, and (2) they think that all three claims are true. But notice what happens if you ask whether the truth of the premises *guarantees* that the conclusion is true. Suppose the premises are true. Could the conclusion not still be false? For example, suppose that some Californians are not Americans. This possibility conflicts in no way with either premise 1 or premise 2. So accepting both premises does not *force* you to accept the conclusion. If this is difficult to take in, consider this next example:

(1)   All men are human.

(2)   All women are human.

∴(3)   All women are men.

The falsity of this conclusion is obviously compatible with the truth of these two premises. But this argument follows the same form as the argument about Californians. Here is what the form looks like schematically:

(1) All A's are B's		(1) All _____ are _____ .
(2) All C's are B's	or	(2) All _____ are _____ .
∴ (3) All C's are A's		∴ (3) All _____ are _____ .

Because it is possible for an argument following this form to move from true premises to a false conclusion, it is easy to see that this form is unreliable. The general name for an unreliable inference is *fallacy*. An inference that is unreliable because it follows an unreliable form or pattern is said to be *formally fallacious* or to commit a *formal fallacy*.

TESTING FOR DEDUCTIVE VALIDITY

The two argument forms we've just been studying resemble each other closely, yet one is deductively valid while the other is formally fallacious, and this is a crucial difference for the purposes of argument evaluation. It is therefore important to be able to reliably distinguish between deductively valid arguments and formally fallacious ones, though they may look very much alike. One way to do this would be to memorize argument forms. But this proves to be an endless and unmanageable undertaking. Fortunately there is a relatively simple and reliable intuitive procedure for determining whether a particular argument is deductively valid. It derives from the essential property of deductively valid forms mentioned above. The procedure consists of asking: "Can we assert the premises and deny the conclusion without contradicting ourselves?" If we *cannot*—that is, if asserting the premises and denying the conclusion results in a contradiction—then the inference *is deductively valid*. If we *can* assert the premises and deny the conclusion without contradiction, the inference is *not* deductively valid.

CRITICAL THINKING TIP 6.1

To test for deductive validity, ask: "Can I assert the premises and deny the conclusion without contradicting myself?"

EXERCISE 6.3 | Testing for Deductive Validity

Which of the following arguments are deductively valid? Which are invalid?

Valid / Invalid	God is perfect. Therefore, God is good.	Explain or give example.
Valid / **Invalid**	Some entertainers are drug users, and all comedians are entertainers, so it stands to reason that some comedians are drug users.	Explain or give example. *Some e's are d's / all c's are e's / ∴ some c's are d's*
Valid / **Invalid**	Some college professors support the idea of a faculty union, an idea supported by many socialists. So at least some college professors must be socialists.	Explain or give example. *Some C's are F's / some S's are K's / ∴ some C's are S's*
Valid / Invalid	Everyone knows that whales live in the sea, and anything that lives in the sea is a fish. Therefore, whales must be fish.	Explain or give example.
Valid / Invalid	All artists are creative people. Some artists live in poverty. Therefore, some creative people live in poverty.	Explain or give example.

Valid	All of the justices on the Supreme Court are lawyers, and all members of the prestigious Washington Law Club are lawyers, so at least some of the Supreme Court justices are members of the Washington Law Club.	Explain or give example.
~~Invalid~~ (circled)		*All J's are L's* *All m's are L's* *∴ Some J's are m's.*

Some people find the validity-testing method just described difficult to conceptualize and tricky to keep straight. Here is a variation that may be easier to grasp intuitively. Try to imagine a scenario in which the premises are all true and the conclusion is false. If you can imagine such a scenario, then the inference is not deductively valid. For example, we can imagine a scenario in which the conclusion of the argument about Americans, Californians, and humans is false. Simply imagine that there are some Californians who are not also Americans. Imagine, for example, that there are some legal residents of the state of California who are not American citizens, let's say because they are foreigners married to Americans. Notice that both premises would still be true. Thus, this "scenario test" shows that the argument is invalid. But be careful. If you can't imagine such a scenario, it doesn't necessarily mean that the inference is deductively valid. It may simply mean that you haven't been imaginative enough.

EXERCISE 6.4 | Using Scenarios to Test for Deductive Validity

Use scenarios to test the validity of the six arguments in the Exercise 6.3.

Valid	God is perfect. Therefore, God is good.	Scenario
Invalid	*All perfect things are good.*	

Valid	Some entertainers are drug users, and all comedians are entertainers, so it stands to reason that some comedians are drug users.	Scenario
Invalid		

Valid	Some college professors support the idea of a faculty union, an idea supported by many socialists. So at least some college professors must be socialists.	Scenario
Invalid		

Valid	Everyone knows that whales live in the sea, and anything that lives in the sea is a fish. Therefore, whales must be fish.	Scenario
Invalid		

	Valid	All artists are creative people.	Scenario
	Invalid	Some artists live in poverty. Therefore, some creative people live in poverty.	

	Valid	All of the justices on the Supreme Court are lawyers, and all members of the prestigious Washington Law Club are lawyers, so at least some of the Supreme Court justices are members of the Washington Law Club.	Scenario
	Invalid		

CONSTRUCTING FORMAL ANALOGIES

One of the best procedures for demonstrating that an inference is unreliable, or fallacious, is to compose an inference that is analogous to it and moves from premises that are obviously true to a conclusion that is obviously false. In the case of the last two examples, the second argument is formally analogous to, or follows the same pattern as, the first (see the figure on page 153) but moves from two premises, each of which is obviously true, to a conclusion that is just as obviously false. By means of this analogy we prove that the original argument—indeed any argument following this pattern—is fallacious. Let's try these procedures on a couple of additional examples:

(1)   Some entertainers abuse drugs.

(2)   All comedians are entertainers.

∴(3)   Some comedians are drug abusers.

Is this a deductively valid argument? In other words, if we assert both of the premises and deny the conclusion, does a contradiction result? Now it may well be true that some comedians abuse drugs, but does it follow from these two premises? No. It is possible for both of the premises to be true and the conclusion false. Let's try to imagine a scenario in which the premises are both true and the conclusion is false. Let's suppose it's true that some entertainers abuse drugs and that all comedians are entertainers. What kind of situation would be compatible with these two assumptions and yet incompatible with the conclusion? Well, suppose that all of the drug-abusing entertainers just happen to be accordion players, while the rest of the entertainment industry is totally clean and sober. This may be hard to imagine because it is so at odds with what you may have heard. But it is possible to imagine it. Try it. Now notice that what you are imagining is at odds with the conclusion but perfectly compatible with each of the premises. This shows that the conclusion does not follow from the premises.

Let's now try to demonstrate that this inference is fallacious by producing a formally analogous inference which moves from obviously true premises to an obviously false conclusion. Step one is to reveal the form of the argument. Using the letter "C" (or _____) to represent the category of comedians, the letter

"A" (or _____) to represent the category of drug abusers, and the letter "E" (or _____) to represent the category of entertainers, we get from this:

    (1)   Some entertainers abuse drugs.

    (2)   All comedians are entertainers.

∴(3)   Some comedians are drug abusers.

to this:

(1) Some E's are A's		(1) Some _____ are _____ .
(2) All C's are E's	or	(2) All _____ are _____ .
∴ (3) Some C's are A's		∴ (3) Some _____ are _____ .

Now, starting with the conclusion, we substitute terms for the abstract placeholders in the formula. We want to pick terms that result in an obviously false conclusion. For example, let "**C**" (or _____) now stand for the category of fathers and let "**A**" (or _____) now stand for the category of women. That results in the obviously false conclusion that some fathers are women. Now simply substitute the same terms wherever the abstract placeholders "**C**" (or _____) and "**A**" (or _____) occur in the formula. This gives us:

(1) Some E's are women.	(1) Some _____ are women.
(2) All fathers are E's.	(2) All fathers are _____ .
∴ (3) Some fathers are women.	∴ (3) Some fathers are women.

Now all we need is a value for "**E**" (or _____) that would make both premises 1 and 2 true. Suppose we let "**E**" stand for the category of parents. That would give us:

    (1)   Some parents are women.

    (2)   All fathers are parents.

∴ (3)   Some fathers are women.

Here's another example:

    (1)   Some mysteries are entertaining.

    (2)   Some books are mysteries.

∴ (3)   Some books are entertaining.

Is this a deductively valid argument? In other words, if we assert both of the premises and deny the conclusion, does a contradiction result? No, it is possible for both of the premises to be true and the conclusion false. This may be hard to appreciate, especially if you think just about the conclusion and your actual experience. The conclusion is no doubt true as a matter of fact. But it does not follow from these two premises. It is possible to imagine a scenario in which both premises are true and the conclusion is false. Imagine, for example, that no books are entertaining (in other words, imagine that the conclusion is false). This does not conflict with the first premise. It could easily be the case that some books are mysteries and that no books are entertaining. Nor does it conflict with the second premise. Suppose that all of the entertaining mysteries are movies.

Now let us demonstrate that this inference is fallacious by producing a formally analogous inference which moves from obviously true premises to an obviously false conclusion. First we reveal the form of the argument. Using the letter "B" (or _____) to represent the category of books, the letter "M" (or_____) to represent the category of mysteries, and the letter "E" (or_____) to represent the category of things which are entertaining, we get from this:

    (1)   Some books are mysteries.

    (2)   Some mysteries are entertaining.

∴ (3)   Some books are entertaining.

to this:

(1)	Some B's are M's		(1)	Some _____ are _____.
(2)	Some M's are E's	or	(2)	Some _____ are _____.
∴ (3)	Some B's are E's		∴ (3)	Some _____ are _____.

Again, starting with the conclusion, we substitute terms for the abstract placeholders in the formula. We want to pick terms which result in an obviously false conclusion. For example, let "B" (or_____) now stand for the category of females, and let "E" (or_____) now stand for the category of males. That results in the obviously false conclusion that some females are male. Now simply substitute the same terms wherever the abstract placeholders "B" (or_____) and "E" (or_____) occur in the formula. This gives us:

(1)	Some females are M's.		(1)	Some females are _____.
(2)	All M's are male.		(2)	All _____ are male.
∴ (3)	Some females are male.		∴ (3)	Some females are male.

Now all we need is a value for "M" (or _____) that would make both premises 1 and 2 true. Again, suppose we let the remaining term "M" stand for the category of parents. That would give us

    (1)   Some parents are male.

    (2)   Some females are parents.

∴ (3)   Some females are male.

EXERCISE 6.5 | Constructing Formal Analogies

For each of the invalid arguments in Exercises 6.3 and 6.4 (Testing for Deductive Validity), construct a formally analogous argument that moves from obviously true premises to an obviously false conclusion.

	Invalid Argument	Formally Analogous Argument
Premise		
Premise		
Conclusion		

	Invalid Argument	Formally Analogous Argument
Premise		
Premise		
Conclusion		

	Invalid Argument	Formally Analogous Argument
Premise		
Premise		
Conclusion		

	Invalid Argument	Formally Analogous Argument
Premise		
Premise		
Conclusion		

CATEGORICAL LOGIC

A "syllogism" is defined as a deductive inference from two premises. The argument forms we have been studying so far in this chapter are called "categorical syllogisms" because they are made up of *categorical statements* (claims about relationships between categories of things). The Greek philosopher Aristotle developed a relatively simple but very powerful system of logic based on categorical syllogisms. One of his insights was that anything one might want to say about the relationships between any two categories can be said in one of the following four ways. In other words, all categorical statements can be reduced to one of the four following standard forms:

	Affirmative		Negative
A:	Universal Affirmative	E:	Universal Negative
e.g.	All mothers are female.	e.g.	No fathers are female.
I:	Particular Affirmative	O:	Particular Negative
e.g.	Some women are mothers.	e.g.	Some women are not mothers.

These forms are arranged above in a matrix that reflects two major distinctions cutting across each other. The categorical statements in the left-hand column *affirm* an *inclusive* relationship between two categories. The categorical statements in the right-hand column each *deny* such a relationship between the two categories; the relationships they indicate are *exclusive*. This is traditionally understood as a "qualitative" distinction and is designated by the terms "affirmative" and "negative." The conventional designation of these statement forms by the letters "A," "E," "I," and "O" derives from this qualitative distinction via the Latin words *AffIrmo* ("I affirm") and n*EgO* ("I deny").

The statements on the top line of the matrix assert the *total* inclusion or exclusion of an entire category in or from another. The statements on the bottom line of the matrix assert the *partial* inclusion or exclusion of one category in or from another. This is traditionally understood as a "quantitative" distinction and is designated by the terms "universal" and "particular."

A way to measure the "theoretical power" of a system would be to divide the number of cases that the system effectively covers by the size of the theoretical apparatus. By this measure, Aristotle's system of categorical logic is extremely powerful. Look at how elemental the theoretical apparatus is: Two major distinctions—Universal (all or none) versus Nonuniversal (some) and Affirmative versus Negative—yield four statement forms, which together cover practically the entire range of claims about category relationships. This is bound to score way up on the scale of theoretical power.

TRANSLATING CATEGORICAL STATEMENTS INTO STANDARD FORM

However, there is a catch. Understandably the power of the system depends heavily on being able to translate the wide variety of things that people actually say about categories in their actual arguments into one or another of the four standard forms. However, because language is *so* flexible and rich in possibilities, and because people are *so* imaginative and innovative in their use of language, translation into standard form is a matter of some complexity and uncertainty. There are a few general rules, with exceptions, and an indefinitely large set of interpretive guidelines, of which we shall now give you the short "starter kit."

The *General Rules* are:

- Categorical statements begin with a "quantity indicator" ("all," "some," or "no").
- There is a verb in the middle (either "are" or "are not") to indicate the "quality" of the statement (whether it is affirmative or negative).

- There are two terms, each denoting a category. The term before the verb is called the "subject term," and the term after the verb is called the "predicate term."
- Subject and predicate terms must be nouns or noun phrases. For convenience in what follows we will use angle brackets < > to set off the subject and predicate terms from the quantity and quality indicators in standard formulations of categorical statements.

The *Exceptions to the General Rules* are:

- You can't say "All <xxx's> are not <yyy's>" as in "All the <computers on campus> aren't <IBM compatible>." This formulation is disallowed because it is ambiguous. It could mean "Not all the <computers on campus> are <IBM compatible>" (which would be the same as saying, "*Some* of the <computers on campus> are *not* <IBM compatible>"); or it could mean, "None of the <computers on campus> are <IBM compatible>." You have to decide whether the statement is supposed to say "Not *all* <xxx's> are <yyy's>" or "Not *any* <xxx's> are <yyy's>." If the meaning is "Not *all* <xxx's> are <yyy's>," use the "O" form: "Some <yyy's> are not <xxx's>." If the meaning is "Not *any* <xxx's> are <yyy's>," use the "E" form: "No <xxx's> are <yyy's>."
- There are categorical statements about individuals. For example, "David Letterman is a talk show host"; or "The Artist Formerly Known as 'Prince' is a musician"; or "The World Series is an annual event." For all practical purposes (and especially because we are at the very beginning of the study of formal logic), it will work best for now to treat any statement like these as though it were a Universal Affirmative (or "A") categorical statement, even though there is only one real "category" involved. Categorical logic can handle such statements quite effectively if we pretend that we're talking, for example, about all members of the category <The Artist Formerly Known as 'Prince'> (a category of which there is only one member) when we say that he's in the category <musicians>.

Some *Interpretive Guidelines* are:

- Turn adjectives into nouns or noun phrases. In some cases this is pretty straightforward and intuitive. For example, "Bill Gates is wealthy" becomes <Bill Gates> is a <wealthy man>.
- Use the context to help determine how to formulate the noun phrase. For example, in the context of this argument: "Wealthy individuals enjoy disproportionate access to power. Bill Gates is wealthy. So he must have disproportionate access to power," the premise expressed in the second sentence makes the most sense if we interpret it to mean that Bill Gates is in *precisely* the category indicated by the subject term in the first sentence, <wealthy individuals>. This makes the logic of the inference easier to see. So here "Bill Gates is wealthy" becomes <Bill Gates> is a <wealthy individual>.
- Turn verbs into nouns or noun phrases. Again, in some cases this is pretty straightforward and intuitive. For example, "Deciduous plants shed their leaves" becomes "All <deciduous plants> are <things that shed their leaves>.

- Use the context to help determine how to formulate the noun phrase. For example, in this context, "All dancing bears are performing animals. Smokey the Bear is dancing the tango. Therefore, Smokey the Bear is a performing animal," the logic of the premise expressed in the second sentence makes sense only if we render it thus: <Smokey> is a <dancing bear>.

- Use the grammar as a guide, but bear in mind that grammatical structure and logical structure often diverge. For example, in the sentence, "Happy is the man who finds work doing what he loves," the subject term <the man who finds work doing what he loves> is contained in the grammatical predicate. Also, notice that although the subject term is grammatically singular, the meaning for the purposes of categorical logic is plural; "the man who finds work doing what he loves" is meant to stand for the whole category of people who find work doing what they love. So the standard formulation of this statement would be "All <people who find work doing what they love> are <happy people>."

TABLE 6.1a   General Rules for Translating into Standard Form

- Categorical statements begin with a "quantity indicator" ("all," "some," or "no").
- There is a verb in the middle (either "are" or "are not") to indicate the "quality" of the statement (whether it is affirmative or negative).
- There are two terms, each denoting a category. The term before the verb is called the "subject term," and the term after the verb is called the "predicate term."
- Subject and predicate terms must be nouns or noun phrases. For convenience below we will use angle brackets < > to set off the subject and predicate terms from the quantity and quality indicators in standard formulations of categorical statements.

TABLE 6.1b   Exceptions to the General Rules

- This formulation, "All <xxx's> are not <yyy's>," as in "All the <computers on campus> aren't <IBM compatible>," is disallowed because it is ambiguous. If the meaning is "Not all <xxx's> are <yyy's>," use the "O" form: "Some <yyy's> are not <xxx's>." If the meaning is "Not any <xxx's> are <yyy's>," use the "E" form: "No <xxx's> are <yyy's>."
- There are categorical statements about individuals. Treat proper names of individuals as names of categories.

TABLE 6.1c   Interpretive Guidelines

- Turn adjectives and verbs into nouns or noun phrases.
- Use the grammar as a guide, but most important: use the context to determine how to formulate the noun phrases.

EXERCISE 6.6 | **Translating Categorical Statements into Standard Form**

Translate each of the following categorical statements into standard form.

All computer hardware has a short shelf life.	C = computer hardware S = things with short shelf life	Standard form: all C's are S's.

Some of my beliefs are false.	B = my beliefs F = things which are false	Standard form: *Some B's are F's*
One major corporation is Microsoft.	C = major corporations M = Microsoft	Standard form: *Some C's is M's*
Some of the members of Heaven's Gate were reasonable people.	M = members of Heaven's Gate R = reasonable people	Standard form: *Some m's were R's.*
Any discipline has rules, or at least regularities of some kind.	D = disciplines R = things with rules or regularities	Standard form: *All D's are R's.*
El Niño is the cause of some of these abnormal weather patterns.	A = these abnormal weather patterns N = things caused by El Niño	Standard form: *Some A are caused by N.*
I like action movies.	A = action movies L = things I like	Standard form: *All A's are L's*
San Francisco is a city in California.	S = San Francisco C = cities in California	Standard form: *All s's are C's*
My favorite actress is a Gemini.	F = my favorite actress G = Geminis	Standard form:
Dogs love trucks.	D = dogs L = lovers of trucks	Standard form: *All d's are L's*

THE SQUARE OF OPPOSITION

Let us now return to the matrix we used above to introduce the four standard forms of categorical statements. This time we will use the same subject and predicate terms in all four examples so as to highlight differences in quality and quantity. Traditionally, in categorical logic two categorical statements that differ from each other in quality or in quantity or both but that are otherwise the same are said to stand in "opposition" to each other. There are several kinds of "opposition," depending on whether the difference is one of quality or quantity or both. Let's start with what might be described as the "strongest" form of opposition. Look at the "A" statement and the "O" statement together:

Affirmative		Negative	
A:	Universal Affirmative	E:	Universal Negative
e.g.	All <bonds> are <secure investments>.	e.g.	No <bonds> are <secure investments>.
I:	Particular Affirmative	O:	Particular Negative
e.g.	Some <bonds> are <secure investments>.	e.g.	Some <bonds> are not <secure investments>.

Notice that they can't both be true *and* they can't both be false. This kind of opposition is traditionally called *contradiction*. Now look at the "E" and "I" statements together. Like the "A" and "O" statement pair, if either "E" or the "I" statement is true, the other one must be false; they also *contradict* each other.

Now look at the "A" statement and the "E" statement together:

Affirmative		Negative	
A:	Universal Affirmative	E:	Universal Negative
e.g.	All <bonds> are <secure investments>.	e.g.	No <bonds> are <secure investments>.
I:	Particular Affirmative	O:	Particular Negative
e.g.	Some <bonds> are <secure investments>.	e.g.	Some <bonds> are not <secure investments>.

Notice that they can't both be true, but they *might* both be false. This is a somewhat weaker form of opposition than contradiction. This kind of opposition is traditionally called *contrariety*. Two categorical statements that stand in this kind of opposition to each other are called *contraries* of each other.

Now look at the "I" statement and the "O" statement together:

Affirmative		Negative	
A:	Universal Affirmative	E:	Universal Negative
e.g.	All <bonds> are <secure investments>.	e.g.	No <bonds> are <secure investments>.
I:	Particular Affirmative	O:	Particular Negative
e.g.	Some <bonds> are <secure investments>.	e.g.	Some <bonds> are not <secure investments>.

Notice that they *could* both be true, but they *can't* both be false. This kind of opposition is traditionally called *sub-contrariety*. Two categorical statements that stand in this kind of opposition to each other are called *sub-contraries* of each other.

There is something a little peculiar about the technical way in which logicians use the word "opposition." So far all of the different kinds of opposition we have discussed seem to involve some sort of "disagreement." But now if you look at the "A" and the "I" statements together you'll see that they seem to agree with each other:

Affirmative	Negative
A: Universal Affirmative e.g. All \<bonds\> are \<secure investments\>.	E: Universal Negative e.g. No \<bonds\> are \<secure investments\>.
I: Particular Affirmative e.g. Some \<bonds\> are \<secure investments\>.	O: Particular Negative e.g. Some \<bonds\> are not \<secure investments\>.

In fact, it seems reasonable to say that if the "A" statement is true, the "I" statement must also be true, "by implication." For example, if it *is* true that all bonds are secure investments, it must surely be true that *some* bonds are secure investments as well. The same relationship also holds between "E" and "O" statements. For example, if it is true that no bonds are secure investments, it must surely be true as well that some bonds are *not* secure investments. Traditionally this kind of opposition is called *sub-alternation.* If two categorical statements with the same subject and predicate terms agree in quality (are both affirmative or both negative) but differ in quantity, the universal statement implies its *sub-alternate* particular statement. Notice that this is a one-way relationship. The particular statement does not imply the universal statement. Even if it is true that some bonds are secure investments, that does not, all by itself, imply that *all* bonds are secure investments. Similarly, even if it is true that some bonds are *not* secure investments, that does not by itself imply that *no* bonds are secure investments. Let us now summarize the above relationships in what is traditionally called the "square of opposition":

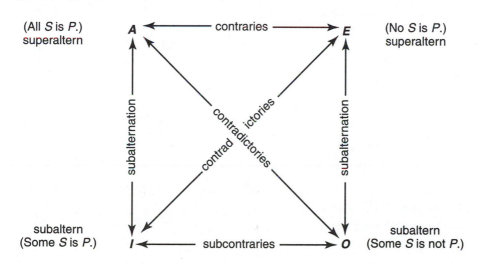

(All *S* is *P*.) superaltern A ← contraries → E (No *S* is *P*.) superaltern

subalternation   contradictories   subalternation

subaltern (Some *S* is *P*.) I ← subcontraries → O subaltern (Some *S* is not *P*.)

IMMEDIATE INFERENCES AND SYLLOGISMS

Based on the relationships described above and represented in the square of op-position, logic traditionally recognizes certain *immediate inferences* as deduc-tively valid. Inferences such as these are traditionally referred to as "immediate," meaning that they proceed directly from one single categorical statement as a premise to another as the conclusion.

- Assuming that a given "A" statement is true: its contradictory "O" statement is false; its contrary "E" statement is false; its sub-alternate "I" statement is true.

- Assuming that a given "E" statement is true: its contradictory "I" statement is false; its contrary "A" statement is false; its sub-alternate "O" statement is true.

- Assuming that a given "I" statement is true: its contradictory "E" statement is false.

- Assuming that a given "O" statement is true: its contradictory "A" statement is false.

Beyond these "immediate inferences" there is larger category of inferences, called *syllogisms,* based on combining two categorical statements as premises. The examples we used above to introduce and illustrate the concept of deductive validity were all syllogisms.

EXERCISE 6.7 | **Immediate Inferences**

In each of the following sets of claims, assume that the first (in **bold**) is true, then highlight the claim(s) from the rest of the set that may be validly inferred from it.

All U.S. Treasury bonds are safe investments.

No U.S. Treasury bonds are safe investments.

Some U.S. Treasury bonds are safe investments.

Some U.S. Treasury bonds are not safe investments.

No U.S. Treasury bonds are safe investments.

Some U.S. Treasury bonds are safe investments.

Some U.S. Treasury bonds are not safe investments.

All U.S. Treasury bonds are safe investments.

> **Some U.S. Treasury bonds are safe investments.**
> Some U.S. Treasury bonds are not safe investments.
> All U.S. Treasury bonds are safe investments.
> No U.S. Treasury bonds are safe investments.

> **Some U.S. Treasury bonds are not safe investments.**
> All U.S. Treasury bonds are safe investments.
> No U.S. Treasury bonds are safe investments.
> Some U.S. Treasury bonds are safe investments.

An immediate inference involves only two categories. A syllogism always involves three. The three categories, and their corresponding terms, have special names. Let us now introduce this terminology, using one of our earlier examples.

All <humans> are <mortals>. *Ma*

All <Americans> are <humans>. *Mi*

_____

∴ All <Americans> are <mortals>.

subject   predicate.

Notice that two of the three terms appear in the conclusion, while the third does not. The term that appears in the ==predicate position== in the conclusion is called the *major term*; the term that appears in the ==subject position== in the conclusion is called the *minor term*. The term that does not appear in the conclusion is called the *middle term*—the term that "mediates" the inference. It appears once in each of the premises. The premise in which the major term appears is called the ==*major premise*;== the premise in which the minor term appears is called the *minor premise*. Syllogisms in standard form always go in this order: major premise, minor premise, conclusion.

EXERCISE 6.8 | Standard Form

Put each of the following syllogisms into standard form: major premise first, followed by minor premise, then conclusion.

All Americans are humans. *M*	All humans are mortals *A* *Ai* All h are M's
All humans are mortals. *Ma*	All ~~Humans~~ Americans are humans; *A*: All A's or H's
∴ All Americans are mortals. S P	∴ All Americans are mortals. *A* ∴ All A's are M's.

All men are human. *Ma*	All m's are H's.
All women are human. *Mi*	All w's are H's. *AAA*
∴ All women are men. S P	All w's are M's

Some books are mysteries. *M₁*

Some mysteries are entertaining. *Ma*

∴ Some books are entertaining.

[handwritten: Some B's are M's / Some M's are E's   III. / Some b's are E's.]

[handwritten annotations: S, P, entertaining things]

MOOD AND FIGURE

Remember, there are only four types of categorical statements—A, E, I, and O—as arrayed in the square of opposition, and three claims in any syllogism: major premise, minor premise, conclusion. Each of these claims may be of any one of the four types. This yields 64 possible combinations (by the formula: 4³); logicians refer to these combinations as *moods*. The *mood* of a syllogism is determined by which of the four statement types appears as the major premise, the minor premise, and the conclusion, when the syllogism is in standard form. The mood is indicated by a series of three letters, representing the three statement types in the inference in standard order (e.g., AAA, EAE, EIO, AOO, etc.).

EXERCISE 6.9 | Mood

Step 1: Using the square of opposition, identify the statement type of the major premise, minor premise, and conclusion in each of the following syllogisms.

Step 2: Test each syllogism for deductive validity using the procedures outlined above (see Critical Thinking Tip 6.1).

All humans are mortals.

All Americans are humans.

∴ All Americans are mortals.

All men are human.

All women are human.

∴ All women are men.

Some mysteries are entertaining.

Some books are mysteries.

∴ Some books are entertaining.

Some mysteries are not entertaining.

Some books are not mysteries.

∴ Some books are not entertaining.

All mysteries are suspenseful.

Some books are not mysteries.

∴ Some books are not suspenseful.

Now look closely at the first two inferences in Exercise 6.8. The mood of each of these syllogisms is AAA. But, as we have seen since the very beginning of this chapter, the first inference is valid while the second one is invalid. What is the difference? The difference has to do with what logicians call the *figure* of each syllogism, which is determined by the *position of the middle term*. Notice that in the first inference (the valid one), the middle term appears in the subject position in the major premise but in the predicate position in the minor premise. In the second inference (the invalid one) the middle term appears in the predicate position in both premises (see the accompanying figure).

All humans are mortals.   All men are humans.

All Americans are humans.   All women are humans.

∴ All Americans are mortals.   ∴ All women are men.

In a standard-form syllogism, the middle term appears once in each premise, but that can be either in the subject or predicate position. Since there are two premises, and each premise has both a subject and a predicate, this gives rise to four possible combinations, or *figures*. Using the letter "S" to indicate the minor term (subject of the conclusion), "P" to indicate the major term (predicate of the conclusion), and "M" to indicate the middle term, the four figures can be depicted as follows:

1st Figure	2nd Figure	3rd Figure	4th Figure
M-P	P-M	M-P	P-M
S-M	S-M	M-S	M-S
S-P	S-P	S-P	S-P

Now, with 64 moods and four figures, the total number of possible syllogistic forms comes to 256 (64 × 4). Of these, 15 turn out to be deductively valid. The remaining 241 are invalid. Once a syllogism has been translated into and arranged in standard form, its formal structure (its mood and figure) determine whether it is deductively valid or not in accordance with the following set of rules:

- The syllogism must contain exactly three terms, each used consistently throughout the inference (no ambiguity allowed).
- The middle term of the syllogism must be *distributed* in at least one premise. (A term is *distributed* when the claim in which it appears says something about *every member of the category* to which the term refers. For example, in the premise "All bonds are safe investments," the term "bonds" is distributed, but the term "safe investments" is not.)
- If either term is distributed in the conclusion, it must be distributed in the premises.
- A valid syllogism may have at most one negative premise.
- If either premise of the syllogism is negative, the conclusion must be negative.
- If the conclusion of the syllogism is negative, one premise must be negative.

EXERCISE 6.10 | **Invalid Syllogisms**

In Exercise 6.8, the first syllogism was valid, but all the rest were invalid. Here again are the invalid syllogisms. Which of the above rules is violated in each case?

All men are human.

All women are human.
_____
∴ All women are men.

Some mysteries are entertaining.

Some books are mysteries.
_____
∴ Some books are entertaining.

Some mysteries are not entertaining.   ⟩ *at most one negative premise*

Some books are not mysteries.
_____
∴ Some books are entertaining.

All mysteries are suspenseful.

Some books are not mysteries.
_____
∴ Some books are not suspenseful.

VENN DIAGRAMS

As you can plainly see, there's quite a bit to keep track of in categorical logic. Just as with argument analysis, many people find graphics and visualization helpful in gaining a grasp of this material. For this purpose, British logician John Venn invented a graphic system for representing categorical statements and testing the validity of categorical syllogisms. The system consists of intersecting circles. Each circle represents a category. A shaded area is "vacant"—an area where there are no examples or members. An X is used to indicate a "populated" area—an area where there is at least one member. Using two intersecting circles and these simple symbols, we can represent any of the four standard forms of categorical statements (A, E, I, and O). In the accompanying figure the circle on the left represents the category of mothers and the circle on the right represents the category of females. The shaded area indicates that there are no members of the category "mothers" who are not also members of the category "females." Thus, the figure diagrams the statement that all mothers are female.

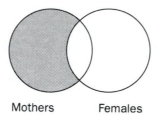

Mothers   Females

In the next figure the circle on the left represents the category of fathers and the circle on the right represents the category of females. The shaded area indicates that there are no members of the category "fathers" who are also members of the category "females." Thus, the figure diagrams the statement that no fathers are female.

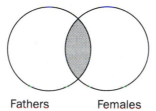

Fathers   Females

In the next two figures the circle on the left represents the category of women and the circle on the right represents the category of mothers. In the first the X indicates that there are some members of the category women who are also members of the category mothers. Thus, the figure diagrams the statement that some women are mothers. In the second figure the X indicates that there are some members of the category women who are not also members of the category mothers. Thus, the figure diagrams the statement that some women are not mothers.

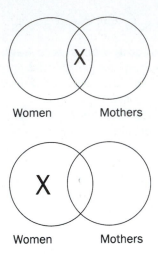

In a categorical syllogism there are three terms, corresponding to three categories, two of which appear in the conclusion. In a categorical syllogism each of the premises states a relationship between one of these two categories, which appear in the conclusion and a third (or "middle") category. Thus, to diagram a categorical syllogism we need three intersecting circles, one for each of the categories in the conclusion and a third for the middle category:

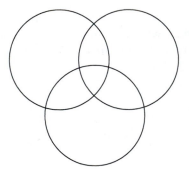

TESTING FOR VALIDITY USING VENN DIAGRAMS

In using the diagram to test for the validity of categorical syllogisms, we should remember what the essential characteristic of deductively valid arguments is: If the premises of an argument that follows the form are taken to be true, then the conclusion of the argument (no matter what it is) must also be true. In a certain important sense, the conclusion of a deductively valid inference is already "contained in" its premises. Thus, if we represent the information contained in the two premises in the diagram, the conclusion should automatically be represented as well, *if* the argument is a valid one. Let's try this with the first of the examples we considered in this chapter:

(1) All Americans are human.

(2) All humans are mortal.

∴ (3) All Americans are mortal.

In the accompanying figure the circle on the left will represent the category of Americans, the circle on the right will represent the category of mortals, and the lower circle will represent the middle category of humans.

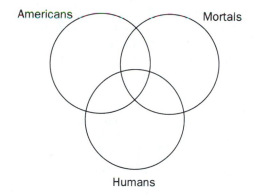

To represent premise 1 in the diagram we shade in all the human circle except where it intersects with the mortal circle:

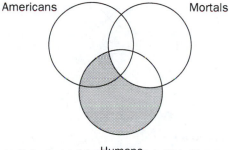

This indicates that there are no members of the category "humans" who are not also members of the category "mortals." Similarly, we represent premise 2 in the diagram by shading in all the American circle except where it intersects with the human circle:

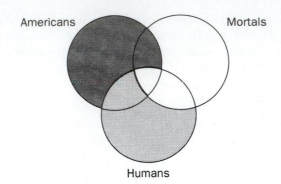

This indicates that there are no members of the category "Americans" who are not also members of the category "humans." Lo and behold, this figure already represents the conclusion because the area inside the American circle but outside its intersection with the mortal circle is shaded in, indicating that there are no members of the category "Americans" who are not also members of the category "mortals." Thus, our diagram demonstrates the validity of the inference.

Now let's try the same procedure with the first formally fallacious example we considered above:

(1) All Americans are human.

(2) All Californians are human.

∴ (3) All Californians are Americans.

In the accompanying figure we'll let the circle on the left represent the category of Californians, the circle on the right will represent the category of Americans, and the lower circle will represent the middle category of humans.

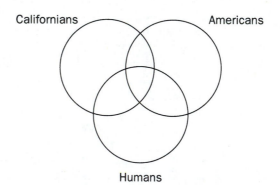

To represent premise 1 we shade in the entire American circle except where it intersects with the circle of humans (see the accompanying figure), indicating that there are no members of the category "Americans" who are not also members of the category "humans."

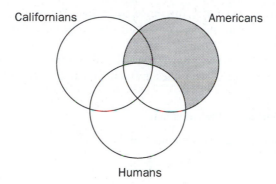

To represent premise 2 we shade in the entire Californian circle except where it intersects with the circle of humans (see the next figure), indicating that there are no members of the category "Californians" who are not also members of the category "humans."

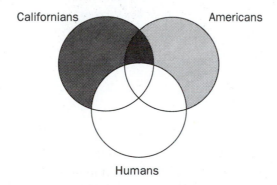

Does this figure represent the conclusion that all Californians are American? It would if the entire area within the California circle were shaded in except where it intersects with the American circle. But there remains an unshaded area inside the California circle but outside the American circle, indicating that there *may be* some Californians who are not American. This shows that even if premises 1 and 2 are both true, the possibility that the conclusion is false is still open. In other words, the inference is not valid.

Some of you may still wonder *why* this is an invalid inference. This may be due to your awareness that California is one of the United States of America. So, you may be thinking, it's not possible to be a Californian without also being an American. But it *is* possible to be a Californian without being an American. One can be a legal, taxpaying, permanent resident of the state of California without being an American citizen. Suppose an American woman who resides in California marries a Frenchman and the couple chooses to reside in California but the husband retains his French citizenship. One can even be a *native-born*, legal, taxpaying, permanent resident of the state of California without being an American citizen. The main point here, however, is that these possibilities don't conflict with either of the premises of the inference. In other words, it's possible for the premises both to be true and the conclusion still to be false, which again, is what the Venn diagram shows.

We've now diagrammed two syllogisms involving universal categorical statements. Let's try a couple of examples involving particular categorical statements as well.

(1)   All entertainers love attention.

(2)   Some drug abusers are entertainers.

∴ (3)   Some drug abusers love attention.

In the figure we'll let the circle on the left represent the category of drug abusers, the circle on the right represent the category of those who love attention, and the lower circle represent the middle category of entertainers.

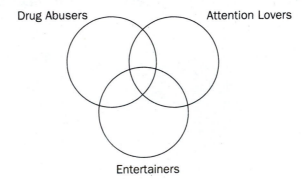

To represent premise 1 we must shade out the entire entertainers circle except where it intersects with the circle of lovers of attention:

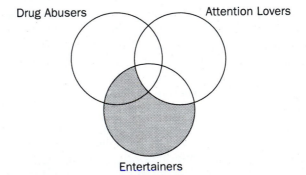

To represent premise 2 we must place an X somewhere in the intersection of the drug abusers and entertainers circles. But only half of that intersection remains open. Thus, the X may appear only in the area where all three circles intersect:

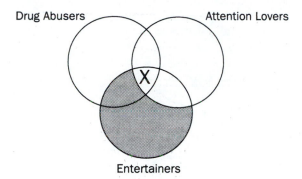

Does this figure represent the conclusion that some drug abusers love attention? Yes, it does. An X already appears in the intersection of the circles representing drug abusers and those who love attention. This shows the inference to be valid.

Compare this last example with the similar one we discussed earlier:

(1) Some entertainers abuse drugs.

(2) All comedians are entertainers.

∴ (3) Some comedians are drug abusers.

In the next figure we'll let the circle on the left represent the category of comedians, the circle on the right represent the category of drug abusers, and the lower circle represent the middle category of entertainers.

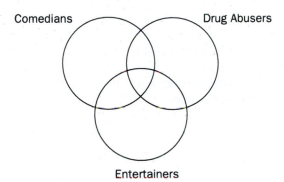

This time we'll start with premise 2, following the guideline to diagram a universal premise before a particular one. To represent premise 2 we shade in the entire area in the comedians circle except where it intersects with the entertainers circle, indicating that there are no comedians who are not also entertainers:

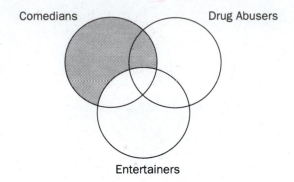

To represent premise 1 we must place an X somewhere in the intersection of the drug abusers and entertainers circles. But do we place it inside or outside the circle of comedians? Nothing in the premises determines the answer to this question. And since we don't know, the X goes on the line:

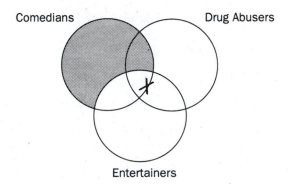

Now, does this figure represent the conclusion that some comedians are drug abusers? It would if the X appeared clearly within the intersection of the comedians and drug abusers circles. But it does not. It appears on the line, indicating that on the basis of our two premises it is not yet clear whether the conclusion is true, and thus that the inference is not valid.

EXERCISE 6.11 | Invalid Syllogisms

Here again are the syllogisms from exercise 6.8. Use Venn diagrams to test for and demonstrate their validity or invalidity.

All humans are mortals.

All Americans are humans.

∴ All Americans are mortals.

All men are human.

All women are human.

∴ All women are men.

Some mysteries are entertaining.

Some books are mysteries.

∴ Some books are entertaining.

Some mysteries are not entertaining.

Some books are not mysteries.

∴ Some books are entertaining.

All mysteries are suspenseful.

Some books are not mysteries.

∴ Some books are not suspenseful.

ADDITIONAL EXERCISES

■ **EXERCISE 6.12**   For each of the following passages, indicate whether it is a deductive argument, an inductive argument, or not an argument.

Deductive	We can't lose. They've got	Explain your answer:
(Inductive)	no offense and they've got	
Nonargumentative	no one to stop our leading	
	scorer. They've lost their	
	last four games, and it'll be	
	on our court.	

(Deductive)	"In a democracy, the poor	Explain your answer:
Inductive	have more power than the	
Nonargumentative	rich, because there are	
	more of them."	
	—Aristotle	

	Deductive	I've been eating corn on the cob for years, and I always count the number of rows. I have never found an ear of corn with an odd number of rows. I'm convinced that ears of corn always have even numbers of rows.	Explain your answer:
	(Inductive)		
	Nonargumentative		

	(Deductive)	Even God makes mistakes. In the Bible, God says, "It repenteth me that I have made man." Now either the Bible is not the word of God, or we must believe that God did say, "It repenteth me that I have made man." But then, if we are to believe the word of God, we must further conclude that He really did repent making man, in which case, either God made a mistake in making man, or He made a mistake in repenting making man.	Explain your answer:
	Inductive		
	Nonargumentative		

	(Deductive)	The theory of the unreality of evil now seems to me untenable. Suppose that it can be proved that all that we think evil was in reality good. The fact would still remain that we think it evil. This may be called a delusion or mistake. But a delusion or mistake is as real as anything else. The delusion that evil exists is therefore real. But then it seems certain that a delusion which hid from us the goodness of the universe would itself be evil. And so there would be real evil after all. — J. M. E. McTaggart	Explain your answer:
	Inductive		
	Nonargumentative		

Deductive Inductive Nonargumentative	First of all, as the 18th-century Scottish philosopher David Hume pointed out, we never directly observe causal relationships. We have to infer them. Next, we can never infer them with deductive certainty. Since the evidence for a causal relationship is always indirect, there will always be some room for doubt when we infer a cause. In other words, we must reason inductively about them.

Explain your answer:

Deductive Inductive Nonargumentative	In the entire history of the stock market, every bull market has been followed by a bear market, and vice versa. Therefore, the stock market behaves cyclically.

Explain your answer:

Deductive **Inductive** Nonargumentative	Grumble County has voted for the loser in every state Senate contest since 1876. Grumble County polls show incumbent Senator Press Fleshman running 27 points behind challenger Mary Kay Weedemout. But I'm tired of always voting for losers and lost causes. I'm going to vote for Fleshman, since it looks like he's going to win anyway.

Explain your answer:

■ **EXERCISE 6.13** Translate each of the following arguments into standard syllogistic form.

All crooks deserve to be punished. But some politicians are not crooks. So some politicians do not deserve to be punished.	C = crooks D = deserve to be punished P = politicians	Standard form: √

All artists are creative people. Some artists live in poverty. Therefore, some creative people live in poverty.	A = artists C = creative people P = people who live in poverty	Standard form: ✓
Some reference books are textbooks, for all textbooks are books intended for careful study and some reference books are intended for the same purpose.	R = reference books T = textbooks S = books intended for careful study	Standard form: ✓
Since all birds eat worms, and chickens are birds, chickens must eat worms.	B = birds W = eaters of worms C = chickens	Standard form: ✓
Most poets drink to excess, and some poets are women. So, some women drink to excess.	P = poets D = people who drink to excess W = women	Standard form: ✓
Everyone who smokes marijuana goes on to try heroin. Everyone who tries heroin becomes a junkie. So everyone who smokes marijuana becomes a junkie.	M = marijuana smokers H = people who try heroin J = people who become junkies	Standard form: ✓
This argument must be valid because its premises are true and its conclusion is true and all arguments with true premises and conclusions are valid.	A = anything that is this argument V = things that are valid T = things with true premises and conclusions	Standard form:
This argument must be invalid because its premises are not true and all arguments with untrue premises are invalid.	A = anything that is this argument I = things that are invalid U = arguments with untrue premises	Standard form:

■ **EXERCISE 6.14**   Using a combination of any two of the procedures discussed in this chapter (the Intuitive Test, the Scenario Method, Venn Diagrams), determine which of the following are valid deductive arguments. For each invalid argument compose a formally analogous argument that moves from obviously true premises to an obviously false conclusion.

	Valid	All crooks deserve to be punished. But some politicians are not crooks. So some politicians do not deserve to be punished.	Explain your answer:
	Invalid		

	Valid	All artists are creative people. Some artists live in poverty. Therefore, some creative people live in poverty.	Explain your answer:
	Invalid		

	Valid	Some reference books are textbooks, for all textbooks are books intended for careful study and some reference books are intended for the same purpose.	Explain your answer:
	Invalid		

	Valid	Since all birds eat worms, and chickens are birds, chickens must eat worms.	Explain your answer:
	Invalid		

	Valid	Most poets drink to excess, and some poets are women. So, some women drink to excess.	Explain your answer:
	Invalid		

	Valid	Everyone who smokes marijuana goes on to try heroin. Everyone who tries heroin becomes a junkie. So everyone who smokes marijuana becomes a junkie.	Explain your answer:
	Invalid		

	Valid	This argument must be valid because its premises are true and its conclusion is true and all arguments with true premises and conclusions are valid.	Explain your answer:
	Invalid		

	Valid	This argument must be invalid because its premises are not true and all arguments with untrue premises are invalid.	Explain your answer:
	Invalid		

EXERCISE 6.15   Take any position on the issue you have been working with so far and design an argument in support of that position using any of the deductively valid argument forms discussed in Chapter 6. Then take an alternative or opposed position and design an argument in support of it using any of the deductively valid argument forms discussed in Chapter 6.

GLOSSARY

categorical statement   a statement about a relationship between categories

categorical syllogism   a syllogism made up of categorical statements

contradiction   in categorical logic: a form of opposition between categorical statements; two categorical statements that cannot both be true and also cannot both be false are contradictories

contrariety   a form of opposition between categorical statements; two categorical statements that cannot both be true but that might both be false are contraries

deductive   reasoning designed and intended to secure its conclusion with certainty so that anyone who fully understands what the statements in the argument mean must recognize that the premises cannot both be true without the conclusion also being true

distribution   a term is "distributed" when the claim in which it appears says something about *every member of the category* to which the term refers; for example, in the premise "All bonds are safe investments," the term "bonds" is distributed, but the term "safe investments" is not

fallacy   an unreliable inference

formal fallacy   an inference that is unreliable because it follows an unreliable form or pattern

inductive   reasoning designed and intended to make the conclusion reasonable, probable, or likely, but not certain

invalidity   in a deductive argument, the absence of the essential formal characteristic of a successful deductive argument (see "validity")

sound   a valid deductive argument based on true or acceptable premises

square of opposition   in categorical logic the array of relationships between the four statement forms showing the immediate inferences that may be drawn on the basis of differences of quality and quantity

sub-alternation   in categorical logic, the relationship between statements with the same subject and predicate terms that agree in quality (both affirmative or both negative) but differ in quantity (not both universal)

sub-contrariety   a form of opposition between categorical statements; two categorical statements that might both be true but that can't both be false are sub-contraries

syllogism   a deductive inference from two premises

validity   the essential formal characteristic of a successful deductive argument; if the premises are taken to be true, then the conclusion must also be true

CHAPTER 7

Evaluating Deductive Arguments II: Truth Functional Logic

The argument forms we have been studying so far have been composed entirely of categorical statements. But of course there are many more kinds of claims in our language out of which arguments can be composed. Arguments often involve claims like these:

- "Either we make a few sacrifices in the area of privacy, or we will continue to be vulnerable to terrorist attacks."

- "If we allow our civil liberties to be destroyed in the name of greater security, then the terrorists will have won."

As powerful as Aristotle's system of categorical logic is, it is hopelessly awkward to try to translate claims like these into categorical statements. So, because claims like these are so important in reasoning, logicians have developed a system known as truth functional logic (often called "symbolic logic") to deal with them. That will be the subject of this chapter.

Farcus

by David Waisglass
Gordon Coulthart

WAISGLASS/COULTHART

© 1997 Farcus Cartoons

**"So, I say if it's not worth doing well,
it's not worth doing at all."**

TRUTH FUNCTIONAL ANALYSIS OF LOGICAL OPERATORS

The two examples above have easily recognizable grammatical structures. The first example is a "disjunction," which from the point of view of grammar means an "either . . . or . . ." statement. The second example is called a "conditional," which from the point of view of grammar means an "if . . . then . . ." statement. However, in studying the role they each play in reasoning and argumentation, we will need to understand not only their grammatical structure but also their *logical* structure. And in order to do this we will need to introduce a bit more of the apparatus of modern logic: truth functional analysis of logical operators.

What in the world is a *logical operator*? As a first step, let us distinguish between simple and compound statements. A *simple statement* is one that does not contain another statement as a component part. A *compound statement* is one that does contain at least one other statement as a component part. For example, "The weather is great" and "I wish you were here" are each simple statements, but "The weather is great and I wish you were here" is a compound statement. Think of logical operators as devices for making compound statements out of simple(r) ones. In this example, the word *and* is used to express the logical operator known as conjunction.

NEGATION

Logical operators are defined and distinguished from each other according to how they affect the "truth values" of the compound sentences we make with them. And truth functional analysis is simply a way of keeping track of this. The simplest of the logical operators and the easiest to understand truth functionally is *negation*. For example, the compound statement "The weather is not great" is produced by negating the simple statement "The weather is great." In this example the word "not" is used to express the logical operator negation. How does the logical operator negation affect the truth value of the compound statement "The weather is not great"? Well, if the simple statement "The weather is great" is true, then the compound statement "The weather is not great" is false, and if the simple statement "The weather is great" is false, then the compound statement "The weather is not great" is true. In other words, negation simply reverses the truth value of the component statement to which it is applied. Here is a simple graphic representation. Let the letter "P" represent any statement. The symbol ~ will be used to represent the logical operator negation. Thus " ~ P" represents the negation of P.

P	~P
T	F
F	T

This sort of graphic representation is called a "truth table." We use it here to define the logical operator negation by showing what the truth value of the compound statement produced by negation would be for each of the possible truth values of its component statement.

CONJUNCTION

A truth table needs to have as many lines as there are possible combinations of truth value for the number of distinct components involved. Negation operates on a single component statement, P. Since P is either true or false (not true), our truth table for negation required only two lines. But most logical operators connect two component statements, each of which might be either true or false. So a truth table defining any such operator will require four lines to represent each of the four possible combinations of truth value for the components. To illustrate, let us use the example of conjunction mentioned above: "The weather is great and I wish you were here." This once again is composed of the two simple statements "The weather is great" and "I wish you were here." The components of a conjunction are called "conjuncts." Let "P" stand for the first conjunct and the letter "Q" stand for the second. The symbol "&" will be used to represent the logical operator conjunction. Thus "P & Q" represents the conjunction of P and Q. It is fairly easy to see intuitively that the conjunction "P & Q" is true only if both of its conjuncts are true. "The weather is great and I wish you were here" is true only if the weather really is great and I really do wish you were here. If either conjunct or both were not true, then the conjunction "P & Q" would also not be true, as indicated in the following truth table:

P	Q	P & Q
T	T	T
T	F	F
F	T	F
F	F	F

CONDITIONALS

We're now ready to examine the logical structure of conditionals. First of all, conditionals are compound statements. And what they assert is that a peculiar kind of relationship (a "truth-dependency" relationship) holds between their component parts. For example, the conditional:

If love is blind, then fools rush in

is composed of the two simple component statements "Love is blind" and "Fools rush in." What it asserts is not that either of them *is* true, only that the truth of the second one *depends on* the truth of the first one. It asserts that the statement "Love is blind" *implies* the statement "Fools rush in." We call both this relationship and the logical operator involved in making conditionals *implication*.

Because this is not a reciprocal relationship—because it only goes in one direction—we'll need terms to keep track of which statement depends on which. In a conditional statement, the component introduced by the word "if" is called the *antecedent,* and the component introduced by the word "then" is called the *consequent.* In this example "Love is blind" is the antecedent and "Fools rush in" is the consequent.

Sometimes conditionals are used to say more than just that one statement implies another. For example, the statement

If abortion is homicide, then by definition it involves the killing of human beings

expresses also that the consequent *follows (by definition)* from the antecedent. For another example, the statement

If the economy doesn't improve, then the President will have a hard time getting reelected

expresses also that the antecedent is *causally* connected to the consequent. And the following statement,

If the Congress overrides the President's last veto, then I'll eat my hat

expresses also that the speaker is *committed* to do something on a certain condition. In each of these cases, though, the statement expresses at a minimum that the truth of the consequent depends on the truth of the antecedent. This is the logical structure at the core of conditionals, represented in the truth table that follows. Let "P" represent the antecedent and "Q" represent the consequent. The symbol "⊃" will be used to represent the logical operator implication. Thus, "P ⊃ Q" represents the conditional "If P then Q."

P	Q	P ⊃ Q
T	T	T
T	F	F
F	T	T
F	F	T

You may have noticed that according to this truth table the conditional "If P then Q" comes out false *only* when the antecedent is true and the consequent is false. In all other cases logic treats conditionals as true. It is intuitively reasonable to suppose that a conditional with a true antecedent and a false consequent is false. Generally this is how conditionals are tested for truth. Take the following example:

If the economy does not improve, then the President will lose his bid for a second term.

We could be certain that this conditional is false only if the economy does not improve (i.e., the antecedent is true) and the President nevertheless wins reelection (i.e., the consequent is false). But you might wonder why we would want to call a conditional true whose antecedent and consequent are both false? Well, suppose you and your friend are scanning the radio dial for something new and you happen to tune into a station broadcasting the very latest in avant-garde electronic music, which sounds to both of you something like the dishwasher full of bone china falling down a flight of stairs. And so your friend says:

If this is music, then I'm the king of Peru.

The *point* of such a statement is to assert the *falsity* of the antecedent, to claim that this isn't (*can't possibly be*) music. Here's how the conditional is being used to make this point: In effect, your friend is saying: "Since the consequent is obviously false (I'm not the king of Peru), if the antecedent *were* true the conditional itself would be false. But what I am now saying is true, so the antecedent has to be false too."

Owing to the complexity and flexibility of language, there is quite a wide variety of ways of expressing this conditional relationship in English. For example, here's a conditional claim: "If I get an A in this class, then my GPA will be a 3.8." And here are several other ways of expressing the same claim:

- If I get an A in this class, my GPA will be a 3.8.
- My GPA will be a 3.8 if I get an A in this class.
- My GPA will be a 3.8, provided I get an A in this class.
- My GPA will be a 3.8, on the condition that I get an A in this class.

By the same token, not every statement containing the word *if* is a conditional. "You're welcome to wait in the drawing room, if you like" would not ordinarily express a conditional relationship between two component statements. As in so many other situations, recognition of conditionals is an interpretive matter; we need to be aware of nuances of meaning in context.

One subtle but important difference to be aware of is the distinction between "if" and "only if." "My GPA will be a 3.8, *only if* I get an A in this class" does *not* say the same thing as "My GPA will be a 3.8 if I get an A in this class." What it really says is "*Unless* I get an A in this class, my GPA *won't* be a 3.8." This is the same as saying "If I *don't* get an A in this class, my GPA *won't* be a 3.8." In other words, "*In order to* get my GPA up to a 3.8, I *must* get an A in this class." This means that if I have a GPA of 3.8, then I will have gotten an A in this class. Thus, "only if" has the effect of reversing the conditional relationship between the antecedent and consequent, as the accompanying figure shows.

P = I get an A in this class   Q = My GPA will be a 3.8

• **If** I get an A in this class, my GPA will be a 3.8.	**P ⊃ Q**
• My GPA will be a 3.8, **if** I get an A in this class.	**P ⊃ Q**
• My GPA will be a 3.8, **provided** I get an A in this class.	**P ⊃ Q**
• My GPA will be a 3.8, **on the condition that** I get an A in this class.	**P ⊃ Q**
• My GPA will be a 3.8 **only if** I get an A in this class.	**Q ⊃ P**
• **Only if** I get an A in this class will my GPA be a 3.8.	**Q ⊃ P**
• **Unless** I get an A in this class, my GPA will **not** be a 3.8	**~P ⊃ ~Q = Q ⊃ P**
• **If** my GPA is a 3.8, I will have an A in this class.	**Q ⊃ P**

DISJUNCTIONS

Like conditionals, disjunctions assert a truth-functional relationship between the two component statements of which they are made up. These component statements are called *disjuncts*. Normally the relationship asserted by a disjunction can be expressed as follows: At least one of the disjuncts is true (possibly both). For example, the statement

Either the battery is dead or there is a short in the ignition switch

asserts that at least one of the two statements "The battery is dead" and "There is a short in the ignition switch" is true. This relationship and the logical operator used to make compound statements that assert it we call *disjunction,* and we can represent it by means of the following truth table. Let the letters "P" and "Q" represent the two disjuncts and the symbol "v" represent the operator disjunction. Thus "P v Q" represents the statement "Either P or Q."

P	Q	P v Q
T	T	T
T	F	T
F	T	T
F	F	F

EXERCISE 7.1

Translate the following claims into truth functional logical format.

Either the governor will veto the bill or she won't be reelected.	V = The governor will veto the bill R = The governor will get reelected.	Truth Functional Format: V v ~R

Judging from that getup, either he's the new Ronald McDonald or he thinks it's Halloween.	R = He's the new Ronald McDonald. H = He thinks it's Halloween.	Truth Functional Format: R v H

We're going to be late and Grandma is not going to be happy.	L = We're going to be late. H = Grandma is going to be happy.	Truth Functional Format: L & ~H

The weather is great and I wish you were here.	G = The weather is great. W = I wish you were here.	Truth Functional Format: G & W

If you're ever going to become a musician, you're going to have to practice.	M = You're going to become a musician. P = You're going to have to practice.	Truth Functional Format: M ⊃ P

Paul will be graduating with honors only if he keeps his GPA above 3.3 this semester.	H = Paul will be graduating with honors. K = Paul keeps his GPA above 3.3 this semester.	Truth Functional Format: H ⊃ K

only if K ⊃ H

Paul will not be graduating with honors unless he keeps his GPA above 3.3 this semester.	H = Paul will be graduating with honors. K = Paul keeps his GPA above 3.3 this semester.	Truth Functional Format: ~K ⊃ ~H = H ⊃ K

ARGUMENT FORMS

MODUS PONENS

Because of their unique structure conditionals are extremely powerful reasoning tools and so they play a crucial role in a great many arguments and argument forms. Let's suppose, for example, that an experimental space probe begins with the following conditional first premise:

(1) If there is life on Mars, then there is adequate life support on Mars.

Now suppose that the space probe establishes that in fact:

(2) There is life on Mars.

From this as an additional premise together with the first premise we can conclude that:

(3) There is adequate life support on Mars.

Notice first that premise 2 is identical with the antecedent of the conditional premise 1 and that the conclusion is identical with its consequent. Notice also that it is impossible to assert 1 and 2 and deny 3 without contradicting yourself. Try it. Thus, this is a deductively valid argument. It follows a form that can be represented schematically as follows:

$$
\begin{array}{l}
(1)\ P \supset Q \\
(2)\ P \\
\hline
\therefore\ (3)\ Q
\end{array}
$$

Logicians traditionally refer to this argument form by the Latin label *modus ponens,* which means "affirmative mood." Because modus ponens is deductively valid, for any argument whatsoever, as long as it follows the form of modus ponens, accepting the premises forces you to accept the conclusion. Try it. Make some up.

FALLACY OF ASSERTING THE CONSEQUENT

Now let us suppose that our space probe turns up another kind of evidence. Suppose the space probe establishes that:

(2a) There is adequate life support on Mars.

Suppose we drew the conclusion from this together with premise 1 that:

(3a) There is life on Mars.

Perhaps conclusion 3a is correct. But do our two premises really guarantee it? No, they don't. It is possible to deny 3a without contradicting the assertion either of 1 or 2a. Try it (using the scenario method).

If you're having trouble with this, consider the following formally analogous argument:

> If a figure is square, then it has four sides.
> This rhombus has four sides.
> _____
> ∴ This rhombus is square.

Thus, this argument is not deductively valid. And the form it follows, which can be schematically represented as follows, is unreliable, or formally fallacious:

$$(1) \quad P \supset Q$$
$$(2a) \quad Q$$
$$\text{_____}$$
$$\therefore (3a) \quad P$$

Logicians traditionally refer to this form as the *fallacy of asserting the consequent* because that's what the second premise does. It asserts the consequent of the conditional first premise.

MODUS TOLLENS

Now let us suppose that our space probe turns up yet another kind of evidence. Suppose the space probe establishes that:

(2b) There is no adequate life support on Mars.

From this together with our first premise it is possible to conclude that:

(3b) There is no life on Mars.

Notice here that premise 2b is the denial of the consequent of premise 1, whereas 3b is the denial of its antecedent. And notice that here again it is impossible to assert 1 and 2b and deny 3b without contradicting yourself. Try it. Thus, this inference is deductively valid. It follows a pattern that can be represented schematically as follows:

$$(1) \quad P \supset Q$$
$$(2b) \quad {\sim}Q$$
$$\text{_____}$$
$$\therefore (3b) \quad {\sim}P$$

Logicians traditionally refer to this argument form by the Latin label *modus tollens*, which means "denying mood." Because modus tollens, like modus ponens, is deductively valid, for any argument whatsoever, as long as it follows the form of modus tollens, accepting the premises forces you to accept the conclusion. Try it. Make some up.

FALLACY OF DENYING THE ANTECEDENT

Next let's suppose our space probe establishes that:

(2c) There is no life on Mars.

Suppose we drew from this and our first premise the conclusion that:

(3c) There isn't adequate life support on Mars.

Again, perhaps 3c is correct, but do premises 1 and 2c guarantee it? No, they don't. It is possible to assert both 1 and 2c and deny 3c without contradicting yourself. Try it (again using the scenario method).

Recall the earlier example. You can demonstrate the invalidity of this inference by means of a formally analogous argument thus:

> If a figure is square then it has four sides.
> This figure (a rhombus) is not a square.
> _____
> ∴ This figure (a rhombus) does not have four sides.

Thus, this argument is not deductively valid. And the form it follows, which can be schematically represented as follows, is unreliable, or formally fallacious:

$$(1) \quad P \supset Q$$
$$(2c) \quad {\sim}P$$
$$\text{-------------}$$
$$\therefore (3c) \quad {\sim}Q$$

Logicians traditionally refer to this form as the *fallacy of denying the antecedent* because that's what the second premise does. It denies the antecedent of the conditional first premise.

The following table summarizes what we've said about these four conditional forms:

	Valid		Invalid	
Modus Ponens	(1) P ⊃ Q (2) P		Asserting the Consequent	(1) P ⊃ Q (2a) Q
	∴(3) Q			∴(3a) P
Modus Tollens	(1) P ⊃ Q (2b) ~Q		Denying the Antecedent	(1) P ⊃ Q (2c) ~P
	∴(3b) ~P			∴(3c) ~Q

EXERCISE 7.2

Demonstrate the fallacious status of affirming the consequent and denying the antecedent by composing arguments of each form that move from intuitively acceptable or obviously true premises to intuitively unacceptable or obviously false conclusions.

EXERCISE 7.3

Analyze and evaluate the following two arguments:

> If astrology is correct, then all people born at the same time would have the same sort of personalities, experiences, and opportunities, yet this is not the case.
> - i. What is the thesis of this argument?
> - ii. The argument is an example of which argument form?
> - iii. Is the argument deductively valid or not?

> If astrology has been refuted, then we should not depend on the predictions in the horoscope. But since astrology has not been refuted, we *should* depend on them.
> - i. What is the thesis of this argument?
> - ii. The argument is an example of which argument form?
> - iii. Is the argument deductively valid or not?

HYPOTHETICAL SYLLOGISM

Another commonly used and important argument form involves two conditional premises. Let's suppose once again, for example, that an experimental space probe begins with the following conditional first premise:

(1) If there is life on Mars, then there is adequate life support on Mars.

This time, however, let's add a second conditional premise:

(2d) If there is adequate life support on Mars, then a manned mission to Mars is feasible.

From this together with our premise 1b it is possible to conclude that:

(3d) If there is life on Mars, then a manned mission to Mars is feasible.

Notice here that premise 2d is a conditional whose antecedent is identical with the consequent of premise 1, whereas the conclusion, 3d, is another conditional, whose antecedent is identical with the antecedent of premise 1 and whose consequent is identical with the consequent of premise 2d. And notice that here again it is impossible to assert 1 and 2d and deny 3d without contradicting yourself. Try it. Thus, this inference is deductively valid. It follows a pattern that can be represented schematically as follows:

$$(1) \quad P \supset Q$$
$$(2d) \quad Q \supset R$$
$$\overline{\therefore (3d) \quad P \supset R}$$

Logicians traditionally refer to this argument form as *hypothetical syllogism* Because hypothetical syllogism, like modus ponens and modus tollens, is deductively valid, for any argument whatsoever, as long as it follows the form of hypothetical syllogism, accepting the premises forces you to accept the conclusion. Try it. Make some up.

But now compare the last example with this one:

(1) If there is life on Mars, then there is adequate life support on Mars.

(2e) A manned mission to Mars is feasible only if there is adequate life support on Mars.

∴ (3d) If there is life on Mars, then a manned mission to Mars is feasible.

This inference is not deductively valid. Remember that "only if" (as in premise 2e) reverses the positions of antecedent and consequent (see the figure on page 190). You can also see the invalidity using the following scenario. Suppose that it's true that the existence of life on Mars presupposes adequate life support on Mars (premise 1). Suppose also that a manned mission to Mars is feasible *only if* there is adequate life support on Mars (premise 2e). Now let us also suppose that there is indeed life on Mars, and so also adequate life support on Mars. And yet intuitively it's pretty clear that the feasibility of a manned mission to Mars is still an open question. So the conclusion (3d) does not follow logically from these two premises.

DISJUNCTIVE SYLLOGISM

Like conditional statements, disjunctions are extremely powerful reasoning tools, and so they play a crucial role in a great many arguments and argument forms. Let's suppose, for example, that we've been trying to diagnose a mechanical problem with the car, and we have eliminated all possible problems but two: the battery and the ignition switch. So we now have good reason to believe that

(1) Either the battery is dead or there is a short in the ignition switch.

Now suppose we check the battery and find that it's fully charged and functioning properly. We now know that

(2) The battery is not dead.

From this together with our first premise it is possible to conclude that:

(3) There is a short in the ignition switch.

Notice here that premise 2 is the denial of one of the disjuncts of premise 1, whereas 3 is identical with the other disjunct. And notice that here again it is impossible to assert 1 and 2 and deny 3 without contradicting yourself. Try it. Thus, this inference is deductively valid. It follows a pattern that can be represented schematically as follows:

$$(1)\ P \lor Q$$
$$(2)\ \sim P$$

$$\therefore\ (3)\ Q$$

Logicians traditionally refer to this argument form as *disjunctive syllogism*.

DILEMMA

One of the oldest and most powerful argumentative strategies combines conditional and disjunctive premises. The strategy aims to prove its point by showing that it is implied by each of two alternatives, at least one of which must be true. The strategy and the argument form that embodies it are called *dilemma*. For example, suppose that during the Monday Night Football pregame commentary you hear John Madden say,

> If the Saints beat the Rams tonight, then the Forty-niners are in the playoffs as division champs.
>> But if the Rams beat the Saints, then the 'Niners are in the playoffs as a wild card.

EXERCISE 7.4

This is an incompletely stated argument. Using the tools presented in Chapter 4, see if you can reconstruct it before reading any further.

- If the Saints beat the Rams tonight, then the Forty-niners are in the playoffs as division champs. But if the Rams beat the Saints, then the 'Niners are in the playoffs as a wild card.

The argument as presented consists of two claims, both conditionals, neither of which seems to support the other. What is the point? Apparently that the 'Niners are in the playoffs (regardless of the outcome of tonight's game). Thus, the implied conclusion of the argument would be "The 'Niners are in the playoffs." But the argument also depends on a third premise, which is unstated because it is so obvious that it "goes without saying," namely, that either the Saints will beat the Rams or the Rams will beat the Saints. When these elements are filled in, the argument goes like this:

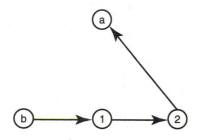

(b) Either the Saints will beat the Rams or the Rams will beat the Saints.

(1) If the Saints beat the Rams, then the 'Niners are in the playoffs (as division champs).

(2) If the Rams beat the Saints, then the 'Niners are in the playoffs (as a wild card).

∴ (a) The 'Niners are in the playoffs.

Notice here that antecedent of claim 1 is one of the disjuncts of the implied premise (b), and the antecedent of claim 2 is the other disjunct, while the consequent of each conditional claim is the argument's implied conclusion. And notice that here again it is impossible to assert the three premises together and deny the conclusion without contradicting yourself. Try it. Thus, this inference is deductively valid. It follows a pattern that can be represented schematically as follows:

(1) P v Q

(2) P ⊃ R

(3) Q ⊃ R

∴ (4) R

EXERCISE 7.5

Identify the logical structure of each of the following examples.

	Modus Ponens	If Paul keeps his GPA above 3.3 this semester, then he will be graduating with honors. And his GPA is 3.7. So he's going to be graduating with honors.
	Asserting Consequence	
	Modus Tollens	
	Denying Antecedent	
	Hypothetical Syllogism	
	Disjunctive Syllogism	
	Dilemma	

	Modus Ponens	Unless Paul keeps his GPA above 3.3 this semester he won't be graduating with honors. But his GPA is 3.7. So he's going to be graduating with honors.
	Asserting Consequence	
	Modus Tollens	
	Denying Antecedent	
	Hypothetical Syllogism	
	Disjunctive Syllogism	
	Dilemma	

	Modus Ponens	Unless Paul keeps his GPA above 3.3 this semester he won't be
	Asserting Consequence	graduating with honors. And his GPA is 2.7. So he's not going to be
	Modus Tollens	graduating with honors.
	Denying Antecedent	
	Hypothetical Syllogism	
	Disjunctive Syllogism	
	Dilemma	

	Modus Ponens	Paul will be graduating with honors only if he keeps his GPA above 3.3 this
	Asserting Consequence	semester. He will keep his GPA above 3.3 only if he studies an extra 20
	Modus Tollens	hours per week. So Paul will be graduating with honors only if he studies
	Denying Antecedent	an extra 20 hours per week.
	Hypothetical Syllogism	
	Disjunctive Syllogism	
	Dilemma	

	Modus Ponens	We're not going to get to sleep unless the dog stops barking. The dog
	Asserting Consequence	won't stop barking until the porch light is turned off. So we'll get to sleep
	Modus Tollens	only if the porch light is turned off.
	Denying Antecedent	
	Hypothetical Syllogism	
	Disjunctive Syllogism	
	Dilemma	

	Modus Ponens	Either we turn the porch light off, or that dog will keep on barking. We're
	Asserting Consequence	not going to get any sleep until the dog stops barking. So we'd better go
	Modus Tollens	turn that porch light off.
	Denying Antecedent	
	Hypothetical Syllogism	
	Disjunctive Syllogism	
	Dilemma	

	Modus Ponens	"Every time we talked to higher level managers, they kept saying they
	Asserting Consequence	didn't know anything about the problems below them. Either the guys at
	Modus Tollens	the top didn't know, in which case they should have known, or they did
	Denying Antecedent	know, in which case they were lying to us."[1]
	Hypothetical Syllogism	
	Disjunctive Syllogism	
	Dilemma	

TESTING FOR VALIDITY WITH TRUTH TABLES

In Chapter 6 we found the system of Venn diagrams useful as a graphic means of testing the validity of categorical syllogisms. Venn diagrams don't accommodate the kind of argument forms we've just been considering very well. But we can use truth tables for this purpose. We conclude this chapter by demonstrating this feature of truth tables. Thus far we have used truth tables to define and explain logical operators. A truth table will list all possible combinations of truth value for all components of a truth functional compound statement on the left, with the corresponding truth value of the compound statement in the far right column, as, for example, in this truth table for implication:

Components		Compound
P	Q	$P \supset Q$
(premise 2)	*(conclusion)*	*(premise 1)*
T	T	T
T	F	F
F	T	T
F	F	T

MODUS PONENS

It so happens that the truth table also represents all of the possible truth value combinations of the premises and conclusion of the argument form modus ponens. The column on the right corresponds to premise 1, the column on the left corresponds to premise 2, and the column in the middle corresponds to the conclusion. So we should also be able to tell from the truth table whether or not it's possible for both of the premises to be true while the conclusion is false. As always, if so, the argument form is not deductively valid, but if not, the argument form is deductively valid. There is only one line (line 1) of the truth table on which both premises are true (see the accompanying figure), and on that line the conclusion is also true. So the argument form is a valid one.

Components		Compound
P	Q	$P \supset Q$
(premise 2)	*(conclusion)*	*(premise 1)*
T	T	T
T	F	F
F	T	T
F	F	T

FALLACY OF ASSERTING THE CONSEQUENT

It turns out also that the truth table for implication represents all of the possible truth value combinations of the premises and conclusion of the fallacy of asserting the consequent. In this case the column on the right corresponds to premise 1, the column in the middle corresponds to premise 2, and the column on the left corresponds to the conclusion. So again we should also be able to tell from the truth table whether or not it's possible for both of the premises to be true while the conclusion is false. This time, there are two lines (lines 1 and 3) of the truth table on which both premises are true (see the accompanying figure), and on line 3 the conclusion is false. In other words, the truth table shows that it is possible for an argument of this form to have true premises and a false conclusion, and therefore that the argument is not valid.

Components		Compound
P	Q	P ⊃ Q
(conclusion)	*(premise 2)*	*(premise 1)*
T	T	T
T	F	F
Ⓕ	T	T
F	F	T

MODUS TOLLENS

Testing the validity of modus tollens and the fallacy of denying the antecedent is only slightly more complicated. This is because none of the truth tables we have generated so far happens to represent all of the possible truth value combinations for the premises and conclusions of either of these two argument forms. However, we need merely add a couple of columns to the truth table for implication to get this accomplished (see the accompanying figure). These two columns are to represent the truth values of ~ P and ~ Q, which, according to the truth table for negation, are simply the reverse of the truth values for P and Q respectively.

Components		Compounds		
P	Q	P ⊃ Q	~P	~Q
		(premise 1)	*(conclusion)*	*(premise 2)*
T	T	T	F	F
T	F	F	F	T
F	T	T	T	F
F	F	T	T	T

To test the validity of modus tollens we simply need to locate the columns representing the premises and conclusion and check to see whether or not it's possible for both of the premises to be true while the conclusion is false. In our truth table the third column now represents premise 1, the column on the far right represents premise 2, and the column between them represents the conclusion. There is only one line (line 4) on which both premises are true. Since the conclusion is also true on this line, the argument form is a valid one.

FALLACY OF DENYING THE ANTECEDENT

Similarly, to test the fallacy of denying the antecedent we simply need to locate the columns representing the premises and conclusion and check to see whether or not it's possible for both of the premises to be true while the conclusion is false. In our truth table the third column now represents premise 1, the column immediately to the right of it represents premise 2, and the column on the far right represents the conclusion (see the accompanying figure). But this time, there are two lines (lines 3 and 4) of the truth table on which both premises are true, and on line 3 the conclusion is false. In other words, the truth table shows that it is possible for an argument of this form to have true premises and a false conclusion, and therefore that the argument is not valid.

Components		Compounds		
P	Q	P ⊃ Q	~P	~Q
		(premise 1)	(premise 2)	(conclusion)
T	T	T	F	F
T	F	F	F	T
F	T	T	T	Ⓕ
F	F	T	T	T

And again we can demonstrate its validity by means of a truth table. This time we are dealing with three distinct components: P, Q, and R. So our truth table (see figure) will need eight lines in order to represent all the possible combinations of truth value for the number of distinct components involved.

Components			Compounds		
P	Q	R	P ⊃ R	Q ⊃ R	P v Q
		(conclusion)	(premise 2)	(premise 3)	(premise 1)
T	T	T	T	T	T
T	T	F	F	F	T
T	F	T	T	T	T
T	F	F	F	F	T
F	T	T	T	T	T
F	T	F	T	T	T
F	F	T	T	T	F
F	F	F	T	T	F

This time, there are three lines (lines 1, 3 and 5) of the truth table on which all of the premises are true. Since the conclusion is also true on each of these lines, the argument form is a valid one.

EXERCISE 7.6

Demonstrate the validity of the argument form hypothetical syllogism by means of the truth table below. Highlight the rows in which the truth values of both premises are true. Then determine whether the argument form is valid as illustrated above.

P	Q	R	P ⊃ R	Q ⊃ R	P ⊃ R
T	T	T	T	T	T
T	T	F	T	F	F
T	F	T	F	T	T
T	F	F	F	T	F
F	T	T	T	T	T
F	T	F	T	F	T
F	F	T	T	T	T
F	F	F	T	T	T

EXERCISE 7.7

Demonstrate the validity of the argument form disjunctive syllogism by means of the truth table below. Highlight the rows in which the truth values of both premises are true. Then determine whether the argument form is valid as illustrated above.

P	Q	P v Q	~P
T	T	T	F
T	F	T	F
F	T	T	T
F	F	F	T

ADDITIONAL EXERCISES

■ **EXERCISE 7.8**   Translate the following claims into truth functional logical format.

If a government harbors terrorists, we will hold that government responsible.	G = a government harbors terrorists H = we will hold that government responsible	Truth Functional Format:

If a government harbors terrorists, we will not hesitate to use military force.	G = a government harbors terrorists H = we will hesitate to use military force	Truth Functional Format:

Either the FBI memo was lost, or CIA analysts misunderstood the memo's implications.	F = the FBI memo was lost C = CIA analysts misunderstood the memo's implications	Truth Functional Format:

Either the FBI memo was lost, or CIA analysts did not understand the memo's implications.	F = the FBI memo was lost C = CIA analysts understood the memo's implications	Truth Functional Format:

The FBI memo was lost, and CIA analysts did not understand its implications.	F = the FBI memo was lost C = CIA analysts understood the memo's implications	Truth Functional Format:

Unless interagency communication is improved, national security will continue to be at risk.	I = interagency communication is improved N = national security will continue to be at risk	Truth Functional Format:

■ **EXERCISE 7.9**   Translate each of the following arguments into standard form using the scheme of abbreviation provided. Then set up and complete a truth table for each argument and determine each argument's validity status.

If Paul keeps his GPA above 3.3 this semester, then he will be graduating with honors. And his GPA is 3.7. So he's going to be graduating with honors.	H = "Paul will be graduating with honors." K = "Paul keeps his GPA above 3.3 this semester." S = "Paul studies an extra 20 hours per week."	1) K ⊃ H ⊕ 2) K H

H	K	S	Premise 1	Premise 2	Conclusion	Valid	Invalid
t	T	t	T	T	T	X	
t	T	f	T	T	T		
t	F	t	T	F	T		
t	F	f	T	F	T		
f	T	t	F	F	F		
f	T	f	F	F	F		
f	F	t	T	F	F		
f	F	f	T	F	F		

Unless Paul keeps his GPA above 3.3 this semester he won't be graduating with honors. But his GPA is 3.7. So he's going to be graduating with honors.	H = "Paul will be graduating with honors." K = "Paul keeps his GPA above 3.3 this semester." S = "Paul studies an extra 20 hours per week."	$\sim K \supset \sim H$ 1) $H \supset K$ 2) K 3) H

H	K	S	Premise 1	Premise 2	Conclusion	Valid	Invalid
t	T	t	T	T	T		
t	T	f	T	T	T		
t	f	t	F	F	T		
t	f	f	F	F	T		
f	t	t	T	F	F		X
f	t	f	T	T	F		
f	f	t	T	F	F		
f	f	f	T	F	F		

Unless Paul keeps his GPA above 3.3 this semester he won't be graduating with honors. And his GPA is 2.7. So he's not going to be graduating with honors.	H = "Paul will be graduating with honors." K = "Paul keeps his GPA above 3.3 this semester." S = "Paul studies an extra 20 hours per week."	

H	K	S	Premise 1	Premise 2	Conclusion	Valid	Invalid
t	t	t					
t	t	f					
t	f	t					
t	f	f					
f	t	t					
f	t	f					
f	f	t					
f	f	f					

Paul will be graduating with honors only if he keeps his GPA above 3.3 this semester. He will keep his GPA above 3.3 only if he studies an extra 20 hours per week. So Paul will be graduating with honors only if he studies an extra 20 hours per week.	H = "Paul will be graduating with honors." K = "Paul keeps his GPA above 3.3 this semester." S = "Paul studies an extra 20 hours per week."	

H	K	S	Premise 1	Premise 2	Conclusion	Valid	Invalid
t	t	t					
t	t	f					
t	f	t					
t	f	f					
f	t	t					
f	t	f					
f	f	t					
f	f	f					

We're not going to get to sleep unless the dog stops barking. The dog won't stop barking until the porch light is turned off. So we'll get to sleep only if the porch light is turned off.	W = we are going to get to sleep D = the dog will stop barking P = the porch light is turned off	

W	D	P	Premise 1	Premise 2	Conclusion	Valid	Invalid
t	t	t					
t	t	f					
t	f	t					
t	f	f					
f	t	t					
f	t	f					
f	f	t					
f	f	f					

Either we turn the porch light off, or that dog will keep on barking. We're not going to get to sleep until the dog stops barking. So we'd better go turn that porch light off.	W = we are going to get to sleep D = the dog will stop barking P = the porch light is turned off

W	D	P	Premise 1	Premise 2	Conclusion	Valid	Invalid
t	t	t					
t	t	f					
t	f	t					
T	f	f					
f	t	t					
f	t	f					
f	f	t					
f	f	f					

■ **EXERCISE 7.10**   At the beginning of this chapter is a Farcus cartoon. Using the tools of truth functional logic, can you explain the point of the cartoon?

■ **EXERCISE 7.11**   Take any position on the issue you have been working with so far, and design an argument in support of that position, using any of the deductively valid argument forms discussed in Chapter 7. Then take an alternative or opposed position and design an argument in support of it using any of the deductively valid argument forms discussed in Chapter 7.

GLOSSARY

antecedent   in a hypothetical statement, the component introduced by the word *if*

conjunction   a compound statement that is true only when both of its components are true; the logical operator *and* used to make such a statement

consequent   in a hypothetical statement, the component introduced by the word *then*

contradiction   in truth functional logic, a conflict between a statement and its negation

dilemma   an argument form or strategy combining hypothetical and disjunctive premises that seeks to prove its point by showing that it is implied by each of two alternatives, at least one of which must be true

disjunct   component of a disjunction

disjunction   a compound statement that is true when either one or both of its components are true; the logical operator *or* used to make such a statement

disjunctive syllogism   a deductively valid argument form based on a disjunction and the denial of one of its disjuncts

fallacy of affirming the consequent   a deductively invalid argument form based on a hypothetical statement and the affirmation of its consequent

fallacy of denying the antecedent   a deductively invalid argument form based on a hypothetical statement and the denial of its antecedent

hypothetical syllogism   a deductively valid argument form based on two hypothetical statements as premises, where the consequent of the first is the antecedent of the second

logical operator   in truth functional logic a device for making a compound statement out of simple(r) ones

modus ponens   a deductively valid argument form based on a hypothetical statement and the affirmation of its antecedent

modus tollens   a deductively valid argument form based on a hypothetical statement and the denial of its consequent

negation   the logical operator that reverses the truth value of the component statement to which it is applied; a statement formed by applying this logical operator

truth functional analysis   system for keeping track of how logical operators affect the truth values of compound sentences made with them

truth functional logic   system of logic based on truth functional analysis

truth table   chart used in truth functional logic for listing variable truth values

truth value   the truth or falsity of a statement

ENDNOTES

[1] Richard Feynman, "Mr. Feynman Goes to Washington: Investigating the Space Shuttle *Challenger* Disaster," *What Do You Care What Other People Think? Further Adventures of a Curious Character* (New York: W.W. Norton, 1988), pp. 212–213.

CHAPTER 8

Evaluating Inductive Arguments I: Generalization and Analogy

As we have seen in the previous two chapters, deductively valid arguments guarantee their conclusions. If the truth of the premises of a deductively valid argument has been established, that leaves no more room for doubt about the argument's conclusion. But many arguments that do not provide this "absolute" level of inferential security nevertheless provide substantial support for their conclusions and are therefore not to be dismissed simply on the grounds that they are not *deductively* valid. There are some arguments whose premises, though they do not *guarantee* the conclusion, nevertheless make the conclusion more reasonable or probable or likely. Here is an example of such an argument:

[Professor Jones has never missed a class. (1)] So chances are [she'll be in class today. (2)]

If the premise (claim #1) is accepted as true, then it would be reasonable to accept the argument's conclusion (claim #2). Of course, even if the premise is true

THE NORM Michael Jantze

WOMEN ARE SO DIFFERENT FROM MEN.

WHAT? LIKE I HAVE TO PROVE IT?

the conclusion may prove to be false: Professor Jones may not show up for class. Perhaps she's ill or has had an accident or been arrested or has an important conflicting appointment. Nevertheless, the premise does provide reasonable support for the conclusion. Here is another example:

> [It's highly unlikely that any female will play football in the National Football League in the near future, ①] for [none has so far. ②]

Again, if the premise (claim #2) is accepted as true, it provides good—though not deductively valid—grounds for accepting the conclusion (claim #1). These are examples of *inductive* inferences. As we explained in Chapter 6, the essential difference between deductive and inductive reasoning is that deductive inferences are designed to achieve "absolute inferential security," whereas inductive inferences are designed to manage risk of error where absolute inferential security is unattainable.

ASSESSING INDUCTIVE STRENGTH

A deductive argument is either valid or not valid. But inductive strength is relative, which means it *admits of degrees*. Some valid inductive arguments are stronger than others. In the absence of *absolute* inferential security—that is to say, when the premises, even if true, leave room for doubt about the conclusion—the essential question becomes "How much room for doubt?" To evaluate inductive reasoning we must estimate the *relative* security of inferences.

EXERCISE 8.1 | **Inductive Strength**

Which is the "stronger" of the following two arguments?

1. The last three cars we have owned have been Chrysler products and they've all been trouble free. So we're probably safe to assume that a new Dodge will be reliable.

2. In Consumers' Union nationwide studies of new cars purchased over the last 10 years, Chrysler had a 30 percent lower frequency-of-repair rate than the other manufacturers. So we're probably safe to assume that a new Dodge will be reliable.

In each argument the premise does provide some reason for accepting the conclusion. But the first argument leaves more room for doubt than the second. So the second argument is that much stronger than the first. If inductive strength is a matter of degree—and the essential question for assessing inductive strength is: "How much room for doubt is there left here?"—the answer to this question is, "It depends." Inductive strength depends on a number of variables, according to the *type* of inductive reasoning involved.

INDUCTIVE GENERALIZATIONS

We will begin with the simplest and most common of inductive reasoning types called *inductive generalization*, or simply "generalization." This type of inductive reasoning is involved whenever we draw a general conclusion from a number of particular instances.

Suppose that you work with computers and you have just opened a new shipment of floppy disks. It will make things easier if we imagine that floppy disks are delivered in shipments of 100. The first disk you try is defective. So you try a second one and it's defective too. So you try a third disk. Also defective. At some point you begin to wonder whether the whole shipment might be defective. So far you've only tried three disks. They've all been defective, but still you can't be very sure that the entire shipment is defective. In fact, at this point you merely suspect that the entire shipment might be defective. That's because you've barely sampled the shipment. Suppose you keep going. You try a fourth disk and a fifth disk. Both defective. This confirms your suspicion. Obviously, the more disks you try (assuming each one is defective) the more certain you become that the entire shipment is defective. By the time you get to the 35th disk (assuming each one is defective), you're going to be much more certain—though still not *absolutely* certain—that the entire shipment is defective. This highlights two of the variables that affect the strength of an inductive generalization. From now on, let's refer to the number of disks you've tried as the *sample* and the entire shipment (the general class you're wondering about) as the *population*. The size of the sample and the size of the population each affect the strength of the inductive inference. *As the size of the sample increases relative to the population, so does the strength of the induction.*

CRITICAL THINKING TIP 8.1

As the size of the sample increases relative to the population, so does the strength of the induction.

Other variables affect inductive strength. If the only variables affecting inductive strength were the size of the sample and the size of the population, then the only way to increase inductive strength—or reduce doubt—would be to keep on plodding along, testing the disks one by one until the sample coincides with the population. But you don't need to test each and every disk to be reasonably certain about the entire population. A commonsense shortcut would be, after the first three or so disks have been identified as defective, to dig down deeper into the shipment and try a disk from the middle and another one from near the bottom. If they too turn out to be defective, you can be more certain—although still not *absolutely* certain—that the entire shipment is defective. But notice also that if you followed this procedure and got these results, you would be *more* certain than if you had just tried the *next two* disks. Why? Because, it is much more *unlikely* that by sampling in this more "random" way you would end up picking just those disks that are defective. This highlights another of the variables that affect the strength of an inductive inference: the degree to which the sample is representative of the population as a whole. *The more representative the sample is of the population as a whole, the stronger the induction.*

CRITICAL THINKING TIP 8.2

The more representative the sample is of the population as a whole, the stronger the induction.

How do we determine the degree to which the sample is representative of the population as a whole? This is a really a matter of variety. In this example, our "expanded for variety sample" is equal in size to our "keep on plodding along sample" but "covers more variables," as the accompanying figure shows.

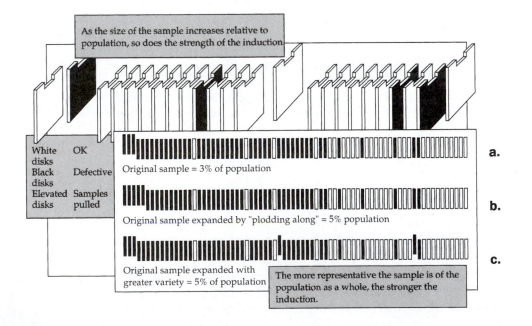

As the size of the sample increases relative to population, so does the strength of the induction.

White disks — OK
Black disks — Defective
Elevated disks — Samples pulled

a. Original sample = 3% of population

b. Original sample expanded by "plodding along" = 5% population

c. Original sample expanded with greater variety = 5% of population

The more representative the sample is of the population as a whole, the stronger the induction.

Suppose the disks are packed in the order that they came off the assembly line, and you began by sampling them in (reverse) order. In sampling the middle and both ends of the shipment rather than just the beginning, what you're doing is adding to the variety of the sample by including within it particular examples representing the entire population, whether packed first, middle, or last. You've added to the variety of the sample in the *dimension* of "numerical order within the shipment." And this is significant because numerical order within the shipment—numerical position in the "packing order"—could have something to do with whether a given disk is defective. Maybe there was a short run of 30 consecutive defective disks. By varying the sample through the dimension of numerical order, you have a way of ruling this out as a possible source of error—a way to reduce the risk of error. Because numerical order within the shipment might have something to do with whether a disk is defective or not, numerical order within the shipment is a *relevant* dimension here. *Generally, you should try to vary the sample as widely and in as many different relevant dimensions as you can think of.* In science this is called *controlling the variables.* These two factors—sample size relative to population size and representativeness of the sample—help explain why the first of our two examples of induction was weaker than the second. A *nationwide* comparative study of frequency-of-repair rates involving *not just* Chrysler products but those of other manufacturers as well constitutes both a larger and more representative sample than the tiny and highly selective "last three cars we have owned."

EXERCISE 8.2 | Inductive Strength II

Rank the following inductive arguments in order of decreasing strength (strongest to weakest). Be prepared to explain your ranking.

- Contrary to current media claims, our schools appear to be doing a superb job of teaching our children to read. A leading news magazine recently tabulated the results of the thousands of responses it received to the survey it published in its May issue. Readers from every state in the union responded. Ninety percent of the respondents believed that their school-aged children's reading skills were good to excellent. Eight percent more believed that their children's reading skills were at least adequate. Less than 1 percent felt that their children were developing less than adequate reading skills. (One percent of the respondents failed to answer this question.)

- In all of the studies that have been done over the past 30 years concerning the relationship between standardized test performance and success in school, involving several hundred thousand school-age subjects from a variety of ethnic, regional, and socioeconomic backgrounds, I.Q. tests have been shown to be the single most reliable predictor of success in school. Therefore, if one scores highly on I.Q. tests, one will probably perform well in school.

- An hour in a hot tub will probably impair a man's fertility for up to six weeks. According to one study, three men who sat in a hot tub with water heated to 102.4°F (most health clubs heat theirs to 104°F) showed reductions in the number and penetrating capacity of their sperm cells. In samples taken 36 hours later, the damage was present, but the most dramatic effects did not show up until four weeks later. This indicated that even immature sperm cells had been harmed by the high heat. (It takes about seven weeks for a newly created sperm cell to mature and pass through a system of storage ducts.) Seven weeks after their dip in the hot tub, their sperm returned to normal.

STATISTICAL GENERALIZATIONS

In our example of the defective computer disks, notice that *all* the members of the sample turned out to be one way: defective. Life is rarely as simple as that. More often, some members of the sample will be one way, and some another. So a variation on simple inductive generalization involves projecting *trends* or *percentages* observed in the sample onto other instances or onto the population as a whole. This is commonly called *statistical generalization*. For instance, suppose we're interested in how likely college students with different majors are to gain admission to law school. We might survey law school admissions for a certain period of time. Suppose our survey shows that 20 percent more of those applicants with philosophy majors were admitted than were admitted from the next most successful major. We might then project inductively that philosophy majors are 20 percent more likely to gain admission to law school than other college students.

The same principles used to evaluate the strength of simple inductive generalizations also apply in evaluating the strength of statistical generalizations. In both simple inductive generalization and statistical induction the strength of the inference increases with the size of the sample relative to the population and with the degree to which the sample is representative of the population as a whole. Suppose our survey of law school admissions was only one year long or was confined to the state of California. Then we might be overlooking variables that might otherwise show up in a 10-year nationwide survey. Perhaps in a particular year more students with law school aptitude happened to elect philosophy as a major. Perhaps the state of California has particularly strong instructional programs in philosophy. In any case, the smaller and more selective the sample, the weaker the induction.

MARGIN OF ERROR

Another variable that affects the strength of statistical generalizations is the degree of precision and certainty attached to the conclusion relative to the evidence contained in the premises. A statistical generalization can generally be strengthened by hedging the conclusion with appropriate qualifications, essentially by toning down the language with which the conclusion is presented. This is one reason why statistical arguments often sound so "wishy-washy" in spite of all the numbers in them. Similarly, the degree of precision with which the figures in the conclusion are stated can affect the strength of a statistical generalization. We may lack sufficient evidence to conclude with very much certainty that precisely 73.86 percent of the electorate favors the president's new economic program. However, the very same data might well be sufficient to conclude with a much higher degree of certainty that *more than two-thirds* or *most* of the electorate favors it. To handle this variable in a systematic way, statisticians use a conceptual tool known as "margin of error," as in:

> The exit polling predicts that Proposition X will pass by a 62 percent majority, with a 3 percent margin of error.

Margin of error is an estimate of the likelihood of error in the conclusion of an inductive inference. You may wonder how it would be possible to estimate such a thing so precisely—especially given the size of the sample relative to the population in most public-opinion polling. To give a detailed and systematic answer to this perfectly reasonable question would require a course in statistics, the branch of mathematics having to do with collecting and interpreting numerical data. Nevertheless, here's a way to begin to think about the problem conceptually: Margin of error is an estimate of how well you think the research has controlled the variables. Notice how closely this relates to both the degree of precision and the certainty with which the results of the polling are presented and understood.

EXERCISE 8.3 | Margin of Error

Topic for Class Discussion: Identify two distinct ways in which each of the following inferences might be strengthened. Be prepared to explain your answer in terms of how each of the ways you suggest would lower the "margin of error."

1. The last three cars we have owned have been Chrysler products and they've all been trouble free. So we're probably safe to assume that a new Dodge will be reliable.

2. In Consumers' Union nationwide studies of new cars purchased over the last 10 years, Chrysler had a 30 percent lower frequency-of-repair rate than the other manufacturers. So we're probably safe to assume that a new Dodge will be reliable.

3. My English teacher has recommended three novels and they've all been wonderful. I think I'm going to enjoy this book of poetry because she just recommended it too.

REASONING BY ANALOGY

An analogy is a kind of comparison—one of the most useful and powerful reasoning tools there is. Why is this? Comparison essentially involves focusing one's attention on similarity. Similarity is an indispensable guide to the environment of any intelligent and sentient being. And there's a lot of similarity in the world to pay attention to.

EXERCISE 8.4 | Thought Experiment

Try to think of two things—*any* two things—that are so completely different from each other that they have *nothing* in common. Then see if you can't find some similarity between them.

Reasoning with analogies involves the application of three of the most basic intellectual concepts: similarity, difference, and relevance. The connection between analogy and similarity is obvious to the point of being overwhelming. The words *analogous* and *similar* are often regarded as synonymous. What is much less obvious, although no less important, is that comparison always implies its inseparable opposite, its "flip side," contrast—which essentially involves focusing one's attention on difference. Difference, too, is an indispensable guide to the environment of any intelligent and sentient being. And there's a lot of difference in the world to pay attention to.

EXERCISE 8.5 | Thought Experiment

Try to think of two things—*any* two things—that are so completely identical to each other that they cannot be told apart in any way. Then see if you can't find some difference between them.

Analogies are comparisons applied to some specific intellectual purpose. There are, of course, many such purposes. Here, for example, trumpet virtuoso Wynton Marsalis uses an analogy to explain the usefulness of analogies in explaining some of the fascinating dimensions of music:

> As we explore the world of music, we'll be looking for similarities. It's kind of like when you try to begin a conversation with someone you don't know. It's better to talk about what you have in common, rather than be stifled by your obvious differences.[1]

Analogies can be used very effectively to *explain* new and unfamiliar or abstract and intangible things by comparing them to more familiar and tangible ones. Analogies can be used simply to give a vivid description or to spice up a narrative. Imagine a recent divorcee telling her sister the story of how she fended off unwanted advances at the office: ". . . and I need a date like a fish needs a bicycle." An analogy can be used as the basis for a joke. Lily Tomlin did this when she pointed out that we get olive oil by squeezing olives and corn oil by squeezing kernels of corn and sesame oil by pressing sesame seeds and peanut oil by mashing peanuts, and then wondered how we get baby oil.

EXERCISE 8.6 | How Many Analogies?

Topic for Class Discussion: How many analogies can you find in the following passage? What is the author trying to accomplish by means of each of the analogies you notice?

In a *Scientific American* column on innumeracy, the computer scientist Douglas Hofstadter cites the case of the Ideal Toy Company, which stated on the package of the original Rubik cube that there were more than three billion possible states the cube could attain. Calculations show that there are more than 4×10^{19} possible states, 4 with 19 zeroes after it. What the package says isn't wrong; there are more than three billion possible states. The understatement, however, is symptomatic of a pervasive innumeracy which ill suits a technologically based society. It's analogous to a sign at the entrance to the Lincoln Tunnel stating: New York, population more than 6; or McDonald's proudly announces that they have sold more than 120 hamburgers.[2]

There are two prominent analogies in the above passage: one involving an imagined sign at the entrance to the Lincoln Tunnel in New York City and one involving McDonald's proudly announcing having sold more than 120 hamburgers. The point of each analogy is to make it easier to grasp the magnitude of an understatement that most of us would otherwise find incomprehensible. "Innumeracy" itself is quite possibly an unfamiliar concept, which the author, John Allen Paulos, introduces by means of an analogy with the more familiar concept of illiteracy. This analogy is compressed into his book's title, *Innumeracy: Mathematical Illiteracy and Its Consequences*. Implied in this analogy is also an argument about the importance of overcoming the handicap of innumeracy.

ARGUMENT BY ANALOGY

Analogies can also be used inferentially or argumentatively, that is, to infer conclusions and to support or defend controversial positions. We call this reasoning by analogy or argument by analogy. Here is an example in which the 18th-century Scottish philosopher Thomas Reid argues for the probability of extraterrestrial organic life in our solar system:

> We may observe a very great similitude between this earth which we inhabit, and the other planets, Saturn, Jupiter, Mars, Venus and Mercury. They all revolve round the sun, as the earth does, although at different distances and in different periods. They borrow all their light from the sun, as the earth does. Several of them are known to revolve round their axis like the earth, and by that means, must have a like succession of day and night. Some of them have moons, that serve to give them light in the absence of the sun, as our moon does to us. They are all, in their motions, subject to the same law of gravitation, as the earth is. From all this similitude, it is not unreasonable to think that those planets may, like our earth, be the habitation of various orders of living creatures. There is some probability in this conclusion from analogy.[3]

Notice that Reid recognized that the inference is not deductively valid—in other words, that this is a form of inductive inference in which there is room for doubt and error. Nevertheless, he expressed cautious confidence in it as an inference. At some points in history, for instance in the middle of the 20th century, it may have appeared that the conclusion Reid was cautiously drawing was not true, though the question remains an open one to this day. But he was not essentially misguided in placing confidence in the argument. He was following a familiar and generally reliable line of reasoning, which a great many of our everyday inferences follow as well. If you try to enroll in Professor Smith's section of the upper-division poetry course because you have taken three of her lower division courses and found her to be a knowledgeable and stimulating instructor, you are following the same reasoning strategy as Reid was. In effect, you are reasoning as follows:

1. I have observed several items: a, b, and c, each of which has the important characteristic 1 in common with target item d. *(I have taken three courses taught by the instructor of the course I'm contemplating.)*

2. The observed items a, b, and c also have characteristics 2 and 3. *(The three courses I've taken were stimulating and imparted knowledge.)*

3. Therefore, it is likely that target item d will have characteristics 2 and 3 as well. *(The course I'm contemplating is likely to be stimulating and to impart knowledge.)*

The basic inferential strategy of an argument by analogy, as illustrated in these examples, is to infer that if things are similar in some way(s), they are probably similar in other way(s) as well.

In the process of analysis and evaluation of arguments by analogy, it is useful to distinguish the items compared by the roles they play in the comparison. For this purpose we will call the item(s) used as the basis of the comparison the *analogue(s)*, and we will refer to the item(s) about which conclusions are drawn or explanations are offered as the *target(s)*. So, for example, in Thomas Reid's argument about extraterrestrial life, the planet Earth is the analogue and the other planets in our solar system are the targets. In the example about Professor Smith's poetry class, the three lower division courses you have taken are the analogues and the target is her upper division class.

EXERCISE 8.7 | Analyzing Analogies

Identify the analogues and targets in each of the following analogies. Which analogies are used inferentially or argumentatively, and which are used for explanatory purposes, or something else like narrative enhancement or entertainment?

"Suppose that someone tells me that he has had a tooth extracted without an anaesthetic, and I express my sympathy, and suppose that I am then asked, 'How do you know that it hurt him?' I might reasonably reply, 'Well, I know that it would hurt me. I have been to the dentist and know how painful it is to have a tooth stopped [filled] without an anaesthetic, let alone taken out. And he has the same sort of nervous system as I have. I infer, therefore, that in these conditions he felt considerable pain, just as I should have.'"[4]

analogue	target	arg	exp	other

"Social Security has given a bunch of money to old people. That's not terrible. But Social Security is a pyramid scheme. People who get in early make out like bandits. People who get in late are screwed. And Social Security is a very sophisticated pyramid scheme. The people who are going to get screwed weren't even born when Social Security was set up. But they have been now. And they're you."[5]

analogue	target	arg	exp	other

"When Dubya wants to sound presidential, he'll try to construct a sentence that suggests some sense of mission, what his father used to call 'the vision thing.' But it's like someone assembling a barbecue—when the sentence is finished there are always a half-dozen parts left over."[6]

analogue	target	arg	exp	other

"What grounds have we for attributing suffering to other animals[?] It is best to begin by asking what grounds any individual human has for supposing that other humans feel pain. Since pain is a state of consciousness, a 'mental event,' it can never be directly observed. No observations, whether behavioral signs such as writhing or screaming or physiological or neurological recordings, are observations of pain itself. Pain is something one feels, and one can only infer that others are feeling it from various external indications. The fact that only philosophers are ever skeptical about whether other humans feels pain shows that we regard such inference is justifiable in the case of humans. Is there any reason why the same inference should be unjustifiable for other animals? Nearly all the external signs which lead us to infer pain in other humans can be seen in other species, especially 'higher' animals such as mammals and birds. Behavioral signs—writhing, yelping, or other forms of calling, attempts to avoid the source of pain, and many others—are present. We know, too, that these animals are biologically similar in the relevant respects, having nervous systems like ours which can be observed to function as ours do. So the grounds for inferring that these animals can feel pain are nearly as good as the grounds for inferring other humans do."[7]

analogue	target	arg	exp	other

"If we were to repeat the same note without accents, it would be like our pulse. But what happens if we accent the first of every four **beats**—one, two, three, four, one, two, three, four? Accenting that first note sets up a rhythm we can count. Each note becomes part of a four-beat rhythm, and every four beats is one unit. This could get confusing if we didn't have a way to organize these units. But other things are that way, too. For example, if I ask you how far from home to school, you might say 5 blocks, but you wouldn't say 6,737 steps. Or you might say 10 minutes, not 600 seconds. You divide the distance or organize the time into convenient units."[8]

analogue	target	arg	exp	other

EVALUATING REASONING BY ANALOGY

The variables that affect the strength of inductive inferences generally also pertain in evaluating reasoning by analogy. The number of analogues relative to the number of targets affects the strength of an argument by analogy just as the size of the sample relative to the size of the population affects the strength of an inductive generalization. An argument based on a large series of analogous cases will tend to be stronger than one based on a single analogue, just as an inductive generalization based on many instances will be stronger than one based on a tiny sample. Similarly, the number of observed similarities between analogue and target affects the strength of the analogy, just as the representativeness of the sample relative to the population affects the strength of an inductive generalization. This is intuitively fairly obvious. In general, the more similar things are *observed to be,* the more likely they are to be similar in additional ways as well. Another variable that affects the strength of both inductive inferences generally and arguments by analogy is the strength of the conclusion relative to the evidence contained in the premises. An argument by analogy can be strengthened by hedging the conclusion with appropriate qualifications, as Thomas Reid did in the example about extraterrestrial life. Had he expressed the conclusion with greater certainty than he did, his argument would have been weaker than it was. These same general considerations apply to differences too, only in reverse. The more differences there are between analogue and target, the weaker the analogy tends to be.

But there is another factor to consider in the evaluation of arguments by analogy, a factor that affects both similarities and differences and is more important than either similarities or differences by themselves. This is the factor of *relevance.* In our earlier example of the defective computer disks, we noted that numerical order within the shipment might have something to do with whether a disk is defective or not. Thus, numerical order within the shipment is a *relevant* variable. Similarly, in evaluating arguments or inferences by analogy, we are most interested in similarities and differences that might reasonably be thought to have something to do with the point of the comparison—the conclusion being inferred about the target. In general, the more relevant the observed similarities between analogue and target are to the conclusion being inferred, the stronger the analogy. And by the same token the more relevant the differences between analogue and target are to the conclusion being inferred, the weaker the analogy. Suppose you are shopping for a new car. You decide that the new Honda Accord is likely to be a reliable low-maintenance vehicle because Hondas you have owned in the past have been reliable and required minimal maintenance. Your inference is based on a relevant similarity, the identity of the manufacturer. Why? On the other hand, suppose someone drew the same conclusion about a car because it was blue, and the blue cars she had owned in the past had been reliable and required minimal maintenance. This inference would be based on an irrelevant similarity. Why? Because there are good reasons for thinking that in general cars made by the same manufacturer will meet similar standards of reliability, but there are no similarly good reasons to suppose that the color of a car makes a difference as to its reliability. There is a plausible explanatory basis for linking the identity of the manufacturer to quality control in the production process. There is no plausible explanatory link between color and reliability.

Thus, to evaluate an argument or inference by analogy we must add up the relevant similarities and differences. This can be accomplished in a systematic way by means of a simple form.

	Analogue	Target	Degree of Similarity or/ Difference	Relevance
Basic points of similarity used as premises				
Conclusion				
Differences				

For purposes of illustration we will use examples from Exercise 8.7, starting with Alfred Jules Ayer's inference to the conclusion that another person besides himself feels pain. Ayer uses himself as the analogue. The target is some other person. There is one basic similarity used as a premise: similar nervous system. And, of course, the conclusion is that the other person would have the same sort of pain that Ayer would.

Ayer's Argument	Analogue: Ayer	Target: Other Humans	Degree of Similarity or/ Difference	Relevance
Basic points of similarity used as premises	Central nervous system basic to physiology of sensory experience of pain	Central nervous system basic to physiology of sensory experience of pain		
Conclusion	Ayer experiences pain when undergoing dental work w/o anaesthetic	Other people experience pain when undergoing dental work w/o anaesthetic		
Differences				

To evaluate this as an argument by analogy we would first want to know whether the similarity Ayer asserts in fact obtains. Is it really the case that people have similar neurophysiology? They do. We should also note that the human central nervous system is a highly complex mechanism with a very high degree of similarity both physically and functionally from person to person. Thus, although there is only one similarity claimed here, that similarity is of a very high degree. Next we want to determine whether this similarity is *relevant* to the conclusion Ayer is trying to draw. And it is, because we have good theoretical grounds and empirical evidence to suppose that a body's neurophysiology is the central mechanism involved in the person's sensory experience. So we might add the following assessments under "Degree of Similarity" and "Relevance":

Ayer's Argument	Analogue: Ayer	Target: Other Humans	Degree of Similarity or/ Difference	Relevance
Basic points of similarity used as premises	Central nervous system basic to physiology of sensory experience of pain	Central nervous system basic to physiology of sensory experience of pain	High degree of similarity	Highly relevant to conclusion
Conclusion	Ayer experiences pain when undergoing dental work w/o anaesthetic	Other people experience pain when undergoing dental work w/o anaesthetic		
Differences				

At this point we would want to determine whether there are significant relevant differences between the analogue and the target. In the case of this particular argument, since the analogy is between Ayer himself and *any* other human being, the differences would have to relate to characteristics unique to Ayer and that would distinguish him from *any* other human being. And, of course, there are many such characteristics, as there are with all human individuals. For example, Ayer was the author of an important work of philosophy published in 1936 entitled *Language, Truth and Logic*. This is true of no other human being. But we can't think of any such differences that would be *relevant* to Ayer's conclusion. So we complete the evaluation as follows:

Ayer's Argument	Analogue: Ayer	Target: Other Humans	Degree of Similarity or/ Difference	Relevance
Basic points of similarity used as premises	Central nervous system basic to physiology of sensory experience of pain	Central nervous system basic to physiology of sensory experience of pain	High degree of similarity	Highly relevant to conclusion
Conclusion	Ayer experiences pain when undergoing dental work w/o anaesthetic	**Other people experience pain when undergoing dental work w/o anaesthetic**		
Differences	Ayer was the author of *Language, Truth and Logic,* published in 1936	No other human being was the author of *Language, Truth and Logic,* published in 1936	True	Irrelevant

So Ayer's argument appears to be quite strong, in spite of the fact that it is based on one lone similarity.

EXERCISE 8.8 | Analyzing an Argument by Analogy

Now look at Singer's very analogous argument about nonhuman animals. Using the above example as a model, set up the form for evaluating Singer's argument by identifying the analogue, the target, the basic points of similarity, and the conclusion in the blank below.

Singer's Argument	Analogue	Target	Degree of Similarity or/ Difference	Relevance
Basic points of similarity used as premises				
Conclusion				
Differences				

In this case the analogue is human beings and the target is nonhuman animals. The conclusion is that nonhuman animals have experiences of pain similar to those of humans. This inference rests on two basic points of similarity: similarity of neurophysiology and similarity in behavioral responses to stimuli.

EXERCISE 8.9 | Evaluating an Argument by Analogy

Now complete the evaluation of Singer's argument by assessing the degree and relevance of similarity in the premises, and the degree and relevance of differences you can identify, to Singer's conclusion.

Singer's Argument	Analogue	Target	Degree of Similarity or/ Difference	Relevance
Basic points of similarity used as premises	Central nervous system basic to physiology of sensory experience of pain	Central nervous system basic to physiology of sensory experience of pain		
	Expressive behavioral responses to sensory stimuli	Expressive behavioral responses to sensory stimuli		
Conclusion	Humans enjoy pleasure and suffer pain	Nonhuman animals enjoy pleasure and suffer pain		
Differences				

Here are our findings: To evaluate Peter Singer's argument as an argument by analogy, we would first want to know whether the similarities Singer asserts in fact obtain. Is it really the case that humans and nonhuman animals have similar neurophysiology? And it turns out they do. How similar are human and nonhuman animals in terms of neurophysiology? In some cases—that is, with so-called higher animals—the similarity is extremely high in complex and sophisticated detail both physically and functionally. Next, do humans and nonhuman animals exhibit similar behavioral responses to stimuli? Again, the answer is "Yes, to a remarkably high and complex degree of similarity in many cases." Next, we want to determine whether these similarities are relevant to the conclusion Singer is trying to draw. And it seems that they are, because we have good theoretical grounds and empirical evidence to suppose that a body's neurophysiology is the central mechanism involved in an organism's sensory experience, and similarly good theoretical and evidentiary grounds to connect behavioral manifestations to inner experience. So we would make the following preliminary assessment:

Singer's Argument	Analogue	Target	Degree of Similarity or/ Difference	Relevance
Basic points of similarity used as premises	Central nervous system basic to physiology of sensory experience of pain	Central nervous system basic to physiology of sensory experience of pain	High degree of similarity	Highly relevant to conclusion
	Expressive behavioral responses to sensory stimuli	Expressive behavioral responses to sensory stimuli	High degree of similarity	Highly relevant to conclusion
Conclusion	Humans enjoy pleasure and suffer pain	Nonhuman animals enjoy pleasure and suffer pain		
Differences				

At this point we would want to determine whether there are significant relevant differences between the analogue and the target. And, of course, there are many differences between humans and other species, several perhaps that people might think relevant to Singer's conclusion. For example, Singer goes on in the essay from which the example was taken to consider the issue of language. Now there may be some controversy over the question whether humans are the only species of animal with the capacity to develop and use languages. But for the sake of the argument let's suppose that this difference genuinely does obtain. Now the question is whether this is a relevant difference. Singer argues that it is not because we do not attribute pain to human beings on the basis of their linguistic behavior but more so on the basis of the sorts of behavior exhibited by other species of animal. So, on this basis we judge Singer's argument to be, like Ayer's quite strong:

Singer's Argument	Analogue	Target	Degree of Similarity or/ Difference	Relevance
Basic points of similarity used as premises	Central nervous system basic to physiology of sensory experience of pain	Central nervous system basic to physiology of sensory experience of pain	High degree of similarity	Highly relevant to conclusion
	Expressive behavioral responses to sensory stimuli	Expressive behavioral responses to sensory stimuli	High degree of similarity	Highly relevant to conclusion
Conclusion	Humans enjoy pleasure and suffer pain	**Nonhuman animals enjoy pleasure and suffer pain**		
Differences	Human beings have linguistic capacity	Nonhuman animals do not have linguistic capacity	Plausible, though open to question	Irrelevant to conclusion

REFUTATION BY ANALOGY

One use of analogy that deserves special mention is the refutation of arguments by comparison. In this strategy the target is usually an argument (occasionally the thesis of an argument) and the goal is to discredit the target by showing that it is analogous to some other argument (or thesis) that is obviously weak or objectionable. In the following passage from *Alice in Wonderland*, Alice gets refuted by the Mad Hatter and the March Hare. The Mad Hatter has told Alice, who has just said something illogical, that she should "say what she means":

"I do," Alice hastily replied; "at least—at least I mean what I say—that's the same thing, you know."

"Not the same thing a bit!" said the Hatter. "Why, you might just as well say that 'I see what I eat' is the same thing as 'I eat what I see'!"

"You might just as well say," added the March Hare, "that 'I like what I get' is the same thing as 'I get what I like'!"[9]

In Chapter 6 we used an example of refutation by formal analogy and explained the concept of a formal fallacy when we compared the two arguments below:

(1) All Americans are human.	(1) All men are human.
(2) All Californians are human.	(2) All women are human.
∴ (3) All Californians are Americans.	∴ (3) All women are men.

And we presented a strategy for demonstrating an argument to be formally fallacious by constructing a formally analogous argument, that is, one that follows an identical formal pattern but has obviously true premises and an obviously false conclusion.

ADDITIONAL EXERCISES

■ **EXERCISE 8.10**   Suppose we were to evaluate the sample in each of the following inductive generalizations. Highlight those among the listed dimensions that would in your opinion be relevant to the generalization and would need to be "controlled" to make the sample more "representative." Compare your answers with those of your classmates. Try to resolve any and all points of disagreement rationally, by explaining your answers to each other.

"In Consumers' Union nationwide studies of new cars purchased over the last 10 years, Chrysler had a 30 percent lower frequency of repair rate than the other manufacturers. So we're probably safe to assume that a new Dodge will be reliable."

- the color of the car
- the age of the principal driver of the car
- the price paid for the car
- the number of miles driven annually
- the size of the car
- the size of the owner's family
- the trim package
- the brand of gasoline used in the car

"Look! The first 10 people to come out of the theater are all smiling and laughing. I guess this is going to be a good show!"

- the ages of the people
- the gender identities of the people
- the racial identities of the people
- the ethnic identities of the people
- the religious affiliations of the people
- the economic status of the people
- the political affiliations of the people
- the class status of the people

■ **EXERCISE 8.11**   Identify and explain as many analogies as you can find in each of the following passages. For each analogy, specify the analogue and the target as well as the purpose (argumentative, explanatory, entertaining, etc.) of the comparison.

- "Well, thish-yer Smiley had rat-tarriers, and chicken cocks, and tom-cats, and all them kind of things, till you couldn't rest, and you couldn't fetch nothing for him to bet on but he'd match you. He ketched a frog one day, and took him home, and said he calculated to educate him; and so he never done nothing for three months but set in his back yard and learn that frog to jump. And you bet he did learn him, too. He'd give him a little punch behind, and the next minute you'd see that frog whirling in the air like a doughnut."[10]

- "So, we need a bit of theory to support, to guide, and to explain our evaluative intuitions. For theoretical purposes we'll make a basic distinction between the structural features of an argument and the materials used in its construction. One way to understand this distinction is to think of an argument as a building. Now suppose we are evaluating buildings; for example, suppose we're buying a house. Some houses are obviously and intuitively better built than others. We can tell 'intuitively' that the White House is a stronger building than the outhouse. But we need a more systematic set of criteria to make reasonable decisions where houses are more closely matched. Buildings are complicated, so there are many criteria relevant to evaluating buildings. That's why we would want to make the set of criteria 'systematic.' The system gives us organization. One way to organize is to divide. And with buildings, a reasonable and powerful first distinction for purposes of evaluation would be between the materials used and how those materials are put together—the design and the execution of the design. So also in evaluating arguments we could look at 'design factors' and 'materials factors.' In this comparison (or 'analogy') the 'materials' are the premises of the argument, the 'design' is the plan according to which the premises are assembled in support of the conclusion."[11]

- "Up to this point we've talked about accents and rests of the same length. But what do musicians like to do most with rhythms? Well, we like to do what everybody likes to do. We like to play. That's right. In basketball, when we first learned how to dribble, it was an achievement just to bounce the ball in a steady motion. You know, you could spend a long time just learning to bounce the ball in one unchanging rhythm. It might take two weeks to learn how to do that comfortably, or a month. But in order to have fun playing, we have to vary the bounces with accents and rests. In a game you would want to fake out an opponent. You wouldn't dribble only at one speed, or in the same predictable rhythm. Sometimes you would go fast, sometimes a little slower, and then maybe real quick between your legs or behind your back. And then sometimes you'd stop dribbling and pass the ball. In a basketball game we dribble the ball to go from one point on the court to another, we hope closer to the basket, and of course we always want to dribble with imagination and style. If you're not going to have imagination and some type of style, it doesn't make sense to play. In music we play with rhythms from tiny fast ones to long slow ones, just like dribbling the ball."[12]

- "When someone writes a piece of music, what he or she puts on the paper is roughly the equivalent of a recipe—in the sense that the recipe is not the food, only instructions for the preparation of the food. Unless you are very weird, you don't eat the recipe. If I write something on a piece of paper, I can't actually 'hear' it. I can conjure up visions of what the symbols on the page mean, and imagine a piece of music as it might sound in performance, but that sensation is nontransferable; it can't be shared or transmitted. It doesn't become a 'musical experience' in normal terms until 'the recipe' has been converted into wiggling air molecules. Music, in performance, is a type of sculpture. The air in the performance space is sculpted into something. This 'molecule-sculpture-over-time' is then 'looked at' by the ears of the listeners—or a microphone."[13]

■ **EXERCISE 8.12**   Evaluate each of the following analogy-based arguments using the tools and procedures outlined in this chapter.

Putting up a traffic light after last week's deadly accident is like locking the barn door after the horse has been stolen.

	Analogue	Target	Comment
Basic points of similarity used as premises			
Conclusion			
Differences			

"Last spring, when Arsenio Hall's new sitcom was yanked from the lineup after a handful of showings, the comic appeared on *The Late Show with Tom Snyder* and told the host that the show was being 'retooled.' This did not mean that Arsenio had been cancelled, he insisted, but only sent back to the shop for more work. Hall ingeniously explained that a flawed sitcom was like an aircraft, which was much easier to repair while parked on the ground than in mid-flight."[14]

	Analogue	Target	Comment
Basic points of similarity used as premises			
Conclusion			
Differences			

One of the most well known instances of argument by analogy is the famous teleological argument for the existence of God. As formulated by the 18th-century theologian William Paley, the argument goes something like this:

> Suppose we happened to find a watch lying on the ground in the woods, or on the moon. How could we explain it? Unlike a rock, which we could easily imagine to have just been lying there indefinitely, a watch, we would be forced to conclude, was the product of some intelligent designer, because no other explanation would be adequate to account for the marvelous degree to which the parts and features of the watch seem to be designed, adapted and coordinated for the purpose of telling time. But now compare the watch to the natural universe or to organic phenomena in the natural universe such as the human eye. The human eye, like the watch, is a complex organ whose parts, like the parts of a watch, seem marvelously well adapted and coordinated for the purpose of enabling visual experience. So it is reasonable to suppose that the human eye, and other similar phenomena in nature, and indeed the entire natural universe, are the products of an intelligent designer: God.

	Analogue	Target	Comment
Basic points of similarity used as premises			
Conclusion			
Differences			

■ **EXERCISE 8.13**   Identify areas within the context of the issue you have been working on where generalizations or statistics would be relevant. Identify reliable sources for such information. Pick one such application of inductive reasoning and design the sort of research program or experiment that would be likely to yield reliable results. Next, take any position on the issue you have been working on and design an argument in support of that position based on an analogy. Then take an alternative or opposed position and design an argument in support of it based on an analogy.

GLOSSARY

analogue   an item used as a basis of comparison in an explanation or argument by analogy

analogy   a comparison

inductive generalization   a variety of inductive reasoning in which general conclusions are projected from a number of particular instances

margin of error   estimate of the likelihood of error in the conclusion of an inductive inference

plausibility   a measure of an idea's likelihood of surviving critical scrutiny

population   the set of instances about which general conclusions are projected in an inductive or statistical generalization

relative   as applied to inferential security, means "admits of degrees"

relevance   in inductive reasoning refers to factors that might reasonably be thought to have something to do with the conclusion being inferred

sample   particular observed instances used in inductive or statistical generalizations

sample size   a measure of the number of particular observed instances relative to the population in an inductive or statistical generalization

statistical generalization   a variety of inductive reasoning in which trends or percentages observed in the sample are projected onto other instances or onto the population as a whole

target   an item about which conclusions are drawn or explanations are offered by analogy

ENDNOTES

[1] Wynton Marsalis, *Marsalis on Music* (New York: Norton, 1995), p. 20.

[2] John Allen Paulos, *Innumeracy: Mathematical Illiteracy and Its Consequences* (New York: Hill and Wang, 1988), pp. 9–10.

[3] Thomas Reid, *Essays on the Intellectual Powers of Man,* Essay 1, Chapter 4.

[4] Alfred J. Ayer, "One's Knowledge of Other Minds," *Theoria,* 19 (1953).

[5] P. J. O'Rourke, "Why I Believe What I Believe," *Rolling Stone,* July 13–27, 1995.

[6] Geoffrey Nunberg, *The Way We Talk Now* (Boston: Houghton Mifflin, 2001), p.130.

[7] Peter Singer, *New York Review of Books,* April 5, 1973.

[8] Wynton Marsalis, *Marsalis on Music,* p. 26.

[9] Lewis Carroll, *Alice's Adventures in Wonderland,* Chapter 7.

[10] Mark Twain, "The Celebrated Jumping Frog of Calaveras County."

[11] Joel Rudinow and Vincent Barry, *Invitation to Critical Thinking* (Belmont, CA: Wadsworth, 2003), pp. 145–146.

[12] Wynton Marsalis, *Marsalis on Music,* pp. 26–27.

[13] Frank Zappa, "All About Music," *The Real Frank Zappa Book* (New York: Poseidon, 1989), p. 161.

[14] Joe Queenan, "The Retooling Channel," *TV Guide,* July 26–August 1, 1997.

CHAPTER 9

Evaluating Inductive Arguments II: Hypothetical Reasoning and Burden of Proof

"When you believe in things that you don't understand, then you suffer. . . .
Superstition ain't the way." STEVIE WONDER

As we explained in Chapter 8, the evaluation of inductive inferences is based on assessing their relative security, which depends on a number of variables, according to the *type* of inductive reasoning involved. In this chapter we will explore two more important and common categories or types of inductive reasoning: hypothetical reasoning and burden-of-proof arguments.

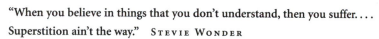

PRESUMPTION AND THE "BURDEN OF PROOF"

"Burden of proof" reasoning is a kind of inductive reasoning useful in resolving disputes that cannot be compromised or reconciled on a win/win basis—in other words, disputes between two parties or "sides" in which a winner must be declared. Many situations like this often arise in legal contexts. One of the most obvious and familiar examples of burden-of-proof reasoning is the "presumption

*"Let me tell you, folks—I've been around long enough
to develop an instinct for these things, and my client is
innocent or I'm very much mistaken."*

of innocence." In many, though by no means all, of the world's legal systems—
for example, in the American system of jurisprudence—the accused is presumed
innocent unless and until the prosecution meets its "burden of proof." The party
(or "side") with the burden of proof is the party (or "side") that has to produce
the argument. It is convenient to think of this as a procedural rule in a structured
contest according to which one side is assigned the role or position of "offense"
while the other side plays "defense." If the side that bears the burden of proof fails
to meet its obligation, the issue is decided in favor of the other side. Thus, in
American criminal law it is the prosecution that bears the burden of proof and
has to "make its case beyond a reasonable doubt." Meanwhile the defense need
not make any argument of its own beyond simply attacking the argument of the
prosecution and getting "the benefit of the doubt."

In most real-life situations, we will find that the procedural rules are already
established, and we just need to be competently informed what they are. Thus, as
jurors we are instructed by the judge what the rules are and how to weigh the evidence and arguments presented to us in court as we deliberate to a verdict. As
plaintiffs and defendants, we will ordinarily be advised by our attorneys what our
best argumentative strategy may be. But thinking of the burden of proof in this
way (as a procedural rule) raises the question of how we decide where—on
which side of any given issue—the burden of proof properly belongs. How is the
presumption of innocence or any other procedural rule of this kind justified?
Why, for example, does the prosecution have the burden of proof in American

criminal law? Why not the defense? Why shouldn't the accused have to prove his or her innocence? Another similar question concerns the size or "weight" of that burden. For example, the burden of proof is heavier in a criminal trial than in a civil trial. In a criminal trial the prosecution must prove guilt "beyond a reasonable doubt" (a deliberately vague but nevertheless very high standard of proof). In a civil trial, the plaintiff (the one who brings the lawsuit, the one making the complaint) has only the obligation of making a *prima facie* case, which then shifts the burden of proof onto the defense. One can imagine many alternatives to such arrangements—many different ways of formulating the procedural rules.

Let us approach these questions at the more general theoretical level. For example, if someone suggested that you invest a small sum of money in a mutual fund, you might want some evidence that the fund is well and profitably managed, but you'd want *more* evidence of the security of your investment if it represented your entire life savings. In general, the greater the risk of error—and the higher the cost of being wrong—the heavier the burden of proof. In general, then, the burden of proof is placed and the standard of proof is set where they "reasonably belong," which is to say where reasonable explanation and argument will support. Thus, the placement and apportionment of the burden of proof, like many of the concepts we have already encountered in this book, is governed by a number of general rules of thumb. One such rule is based on the concept of "plausibility" (as introduced in Chapter 4). In general, the less plausible the arguer's position, the heavier the burden of proof.

Another general rule, derived from the discipline and traditions of rhetoric, has to do with the distinction between the "affirmative" and "negative" positions in a debate. In general, the affirmative side in a debate has the burden of proof. The reason for this is that it is in general so much harder to "prove the negative." For example, someone who believes in the healing power of the mind, or the therapeutic efficacy of marijuana, or the existence of intelligent extraterrestrial life is expected to produce the evidence. All the affirmative side would need to do to prove conclusively that extraterrestrial intelligent life exists would be to bring forward one specimen. You can see how much harder it would be to prove *conclusively* that extraterrestrial intelligent life does *not* exist. So, in fairness, the general rule is to place the burden of proof on the affirmative position in a dispute.

Fairness is also behind the placement of the burden of proof on the prosecution in American criminal and civil law. In civil law it seems fair to place the burden of proof initially on the party making the complaint but then to have it shift to the other party if there's enough evidence to support reasonable suspicion. In criminal law the accused is (usually) an individual, whereas the prosecution is the "people" acting collectively through the agency of the government, and the stakes are almost always some form of punishment. Fairness seems to call for the prosecution to produce conclusive proof of guilt. There is another rationale for placing the burden of proof on the prosecution. Consider the question of how justice could be miscarried. It seems that there are only two kinds of miscarriage of justice: A guilty party gets off without penalty and an innocent party gets penalized. Which of these two kinds of miscarriage of justice is worse? Some legal traditions—the American system, for example—are based on the idea that it's worse to punish an innocent person than to let a guilty person go unpunished.

Not everyone agrees with this idea. Question: Is it worse to punish an innocent person than to let a guilty person go unpunished? Or is it the other way around? Or are the two equally bad? An interesting exercise would be to consider the arguments that might be made on all sides.

REASONING HYPOTHETICALLY

A subtle and complex, but crucial, variety of inductive reasoning consists in reasoning from facts or observations to explanatory hypotheses. An explanation is an idea or set of ideas that succeeds in reducing or eliminating puzzlement. An "explanatory hypothesis" is an idea or set of ideas put forward for that purpose. The word *hypothesis* means "supposition" or "conjecture." It comes originally from the Greek word *thesis,* which means "idea proposed or laid down for consideration," and the Greek root *hypo-,* which means "under." Here the "under" is meant to indicate that the proposed idea is "under investigation."

As the terms suggest, this variety of inductive reasoning, "hypothetical reasoning," is used primarily in trying to better understand the many puzzling things there are in life—the many things that prompt the question "Why?" Why is the water salty in the Pacific Ocean but not in Lake Tahoe? Why do so many incumbents continue to win reelection in spite of overwhelming anti-incumbent sentiment in the polls? Why does the Dow Jones index continue rising while fundamental economic indicators such as the unemployment rate indicate a recession? Why does the sound of an approaching train whistle appear to drop in pitch as the train passes by? We draw inferences to explanations constantly in all sorts of situations, and when we do, just as when we generalize, we risk error—that is, we reason inductively.

A simple example will illustrate the general structure of inferences to explanatory hypotheses. A customs inspector is examining the contents of a crate. In it she finds several plastic bags of white powder. What is it? Heroin? Cocaine? Flour? She tests it by tasting it and finds that it is sweet, identifying it as powdered sugar. We might represent her reasoning in the form of the argument or inference:

This tastes sweet.
_____

∴ This is sugar.

In identifying the powder as sugar, the customs inspector has not reasoned deductively. The conclusion does not follow deductively from the premise. But the inference from the taste of the substance to its classification is a reasonable induction. Though there remains room for doubt about the truth of the conclusion, the premise does make it *reasonable to suppose* that the conclusion is true. What makes the inference reasonable? How does the premise make it reasonable to suppose that the conclusion is true? What makes the inference reasonable is the idea that *if the conclusion were true, that would explain the truth of the premise—or—if the conclusion were not true, that would make the premise much more puzzling.* In other words, the observed fact that the substance tastes sweet *can be best explained* by assuming that it is sugar. This is the general structure of inferences to explanatory hypotheses, or hypothetical reasoning.

The importance of hypothetical reasoning lies in its capacity to extend or expand our knowledge of the world. Since hypothetical reasoning always takes us beyond what we already know, it always involves the risk of error. Just as with inductive generalizations, the strength of an inference to an explanatory hypothesis is essentially a matter of how well the risk of error is managed or controlled. There really is no way to manage the risk of error in hypothetical reasoning on an individual inference-by-inference basis. To manage the risk of error in hypothetical reasoning, we must engage in more and more of it—in effect, using hypothetical reasoning to evaluate hypothetical reasoning. More precisely, the risk of error is measured and managed in terms of the relative plausibility of competing explanatory hypotheses, their relative explanatory power, and the degree to which a given hypothesis can be supported by experimental evidence.

PLAUSIBILITY

In Chapter 4 we introduced the idea of plausibility as a measure of how well we think an idea is likely to survive critical scrutiny. How well would the idea hold up were we to devise strenuous tests designed to expose any falsity in the idea? A plausible idea is one that we think would hold up well. An implausible idea is one that we think would not hold up so well. Neither plausibility nor implausibility is "absolute." They both admit of degrees. Some claims are more plausible than others. A good place to look for examples to illustrate this point (implausible though this may sound) is in tabloids like the *National Enquirer*. In these publications you will find a steady diet of highly *im*plausible claims, like "Confederate Flag Sighted on Bottom of UFO" and "Elvis Presley Planning Return to United States from Seclusion in Brazil to Expose His Death as Hoax"; and a good many claims that are somewhat less implausible, like "Hypnosis Cures Urge to Smoke"; alongside a few claims that might be quite a bit more plausible, like "Madonna Has New Love Interest" or "Royal Family Locked in Power Struggle over Engagement of Prince William." Moreover, our estimates of a claim's plausibility or implausibility are not static. Rather, they are subject to adjustment in accordance with new incoming information. What may appear initially to be a plausible idea may, on further investigation, seem more and more or less and less plausible. And plausibility is only loosely correlated with truth. A plausible idea may well turn out not to be the case. And there are a good many cases throughout history of initially implausible ideas that have nonetheless been confirmed as true. *In general, the more plausible the explanatory hypothesis, the stronger the inference.* Here we are interested in *relative* plausibility. We need to know how the explanatory hypothesis under investigation compares with others. Is there another hypothesis that is just as or even more likely to survive critical scrutiny? If not, that strengthens the inference.

CRITICAL THINKING TIP 9.1

The more plausible the explanatory hypothesis, the stronger the inference.

For example, remember the customs inspector. As soon as she tastes the powder, she has occasion to consider the explanatory hypothesis that the powder is sugar. This, of course, is not the only hypothesis that might account for the observed fact that the powder tastes sweet. It could possibly be a new derivative of coca, genetically engineered to have a taste indistinguishable from powdered sugar so as to escape detection as a variety of cocaine. This hypothesis, if true, would account for the observed fact that the powder tastes sweet, and it is certainly within the realm of the "possible," but it is much less plausible than the simple powdered-sugar hypothesis.

Here's another hypothesis that might account for the observed fact that the powder tastes sweet. Perhaps the powder is cocaine and the customs inspector has suddenly developed a "taste blindness" so that cocaine and powdered sugar taste identical to her. Again, this hypothesis, if true, would account for the observed fact that the powder tastes sweet. This hypothesis, too, is within the realm of the "possible"—but, like the "sweet cocaine hypothesis," also much less plausible than the simple powdered-sugar hypothesis.

An interesting theoretical problem arises when you compare the taste-blindness hypothesis and the sweet-cocaine hypothesis against each other. Is one of them more plausible than the other? If so, which one? Or are they equally implausible? How do we tell? In this case it doesn't matter a whole lot, since there's a much more plausible option available in the simple powdered-sugar hypothesis. But what if we had to choose between competing hypotheses that seemed about equally plausible—or equally implausible? Or what if we couldn't agree which of several competing hypotheses was the most plausible—or the least plausible? Fortunately plausibility is not the only standard we have to appeal to.

EXERCISE 9.2 | Plausibility

Topic for Class Discussion: Several theories have arisen since the assassination of President Kennedy, which remains shrouded in mystery and controversy nearly 40 years after the fact. Rank the following theories in descending order of plausibility. Compare your rankings with those of your classmates. Try to resolve any points of disagreement by explaining your answers to each other.

	Lee Harvey Oswald, acting alone, assassinated the President.
	The assassination was planned and executed by the Mafia.
	The assassination was planned and executed by officials of the U.S. government.

	The assassination was planned and executed by officials of the U.S. government in collaboration with the Mafia.
	The assassination was planned and executed by officials of a foreign government.
	The assassination was planned and executed by officials of a foreign government in collaboration with officials of the U.S. government.
	The assassination was carried out by aliens from outer space.

EXPLANATORY POWER

Remember that an explanatory hypothesis is an idea or set of ideas put forward to reduce or eliminate puzzlement. And a good explanation is one that succeeds in reducing or eliminating puzzlement. The "explanatory power" of a given hypothesis is the capacity it has to reduce or eliminate puzzlement. *In general, the greater the explanatory power of a given hypothesis, the stronger the inference.* Here, as with plausibility, we are interested in *relative* explanatory power. We need to know how the explanatory hypothesis under investigation compares with others. Is there another hypothesis that would explain the observed fact(s) in the premise(s) equally well or better? If not, that strengthens the inference. Are there other observed facts besides the one(s) in the premise(s) that the hypothesis explains better than competing hypotheses? If so, that, too, strengthens the inference.

CRITICAL THINKING TIP 9.2

The greater the explanatory power of a given hypothesis, the stronger the inference.

For example, consider the following case: The neighbors have discovered the body of a well-known but reclusive novelist. The homicide inspector arrives at the scene. The body of the deceased is slumped over the typewriter, in which there is a sheet of paper with what appears to be an unfinished suicide note. Beside the body is a hypodermic syringe. Traces of white powder are recovered from the table beside the typewriter. The autopsy establishes the cause of death as heroin overdose and fixes the time of death at around 3:00 A.M. A psychiatric history of the deceased reveals several bouts of depression over a 10-year period and two previous suicide attempts. One plausible hypothesis, the obvious one, is that the novelist committed suicide by injecting himself with heroin and lost consciousness while at the typewriter composing the suicide note. Still, the inspector is puzzled. She cannot account for the fact that the typewriter, an IBM Selectric, is switched off. Nor can she account for the fact that neither the reading lamp nor the overhead light was on in the room at the time the body was discovered. If the novelist died at 3:00 A.M. while typing, how did he manage to turn off the typewriter and all of the lights?

What the inspector needs now is an explanatory hypothesis with greater explanatory power. Perhaps the novelist was murdered by someone who tried to make the murder look like a suicide. Perhaps the murderer was surprised at the scene of the crime by approaching footsteps, and, in order to discourage the approaching party from intruding upon the scene and discovering the crime, turned off the lights and the typewriter. This hypothesis, though not nearly as plausible as the suicide hypothesis, nevertheless has greater explanatory power because it accounts for everything that the suicide hypothesis accounts for plus the fact that the typewriter and lights were switched off.

Just as with plausibility, a theoretical problem arises in connection with explanatory power when we have to compare competing hypotheses that seem about equally powerful, or when we can't agree which of several competing hypotheses is the most powerful. Just as with the earlier problem, we can appeal to the plausibility standard when the explanatory power standard is not decisive. But we're still left with the problem of what to do when competing hypotheses seem to measure up roughly equally in both areas. And there is another theoretical problem. In our present example, the murder hypothesis is less plausible but more powerful as an explanatory hypothesis. This raises the question: How do we determine the strength of a hypothetical inference when our standards conflict? Does explanatory power outweigh plausibility? Or is it the other way around? Or does it depend? Maybe explanatory power outweighs plausibility when the explanatory-power-gap is bigger than the plausibility-gap, and vice versa. It would be nice if there were a good answer to this question that is both simple and straightforward. But as far as we know, the best approach to resolving any of these problems is just to test hypotheses experimentally.

EXERCISE 9.3 | **Explanatory Power**

Topic for Class Discussion: Here once again are the theories mentioned in Exercise 9.2. This time rank the theories in descending order of explanatory power. Compare your rankings with those of your classmates. Try to resolve any points of disagreement by explaining your answers to each other.

	Lee Harvey Oswald, acting alone, assassinated the President.
	The assassination was planned and executed by the Mafia.
	The assassination was planned and executed by officials of the U.S. government.
	The assassination was planned and executed by officials of the U.S. government in collaboration with the Mafia.

	The assassination was planned and executed by officials of a foreign government.
	The assassination was planned and executed by officials of a foreign government in collaboration with officials of the U.S. government.
	The assassination was carried out by aliens from outer space.

TESTING HYPOTHESES

The word *hypothesis* means an idea (or set of ideas) "under investigation." To investigate hypotheses is to search for experimental evidence relevant to their truth or falsity. And the "scientific method" for doing this boils down to first using the hypothesis under investigation to predict things, and then seeing whether or not the predictions turn out to be true. *If what the hypothesis predicts turns out to be true, that counts in favor of, or "confirms," the hypothesis. If what the hypothesis predicts turns out not to be true, that counts against, or "disconfirms," the hypothesis.*

For example, let's go back to the customs inspector's first hypothesis, that the white powder is sugar. What else do we know about sugar that we could use to test this hypothesis? We know that sugar is soluble in water. So, using the hypothesis, along with this knowledge, we might predict that the powder will dissolve in water. Now if we place the powder in water and it does dissolve, this counts as evidence confirming the hypothesis that the powder is indeed sugar. If we place the powder in water and it does not dissolve, this counts as evidence disconfirming the hypothesis that the powder is sugar. Confirming and disconfirming evidence each vary in strength according to the strength of the prediction involved. *The more certain the prediction, the stronger the evidence. In testing hypotheses, we should search for both confirming and disconfirming evidence.*

In quite a few cases we may expect to find evidence of both kinds. For example, in the case of the deceased novelist there is some evidence that confirms the suicide hypothesis and some evidence that disconfirms it. Naturally, we would be interested in the relative weight of the evidence for and against a given hypothesis. At first there seems to be more evidence in favor of the suicide hypothesis than there is against it. But when the disconfirming evidence first emerges, the homicide inspector quite correctly becomes suspicious. She not only begins to consider other hypotheses but also begins to focus her investigation in search specifically of more evidence disconfirming the suicide hypothesis. Why does she proceed in this way instead of simply concluding that the suicide hypothesis is correct because there is more confirming evidence than disconfirming evidence? The homicide inspector is following the general principle that *disconfirming evidence weighs more heavily than confirming evidence.*

Disconfirming evidence weighs more heavily than confirming evidence.

Why does disconfirming evidence outweigh confirming evidence? Again, let's consider the customs inspector and the white powder. To test the sugar hypothesis, we derived the prediction that the powder will dissolve in water. And so, if it does, we have confirming evidence; if it does not, disconfirming evidence. Confirming evidence does not completely verify the hypothesis. But notice that disconfirming evidence completely refutes it. Here's why. Our prediction that the powder will dissolve takes the form of the hypothetical statement:

If our hypothesis that the powder is sugar is correct, then the powder will dissolve in water.

When our test confirms the hypothesis, what we observe is, in effect, the consequent of this hypothetical statement coming true:

The powder does dissolve in water.

You'll remember that from these two statements we cannot validly deduce the conclusion that the powder is sugar. If we simply inferred this as a conclusion, we would be committing the fallacy of affirming the consequent. This makes sense when you consider that there may well be other white powdered substances (like artificial sweeteners) that taste sweet and dissolve in water. Nevertheless, the combination of the two statements does, in this sort of situation, provide relevant though not absolutely conclusive evidence in support of the hypothesis under investigation. On the other hand, when our test disconfirms the hypothesis, what we observe is, in effect, the negation of the consequent coming true:

The powder does not dissolve in water.

You'll remember that from these two statements we can validly deduce the conclusion that the powder is not sugar by modus tollens. This is why disconfirming evidence is stronger than confirming evidence, and also why this inferential method is often referred to as the "hypothetical deductive" method.

An interesting application of the principle that disconfirming evidence outweighs confirming evidence generates an additional form of confirming evidence. If we search thoroughly for disconfirming evidence and find none, that in itself constitutes a kind of confirming evidence. This is sometimes referred to as "indirect confirmation." Every *unsuccessful* attempt to falsify a hypothesis has the effect of strengthening it. This is why scientists try so hard to *disprove* their hypotheses. Every time they fail, the hypothesis succeeds.

EXERCISE 9.4 | Testing Hypotheses

Essay Assignment: The following is an argument from businessman (and former presidential candidate) H. Ross Perot. Write a short essay in which you explain Perot's argument using the concepts discussed above. What hypotheses is Perot considering? What evidence does he present? Explain how Perot is using the evidence to confirm or disconfirm the hypotheses he's considering.

> "We have unfairly blamed the American worker for the poor quality of our products. The unsatisfactory quality is the result of poor design and engineering—not poor assembly. If you take a car made in Japan by Japanese workers and place it alongside a Japanese car made in a U.S. plant by U.S. workers (led by Japanese executives) there is no difference in quality. The Honda cars made in this country by U.S. workers are of such high quality that Honda intends to export them. Obviously the American worker is not the problem. The problem is failure of leadership."

CAUSAL REASONING

One of the most widespread and important applications of hypothetical inductive reasoning has to do with figuring out how things work—determining the causes and effects of things. Why is the left channel of the stereo intermittently fuzzy and distorted? What is causing that little clicking noise at 40 miles per hour? What will be the environmental, psychological, and social consequences of the development of virtual-reality technology? These are typical of the kind of causal reasoning problems we encounter so frequently in so many aspects of our lives. But reasoning about causes and effects is tricky. First of all, as the 18th-century Scottish philosopher David Hume pointed out, we never directly observe causal relationships. We have to infer them. Next, we can never infer them with deductive certainty. Since the evidence for a causal relationship is always indirect, there will always be some room for doubt when we infer a cause. In other words, we must reason inductively about them. Finally, reasoning about causes by means of simple inductive generalization turns out not to be very reliable because inductive generalization by itself provides no basis for distinguishing between a causal relationship and a mere coincidence.

MILL'S METHOD OF AGREEMENT

The 19th-century English philosopher John Stuart Mill, best known for his work in moral and political philosophy, also made significant contributions to inductive logic, particularly in its applications to causal reasoning. Mill spelled out a number of guidelines—extensions of the above evaluative principles for inductive generalization—designed to make reasoning about causes and effects more reliable. These guidelines, often referred to as "Mill's Methods," are widely respected and followed as part of what we now call the "scientific method." Mill's method of agreement is a variation of simple inductive generalization. It consists of seeking out some common antecedent condition in all cases of the effect whose cause we are trying to determine. It is based on the (reasonable) assumption that *the cause will be present in every instance in which the effect occurs.* Thus, if we can identify some such common antecedent condition, it is a likely candidate for the cause.

Suppose, for example, that certain people start showing a strange new set of debilitating symptoms in several major cities at around the same time. What is the cause of the strange new disease? Right away we would want to know what these people have in common that might account for their symptoms. We know they live in different parts of the world. Let's suppose that no two individuals live within 500 miles of each other, that they range in age from 5 to 75 years old, that some of them are male, some female, that they have no common occupation, and so on. Now if we were to discover that all of the people suffering from these symptoms had traveled during the month of June to a particular vacation spot (let's call it Fantasy Island), then we might suppose that the cause of the symptoms is related in some way to vacationing on Fantasy Island in June. The accompanying table illustrates the method of agreement. Let the 10 "instances" represent the 10 individual cases under investigation, the letter *s* represent the "effect" of suffering from the symptoms, and the letters A, B, C, D, E, F, and G represent a range of antecedent conditions, F representing having vacationed on Fantasy Island in June.

MILL'S METHOD OF AGREEMENT

Instance	Antecedent Conditions							Effect
1	A	B		D	E	F		s
2	A		C		E	F	G	s
3		B		D	E	F	G	s
4			C	D	E	F		s
5	A	B				F		s
6				D		F	G	s
7						F		s
8	A	B	C	D	E	F	G	s
9	A	B				F		s
10			C			F	G	s

Of course, the fact that all of the symptom sufferers vacationed on Fantasy Island in June does not *prove* (deductively) a causal connection. But it does make it *reasonable to suppose* that such a causal relationship exists, and that is all we can expect from an inductive inference. If having vacationed on Fantasy Island were the *only* common factor we could find among all of the symptom sufferers, we could be even more confident of a causal connection. *In general, the more isolated the common antecedent condition, the more likely it is to be causally related to the effect.*

CRITICAL THINKING TIP 9.4: MILL'S METHOD OF AGREEMENT

In general, the more isolated the common antecedent condition, the more likely it is to be causally related to the effect.

MILL'S METHOD OF DIFFERENCE

The problem, of course, is that any collection of individuals will have not one but very many different antecedent conditions in common, most of which will turn out not to have any causal connection with the effect we are seeking to understand. In this example, having been on Fantasy Island in June together means having not just one but many things in common: exposure to common sources of food and water, exposure to the full range of substances and organisms present in the environment, including the other vacationers, and so on. So we need a way of narrowing the field, of eliminating some of the many candidates we're likely to identify by means of the method of agreement.

For this purpose Mill formulated the method of difference. The method of difference is based on the reasonable assumption that *the cause will be absent from every instance in which the effect does not occur.* To continue with our example, let us suppose that we get a list of all of the people who traveled to Fantasy Island in June and it turns out that some of them have not suffered any of the symptoms we're investigating. So next we would want to know what differences there are between these people and the symptom sufferers. Now suppose we discover that the Fantasy Island vacationers who did not get sick also did not go swimming. This would suggest that the cause of the symptoms has something to do with swimming.

The accompanying table illustrates the method of difference. Let the 12 "instances" represent the 12 individuals who vacationed on Fantasy Island in June, the letter *s* represent the "effect" of suffering from the symptoms, and the letters L, M, N, O, P, R, and S represent a range of activities like attending the luau, beach volleyball, cycling, drinking rum, and so on, S representing swimming.

METHOD OF DIFFERENCE

Instance	Antecedent Conditions							Effect
1	L	M	N	O	P	R	S	s
2	L		N	O	P		S	s
3	L	M	N	O	P		S	s
4		M		O	P	R	S	s
5	L	M	N		P	R	S	s
6	L	M	N	O	P	R	S	s
7	L	M		O		R	S	s
8			N	O	P		S	s
9	L		N	O	P	R	S	s
10	L	M		O	P	R	S	s
11	L	M	N	O	P	R	–	–
12	L	M	N	O	P		–	–

Like the method of agreement, the method of difference is a variation of sim-ple inductive generalization. Instead of looking for a correlation between in-stances of the effect and some common antecedent condition, here we are look-ing for a correlation between the *absence* of the effect and the *absence* of an antecedent condition. Like the method of agreement, the method of difference is not absolutely conclusive. The discovery of such a correlation—in this example between not having gone swimming and not suffering the symptoms—does not *prove* (deductively) that the symptoms and swimming are causally related, but it does make it reasonable to suppose that they are. If having gone swimming were the *only* difference we could find between the symptom sufferers and the vaca-tioners who did not get sick, we could be even more confident of a causal con-nection. *In general, the more isolated the difference, the more likely it is to be causally related to the effect.*

CRITICAL THINKING TIP 9.5: MILL'S METHOD OF DIFFERENCE

In general, the more isolated the difference, the more likely it is to be causally related to the effect.

Since the method of agreement and the method of difference each enhance the reliability of inductive inferences about causal relationships when used sepa-rately, it is reasonable to suppose that using them together in the same investigation (as in our example) would strengthen the inductive inference to a causal relationship even further. In other words, if some antecedent condition is *both* common to all instances of the effect whose cause is under investigation *and* absent from instances where the effect is also absent, that makes a causal connection even more likely.

METHOD OF CONCOMITANT VARIATION

Now suppose we turn up a Fantasy Island vacationer who went swimming but didn't get sick or a Fantasy Island vacationer who got sick but didn't go swimming. We saw earlier how the method of agreement is limited by the fact that any collection of individuals will have not one but many common antecedent conditions, most of which will have no causal connection with the effect we are seeking to understand. For this reason the method of agreement, by itself, is rarely adequate to identify the cause of any phenomenon. And we have now seen how the method of difference helps to identify the cause by a process of elimination. But the method of difference has a limitation of its own, which in turn limits the joint method of agreement and difference. The method of difference—and therefore also the joint method of agreement and difference—depends upon being able to observe instances from which a suspected cause is *absent*. To apply the method of difference we need to find, or experimentally bring about, an instance in which an antecedent condition that is suspected as a cause is out of the picture.

Let's suppose that by the method of agreement we have discovered that there are five antecedent conditions common to all instances in which the effect we're investigating has been observed. To apply the method of difference thoroughly we would need to be able to observe what happens when each of these five antecedent conditions is missing. And this is not always easy to do. Sometimes it's practically impossible. Mill's own example of isolating the cause of tides shows this. When it was suspected that one of the many antecedent conditions that accompanies the ebb and flow of the tides—the position of the moon—was the actual cause of tidal motion, it was nevertheless impossible to confirm this suspicion by the method of difference. As Mill said, "We cannot try an experiment in the absence of the moon, so as to observe what terrestrial phenomena her annihilation would put an end to."[1] To overcome this limitation Mill formulated the method of concomitant variation. When it is difficult or impossible to eliminate a suspected cause, it may nevertheless still be possible to *vary* it, or to observe its natural variations, and see whether these variations are accompanied by corresponding variations in the effect under investigation. In the case of the moon and the tides, it turns out that the closer the moon is to a particular coastal region, the higher the tide, and the further the moon is from a particular coastal region, the lower the tide, which makes it reasonable to suppose that there is a causal connection.

The accompanying table illustrates the joint method of agreement and difference supplemented by the method of concomitant variation for three instances of some effect *s*. The letters L, M, N, O, P, R, and S represent a range of antecedent conditions. By the method of agreement we determine that five of these conditions—L, N, O, P, and S—are present in all cases where *s* is observed. So these are our causal candidates. But there are no cases where any of these conditions, or the effect *s*, is absent. So we cannot isolate a cause by the method of difference. But each of the antecedent conditions varies in degree (represented by the plus and minus signs). And only one of them varies in a way that corresponds to variations in the effect. So that condition, O, is most likely to be causally connected to *s*.

MILL'S JOINT METHOD OF AGREEMENT
AND DIFFERENCE WITH CONCOMITANT VARIATION

Instance	Antecedent Conditions							Effect
1	L+	M	N−	O	P−	R	S+	s
2	L		N+	O+	P		S−	s+
3	L−	M	N	O−	P+		S	s−

The method of concomitant variation is a widely used experimental strategy in the sciences. For example, pharmacology researchers routinely study the efficacy of experimental drugs by varying the dosage. If the observed effects on the alleviation of symptoms vary with the dosage, going up when the dosage is increased and going down when the dosage is decreased, that counts as confirmation of the causal efficacy of the drug. If the alleviation of symptoms does not vary with the dosage—if, for example, the symptoms are alleviated slightly with small doses, slightly more with slightly larger doses, but not at all with large doses—that would raise doubts about the causal efficacy of the drug. (See figure on p. 251.)

EXERCISE 9.5 | Causal Reasoning

Agenda for Class Discussion:

- Think of all the different areas of common routine human interest and concern within which causal reasoning plays a crucial role. Brainstorm a list of such areas.

- Now as a group, pick some phenomenon of common interest or concern to you whose cause(s) are not yet known.

- Now, develop a list of reasonable causal hypotheses.

- Finally, discuss the design of experiments to test these hypotheses.

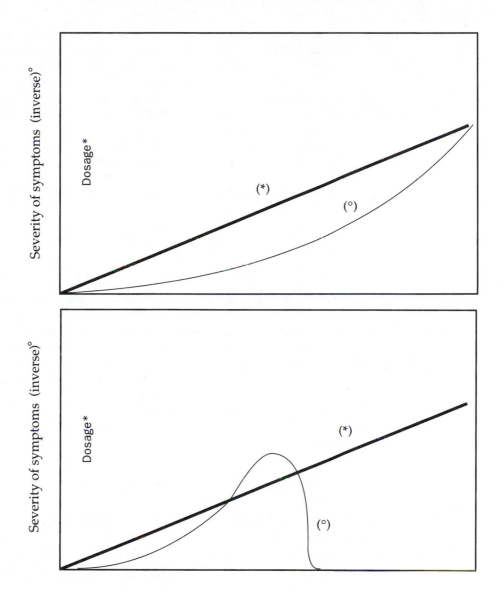

ADDITIONAL EXERCISES

■ **EXERCISE 9.6**   According to Paul and Nathalie Silver of the Carnegie Institute, California's "Old Faithful" geyser can predict large earthquakes within a radius of 150 miles. They argue for this conclusion on the basis of a 20-year record of geyser eruptions. Ordinarily, the geyser erupts at very regular intervals (which is why it came to be known as "Old Faithful"). On the day before the Oroville earthquake of August 1, 1975, the interval between geyser eruptions suddenly changed from 50 minutes to 120 minutes. In 1984 the geyser was erupting every 40 minutes. But the day before the April 24 Morgan Hill tremor, the pattern became irregular, fluctuating between 25-, 40-, and 50-minute intervals. A change was also noted before the 1989 Loma Prieta quake in the San Francisco area. Two and a half days before the quake, eruption intervals at the geyser suddenly shifted from 90 minutes to 150 minutes. The researchers noted that a number of things, including rainfall, can affect the regularity of eruptions in geysers. However, an analysis of rainfall amounts in the Calistoga area rules this out as an explanation of the abrupt pattern changes preceding each of these earthquakes.

Evaluate the evidence and the reasoning involved here. What strengths can you identify? What weaknesses? What kinds of further evidence would confirm the hypothesis that Old Faithful is an effective earthquake predictor? What kinds of further evidence would disconfirm the hypothesis? What kinds of experiments can you think of to discover such evidence?

■ **EXERCISE 9.7**   Fifteen years ago the upstart Fox television network surprised a lot of people in the television industry by running a rather primitively drawn cartoon about a dysfunctional family at the same time as the nation's consistently top-rated prime-time television program, *The Bill Cosby Show. The Simpsons* knocked *The Cosby Show* out of first place and went on to several successful seasons, establishing the Fox network as a force to be reckoned with. What accounts for the success of *The Simpsons*? Consider the following list of explanatory hypotheses in terms of plausibility and explanatory power. On this basis narrow the list down to two leading hypotheses. Describe the kinds of experimental evidence that would then be needed in order to choose between the two finalists.

- *The Simpsons* was more daring in its humor than the safe and mainstream *Cosby Show.*

- It was racism. *The Simpsons* is about a white family and *The Cosby Show* was about a black family.

- It was just a fluke.

- It was novelty appeal. *The Cosby Show* was getting old. People were looking for something new.

- *The Simpsons* was more challenging and rewarding intellectually than *The Cosby Show.*

■ **EXERCISE 9.8**   Using the concepts and terminology of Mill's Methods, explain how, in the following story from the history of medicine, 19th-century medical researcher Ignaz Semmelweis discovered and demonstrated the importance of physician hygiene in patient care.

Between 1844 and 1846, the death rate from a mysterious disease termed "childbed fever" in the First Maternity Division of the Vienna General Hospital averaged an alarming 10 percent. But the rate in the Second Division, where midwives rather than doctors attended the mothers, was only about 2 percent. For some time no one could explain why. Then one day a colleague accidentally cut himself on the finger with a student's scalpel while performing an autopsy. Although the cut seemed harmless enough, the man died shortly thereafter, exhibiting symptoms identical to those of childbed fever. Semmelweis formed the hypothesis that doctors and medical students, who spent their mornings doing autopsies before making their divisional rounds, were unwittingly transmitting to the women something they picked up from the cadavers. Semmelweis tested this hypothesis by requiring the doctors and students to clean their hands before examining patients. Doctors and students were forbidden to examine patients without first washing their hands in a solution of chlorinated lime. The death rate in the First Division fell to less than 2 percent.

■ **EXERCISE 9.9**   Identify areas within the context of the issue you have been working on where causal or hypothetical reasoning would be relevant. Formulate causal, interpretive, or other appropriate hypotheses. Evaluate these for plausibility and explanatory power. On this basis select a "leading hypothesis." Finally, design an experiment by means of which to test the leading hypothesis.

GLOSSARY

burden of proof   obligation to produce the argument in a dispute over an issue; failure to meet the burden of proof settles the issue in favor of the other side

confirming evidence   evidence consistent with what a hypothesis predicts

disconfirming evidence   evidence inconsistent with what a hypothesis predicts

explanatory power   an idea's capacity to reduce or eliminate puzzlement

hypothesis   an idea or set of ideas under investigation

hypothetical deductive method   a method of scientific investigation involving both hypothetical inductive reasoning and deductive reasoning

inductive generalization   a variety of inductive reasoning in which general conclusions are projected from a number of particular instances

joint method of agreement and difference   a principle of causal reasoning that combines the method of agreement with the method of difference

method of agreement   a principle of causal reasoning that consists of seeking out some common antecedent condition in all cases of the effect whose cause we are trying to determine

method of concomitant variation   a principle of causal reasoning that consists in varying a suspected cause and checking for corresponding variations in the effect, useful for situations where it is difficult or impossible to eliminate a suspected cause

method of difference   a principle of causal reasoning that consists in looking for a correlation between the *absence* of the effect and the *absence* of an antecedent condition

Mill's Methods   guidelines for reliable causal reasoning formulated by philosopher John Stuart Mill

plausibility   a measure of an idea's likelihood of surviving critical scrutiny

ENDNOTES

[1] John Stuart Mill, *A System of Logic,* Book III, Chapter 8, Section 6.

Evaluating Whole Arguments

CHAPTER 10

Evaluating Premises: Self-Evidence, Consistency, Indirect Proof

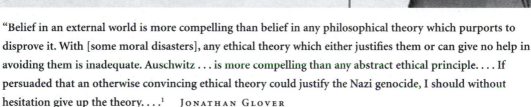

"Belief in an external world is more compelling than belief in any philosophical theory which purports to disprove it. With [some moral disasters], any ethical theory which either justifies them or can give no help in avoiding them is inadequate. Auschwitz . . . is more compelling than any abstract ethical principle. . . . If persuaded that an otherwise convincing ethical theory could justify the Nazi genocide, I should without hesitation give up the theory. . . .[1] JONATHAN GLOVER

In Chapter 6 we distinguished between the structural features of arguments and the materials out of which they are constructed. In Chapters 6 and 7 you learned how to evaluate deductive arguments structurally for validity. In Chapters 8 and 9 you learned how to assess the strength of inductive arguments. Now that you have studied the structural features of arguments in both of these two main argument-design categories, it's time to look at the standards and practices of evaluating premises. You'll be happy (we imagine) to know that there's not much new for you to learn at this stage about evaluating the premises of an argument. Because the premises of any argument are themselves each conclusions of subarguments—or potential conclusions of potential subarguments—evaluating the premises of an argument turns out to be more or less simply a matter of applying what you've already learned about issues and arguments. If there is support for a particular premise offered in the text of

the argument itself, then in effect what we have is a subargument whose conclusion is the premise we're interested in evaluating, and so we can evaluate the subargument. But eventually you will run into premises that aren't supported in the text of the argument itself. All arguments have to start somewhere, and this means that every argument will have unsupported premises in it.

In designing and constructing an argument, common sense would suggest we establish as firm a foundation as possible. So, experienced arguers generally try to use as their most "basic" premises claims that are as uncontroversial, as easy to accept, and as hard to challenge or refute as possible. For example, when Thomas Jefferson wrote in the Declaration of Independence, "We hold these truths to be self-evident," he meant, "Here are some basic premises we don't think we *need* to argue for. These are claims (for example, that basic human rights belong equally to each and every human being) that can and should be accepted at face value by any rational human being."

EXERCISE 10.1 | Topic for Class Discussion

Even if you agree with Jefferson that a claim as basic as "All people are equal when it comes to basic human rights" doesn't (or shouldn't) need to be argued for, it's still an interesting question: Why not? Do you think it's true that basic human rights belong equally to each and every human being? Suppose someone challenged this claim. How would you go about supporting a claim as basic as this?

All arguments have to start somewhere. But is there anywhere for an argument to start where it can move forward without having to back up? The problem Critical Thinking faces at this point is how to avoid an "infinite regress" of argument evaluation. "Infinite regress" means a kind of "bottomless pit" of premises supported by more premises, supported by more premises, and so on to infinity—so that it becomes logically impossible to complete the evaluation of any argument.

EXERCISE 10.2 | Topic for Class Discussion

One version of one of Zeno's famous "Paradoxes of Motion" goes like this: Try to go from wherever you are (Point A) to anywhere else (Point B). First you have to go half the distance from Point A to Point B. But before you can go half the distance from Point A to Point B you have to go half that distance. But before you can go half of half the distance from Point A to Point B you have to go half of that distance, and so on to infinity. So not only can you not ever go from Point A to Point B, you can't even start! Now, everybody knows from experience that motion is possible, so something's got to be wrong with the reasoning in Zeno's Paradox. What can it be?

Philosophers, and other theorists generally, tend to run from infinite regresses like the plague. In fact, there is a kind of general theoretical rule of thumb in many disciplines to the effect that if some hypothesis can be shown to lead to an infinite regress, then that hypothesis is untenable (must be considered incorrect). We can easily understand the urge to apply such a rule of thumb here in Critical Thinking. If there are no "first premises"—if the demand for deeper support can be made over and over at increasing levels of depth ad infinitum—then no resolution to any issue could ever be achieved. And that's not reasonable. Consequently, *some* way of avoiding an infinite regress of argument evaluation *must* be found. So it is worth inquiring whether there are "self-evident truths" beneath which the inquiry cannot or need not go. So, first, are there any claims that are *completely* beyond question or dispute?

NECESSARY TRUTHS

Are there *any claims at all,* available for use as premises, that *don't* require their own additional support?

EXERCISE 10.3 | Topic for Class Discussion

Try to deny the following claim:

   "Either the President knew of the arms-for-hostages deal before it was negotiated or he didn't." What do you notice when you attempt to deny this claim?

TAUTOLOGIES

Some people consider certain claims to be "necessarily true," meaning that these claims can't be denied in a coherent way. For example, when you try to deny the claim in Exercise 10.3, a contradiction results. To deny this claim would be in effect to say that the President both knew of the deal in advance and did not know of the deal in advance, which is logically impossible. What "logically impossible" means is that the impossibility can be traced to the logical form of the contradiction. Thus, *any* statement whose formal structure is "either P or not P" must necessarily be true, because the negation of any statement of the form "either P or not P" is self-contradictory (and therefore necessarily false). A claim that you can't deny without formally contradicting yourself is called a *tautology* and considered to be necessarily true. This can be demonstrated by means of a truth table:

P	~P	P v ~P	~(P v P)
T	F	T	F
F	T	T	F

But even though tautologies always carry the value "true," they don't convey much "information." The claim "either the President knew in advance or he didn't" doesn't by itself tell us very much, does it? For this reason, tautologies are often referred to as *"trivially* true." Nevertheless, they *can* occasionally play a crucial role in an argument. For example:

- Either the President knew in advance of the arms-for-hostages deal or he didn't.
- If he did know of the arms-for-hostages deal in advance, then he's involved in the cover-up and therefore unworthy of his office.
- If he didn't know of the arms-for-hostages deal in advance, then he's not in control of his own administration and is therefore unworthy of his office.
- Therefore, either way, he's definitely unworthy of his office.

EXERCISE 10.4 | **Topic for Class Discussion**

Do you think that Jefferson's claim that all men are created equal is a "tautology"? Do you think it is "trivially true"? Can you deny it without contradicting yourself?

TRUISMS BY DEFINITION

Are there any other kinds of statement that are "necessarily true"—that "cannot coherently be denied"? Perhaps there are. For example, consider the statement "Murder is a form of homicide," or "All bachelors are unmarried," or "'Phonetic' isn't." It seems it would be impossible to deny any of these statements without contradicting yourself, although this would be due not so much to the formal structures of the statements as to the meanings of the terms in them. Murder is, by definition, a subset of the larger category "homicide"; "unmarried" is part of the meaning of "bachelor"; and the word "phonetic" means "spelled the way it sounds." Thus, to deny any of these statements would be a "contradiction *in terms.*" So we would expect anyone who understands the meanings of the terms involved to immediately recognize any such statement as true. Such statements might be called "truisms by definition."

EXERCISE 10.5 | **Topic for Class Discussion**

Do you think that Jefferson's claim that all men are created equal is a "truism by definition"? Do you think it would be a "contradiction in terms" to deny it?

EXERCISE 10.6 | **Necessary Truths**

Sort the following statements into the following categories: (1) Tautologies; (2) True by Definition; (3) Formal Contradictions; (4) Contradictions in Terms; (5) Statements That Are Neither Necessarily True nor Self-Contradictory. Compare your results with those of your classmates. Be prepared to explain your answers.

	Tautologies	True by Definition	Formal Contradictions	Contradictions in Terms	Neither
A rectangle has four sides.		✓			
This rectangle has only three sides.				✓	
Either she's married or she's not married.	✓				
She is both married and unmarried.			✓		
She is either married or engaged.					✓
She is neither married nor engaged.					
Abortion is murder.					✓
Murder is wrong.					✓
White is a color.		✓			
White is a shape.				✓	
No statement that contradicts itself is true.		✓			
The White House is white.		✓			✓
This sentence has seven words in it.		✓			
This sentence has eight words in it.			✓		
All men are created equal.		✓			✓
Wherever you go, there you are.	✓	✓ ✓			
All arguments have to start somewhere.		✓			

CONTINGENT CLAIMS

==Most claims are neither self-contradictory nor necessarily true. Claims that are neither self-contradictory nor necessarily true are called *contingent*, meaning that their truth or falsity *depends on* something outside of themselves, something beyond their formal structures or the meanings of their terms.== Let's return now to consider Jefferson's "self-evident truth" that all men are created equal. Is it a tautology? If someone were to deny it, would that result in a formal contradiction? We think not. There is no formal inconsistency in the claim that "Not all men are created equal," or the logically equivalent claim "Some men are created unequal." Nor is Jefferson's claim that all men are created equal "trivially true," as we would expect a tautology to be. It seems to actually say something important. Is it true by definition? Would its denial constitute a contradiction in terms? Again, apparently not. So, by "self-evident" Jefferson evidently means something other than "necessarily true." Let's therefore suppose that Jefferson's "self-evident truth" that all men are created equal is a contingent claim. That would mean that its truth value depends on something outside its formal structure and the meanings of its terms. What does its truth value depend on?

Suppose someone were to deny the claim that all men are created equal. The first question to ask when we come to the evaluation of a contingent claim that has been used as an unsupported premise is: What *kind* of claim is being made here? Does the premise make a factual claim? An evaluative claim? Does it offer an interpretation? This is like asking: If someone were to challenge this claim, what sort of issue would that raise? A factual issue, an evaluative issue, an interpretive issue, a complex issue involving more than one of these categories? Thinking about these questions helps to determine what sorts of additional support may be needed to establish a given contingent claim as a premise in an argument.

EXERCISE 10.7 | Review

We highly recommend at this point that you review the section in Chapter 1 on issues and issue analysis. It's especially relevant at this point, and it may make even better sense now than it did at the beginning.

FACTUAL CLAIMS

As we pointed out in Chapter 1, most issues are complex and involve elements from all three issue categories. Factual issues often give rise to both evaluative and interpretive issues as well. Thus, establishing a particular premise as a "matter of fact" can turn out to be a tall and complicated order. For example, suppose we're trying to determine as a matter of fact what caused the stock market to suddenly lose 500 points. Right away we are deep into the realm of hypothetical reasoning with all of its nuances and complexities as described in Chapter 9, and a long way from anything that might be considered "self-evident." But there are many factual claims that are much simpler and more directly linked to our own firsthand experience. Thus, for example, in law, firsthand eyewitness testimony carries great weight in any fact-finding process. "I was there. I saw the crime being committed with my own eyes, . . . " sworn under oath and subject to the penalty for perjury, is very hard to overcome as evidence at trial. Even here, though, there are ways on occasion to undermine the force of eyewitness testimony. A witness's memory, or reliability as an observer, or sanity may be impeached, or there may be contradictory eyewitness testimony. So even eyewitness testimony, as probative and as fundamentally unassailable as it may be generally, can still be doubted and overturned, and therefore probably ought not be considered "self-evident." Still, perhaps there are *some* factual claims *so basic* that they might be considered "self-evident." Suppose, for example, you were to say,

My best friend is over 5 feet tall.

The claim made here is a contingent statement of fact. Its truth value depends upon the height of your best friend, something "out there in the world" that can be tested empirically, that is, by reference to sense experience, or to what scientists call "observations." Whenever scientists weigh, measure, or take the temperature of something, they are making observations. Then when they record or report these observations, they are making "observation claims." Suppose someone now challenges your claim that your best friend is over 5 feet tall. How do you respond? Well, suppose you say, "I'm 5'2" tall and my best friend is taller than I am, so my best friend is over 5 feet tall." Now suppose you are challenged to defend these two claims. How do you know you are 5'2" tall? The truth of this sort of observation claim in general would depend on the conditions under which the measurements had been made and so on. In this rather basic and simple instance it would be more than sufficient to know that you had been measured, when standing erect, using an accurate standard instrument of measurement, by someone who knew how to use it, in circumstances that didn't impair the user's performance. OK, so how do you know you were standing erect when your height was being measured? And how do you know your best friend is taller than you are? At some point, you wind up saying something like, "Look. There isn't anything *more basic* for me to appeal to here in support of this claim. We stand next to each other, and I look up and he looks down. That's all there is to it! It's a *basic observation!!* It's *self-evident!!!*" Notice that if you say something like this, you're also admitting that there *are indeed* further claims that you could appeal to in support of the observation that your best friend is taller than you are. You've even specified a little empirical experiment (standing next to each other) whose results support the claim. "Self-evident" in this context seems to mean something like this: The supporting claims are no more basic or evident than what they support. This may well be close to what Jefferson meant when he called the claim that all men are created equal "self-evident," but it is also pretty clearly evident that he was neither reporting a basic observation nor making any other sort of factual claim.

EVALUATIVE CLAIMS

Probably the best short answer to the question what sort of claim "all men are created equal" *does* express is a "basic moral principle," which would put it in the category of evaluative claims. And if the principle were challenged, the issue that would arise would be an evaluative issue. So, on what rational foundation are evaluative issues to be resolved? On what rational foundation are evaluative claims to be established as true? There is a widely held position (which we will call "values relativism") to the effect that it can't be done because of the essential difference and an unbridgeable gap between facts and values. Facts are "objective," values are "relative" or even "subjective." The best argument we can think of in support of values relativism goes something like this:

- Factual claims can be rationally supported empirically.
- This means they are established as true ultimately on the basis of verifiable observations.
- Evaluative claims cannot be rationally supported empirically, nor can they be derived from factual claims alone.
- There is no other basis besides empirical observations on which issues may be rationally resolved or claims rationally established as true.
- Therefore, there *is no* rational basis for the resolution of evaluative issues nor any rational foundation for the establishment of evaluative claims as true.

What we have to say about this view is an extension of what we said about relativism in Chapter 1.

EXERCISE 10.8 | **Review**

We highly recommend at this point that you review the section in Chapter 1 on relativism and limited relativism, under Obstacles to Critical Thinking (pp. 13–15).

Values relativism is a specific version of what we referred to in Chapter 1 as "limited relativism." As such it is inherently more reasonable and understandable than relativism in general, and even more reasonable still because evaluative issues—which *cannot* be resolved by doing science or looking things up—generally *are* harder to resolve than factual issues. Still, it doesn't follow from the fact that evaluative claims can't be established *empirically* that they can't be established at all. The weakness in the above argument for values relativism is in the last premise, which claims that there is no basis other than empirical observation on which issues may be rationally resolved or claims rationally established as true. We deny this claim. There *is* another rational basis for resolving issues and establishing claims as true: *by considering and evaluating the best available arguments on all sides of the issue (like we're doing here).*

In fact, we'll go a step further and argue that certain evaluative claims are already *much more firmly established as true* than certain factual claims are or can hope to be.

EXERCISE 10.9 | **Topic for Class Discussion**

Of the following two claims, which one is evaluative? Which one is factual? Which one do you think is more firmly established as true? Why?

1. Gandhi's political leadership of his people was morally superior to Hitler's political leadership of his.
2. There is intelligent extraterrestrial life elsewhere in our galaxy.

We think claim #1 clearly expresses a value judgment. Yet we think it is also much more firmly established as true than (clearly factual) claim #2 either is or will likely be in the foreseeable future. How can this be? Of course, it isn't *absolutely certain* that Gandhi's leadership of his people was morally superior to Hitler's. But even though this claim expresses a value judgment and even though it may yet be open to challenge and debate, we nevertheless consider it to be quite firmly established as true. How so?

EXERCISE 10.10 | **Facts and Values**

The following argument—or pair of arguments—adds up in our opinion to a very powerful and persuasive case, even though it is chock-full of evaluative claims. How many evaluative claims can you count? Highlight all the evaluative claims you can find. How many factual claims? Highlight all the factual claims you can find. Can you think of any counterarguments? How do the best counterarguments you can find—or think of— compare? Are they as powerful? Anywhere close?

- Gandhi led his people out of the bondage of colonial rule. He also guided that struggle away from violence. To do this required great courage and wisdom, saved a great many human lives, and provided a model to the world of an effective and humane way to engage in political struggle. Human life is precious. Freedom is better than colonial bondage as a way of life. Therefore, Gandhi was a great leader.

- By contrast, Hitler led his people into World War II. He directed his people to invade and forcibly occupy the territory of neighboring states. He directed his people to exterminate several million civilian noncombatants. He led the world to develop nuclear and other weapons of mass destruction. Human life is precious. Peace is precious. Therefore, Hitler was a terrible leader.

The example in Exercise 10.10 illustrates how it is in general that evaluative issues are resolved and evaluative claims established as true—*by considering and evaluating the best available arguments on all sides of the issue (like we're doing here).*

This brings us back to the problem posed at the beginning of this chapter—how to avoid an infinite regress of argument evaluation. In order to evaluate an argument we have to evaluate the premises. But in order to do that we have to evaluate arguments. Does one ever get to the bottom of this? Perhaps not. But once you learn how to swim you stop worrying about "getting (or sinking) to the bottom."

Let's not forget either that the infinite-regress problem arose also in connection with contingent statements of fact. Yet this does not prevent us from determining matters of fact. At some point, we encounter observation claims so "basic" that, even though we *could* go on to support them by appeal to further observations, these would be no more basic or evident than what they support. And so, unless there is *good* reason for doubting them, such claims may be taken as "self-evident." Similarly, with value judgments, at some point you get down to an evaluative claim so *basic* that, even if you *could* go on to support it with further arguments based on further claims, these arguments and claims would be no more convincing than the claims they support. So, even if we can't "get to the *absolute bottom*" of the theoretical heap of premises supported by other premises, supported by other premises, supported by other premises, perhaps we *do* eventually get to a level where the burden of proof shifts decisively in favor of some very basic claim.

EXERCISE 10.11 | **Topic for Class Discussion**

Pick any of the following evaluative claims. Compose (a) the best argument you can in support of it and (b) the best argument you can against it.

- Human life is precious.
- Peace is precious.
- Freedom is better than colonial bondage as a way of life.
- Basic human rights belong equally to each and every human being.

Take a claim like "Human life is precious." If all arguments have to start somewhere, this would be the sort of claim one would want to start with. It's not that one couldn't possibly argue in support of such a claim, but what would the argument add to the strength of the claim itself? Moreover, what sort of argument can be made against such a claim? The burden of proof does clearly fall on the challenger here. And for at least some such claims the burden of proof seems so substantial that intuitively it is hard to imagine how one might overturn it.

EXERCISE 10.12 | **Topic for Class Discussion**

Here is an argument in support of the claim that basic human rights belong equally to each and every human being. Compare the argument to the claim that it supports. Which do you find more convincing? The argument, or the conclusion itself?

1. Morality presumes consistency.
2. In other words, in the absence of a justification for differential treatment, all moral rules and considerations apply equally to all parties.
3. This includes basic human rights.
4. There is apparently no justification for differential treatment between individual human beings with respect to basic human rights.
5. Therefore, basic human rights belong equally to each and every human being.

Here is what we would say: The first two premises of the above argument *appear* to reach higher levels of generality and abstraction than the conclusion does, but that doesn't make them any more convincing than the conclusion itself. Premise #4 makes this a "burden-of-proof" argument, and as such inherently inconclusive. The conclusion itself is much more convincing on its face than *any* "burden-of-proof" argument. This is what we think Jefferson had in mind when he called his first premises "self-evident truths": not that they *can't* be argued for but that an argument has to start somewhere, and *these* claims seem as good as *any* candidates for the office of "first premise."

BEYOND "SELF-EVIDENCE"

By far, most claims you will find as premises in the arguments you encounter will be neither necessarily true nor self-evident. For example, we doubt that the question of "self-evidence" really arises in connection with interpretive claims. To recognize a given claim as an "interpretation" is to recognize the possibility of other interpretations and therefore also the presence of an interpretive issue. And this puts the claim beyond consideration as "self-evident." An interpretation, in other words, is the kind of claim one can always legitimately be challenged to argue for. Nor is there a single simple procedure for resolving interpretive issues. And so there is no single simple procedure for establishing interpretive claims as premises in an argument. Rather, as with evaluative claims and indeed with contingent claims generally, it is a matter of considering the best arguments that can be made for and against them and weighing up the arguments and the evidence on all sides. And again, don't worry too much about "getting to the bottom" of this process of rational evaluation of arguments in support of premises in arguments. Just do it.

Here are some additional techniques and strategies, using concepts we've already discussed. Following these procedures can streamline the process and significantly improve results.

CONSISTENCY

One of the most powerful tools for both formal and informal argument evaluation is the concept of consistency. Two statements are "consistent" if they *could* both be true. Two statements are "inconsistent" if there are no possible circumstances in which they could both be true. A group of statements is inconsistent if any two statements in the group are inconsistent. Not only is the concept of consistency crucial to our understanding of deductive validity, but because *inconsistency* is always a sign that something is wrong somewhere, it can also be applied to the evaluation of premises in several very useful ways. We used it above to explain the concept of a tautology as necessarily true. Similarly, just as a self-contradiction must necessarily be false, and hence its denial or negation necessarily true, a good rule of thumb is to check an argument's entire set of claims *as a group* for consistency. If a given *set* of claims as a group is internally inconsistent, then although you may not know *which* of the premises is false, you know they can't *all* be true.

Check for consistency. If an argument's premises are not internally consistent as a group, they can't all be true.

IMPLICATIONS

While the truth value of a claim remains to be determined, one effective strategy is to treat it hypothetically. That is, assume that the claim is true, and trace out its further implications. What follows logically from the claim? What further claims does it entail or lead us to suppose? The "implications" of a claim are those additional claims that either follow from it by logic or are strongly supported by it inductively. If a claim leads by implication to any further claim that is self-contradictory, or otherwise absurd or known to be false, then there is good reason to doubt the claim. This strategy has traditionally been known by its Latin name *reductio ad absurdum* (which means "to reduce to absurdity"). The strategy can also be inverted to use in defense of a position. This is sometimes referred to as the *method of indirect proof*. In this strategy we assume that the conclusion we want to argue for is *false*. We then trace the implications of that assumption, hoping to find that it leads to some absurd or contradictory conclusion. This then constitutes good reason to reject the original assumption, which leaves our hoped-for conclusion standing. Here is an example drawn from earlier in this chapter: *"If there are no 'first premises'—if the demand for deeper support can be made over and over at increasing levels of depth ad infinitum—then no resolution to any issue could ever be achieved. And that's not reasonable. Consequently, some way of avoiding an infinite regress of argument evaluation must be found."*

| **Topic for Class Discussion**

The following passage makes a host of interesting claims, each with its own set of implications. Trace the implications to highlight any apparent inconsistencies.

> *"Most therapies are dualistic. They try to do what seems good and to correct or avoid what seems bad. If they confuse good and bad, as they are sometimes bound to do, their attempt to do good will compound problems and make them harder to resolve. Non-dualistic therapy makes no value judgment about possible alternatives. It looks at the facts, does experiments, and views the results with an open mind. In this way, it is like science, while dualistic therapy is like moralism. Paradoxes should not disturb us. Awareness, if there is enough of it, can always reach the underlying unity of life and merge apparent opposites."[2]*

ADDITIONAL EXERCISES

EXERCISE 10.14   What are the most "basic" premises of each of the following arguments? Include in your analysis any hidden inferential assumptions. If these premises were challenged, how might they be defended?

- "According to modern physics, radio is our only hope of picking up an intelligent signal from space. Sending an interstellar probe would take too long—roughly 50 years even for nearby Alpha Centauri—even if we had the technology and funds to accomplish it. But radio is too slow for much dialogue. The most we can hope from it is to establish the existence (or, more accurately, the former existence) of another civilization."[3]

- How important are professional athletes to society? Not very. They're mere entertainers. They often present bad role models for children—for every Dave Dravecky there's a Pete Rose, or a Steve Garvey, or a Jose Canseco; for every Michael Jordan or Grant Hill there's a Dennis Rodman. And, given the attention they get, they tend to distract us from serious social concerns. At the very least then, the salaries of these prima donnas should be drastically reduced to reflect their social insignificance.

- "If a being suffers, there can be no moral justification for refusing to take that suffering into consideration, and, indeed, to count it equally with the like suffering (if rough comparisons can be made) of another being. So the only question is: Do animals other than man suffer? Most people agree unhesitatingly that animals like cats and dogs can and do suffer, and this seems also to be assumed by those laws that prohibit wanton cruelty to such animals."[4]

- "Proposition 215 will allow seriously and terminally ill patients to legally use marijuana, if, and only if, they have the approval of a licensed physician. We are physicians and nurses who have witnessed firsthand the medical benefits of marijuana. Yet today in California, medical use of marijuana is illegal. Doctors cannot prescribe marijuana, and terminally ill patients must break the law to use it. Marijuana is not a cure, but it can help cancer patients. Most have severe reactions to the disease and chemotherapy—commonly severe nausea and vomiting. One in three patients discontinues treatment despite a 50% chance of improvement. When standard anti-nausea drugs fail, marijuana often eases patients' nausea and permits continued treatment. . . . University doctors and researchers have found that marijuana is also effective in: lowering internal eye pressure associated with glaucoma, slowing the onset of blindness; reducing the pain of AIDS patients, and stimulating the appetites of those suffering malnutrition because of AIDS 'wasting syndrome'; and alleviating muscle spasticity and chronic pain due to multiple sclerosis, epilepsy, and spinal cord injuries. When one in five Americans will have cancer, and 20 million may develop glaucoma, shouldn't our government let physicians prescribe any medicine capable of relieving suffering? . . . Today, physicians are allowed to prescribe powerful drugs like morphine and codeine. It doesn't make sense that they cannot pre-scribe marijuana, too."[5]

- There are an estimated 2 billion children (persons under age 18) in the world. Since Santa Claus is apparently not responsible for visiting the Muslim, Hindu, Jewish, and Buddhist children, that reduces his workload to 15 percent of the total, or 378 million children, according to the Population Reference Bureau. As-suming an average of 3.5 children per household, that means 91.8 million homes (assuming at least one good child per household). Assuming Santa trav-els from east to west, and factoring in the earth's rotation and the different time zones, Santa has 31 hours of Christmas to work with. This works out to 823 visits per second, which means that Santa has a little more than 1/1000th of a second to park, get out of the sleigh, get down the chimney, fill stockings, distribute presents under the tree, eat the snacks left for him, get back up the chimney and into the sleigh and fly to the next house. Assuming each of the 91.8 million stops to be evenly distributed geographically, each stop would be .78 miles apart, which means that Santa's sleigh will be traveling at 650 miles per second, thousands of times the speed of sound. Assuming that each child gets nothing more than a medium-sized Lego set (approximately 2 pounds), the payload of the sleigh, not counting Santa, would be 321,300 tons. On land, conventional reindeer can pull about 300 pounds. Assuming even that "flying reindeer" could pull 10 times that amount, the team required to pull Santa's payload would be 214,200 reindeer, which increases the weight of the loaded sleigh and team to 353,430 tons (four times the weight of the *Queen Eliza-beth*). An object weighing 350,000 tons traveling at 650 miles per second cre-ates enormous air resistance, with resultant friction and heat, enough to va-porize a reindeer in about 4/1000ths of a second. In conclusion, if Santa ever did deliver presents on Christmas Eve, he's dead now.

■ **EXERCISE 10.15** *Essay Question:* One of the principles on which the American system of criminal justice is theoretically based is that it's worse to punish innocent people than to let guilty people escape punishment. This principle can be understood to express a value judgment. Do you agree with this principle and the value judgment it expresses? If so, formulate three distinct justifications for them. If not, construct three distinct justifications for rejecting them. Write a short essay in which you explain your position.

■ **EXERCISE 10.16**   Here are several justifications for the principle mentioned in Exercise 9.1. For each justification, identify the elements that appeal to consequences and those that appeal to principle. (Don't forget to consider missing premises.) Can you identify any elements that appeal neither to consequences nor to principle? What are the most "basic" premises of each of the above arguments? If these premises were challenged, how might they be defended? Which of the above arguments, a, b, or c, do you find most firmly persuasive? Explain why.

- When a society punishes an innocent person, it inevitably increases the unwarranted suffering in the world. It is always wrong to increase the unwarranted suffering in the world.

- When you punish an innocent person, you turn that person against society, and this leads to an increase in antisocial behavior.

- Punishing the innocent is inherently wrong because they've done nothing to deserve punishment. Letting the guilty escape punishment is inherently wrong because they don't get what they deserve. But punishing the innocent is worse because when you punish an innocent person, you are also letting a guilty person escape punishment.

EXERCISE 10.17   Check for overall consistency and trace the implications of this excerpt from George W. Bush's State of the Union address (January 29, 2002).

... As we gather tonight, our nation is at war, our economy is in recession, and the civilized world faces unprecedented dangers. Yet the state of our Union has never been stronger. (Applause.)

We last met in an hour of shock and suffering. In four short months, our nation has comforted the victims, begun to rebuild New York and the Pentagon, rallied a great coalition, captured, arrested, and rid the world of thousands of terrorists, destroyed Afghanistan's terrorist training camps, saved a people from starvation, and freed a country from brutal oppression. (Applause.)

The American flag flies again over our embassy in Kabul. Terrorists who once occupied Afghanistan now occupy cells at Guantanamo Bay. (Applause.) And terrorist leaders who urged followers to sacrifice their lives are running for their own. (Applause.)

America and Afghanistan are now allies against terror. We'll be partners in rebuilding that country. And this evening we welcome the distinguished interim leader of a liberated Afghanistan: Chairman Hamid Karzai. (Applause.)

The last time we met in this chamber, the mothers and daughters of Afghanistan were captives in their own homes, forbidden from working or going to school. Today women are free, and are part of Afghanistan's new government. And we welcome the new Minister of Women's Affairs, Doctor Sima Samar. (Applause.)

Our progress is a tribute to the spirit of the Afghan people, to the resolve of our coalition, and to the might of the United States military. (Applause.) When I called our troops into action, I did so with complete confidence in their courage and skill. And tonight, thanks to them, we are winning the war on terror. (Applause.) The men and women of our Armed Forces have delivered a message now clear to every enemy of the United States: Even 7,000 miles away, across oceans and continents, on mountaintops and in caves— you will not escape the justice of this nation. (Applause.) . . .

Our cause is just, and it continues. Our discoveries in Afghanistan confirmed our worst fears, and showed us the true scope of the task ahead. We have seen the depth of our enemies' hatred in videos, where they laugh about the loss of innocent life. And the depth of their hatred is equaled by the madness of the destruction they design. We have found diagrams of American nuclear power plants and public water facilities, detailed instructions for making chemical weapons, surveillance maps of American cities, and thorough descriptions of landmarks in America and throughout the world.

What we have found in Afghanistan confirms that, far from ending there, our war against terror is only beginning. Most of the 19 men who hijacked planes on September the 11th were trained in Afghanistan's camps, and so were tens of thousands of others. Thousands of dangerous killers, schooled in the methods of murder, often supported by outlaw regimes, are now spread throughout the world like ticking time bombs, set to go off without warning.

Thanks to the work of our law enforcement officials and coalition partners, hundreds of terrorists have been arrested. Yet, tens of thousands of trained terrorists are still at large. These enemies view the entire world as a battlefield, and we must pursue them wherever they are. (Applause.) So long as training camps operate, so long as nations harbor terrorists, freedom is at risk. And America and our allies must not, and will not, allow it. (Applause.)

Our nation will continue to be steadfast and patient and persistent in the pursuit of two great objectives. First, we will shut down terrorist camps, disrupt terrorist plans, and bring terrorists to justice. And, second, we must prevent the terrorists and regimes who seek chemical, biological or nuclear weapons from threatening the United States and the world. (Applause.)

Our military has put the terror training camps of Afghanistan out of business, yet camps still exist in at least a dozen countries. A terrorist underworld—including groups like Hamas, Hezbollah, Islamic Jihad, Jaish-i-Mohammed—operates in remote jungles and deserts, and hides in the centers of large cities.

While the most visible military action is in Afghanistan, America is acting elsewhere. We now have troops in the Philippines, helping to train that country's armed forces to go after terrorist cells that have executed an American, and still hold hostages. Our soldiers, working with the Bosnian government, seized terrorists who were plotting to bomb our embassy. Our Navy is patrolling the coast of Africa to block the shipment of weapons and the establishment of terrorist camps in Somalia.

My hope is that all nations will heed our call, and eliminate the terrorist parasites who threaten their countries and our own. Many nations are acting forcefully. Pakistan is now cracking down on terror, and I admire the strong leadership of President Musharraf. (Applause.)

But some governments will be timid in the face of terror. And make no mistake about it: If they do not act, America will. (Applause.)

Our second goal is to prevent regimes that sponsor terror from threatening America or our friends and allies with weapons of mass destruction. Some of these regimes have been pretty quiet since September the 11th. But we know their true nature. North Korea is a regime arming with missiles and weapons of mass destruction, while starving its citizens.

Iran aggressively pursues these weapons and exports terror, while an unelected few repress the Iranian people's hope for freedom.

Iraq continues to flaunt its hostility toward America and to support terror. The Iraqi regime has plotted to develop anthrax, and nerve gas, and nuclear weapons for over a decade. This is a regime that has already used poison gas to murder thousands of its own citizens—leaving the bodies of mothers huddled over their dead children. This is a regime that agreed to international inspections—then kicked out the inspectors. This is a regime that has something to hide from the civilized world.

States like these, and their terrorist allies, constitute an axis of evil, arming to threaten the peace of the world. By seeking weapons of mass destruction, these regimes pose a grave and growing danger. They could provide these arms to terrorists, giving them the means to match their hatred. They could attack our allies or attempt to blackmail the United States. In any of these cases, the price of indifference would be catastrophic.

We will work closely with our coalition to deny terrorists and their state sponsors the materials, technology, and expertise to make and deliver weapons of mass destruction. We will develop and deploy effective missile defenses to protect America and our allies from sudden attack. (Applause.) And all nations should know: America will do what is necessary to ensure our nation's security.

We'll be deliberate, yet time is not on our side. I will not wait on events, while dangers gather. I will not stand by, as peril draws closer and closer. The United States of America will not permit the world's most dangerous regimes to threaten us with the world's most destructive weapons. (Applause.)

Our war on terror is well begun, but it is only begun. This campaign may not be finished on our watch—yet it must be and it will be waged on our watch.

We can't stop short. If we stop now—leaving terror camps intact and terror states unchecked—our sense of security would be false and temporary. History has called America and our allies to action, and it is both our responsibility and our privilege to fight freedom's fight. (Applause.) . . .

This time of adversity offers a unique moment of opportunity—a moment we must seize to change our culture. Through the gathering momentum of millions of acts of service and decency and kindness, I know we can overcome evil with greater good. (Applause.) And we have a great opportunity during this time of war to lead the world toward the values that will bring lasting peace.

All fathers and mothers, in all societies, want their children to be educated, and live free from poverty and violence. No people on Earth yearn to be oppressed, or aspire to servitude, or eagerly await the midnight knock of the secret police.

If anyone doubts this, let them look to Afghanistan, where the Islamic "street" greeted the fall of tyranny with song and celebration. Let the skeptics look to Islam's own rich history, with its centuries of learning, and tolerance and progress. America will lead by defending liberty and justice because they are right and true and unchanging for all people everywhere. (Applause.)

No nation owns these aspirations, and no nation is exempt from them. We have no intention of imposing our culture. But America will always stand firm for the non-negotiable demands of human dignity: the rule of law; limits on the power of the state; respect for women; private property; free speech; equal justice; and religious tolerance. (Applause.)

America will take the side of brave men and women who advocate these values around the world, including the Islamic world, because we have a greater objective than eliminating threats and containing resentment. We seek a just and peaceful world beyond the war on terror.

In this moment of opportunity, a common danger is erasing old rivalries. America is working with Russia and China and India, in ways we have never before, to achieve peace and prosperity. In every region, free markets and free trade and free societies are proving their power to lift lives. Together with friends and allies from Europe to Asia, and Africa to Latin America, we will demonstrate that the forces of terror cannot stop the momentum of freedom. (Applause.)

The last time I spoke here, I expressed the hope that life would return to normal. In some ways, it has. In others, it never will. Those of us who have lived through these challenging times have been changed by them. We've come to know truths that we will never question: evil is real, and it must be opposed. (Applause.) Beyond all differences of race or creed, we are one country, mourning together and facing danger together. Deep in the American character, there is honor, and it is stronger than cynicism. And many have discovered again that even in tragedy—especially in tragedy—God is near. (Applause.)

In a single instant, we realized that this will be a decisive decade in the history of liberty, that we've been called to a unique role in human events. Rarely has the world faced a choice more clear or consequential.

Our enemies send other people's children on missions of suicide and murder. They embrace tyranny and death as a cause and a creed. We stand for a different choice, made long ago, on the day of our founding. We affirm it again today. We choose freedom and the dignity of every life. (Applause.)

Steadfast in our purpose, we now press on. We have known freedom's price. We have shown freedom's power. And in this great conflict, my fellow Americans, we will see freedom's victory.

Thank you all. May God bless. (Applause.)

■ **EXERCISE 10.18**   All of the work you have invested so far in this series of exercises should now be paying off. By carefully stating and researching the issue you have been studying, by finding and analyzing opposed arguments, and by exploring various argument design options, you naturally become much "better informed" about the issue than when you started. Now it is time to make some decisions. Answer the following question for yourself in 100 words or less. "Where do I stand on this issue?"

GLOSSARY

consistent   two statements are "consistent" if they could both be true

contingent statement   a claim whose truth value depends on something outside itself

implications   additional claims that either follow logically from or are strongly supported inductively by a given claim

inconsistent   two statements are "inconsistent" if there are no possible circumstances in which they could both be true; a group of statements is inconsistent if any two statements in the group are inconsistent

indirect proof   argumentative strategy of assuming the negation of some hypothesis and deriving from that assumption a clearly false or self-contradictory implication that then provides a reason to overturn the original assumption

necessary truth   a claim that is impossible to deny in a coherent way

reductio ad absurdam   use of the method of indirect proof to refute an opposing position

tautology   a claim that is necessarily true because to deny it would be self-contradictory

---

ENDNOTES

[1] Jonathan Glover, *Humanity: A Moral History of the Twentieth Century* (New Haven, CT: Yale University Press, 1999), p. 406.

[2] Ishvara, *Oneness in Living: Kundalini Yoga, the Spiritual Path, and Intentional Community* (Berkeley, CA: North Atlantic Books, 2002).

[3] Patrick Moore, "Speaking English in Space: Stars," *Omni*, November 1979, p. 26.

[4] Peter Singer, "Animal Liberation," in James Rachels (ed.), *Moral Problems*, 2d ed. (New York: Harper & Row, 1975), p. 166.

[5] Excerpt from the Argument in Favor of Proposition 215, *State of California Voter Manual*, 1996.

CHAPTER 11

Informal Fallacies I: Language, Relevance, Authority

In Chapter 6 we introduced the concept of a *fallacy* as an unreliable inference—a very important concept for argument criticism. Why so important? First, because fallacies are *inferences,* they tend to *appear* reasonable. Second, their unreliability tends not to be apparent on the surface. In fact, they can be very persuasive. As a result of their persuasive power they're quite widespread and prevalent in all sorts of everyday discourse, both public and private. And this leads to a lot of confusion and mistakes. So understanding how fallacies work and knowing how to spot them are useful to the critical thinker. We started with formal fallacies because within the framework of formal logic it is possible to demonstrate very clearly that a fallacy is unreliable and it is relatively easy to show the formal structure of the fallacy and thus how the fallacy works. But other aspects of reasoning besides the formal structure of inferences can undermine reliability. Thus, an *informal*

fallacy is an unreliable inference whose unreliability results from something other than its formal structure.

The informal fallacies constitute a large and very mixed bag. The author of one Critical Thinking textbook estimates that if you were to consult a random selection of informal logic texts, you would likely find several hundred different informal fallacy categories listed. One such text distinguishes over 90 all by itself. This proliferation of categories and terminology makes the study of the informal fallacies bewildering and intimidating for many students. And it leads many students of Critical Thinking, even quite a few instructors, to approach the informal fallacies as essentially a memory challenge—a long list of labels to memorize. This is a terrible way to approach the informal fallacies. Try very hard not to fall into this trap. We must be honest here and tell you that one main reason so many categories are out there is that there is no agreed-upon common standard classification system for the informal fallacies. This is a very good reason *not* to try memorizing a list of fallacy labels.

Here is a much better approach. Think of the informal fallacy terminology as part of a tool kit for doing a certain kind of work. Just as a carpenter has carpentry tools, you are assembling a set of tools for critiquing arguments. Your goal should be to attain mastery in their employment, and the best way to pursue this goal is by working with the tools. The tools are mind tools rather than hand tools— concepts rather than hardware. You already have the tools. They are concepts you've studied. In this chapter we will demonstrate a few applications of the tools. From time to time we will also give you a few tips about using the tools. Like this:

CRITICAL THINKING TIP 11.1

The work of the carpenter is to construct things out of wood. The mastery of the carpenter shows in the work product. The work of the Critical Thinker is to produce a form of understanding.

FALLACIES OF LANGUAGE

AMBIGUITY

If a genie came out of a lamp and offered you the gift of everlasting perfect happiness, would you accept? And now suppose the same genie came back a second time and said, "I'll trade you what I gave you last time for this ratty old bowl of leftover party mix," would you accept the offer? In Chapter 2, the concept of ambiguity was presented as a flexibility feature of language that enables it to handle multiple meanings at once. Although this kind of flexibility is essential to effective communication, here we will focus on the downside of ambiguity—the ways it can undermine the reliability of a piece of reasoning. All right, so now suppose the genie offered you the following argument:

> Look, nothing is better than everlasting perfect happiness, but this ratty old bowl of leftover party mix is better than nothing, so you'd really be better off accepting my generous offer.

EXERCISE 11.1 | **Equivocation**

What is wrong with the genie's argument? Can you explain the trick?

> "Nothing is better than everlasting perfect happiness, but this ratty old bowl of leftover party mix is better than nothing, so the party mix is better than everlasting perfect happiness."

Obviously, *something* is wrong with this argument. But what can it be? It *looks* so logical. Here's a hint. Go back and highlight the terms that appear in both of the premises of the argument. Do these terms each carry the same meaning consistently from premise 1 through premise 2, or do the meanings change? And if so, how? The "trick" here is that the word *nothing*, on which the apparently logical comparison hinges, actually changes meaning from the first premise to the second. The first premise can be paraphrased as follows:

Everlasting perfect happiness is better than *anything else.*

And the second premise can be paraphrased as follows:

Having this ratty old bowl of leftover party mix is better than *not having anything at all.*

When the premises have been paraphrased in this way, we're no longer tempted to think that everlasting perfect happiness and this ratty old bowl of leftover party mix are both being compared to *the same thing,* and the apparent logic of the argument falls away. When an argument depends on switching the meanings of an ambiguous crucial term or expression, as in this example, the argument commits the *informal fallacy of equivocation.* The conceptual tool we are using in diagnosing this fallacy is the concept of ambiguity. In critiquing an argument as an instance of this fallacy, one should be able to identify the term(s) or expression(s) being used ambiguously and demonstrate the ambiguity by making clear at least two distinct meanings for each ambiguous item. The best way to do this is to paraphrase the claims in which it is used, as we did here.

EXERCISE 11.2 | **Your Turn**

- OK, now you try it. Use the cartoon on page 276.

- Then, for comparison, try the following passage from Lewis Carroll's *Through the Looking Glass.* See how well you can explain the tricks in the Queen's reasoning.

  "You couldn't have it if you did want it," the Queen said. "The rule is jam tomorrow and jam yesterday—but never jam today."

  "It must sometimes come to jam today," Alice objected.

  "No it can't," said the Queen. "It's jam every other day: today isn't any other day, you know."

VARIETIES OF AMBIGUITY

A good basic understanding of language—for example, the distinction between syntax and semantics—is obviously helpful in diagnosing and explaining informal fallacies of ambiguity. Some ambiguity arises at the verbal level as a result of the capacity of individual words or idiomatic expressions to support more than one interpretation. Such ambiguity is called "semantic." Thus, the example used above, which we called "equivocation," results from semantic ambiguity—a matter of semantics. Ambiguity can also arise at the grammatical level as a result of grammatical structure or word order. For example:

EXERCISE 11.3 | **Amphibole**

Can you explain the how the ambiguity arises in the following example?

  The loot and the car were listed as stolen by the Los Angeles Police Department.

In the example in Exercise 11.3 there is an ambiguity of reference. Which of the two verbs in the sentence is modified by the prepositional phrase? The expression is presumably intended to indicate that the police *listed* the loot and car as stolen, not that they *stole* it. This would be an example of "syntactical" ambiguity—a matter of syntax. The technical term for an expression whose ambiguity is the result of its grammatical structure or word order is "amphibole." The same sort of thing is going on in the accompanying cartoon.

Reprinted with special permission of King Features Syndicate.

Lance couldn't understand why they had to be licensed, but he brought his plates in anyway.

An argument that exploits or depends on this sort of ambiguity commits the *informal fallacy of amphibole*. Such fallacies are almost always deliberate—for example, in certain sales gimmicks that verge on fraud. For instance, at the end of a direct mail sales offer appears the following guarantee: "We're convinced that you will love your new Acme widget even more than you could begin to imagine. But rest assured. If for any reason you are the least bit dissatisfied, just send it back. We'll give you a prompt and a full refund." Does this mean that you get a full refund promptly? When a dissatisfied customer applies for the refund and receives a nominal reimbursement along with a statement of "service charges," it becomes evident that this is not what the guarantor had in mind—even if it *is* what the guarantor expects *you* to think. Should the customer insist upon a *full* refund, she may expect to wage an indefinitely long and unpleasant battle.

ADVANCED APPLICATIONS

The genie's argument we used above to illustrate the fallacy of equivocation is, shall we say, bogus on its face. In other words, it is immediately obvious to nearly any reader that there's a trick in it of some kind—even if what the trick is exactly is harder to say. But fallacies can be much more seductive and difficult to spot.

EXERCISE 11.4 | False Implication

Here is an example of a widely used ad strategy known as "false implication." Recently we spotted it on a candy bar wrapper with the words "BIGGEST EVER!" imprinted in bright orange 64-point type. Guess the trick if you can.

The widely used ad strategy known as "false implication" consists in *stating* something true while at the same time *implying* something altogether different and false. Of course, it's the implied falsehood that motivates the consumer. The implication in this case is that the candy bar is bigger now than it was before—that it has been *increased in size*. The literal truth of the matter is that the candy bar is exactly as big as it has ever been—and also as small as it has ever been—because it's the same size as it has always been.

This maneuver is standard procedure in writing advertising copy. It explains the conventional advertising industry usage of superlative adjectives, especially in promoting so-called parity products. A "parity product" is one that is practically the same regardless of brand name. Aspirin is a good example of a parity product. Aspirin is aspirin is aspirin. It doesn't matter whether you buy it in the bottle that says "Bayer" on it or in the bottle with the regional brand name or the bottle with the generic label. You get the same number of milligrams of the same chemical formula per tablet. Understandably, producers of parity products work very hard in their ads to promote name recognition and brand loyalty and frequently use superlatives such as "best," "strongest," "most powerful," and so on to describe their products. "How can this be!" you may ask. "If all of the products are identical, they must all be equally good, equally strong, equally powerful, and so on." Quite right. If you have this doubt, it's probably because you recognize that normally a superlative implies a comparison. For example, consider the following sets of adjectives:

Superlative:	Best	Strongest	Sweetest	Biggest	Fastest
Comparative:	Better	Stronger	Sweeter	Bigger	Faster
Descriptive:	Good	Strong	Sweet	Big	Fast

Normally, as you read down the list, each adjective implies the one below. If something is better than something else, this implies that it is good. If something is best, this implies it is better than the rest. But as employed in advertising, the superlative "best" is taken to mean "there is none better"; the superlative "strongest" is taken to mean "there is none stronger"; and so on. The literal truth of the matter is that the pain reliever is "just as strong as any of the other over-the-counter pain relievers." You are simply getting the maximum dosage legally dispensable without a doctor's prescription, the same as with all of the other over-the-counter pain pills.

A special kind of ambiguity is frequently involved in our references to groups of individuals or things. It is not always clear whether the members of the group are being referred to individually or collectively. This can result in one or the other of two common informal fallacies. The *informal fallacy of composition* consists in incorrectly inferring characteristics of the group as a collective whole from characteristics of its individual parts or members. For example, a man observes that every member of a local club is wealthy and therefore infers that the club itself must be wealthy. Not necessarily. The confusion results from assuming that what is true of the part must also be true of the whole. In fact, the whole represents something different from simply the sum or combination of its parts. Of course, it is sometimes true that a collective whole has the characteristics of its individual members. It may be the case, for example, that a series of good lectures is a good series of lectures. But there is no generally reliable equation here. For example, a program of short pieces of music can be a very long program. A team of highly efficient workers may nonetheless be hopelessly inefficient as a team.

The *informal fallacy of division* works in the opposite direction, incorrectly inferring characteristics of the individual parts or members of a group from characteristics of the group as a collective whole. Observing that a club is wealthy, a man infers that each club member must be wealthy or that a particular member must be wealthy. But just as a property of the part need not imply a property of the whole, so a property of the whole need not imply a property of the part. That a book is a masterpiece doesn't mean that each chapter is one; that an orchestra is outstanding doesn't imply that each member is an outstanding musician. Again, it is sometimes the case that the individual parts or members of a group have some of the characteristics of the group as a whole, but again not always. A million-dollar inventory, for example, might be made up out of a great many 5- and 10-cent items.

EXERCISE 11.5 | Fallacies of Ambiguity

Cartoonists sometimes provide the most "artful" examples of fallacious reasoning. Here's a wonderful example drawn by the great satirist Jules Feiffer, in which the politically ambitious leader of the Christian right, Reverend Jerry Falwell, arrives by a suspect line of argument at the seemingly contradictory conclusion that in order to remain part of the free world South Africa must continue to enslave its black population. Can you explain what is wrong with Falwell's reasoning?

FEIFFER®

VAGUENESS

Chapter 2 presented the concept of vagueness as a feature of language in which questions of definition are left open. Like ambiguity, vagueness is very useful. We often need the flexibility to use discretion in applying familiar terms and concepts in new and unforeseeable situations. However, for the very same reason, vagueness is also prone to certain forms of abuse. Because vague terms and expressions are essentially undefined, they lend themselves rather easily and naturally to evasive and manipulative applications. To criticize a piece of reasoning as a case of the abuse of vagueness depends on identifying an instance of vagueness and arguing that it is unreasonably so.

EXERCISE 11.6 | **Topic for Class Discussion**

Highlight the terms and concepts you find used in vague ways in the following passages. Then compare and contrast—where is the vagueness warranted and reasonable, where is it unwarranted or problematic?

Excerpt from President George W. Bush's Address to the nation on October 7, 2001, announcing the military campaign against the Taliban government of Afghanistan.

This military action is a part of our campaign against terrorism, another front in a war that has already been joined through diplomacy, intelligence, the freezing of financial assets and the arrests of known terrorists by law enforcement agents in 38 countries. Given the nature and reach of our enemies, we will win this conflict by the patient accumulation of successes, by meeting a series of challenges with determination and will and purpose. Today we focus on Afghanistan, but the battle is broader. Every nation has a choice to make. In this conflict, there is no neutral ground. If any government sponsors the outlaws and killers of innocents, they have become outlaws and murderers, themselves. And they will take that lonely path at their own peril.

Excerpt from President George W. Bush's radio address to the nation on April 20, 2002, reporting on Secretary of State Colin Powell's diplomatic mission to the Middle East during a period of intensified violence in Israel and the occupied territories of Palestine.

The time is now for all of us to make the choice for peace. America will continue to work toward this vision of peace in the Middle East, and America continues to press forward in our war against global terror. We will use every available tool to tighten the noose around the terrorists and their supporters. And when it comes to the threat of terror, the only path to safety is the path of action.

In the days just after September the 11th, I told the American people our war against terrorism would be a different war, fought on many fronts. And we are making progress on many fronts. Yesterday the United States and the world's other leading industrialized nations blocked the financial assets of another 10 terrorists and terrorist organizations. This joint action among close allies is an important step in choking off the financial pipeline that pays for terrorist training and attacks.

A total of 161 nations around the world have joined together to block more than $100 million of suspected terrorist assets. The United States also continues to work with our friends and allies around the world to round up individual terrorists, such as Abu Zubaydah, a top al Qaeda leader captured in Pakistan. From Spain to Singapore, our partners are breaking up terrorist cells and disrupting their plans. Altogether, more than 1,600 terrorists and their supporters have been arrested or detained in 95 foreign nations.

In Afghanistan, the United States and its partners are pressing forward with a military campaign against al Qaeda and the Taliban. More than a dozen of our NATO allies are contributing forces to this fight. Right now, hundreds of Royal Marines from Great Britain are leading an operation to clear and seal off regions where our enemies are trying to regroup to commit murder and mayhem, and to undermine Afghanistan's efforts to build a lasting peace.

And we're working with nations such as Yemen, the Philippines and Georgia that seek our help in training and equipping their military forces to fight terror in some of the world's distant corners.

We're making progress. Yet nothing about this war will be quick or easy. We face dangers and sacrifices ahead. America is ready; the morale of our military is high; the will of our people is strong. We are determined, we are steadfast, and we will continue for as long as it takes, until the mission is done.

No doubt you can see that there is considerable room here for discussion. There are, first of all, quite a few terms and concepts in play in each of the above passages, many of which are used in ways that could be defined more precisely and are thus arguably vague. For purposes of illustration we will focus only on three central ones: "peace," "war," and "terrorism." So, now the question arises as to the precise definitions of these terms. In what ways are these terms left open to interpretation?

The concept "peace" is not defined, but it is reasonable to assume that it means at least "the absence of war." Among the ways the concept "war" is left open to interpretation are the specific goals, objectives, and means to be used. At the outset, the goals and objectives are defined simply in the phrase "campaign against terrorism." But suppose we want to know more specifically how long this war will go on. How far will it extend geographically? What precisely is our mission? How will we know when we have completed it? The means of achieving these goals are also unspecified. However, it is clear that they are not confined to the use of conventional military force, since they include the use of diplomatic, law enforcement, surveillance, and intelligence procedures. This raises a question as to what additional, perhaps covert, means of achieving the goals and objectives may be under consideration as well. How are we to know whether we are "at war" or not? The concept "terrorism" is given what sounds like a very definitive statement in the context of an ultimatum delivered to all nations in stark black-and-white terms. There is no gray area. Either you are in support of "the outlaws and killers of innocents" or not. But *acting and speaking as though* there are no gray areas does not guarantee that there are no gray areas. Questions may arise as to precisely *who* are the outlaws and killers of innocents in many cases, including the aftermath of September 11, 2001. So just how precise can we make the definition of *terrorism*, after all?

EXERCISE 11.7 | **Topic for Class Discussion**

Review Exercise 2.11 (Chapter 2, page 58). Then read the "official" U.S. government definition of *terrorism* below and consider the following questions: Does the U.S. government or any of its allies ever engage in acts of violence and/or commit homicide against civilian populations for coercive political purposes? Does the U.S. government or any of its allies ever take political hostages? Does the U.S. government or any of its allies ever commit or issue contracts for political assassination?

"[An] act of terrorism means any activity that [A] involves a violent act or an act dangerous to human life that is a violation of the criminal laws of the United States or any State, or that would be a criminal violation if committed within the jurisdiction of the United States or of any State; and [B] appears to be intended (i) to intimidate or coerce a civilian population; (ii) to influence the policy of a government by intimidation or coercion; or (iii) to affect the conduct of a government by assassination or kidnapping."[1]

The questions posed in Exercise 11.7, whether the U.S. government or any of its allies (Israel, for example) ever engage in activities that would count as terrorism under its own official definition of that term, are questions the Bush administration would surely find troublesome and would therefore understandably prefer to avoid. Better to leave the concept of terrorism more loosely defined. There are also understandable reasons why the Bush administration would prefer to keep military options both open and unspecified even if they have been determined. But we can be pretty sure that vagueness is being abused when the interpretations of the crucial concepts get so loose and broad as to be internally inconsistent. (Peace is war, war is peace, war is a means to peace, etc.)

VAGUENESS IN ADVERTISING

Puffery is advertising that praises with vague exaggerations. *Hyperbole,* or "hype" for short, is exaggeration or extravagance as a figure of speech. In advertising, such exaggerations and extravagances are there to create *excitement,* not to convey information. In his book *The Great American Blowup,* Ivan L. Preston gives a long list of examples, including, "When you say Budweiser, you've said it all"; "You can be sure if it's Westinghouse"; "Toshiba—in touch with tomorrow"; "Waterford—the ultimate gift"; "Diamonds are forever!" The general strategy being pursued here is to raise the level of enthusiasm and excitement without actually making any substantive claims.

EXERCISE 11.8 | Topic for Class Discussion

Here is an excerpt from an unsolicited direct mail brochure we received while we were working on this chapter. How many instances of hype and puffery can you find?

> This two-day weekend seminar will open you to the wonders of the contemporary experience of modern High-Tech Serendipity Meditation, as your seminar leader and originator of the High-Tech Serendipity Meditation Experience personally conducts this expansive program, demonstrating the power and potential of this contemporary meditative technology. The weekend includes four power-packed sessions of Holodynamic Serendipity material presented in such a way as to enable each participant to personally experience the contemporary ease and the full potential of High-Tech Meditation.

The pitch in the above example sounds intriguing, beneficial, attractive, but what does it all mean? The terminology, though it *sounds* not only positive but technically precise, is hopelessly vague. That's the important thing to notice here. Because it is so vague, it invites the reader to project onto it whatever meanings are most closely connected with the reader's own fantasies and longings. Of course, if you want to find out in detail what High-Tech Holodynamic Serendipity Meditation is all about, you can sign up for the two-day weekend seminar for a fee of $250. Assuming you can afford it, this might not be such a bad deal for two full days of whatever you want to believe you're hearing.

Already we have seen how ambiguity can be exploited to enable an advertiser, by leaving a comparison unfinished, to imply a claim that cannot truthfully be stated in an explicit and straightforward way. In one famous ad we are told, "Ford LTD— 700% quieter!" Compared to what? Viewers of this ad are understandably inclined to complete the comparison for themselves in one or another of several ways relevant to choosing a new car. So, for example, many viewers naturally assume that the ad means that this year's model is 700 percent quieter than last year's model, or that the Ford LTD is 700 percent quieter than the competitors in its price category. When the FTC challenged the claim, Ford admitted that the real basis of the comparison was exterior noise. The inside of the car was 700 percent quieter than the outside.

Another such device is known as the *weasel word.* The expression is derived from the egg-eating habits of weasels. A weasel will bite into the eggshell and suck out the contents, leaving what appears to the casual observer to be an intact egg. Similarly, a weasel word sucks out the substance of what appears on the surface to be a substantial claim. In effect, what the weasel word does is to make the claim in which it is used a *vague* claim, while at the same time at least partially concealing the vagueness. "Help" functions in advertising as a weasel. *Help* means literally "aid" or "assist" and nothing more. Yet as one author has observed, "'help' is the one single word which, in all the annals of advertising, has done the most to say something that couldn't be said."[2] Once "help" is used to qualify a claim, almost anything can be said after it. Accordingly we are exposed to ads for products that "*help* keep us young," "*help* prevent cavities," and "*help* keep our houses germ free." Just think of how many times a day you hear or read pitches that say "*helps* stop," "*helps* prevent," "*helps* fight," "*helps* overcome," "*helps* you feel," and "*helps* you look." But don't think "help" is the only weasel in the advertiser's arsenal. "Like" (as in "makes your floor look *like* new"), "virtual" or "virtually" (as in "*virtually* no cavities"), "up to" (as in "provides relief *up to* eight hours"), "as much as" (as in "saves *as much as* one gallon of gas"), and other weasels say what cannot be said. Studies indicate that on hearing or reading a claim containing a weasel word, we tend to screen out the weasel word and just hear the claim. Thus, on hearing that a medicine "can provide up to eight hours' relief," we screen out the "can" and the "up to" and infer that the product will give us eight hours' relief, because that's what we want—relief. In fact, according to a strict reading of the wording of the ad, the product may give no relief at all; and if it does give relief, the relief could vary in length from a moment or two to anywhere under eight hours.

DENOTATION

Many issues turn on how things are grouped together in categories. In Chapter 2 we considered several examples, including what we classify as "terrorism" and whether a particular music video is or isn't in the category of "pornography." When an argument depends on a claim that either amounts to or presupposes a questionable classification, it is appropriate to challenge that classification. If a premise in an argument has been challenged in this way and this challenge is not met by a defensible essential definition, we may say that some *informal fallacy of classification* has occurred. Of course, all of this depends on the essential definition of the category in question. Thus, making such a criticism will have the effect of opening the issue of defining the category. And this will in many cases be a formidable issue in its own right.

EXERCISE 11.9 | **Topic for Class Discussion**

Review the section on "essential definitions" and Exercises 2.8–2.11 in Chapter 2 (pp. 56–63). Then consider the following example:

Look around the neighborhood and count the houses and cars. Do you have any trouble deciding which is which? Not likely. But an interesting case in Constitutional law called even this seemingly obvious classification into question. It seems that police officers had observed a certain vehicle parked for several days during which time individuals and small groups of people were also observed coming and going to and from the vehicle. Suspecting possible drug activity, the police investigated further and indeed found the occupant of the vehicle had drugs in his possession. The occupant was arrested and brought to trial on drug charges. The hitch for the prosecution was that the police had not obtained a search warrant before moving to investigate the vehicle. Why would that be necessary? Police don't need a search warrant to inspect a motor vehicle. But it turned out that the occupant was *living in* the vehicle (a motor home), and it was argued that since the vehicle was the occupant's place of residence, it should be covered by the 4th Amendment provision which protects "the right of the people to be secure in their *houses* . . ." against unreasonable search and seizure.[3]

Does this argument commit an informal fallacy of classification?

CONNOTATION

In the heat of debate over an issue in which people are passionately engaged it may be expected that they will use the most powerful language they can muster to make and present their case. So it is well advised to be aware of the connotations of the labels and descriptions used in an argument's text, bearing in mind Critical Thinking Tip 2.1 (p. 43). We may say that some sort of *informal fallacy of loaded language* has occurred when the language distorts the issue under discussion or when the argument leans more heavily on the connotations of the language than it does on the reasoning itself.

A good example of issue-distorting language is the common rhetorical device of *euphemism*. The term *euphemism* derives from the Greek for "good speech" or "good word." It refers to a figure of speech in which things are labeled or described in overly positive terms or terms that understate the negative. The tendency to use and favor euphemisms is natural and understandable as a psychological defense mechanism in many situations. It is nice to be able to put things in a polite way that is respectful of people's feelings. But euphemisms can also be used to obscure and to mislead and to confuse—as, for example, when a politician refers to a "tax" as a "revenue enhancement." Nor are euphemisms confined to the political sphere. Euphemism is a strategy of first resort throughout public relations—for instance, when "human resource managers" (i.e., the boss) devise more and more artful and evasive ways of saying "you're fired," like, "your functions have been outsourced" (huh?), or "you've been made redundant." Or here's one from the wonderful world of customer service. It seems that Blockbuster Video has stopped charging a "late fee" for videos returned after they're due. Instead they assess "extended viewing fees." Sounds much more agreeable. If we think of euphemism as exaggeration in the positive direction, an obvious and equally powerful strategy consists in exaggerating the negative. This strategy is particularly useful in "demonizing official enemies" of state and thereby motivating public support for aggressive and hostile foreign policy. Following the etymology of euphemism, we might call such negative exaggeration *dysphemism*, from the Greek for "bad speech" or "bad word."

EXERCISE 11.10 | **Euphemisms**

Here is a collection of 20th-century military euphemisms. See if you can match the euphemism (left column) with the thing described (right column).

This euphemism	means
a "Pacification Center"	to spy
a "protective reaction strike"	retreat
"incontinent ordnance"	a bombing raid
"friendly fire"	bombs
"force packages"	a concentration camp
"strategic withdrawal"	bombing or shooting someone on your side
to "gather intelligence"	off-target bombs
to "terminate"	to destroy by bombing
to "degrade" the target	civilian casualties caused by our side
"collateral damage"	to kill

LANGUAGE FUNCTIONS

Just as loaded labels can distort an issue, so can inappropriate applications of rhetorical features and persuasive capacities of language. So, we are also well advised to focus our attention on language functions, again bearing in mind Critical Thinking Tip 2.1 (p. 43). Be on the lookout for extreme quantifiers ("all," "every," and so on), extreme intensifiers ("absolutely," "totally," "completely," and the like), and other universalizing expressions. Heavy reliance on this sort of language often masks weakness in the reasoning. If an argument is really strong, it shouldn't need exaggeration in order to make its point. Again, we may say that some sort of *informal fallacy of loaded language* has occurred when the argument leans more heavily on the intensity of the language than it does on the reasoning itself.

Sometimes language functions are exploited as negotiating tactics or as strategic means of eliciting agreement. For example, a question is a request or invitation to respond, ordinarily at the voluntary discretion of the respondent. But we sometimes run across questions—called "rhetorical questions"—that are worded in such a way that only one of the possible answers is invited because all other possible answers are discredited. In "polite" discourse this device can be quite useful for creating an air of "understatement," don't you agree? But rhetorical questions can also amplify and overstate the case. How in the world could you possibly imagine otherwise?! Rhetorical questions are often deployed in lieu of any better argument. When you see this happen, you may say that the *informal fallacy of rhetorical question* has been committed.

EXERCISE 11.11 | **Informal Fallacies of Language**

In each of the following examples, check all fallacy categories that apply. Most important, explain each fallacy you identify.

Airplanes are used for getting high. And airplanes are perfectly legal. Drugs are used for getting high. So they should be legal too.

		Explain your answer:
	Equivocation	
	Amphibole	
	Abuse of vagueness	
	Weasel words	
	Faulty classification	
	Loaded language	
	Euphemism/dysphemism	
	Rhetorical question	

"I passed nobody on the road. Therefore nobody is slower than I am." — Lewis Carroll

		Explain your answer:
	Equivocation	
	Amphibole	
	Abuse of vagueness	
	Weasel words	
	Faulty classification	
	Loaded language	
	Euphemism/dysphemism	
	Rhetorical question	

"It's not a pay raise. It is a pay equalization concept." (U.S. senator Ted Stevens explaining a congressional measure to increase the compensation of members of the U.S. Congress)

	Explain your answer:
Equivocation	
Amphibole	
Abuse of vagueness	
Weasel words	
Faulty classification	
Loaded language	
Euphemism/dysphemism	
Rhetorical question	

Look! The notice on his office door says "Back Soon." But I've been waiting here for over an hour and a half!

	Explain your answer:
Equivocation	
Amphibole	
Abuse of vagueness	
Weasel words	
Faulty classification	
Loaded language	
Euphemism/dysphemism	
Rhetorical question	

God is Love. Love is blind. Therefore, God is blind.

	Explain your answer:
Equivocation	
Amphibole	
Abuse of vagueness	
Weasel words	
Faulty classification	
Loaded language	
Euphemism/dysphemism	
Rhetorical question	

News report: "High-level FBI sources and Defense Department officials will neither confirm nor deny that a would-be terrorist suspect with possible links to al-Qaeda has been apprehended."

	Explain your answer:
Equivocation	
Amphibole	
Abuse of vagueness	
Weasel words	
Faulty classification	
Loaded language	
Euphemism/dysphemism	
Rhetorical question	

FALLACIES OF RELEVANCE

Suppose that someone came up to you and said, "Now that I know how to construct a deductively valid argument, I can finally settle the abortion issue once and for all! Here's my argument:"

EXERCISE 11.12 | Brain Teaser

Clearly something is wrong with the following argument. Can you explain what it is?

> If *abortion* is an eight-letter word, then abortion should be against the law. *Abortion is* an eight-letter word. Therefore, abortion should be against the law.

Are you convinced by the argument in Exercise 11.12? No reasonable person would be, but what is wrong with the argument? Since the argument is in the form modus ponens, it can't be faulted formally. So what else might be wrong with it? Are the premises false? The second one is true. Count the letters. That verifies that. That leaves premise 1. Is premise 1 false? Before you answer this question, just suppose for a moment that the conclusion of the argument is true. Now, is premise 1 false? Hard to tell, isn't it? You don't know yet whether the conclusion is true, but it might be, and in that case you can't really be sure that premise 1 is false. (See the section in Chapter 6 on using truth tables to test for deductive validity.) So what *is* wrong with the argument? The problem here is that both premises are *irrelevant to the issue.* Why? Because the number of letters in the word *abortion* is irrelevant to the moral status of the act of abortion and therefore also to the question of abortion law. Here you can see the concept of relevance in bold relief. An important informal consideration in evaluating arguments is whether the premises offered are relevant to what is at issue. If they are, so much the better for the argument. If not, some sort of *informal fallacy of relevance*, or *irrelevant appeal,* has been committed. The conceptual tools we use in detecting and diagnosing fallacies of relevance are the concept of relevance and the tools of issue analysis presented in Chapter 1. Generally speaking, the relevance of any premise of any argument to the issue in question may be challenged at any point. Bear in mind, however, that to challenge the relevance of a premise is not the same as establishing that it *is* irrelevant. Relevance is not always obvious on the surface. So it remains open to the arguer to meet the challenge by explaining how the premise bears on the conclusion or issue. But if a premise *is* relevant, it should be possible to explain the connection. Thus, the most important thing to do is keep the issue(s) clearly in focus as you go.

CRITICAL THINKING TIP 11.2

Keep the issue(s) in focus.

AD HOMINEM

The relevance problem in the argument in Exercise 11.11 is so glaring that the argument is an "obvious" fallacy. Other instances may well be less obvious, though no less fallacious. *Ad hominem,* the Latin phrase for "to the man," refers to the rhetorical strategy of irrelevant personal attack. When people argue ad hominem, they argue that the *person,* not her reasoning or position, is faulty. Ad hominem's prevalence and remarkable rhetorical force both probably stem from the general human psychological tendencies to personalize conflict and escalate hostility. As natural as it may be for us to turn attention to the personal weaknesses, flaws, and failures of others, these things—whether real or imagined—are almost always and with only very rare exceptions irrelevant to whatever the issue is under discussion.

EXERCISE 11.13 | **Ad Hominem**

Topic for Class Discussion: Here is an excerpt from right-wing radio personality Rush Limbaugh's book *The Way Things Ought to Be* (Chapter 10). Identify and explain the ad hominem elements.

I have spoken extensively in this book about the various fringe movements and the spiritual tie that binds them: radical liberalism. Two groups that are particularly close, to the point of being nearly indistinguishable, are the environmentalists and the animal rights activists. Because I devoted a chapter to the environmentalists I thought it only fair to include one about animal rights activism. I certainly do not want to be accused of discrimination. Every wacko movement must have its day in my book. . . .

The animal rights movement, like so many others in this country, is being used by leftists as another way to attack the American way of life. They have adopted two constituencies who cannot speak and complain about the political uses to which they are put. One of them is trees and other plant life; the other is the animal kingdom. People for the Ethical Treatment of Animals (PETA) takes in over $10 million every year by preying on people's concern for animals. Most of its contributors think most of the money goes to making sure animals are treated kindly . . . but PETA's real mission is destroying capitalism, not saving animals.

The basic right to life of an animal—which is the source of energy for many animal rights wackos—must be inferred from the anticruelty laws humans have written, not from any divine source. Our laws do not prevent us from killing animals for food or sport, so the right to life of an animal is nonexistent.

The Limbaugh passage in Exercise 11.13 contains a good example of what is often called *abusive ad hominem*—where the personal attack is baseless (for example, "wacko") as well as irrelevant. Think of *abusive ad hominem* as essentially a kind of gratuitous name-calling. The Limbaugh passage also contains a good example of a somewhat more sophisticated strategy, often called *circumstantial ad hominem,* where some piece of actual information about a person that carries unfavorable but irrelevant personal implications (for example, "leftist") is the means of attack.

A special case of *circumstantial ad hominem*, in which the attack is based on the person's relationships with others, is often appropriately called the *informal fallacy of guilt by association.* A similar strategy—a sort of *circumstantial ad hominem* in advance—attempts to discredit a position before any argument for it has a chance to get a hearing. This strategy is often called *poisoning the well*. The "well" is the reasoning. The "poison" is prejudice, which literally means "prejudgment." A good critical thinker gives due and open-minded consideration to the reasoning *before* arriving at judgment. Anyone who tries to discourage this is committing the *informal fallacy of poisoning the well.* For example, 19th-century philosopher/theologian John Henry Cardinal Newman engaged in frequent dispute with clergyman/novelist Charles Kingsley. During the course of one of these, Kingsley suggested that Newman could not possibly value truth above all else because of his Catholicism. Newman rightly objected that this was poisoning the well, since it made it impossible for him (or any Catholic) to state his case. No matter what reasons or arguments Newman might offer to show that he did value the truth and that this value was basic to his faith, Kingsley would have already ruled them out because they had come from a Catholic.

PHILOSOPHICAL DIFFERENCES

Used by permission of Norman Dog.

A similar fallacy, often called *genetic appeal*, consists in evaluating something strictly in terms of its origin or sources (or "genesis"). For example, it has been argued by certain religious fundamentalists that dancing is evil and should be forbidden because it originated as a form of pagan worship. We have heard conservative arguments against parent cooperative day-care programs based primarily on the grounds that the idea originated among socialists.

EXERCISE 11.14 | **Fallacies of Relevance I**

In each of the following examples, check all fallacy categories that apply. Most important, explain each fallacy you identify.

"No man can know anything about pregnancy and childbirth, because no man can ever go through the experience. So no man is qualified to render an opinion about abortion."

		Explain your answer:
	Abusive ad hominem	
	Circumstantial ad hominem	
	Guilt by association	
	Genetic appeal	
	Poisoning the well	

"How can you believe anything that this bimbo has to say? Can't you see that she has everything to gain by implicating the President in this scandal? Look, she's sold her story to *Hard Copy*!"

		Explain your answer:
	Abusive ad hominem	
	Circumstantial ad hominem	
	Guilt by association	
	Genetic appeal	
	Poisoning the well	

Letter to the Editor: "I was profoundly dismayed by the badgering of witnesses during the hearings by Senator D. "Mo" Cratic. Doesn't he realize that such criticism reflects badly on the President? If we can't expect the members of our own party to support the President in a time of crisis, just who can we turn to?"

		Explain your answer:
	Abusive ad hominem	
	Circumstantial ad hominem	
	Guilt by association	
	Genetic appeal	
	Poisoning the well	

"I can't vote for the man, because I remember some years ago in his law practice he defended that wacko Unabomber guy."

		Explain your answer:
	Abusive ad hominem	
	Circumstantial ad hominem	
	Guilt by association	
	Genetic appeal	
	Poisoning the well	

POSITIONING, PROVINCIALISM, TRADITION, AND NOVELTY

Watch for ad hominem tactics like those described above wherever partisan lines are well known—wherever there's a well-established "us" and "them." In such all-too-frequent contexts also be on the alert for language that raises considerations of group loyalty, patriotism, nationalism, and so on. Sometimes the group identified with is considerably smaller than a nation—a region, or a city, or perhaps a professional, occupational, or religious group, or a school, or a team. Sometimes the group is even larger than a nation: a gender, for example. The general term for discourse that leans too heavily on irrelevant considerations of loyalty is *provincialism.*

Provincialism is often coupled with an *appeal to tradition*, in which the argument rests heavily on whether something adheres to or departs from tradition. During the Watergate scandal in 1974 there were frequent appeals to tradition surrounding the attempt to impeach President Richard Nixon. Many insisted that Nixon should not be impeached simply because it had never been done before. But the fact that a president had never before been removed from office was irrelevant to the issues of corruption and betrayal of public trust that undermined the Nixon presidency.

In contrast to the *appeal to tradition* but just as fallacious is the *appeal to novelty,* which consists of assuming or arguing that something is good or desirable just because it is new or different. Watch for this tactic around election time. Candidates who use slogans like "Leadership for a Change" or "It's Time for New Ideas" *may* have something new and different to offer, something that would advance the public interest, but the *claim* of novelty by itself is irrelevant.

Just as people sometimes attempt to discredit others through *guilt by association,* they can just as effectively promote themselves and others by *positioning*—by appropriating the reputation of a leader in a field to sell a product, candidate, or idea. Here's how it works. In advertising, positioning creates a spot for a company in the prospective buyer's mind by invoking not only the company's image but that of its leading competitor as well. The assumption here is that the consumer's mind has become an advertising battleground. So a successful advertising strategy involves relating to what has already been established in the consumer's mind. Thus, although RCA and General Electric tried in vain to buck IBM directly in the early years of the mainframe computer market, the smaller Honeywell succeeded using the theme "The *Other* Computer Company." *Positioning* is hardly confined to advertising. During presidential election years, many a congressional campaign is based almost entirely on party affiliation with the incumbent president or the front-runner. This is called "riding on the coattails." In politics, part of waging a successful campaign often means trading on the reputation of another well-known, popular political figure. Thus, candidates of both parties are forever attempting to appropriate the mantle of a Lincoln or a Kennedy by invoking lines from their famous speeches and forging all sorts of tenuous connections. One of the most famous attempts at positioning was Dan Quayle's attempt to link himself with JFK in the 1988 vice-presidential debate, saying that he was as seasoned and experienced a potential leader as Kennedy had been prior to his election as president. The attempt backfired when Democratic candidate Lloyd Bentson positioned himself even closer to Kennedy, saying, "I served with Jack Kennedy in the Senate. Jack Kennedy was a friend of mine. Senator, you're no Jack Kennedy." Bentson's response to Quayle was a devastating rhetorical punch. Yet it was no less an instance of the *informal fallacy of positioning* than Quayle's.

CRITICAL THINKING TIP 11.3

As an antidote to any and all of these corruptions of Critical Thinking, remember Critical Thinking Tip 11.2: Keep the issues in focus.

EMOTIONAL APPEALS

Emotions can exert a powerful influence over our thinking, but they are not always relevant to the issue at hand. One of the most powerful emotions is anger. Often, anger is powerful enough to overwhelm reason and good common sense, as we recognize, for example, when we speak of crimes of passion and distinguish them from premeditated crimes. Thus, a very powerful persuasive strategy consists in arousing and mobilizing anger in support of a position—a favorite of political campaign strategists, especially where the electorate is relatively poorly informed. When this strategy is pursued in place of reasoning, the *informal fallacy of appeal to anger* is being committed. To be sure, there is often good reason to be angry. And anger, when it's reasonably justified, is a powerful and appropriate motivator. But when little or no specific reason is presented for being angry, and instead a vague and rhetorical appeal to general frustration is used to arouse anger, watch out. This is the sort of urging that often leads people to "shoot themselves in the foot." A similar strategy involves attempting to *intimidate* people into accepting a position. The *informal fallacy of appeal to fear* takes the basic form, "Believe this (or do this), or else!"

A similar strategy consists in attempting to persuade people by making them feel sorrow, sympathy, or anguish where such feelings, however understandable and genuine, are not relevant to the issue at stake. The *informal fallacy of appeal to pity* is frequently used in attempts to get special dispensation or exemption from deadlines and penalties. For example, the student who deserves a C in history might try to persuade his teacher to raise his grade for a variety of lamentable reasons: It's the first grade below a B he's ever received; it spoils a 3.85 GPA; he needs a higher grade to qualify for law school and his family has taken a third mortgage to finance his prelaw education. Pity is not *always* irrelevant. For example, when an attorney asks a judge to take into consideration the squalid upbringing of a client in determining a criminal sentence, this is probably not a fallacious appeal to pity. Although such an appeal would be irrelevant and fallacious in arguing for the person's innocence, it may be perfectly germane to the question of the severity of the sentence. Think of the German youth who in the summer of 1987 flew a small plane into the middle of Red Square in Moscow. That he may have been acting out of simple youthful exuberance rather than some motive more threatening to Soviet national security is irrelevant to whether he acted illegally, but it's not irrelevant to how severely he should be punished.

CRITICAL THINKING TIP 11.4

Pay attention to the *relevance* (or lack thereof) of the emotional appeal. Remember that relevance is not always obvious or apparent on the surface. But it *should* always be explainable.

EXERCISE 11.15 | **Emotional Appeals**

Identify and explain the fallacious appeal to emotion in each of the following:

> In the late 1980s, as the public policy issue over secondhand smoke swung more and more in the direction of segregating smokers and restricting them to designated smoking areas, the Philip Morris corporation placed the following full-page ad in major newspapers like *The New York Times:*
>
> > $1 trillion is too much financial power to ignore.
> >   America's 55.8 million smokers are a powerful economic force. If their household income of $1 trillion were a Gross National Product, it would be the third largest in the world. The plain truth is that smokers are one of the most economically powerful groups in this country. They help fuel the engine of the largest economy on the globe. The American Smoker—an economic force.

	Appeal to anger	Explain your answer:
	Appeal to fear	
	Appeal to pity	

"It may be that some of you, remembering his own case, will be annoyed that whereas he, in standing trial upon a less serious charge than this, made pitiful appeals to the jury with floods of tears, and had his infant children produced in court to excite the maximum of sympathy, I on the contrary intend to do nothing of the sort." — Socrates, in *The Apology,* line 34c.[4]

	Appeal to anger	Explain your answer:
	Appeal to fear	
	Appeal to pity	

DIVERSIONARY TACTICS

A common argumentative strategy consists in attempting to divert attention from the issue, especially when one lacks relevant and effective arguments. A general label for diversionary tactics in argument is *red herring.* This colorful term derives from an old ruse used by prison escapees to throw dogs off their trails. (They would smear themselves with herring—which turns red when it spoils—to cover their scent.) Stuck for a good argument? Make a joke. Stuck for a good defense? Attack! No good answer? Evade the question. "Before I answer this question, Ted, let me make a few things clear: . . ." This sort of thing, followed by a long and winding excursion through a number of relatively complicated points, may effectively leave the original topic buried in obscurity. Can't prove your point? Change the subject. Sometimes when people are having trouble making a cogent argument in favor of a position, they distort the issue or address some alternative issue instead. For example, in opening arguments charging an executive with embezzlement, the prosecutor quotes harrowing statistics about white-collar crime. Although her statistical evidence may influence the jury, it is irrelevant to establishing the guilt of the defendant. Sometimes, when people are having trouble making a cogent objection or argument against a position, they distort the position, or in effect set up some alternative position as a target for their objections. This distorted or alternative position is sometimes called a *straw person,* because, like a person made out of straw, it is not real and therefore much easier to "knock down" than the real position. When blame is at issue, watch for an attempt to shift the blame. A police officer stops a speeding motorist. "Why stop me?" the driver asks. "Didn't you see that Jaguar fly by at 80 mph?" (This probably won't get the driver off the hook.) This kind of *red herring* is often referred to as the *informal fallacy of two wrongs,* which comes from the proverb "Two wrongs don't make a right." A variation of this move is spreading the blame. Caught using company stationery for personal use, an office worker says, "Everybody else does it." This kind of *red herring* is often referred to as the *informal fallacy of common practice.*

CRITICAL THINKING TIP 11.5

Remember that issues are complex, so a diversion may on occasion be warranted and reasonable. A warranted and reasonable diversion should eventually return to the issue. Keep the issue(s) in mind.

EXERCISE 11.16 | Fallacies of Relevance II

In each of the following examples, check all fallacy categories that apply. Most important, explain each fallacy you identify.

And the Lord God commanded man, saying, "You may eat freely of every tree of the garden; but the tree of the knowledge of good and evil you shall not eat, for in the day that you eat of it you shall die." (Genesis 2: 16–17)

		Explain your answer:
	Appeal to anger	
	Appeal to fear	
	Appeal to pity	
	Straw person	
	Two wrongs	
	Common practice	

"Precisely what is Nixon accused of doing that his predecessors didn't do many times over? The break in and wire-tapping at the Watergate? Just how different was that from the bugging of Barry Goldwater's apartment during the 1964 presidential campaign?"[5]

		Explain your answer:
	Appeal to anger	
	Appeal to fear	
	Appeal to pity	
	Straw person	
	Two wrongs	
	Common practice	

"[The fight for the Equal Rights Amendment in Iowa] is about a socialist, anti-family political movement that encourages women to leave their husbands, kill their children, practice witchcraft, destroy capitalism, and become lesbians." (Televangelist and former candidate for president Pat Robertson)

		Explain your answer:
	Appeal to anger	
	Appeal to fear	
	Appeal to pity	
	Straw person	
	Two wrongs	
	Common practice	

Topic for Class Discussion: In this cartoon the great satirist Jules Feiffer takes a satirical look at journalism. The relevant background information is this: *Time* magazine once published a controversial story about the career of Israeli leader Ariel Sharon. Before Sharon became Israeli prime minister, he served as Israeli defense minister. And before that he was a general in the Israeli army. In that capacity he was commander of Israeli forces during an episode in West Lebanon in which a number of civilian noncombatants in a refugee camp were killed. Sharon brought a libel suit against *Time* over the story. This lawsuit frightened a good many working journalists into some rather extravagant defenses of *Time* in particular and journalistic practice and the freedom of speech in general. We count no less than seven distinct fallacious moves. How many fallacies can you find in the columnist's argument?

FALLACIOUS APPEALS TO AUTHORITY

As we discussed in Chapter 1, reliance upon authority is appropriate and understandable in many circumstances. Most of what we learn comes from some authority or other. And since we never arrive at the stage of knowing everything or being expert in *every* field, we continue to rely on authority from time to time throughout our lives. But we also noted a risk inherent in reliance upon authority. The risk is that we might rely *too heavily* on authority or rely on authority *when we* shouldn't. To the extent that we wind up relying upon unreliable authority, or upon authority whose reliability is open to serious question, we undermine the reliability of our reasoning and may be said to be committing some *informal fallacy of appeal to authority.* How do we know that the authority we are relying upon is in fact reliable? How do we tell when we are relying too heavily on authority or relying on authority when we shouldn't? Let us now look more closely at these questions and develop some guidelines.

Let us begin with the example we used in Chapter 1 to illustrate the general risk of overreliance on authority. The Heaven's Gate mass suicide presents a particularly chilling example of overreliance on authority, but by no means the only such example. Vivid and scary accounts come to light from time to time of cults such as Scientology, the Moonies, the Rajneeshees, Jonestown (where several hundred followers of Reverend Jim Jones were led to commit mass suicide), and David Koresh's Branch Davidians. All of these accounts illustrate the danger of allowing reality to be defined by appeal to the unassailable pronouncements of some "spiritual leader." When an appeal to authority wipes out all other considerations, it constitutes a fallacious appeal to authority. Such *appeals to invincible authority* have a notorious kind of currency within cults, or groups whose organizational principles or doctrines depend upon subordinating all personal autonomy. But such appeals are not confined to the dark and sinister world of spiritual fascism. Believe it or not, such *appeals to invincible authority* can be found of all places in the history of science. Some of Galileo's colleagues refused to look into his telescope and see for themselves because they were convinced that no evidence whatsoever could possibly contradict Aristotle's accounts of astronomy. This is no isolated aberration, by the way. Galileo himself made a similar argument when he said, "But can you doubt that air has weight when you have the clear testimony of Aristotle affirming that all the elements have weight including air, and excepting only fire?"6 This suggests that perhaps we should adopt a general rule to the effect that any authority worth relying on will remain open to question or challenge.

CRITICAL THINKING TIP 11.6

Any authority that places itself beyond question is unreliable. Any authority worth relying on remains open to question.

Think for a moment about Critical Thinking "Tip" 11.6. If we regard the reliability of any authority as depending on that authority's remaining open to question, it becomes obvious that any reliable authority must be identifiable. How can we question an authority if we don't know who the authority is? In spite of this obvious point, expert opinion is frequently merely *alluded to,* or identified in such a vague and incomplete way as to make any verification of reliability impossible. This is a favorite device of tabloids such as the *National Enquirer* that use phrases like "experts agree," "university studies show," or "a Russian scientist has discovered" to lend the weight of authority to all sorts of quackery. When an authority is left unspecified, we may say that an *informal fallacy of appeal to unidentified authority* has occurred.

These days real expertise tends to be more or less specialized. And although some remarkable individuals excel in more than one area of expertise, there is probably no such animal as an "expert on *everything.*" Accordingly, whenever an appeal to authority is introduced, it is wise to be aware of the area of expertise of any given authority—and to be mindful of the *relevance* of that particular area of expertise to the issue under discussion. When the appeal is to an authority whose expertise is in some field other than the one at issue, we may say that an *informal fallacy of appeal to irrelevant authority* has occurred. A common variety of appeal to irrelevant authority is the celebrity testimonial used throughout advertising for products ranging from aspirin to presidential candidates.

Especially where controversial issues are involved, we may expect to find disagreement even among the experts. What then? We could, of course, simply quote the experts with whom we are in agreement, but the weakness of this as a reasoning strategy is easy to see. Those who disagree with us can quote their own experts, and this leads to a standoff. The simple fact that we find ourselves in agreement with one authority does not by itself make this a more reliable authority than a competing authority with whom we are at odds. Simple appeal to congenial authority, where expert opinion is divided, can be dismissed as the *informal fallacy of division of expert opinion.* But it's not as though there is never a way to move beyond this sort of standoff. When expert opinion is divided, look into the credentials and affiliations of the experts. See if you can learn anything about their reputations. How are they regarded by their peers in their areas of expertise? This may be of some use in sifting through competing appeals to authority.

Sometimes claims are advanced by appeal to experts who do have impressive and genuinely relevant credentials but whose testimony may legitimately be suspect because of a demonstrable *conflict of interest*. The reliability of any authority, even in her own area of specialized expertise, depends also upon her being "impartial." An authority whose impartiality has been compromised is no longer reliable, regardless of the degree or relevance of her expertise. For example, if we find that some scientific study of the effects of secondhand tobacco smoke was underwritten by a research grant from the Tobacco Institute, we should at least look for other studies to compare this one with.

EXERCISE 11.17 | Appeals to Authority

In each of the following examples, check all fallacy categories that apply. Most important, explain each fallacy you identify.

At the beginning of this chapter there is a cartoon in which a lawyer makes a very dubious argument for his client's innocence. Which particular fallacies does the cartoon illustrate?

	Invincible authority	Explain your answer:
	Unidentified authority	
	Irrelevant authority	
	Division of expert opinion	
	Conflict of interest	

"We are, quite bluntly, broke. We don't have the money to sustain the dreams and experiments of liberalism any longer. We have a $400 billion a year budget deficit and a $4 trillion debt. The economist Walter Williams points out that with the money we've spent on poverty programs since the

1960s we could have bought the entire assets of every Fortune 500 company and virtually every acre of U.S. farmland."[7]

		Explain your answer:
	Invincible authority	
	Unidentified authority	
	Irrelevant authority	
	Division of expert opinion	
	Conflict of interest	

ADDITIONAL EXERCISES

■ **EXERCISE 11.18**   In our experience, the best way to study the material in this and the next chapter is in conversation with other people—in a facilitated discussion section, or in a small autonomous study group, or with a study partner. Take turns critically examining the following examples, using the tools and terminology covered in this chapter. Listen to each others' critical assessments and weigh them for their clarity, their explanatory power, and their fairness. As you work your way through the following examples, alternately play the role of finding and explaining the flaw in the argument, and the complementary role of trying to defend the argument against the proposed criticism. Don't forget, sometimes the difference between a fallacy and a reasonable argument is a matter of considerable subtlety and delicacy. An argument may look a lot like a fallacy of some kind and yet deeply defensible. And on the other hand a given argument can have more than one thing wrong with it. The discussion of these examples may well prove to be of greater importance than the "answer" to the question which fallacy, if any, has been committed. If you arrive at a consensus criticism, move on to the next example.

- The end of anything is its perfection. Therefore, since death is the end of life, death must be the perfection of life.

- Pushy father-in-law to new bride: "So, when are you kids planning to make us grandparents?"

- "Repressive environmentalists and population and economic zero-growthers have requested President Reagan to oust James G. Watt as Secretary of the Interior. Those stop-all-progress destructionists have thick-skinned craniums. They lack the intelligence to realize that the United States of America is no longer a subsidiary of the baby-and-people hating and business-repressive do-gooders. President Reagan and Secretary Watt have done what should have been done long ago. Their critics can go to blazes on a one-way ticket."[8]

- "For three decades [1960s, 1970s, 1980s] the environmentalists, Greens, tree huggers—choose any epithet that suits your fancy but mainly descriptions of those who've ranted and railed against growth—have managed to defeat every attempt to modernize Sonoma County transportation to handle the growing load. I would like to point out that sticking your head in the sand and saying you're against growth simply won't cut the mustard. You cannot pass a law (urban growth boundaries) against growth; stupid even to think of it. If you can manage to come up with an elixir that can be delivered in the water system a la Big Brother, which will prevent human sexuality, then you can slow growth."[9]

- "Bill Clinton has ceased promising that the missus will play a key role in his White House. The reason is clear from [a recent] profile of Hillary in *American Spectator*. Since her Yale days, Hillary has been enthusiastically engaged with the radical Left. While she headed the New World Foundation, it gave grants to such leftist organizations as the fellow-traveling National Lawyers Guild and CISPES (the Committee in Support of the People of El Salvador)."[10]

- "Should we not assume that just as the eye, the hand, the foot, and in general each part of the body clearly has its own proper function, so man too has some function over and above the function of his parts?"[11]

- From a letter to the editor: "I was most disappointed with your paper for publishing that article about Madonna's book *Sex* in your 'Teen Life' section. I feel that the article is encouraging teens to buy and view sordid material on the basis that it is only 'fantasy.' Perhaps we need to remind ourselves that Ted Bundy's career started by viewing soft-core pornography, escalated to hard-core and then, when "fantasy" was not enough, he decided that only the real thing would do."

- "Many of my colleagues in the press are upset about the growing practice of paying newsmakers for news. The auction principle seems to them to strike somehow at the freedom of the press, or at least the freedom of the poor press to compete with the rich press. But I find their objections pious and, in an economy where everything and everybody has its price, absurd."[12]

- Republican presidential candidate Jack Kemp in a 1988 televised presidential primary debate, attacking the eventual Republican nominee, George Bush (who was supporting the ratification of the INF Treaty with the Soviet Union): "I can't believe I'm hearing a Republican say 'Let's give peace a chance'!"

- Lt. Colonel Oliver North campaigning in 1992 against Senator Barbara Boxer (Democrat from California): "[She's a] check-kiting, pay-raising, self-promoting, defense-cutting, tax-raising, free-spending permanent political potentate of pork. Who are Barbara Boxer's buddies? They are environmental radicals, people who believe in lifestyles we wouldn't even talk about, much less embrace. She believes spotted owls are higher on the food chain than we are, and that's not how I read Genesis."

- Former President George Bush, in the final days of his unsuccessful run for re-election: "My dog Millie knows more about foreign policy than these two Bozos," referring to Democratic running mates Bill Clinton and Albert Gore. In the same speech, this time about Gore in particular: "You know why I call him Ozone Man? This guy is so far out in the environmental extreme, we'll be up to our neck in owls and outta work for every American. He is way out, far out, man."

- "Can the universe think about itself? We know that at least one part of it can: we ourselves. Is it not reasonable to conclude the whole can?"[13]

- "A term I use to describe the mess that surrounds most issues in the world today and prevents us from getting at what is really so about the world's problems is 'pea soup.' The pea soup is a mass of confusion, controversy, argument, conflict, and opinions. As long as you are asking what more can you do, what better solution have you got, what have you come up with that's different, you cannot see that the confusion, controversy, conflict, doubt, lack of trust, and opinions surrounding the problem of hunger and starvation result inevitably from any position you take. Once you are clear that you cannot take any position that will contribute in any way to the end of hunger and starvation, that any position you take will only contribute to the pea soup that engulfs the problem of hunger and starvation, then hope dies. And when hope dies, hopelessness dies with it: Without hope you can't have hopelessness. You are now close to the source of the problem of hunger and starvation on the planet. If you can see that the problem is without hope, you are no longer hopeless and frustrated. You are just there with whatever is so."[14]

- In President Bill Clinton's second term in office, issues were raised in Congress about the integrity of his campaign fund-raising practices. During a press conference Clinton offered the following response, carefully worded in the passive voice. "No one is blameless here. At the edges errors are made, and when they're made they need to be confessed."[15]

- Take another look at the example in Exercise 11.16 from the Philip Morris ad campaign. Now look at this quote from Philip Morris vice president for corporate affairs, Guy L. Smith, defending the ad against the criticism that it was designed to appeal to fear. "[The ads were] an attempt to raise the level of awareness, but certainly not to scare anybody."

- "How can you deny that abortion is murder? The fetus is certainly alive, isn't it? And it certainly is human, isn't it? And it hasn't done anything wrong, has it? So you're talking about taking an innocent human life. And that's murder! What else is there to say?"

- People object to sexism and racism on the ground that they involve "discrimination." But what is objectionable about discrimination? We discriminate all the time—in the cars we buy, the foods we eat, the books we read, the friends we choose. The fact is there's nothing wrong with discrimination as such.

- "The Dalai Lama says that outer disarmament can only take place through inner disarmament. If the individual doesn't become more peaceful, a society that's the sum total of such individuals can never become more peaceful either."[16]

Calvin and Hobbes
by Bill Watterson

■ **EXERCISE 11.19**   *Essay Assignment:* Is gender relevant? Perhaps an even better question would be *"When* is gender relevant?" Do you think Susie commits a fallacy in the Calvin and Hobbes cartoon? Write a short essay in which you explain why. Are there any circumstances in which you think gender is relevant?

■ **EXERCISE 11.20**   *Essay Assignment:* The 1990 general election in the state of California included two measures concerning liquor taxation. Proposition 134, the "nickel-a-drink" initiative, qualified for the ballot by a citizen petition campaign organized by a coalition led by Mothers Against Drunk Driving (MADD). It was pitted against Proposition 126, which was lobbied onto the ballot through the state legislature. Below you will find a portion of the argument supporters of Proposition 134 used against Proposition 126. Our question for you is: Is this argument an instance of the fallacy of genetic appeal or not? Explain.

"Proposition 126 is sponsored by the liquor industry. The reason they say Proposition 126 is a better approach to taxing the liquor industry than Proposition 134, the "Nickel-a-Drink" proposal, is that Proposition 126 taxes them less.

   "The only reason Proposition 126 is on the ballot is that the liquor industry spends $1,000,000 each year lobbying the Legislature and has contributed over $1,600,000 to politicians since 1988. What the liquor industry wants, the Legislature gives. That's why the Legislature has not changed the wine tax from 1 cent per gallon since 1937.

   "The sole purpose of Proposition 126 is to defeat Proposition 134, the "Nickel-a-Drink" Alcohol Tax Initiative. When reading the argument in favor of Proposition 126, CONSIDER THE SOURCE—IT IS THE LIQUOR INDUSTRY!"

■ **EXERCISE 11.21**   At the end of Chapter 10 you were challenged to take a position on your issue in a 100-word "Position Statement" (Exercise 10.18). We bet that what you came up with is an argument. That is, it is a composition designed to be persuasive at a rational level, and it has a thesis or conclusion in it somewhere and some other ideas and claims that support it. Let's say, then, it's a draft of an argument—in the "abstract." This means, it's short and could be developed more deeply, and it's still open to critique and revision. OK? So, first, analyze your own argument. Then ask, "Is my argument open to any of the kinds of criticisms (Does it commit any of the fallacies?) we have just studied?

GLOSSARY

ad hominem   fallacy consisting of irrelevant personal references or attacks

ad hominem, abusive   fallacy consisting of baseless and irrelevant personal references or attacks

ad hominem, circumstantial   fallacy consisting of irrelevant personal references or attacks based on actual information about a person that carries unfavorable but irrelevant personal implications

amphibole   grammatical ambiguity, or a fallacy based on grammatical ambiguity

appeal to anger   fallacious strategy of arousing irrelevant anger in support of a position

appeal to authority   fallacious use of authority in support of a claim

appeal to fear or force   fallacy of attempting to intimidate people into accepting a position

appeal to novelty   fallacy of assuming or arguing that something is good or desirable simply because it is novel or new

appeal to pity   fallacious strategy of arousing irrelevant pity in support of a position

appeal to popularity   fallacy of assuming or arguing that something is true, good, or desirable simply because it is popularly believed or esteemed

appeal to tradition   fallacy of assuming or arguing that something is good or desirable simply because it is old or traditional

common practice   variety of the "two wrongs" fallacy in which one's own wrongdoing is excused by assimilation to widespread practice

composition   fallacy of inferring characteristics of the whole from characteristics of the parts

conflict of interest   any combination of interests that interferes with impartiality; hence, a variety of fallacious appeal to authority where the authority cited has such a combination of interests

division   fallacy of inferring characteristics of a part from characteristics of the whole

division of expert opinion   variety of fallacious appeal to authority where the authorities with relevant expertise are divided over the question at issue

dysphemism   negative exaggeration

equivocation   inconsistent use of an ambiguous expression, or a fallacy based on such usage

euphemism   positive exaggeration

false implication   advertising strategy in which important claims are strongly implied but remain literally unstated, often because they are known to be false

genetic appeal   fallacy of assessment simply in terms of origin, sources, or genesis

guilt by association   fallacy of supporting negative claims about people or their views or positions solely on the basis of their relationships with others

hyperbole   advertising and public relations strategy in which exaggerated (hyperbolic) terminology is used to promote excitement

informal fallacy   unreliable inference whose flaw or weakness is attributable to something other than its formal structure

invincible authority   variety of fallacious appeal to authority where the authority is taken to outweigh any conflicting consideration

irrelevant expertise   variety of fallacious appeal to authority where the authority cited lacks expertise relevant to the question at issue

poisoning the well   fallacious strategy of attempting to discredit a position, or its advocate, before the argument for the position can be considered

positioning   fallacy of supporting positive claims about people or their views or positions solely on the basis of their relationships with others

provincialism   fallacy of appealing to considerations of group loyalty in support of a claim

puffery   advertising strategy in which vague terminology is used to promote enthusiasm

red herring   fallacious argument strategy of diverting attention from the real issue to another one

rhetorical question   question used to mask a claim, or a fallacy based on such usage

straw person   fallacious argument strategy of attacking a weak or distorted representation of an opponent's position

testimonial   advertising and public relations strategy based on testimony of a celebrity, often an instance of the fallacy of irrelevant expertise

two wrongs   fallacy of excusing one's own wrong by comparing it to others'

unidentified experts   variety of fallacious appeal to authority where the authority is not identified sufficiently to make assessments of expertise, impartiality, or other relevant variables

weasel word   a vague word or expression, often part of advertising and public relations strategies, used to evade responsibility for an implied claim

ENDNOTES

[1] 98th Congress, 2nd Session, 1984, October 19.

[2] Paul Stevens, "Weasel Words: God's Little Helpers," in Paul A. Eschol, Alfred A. Rosa, and Virginia P. Clark (eds.), *Language Awareness* (New York: St. Martin's Press, 1974).

[3] In the early days of the automobile the Supreme Court created an exception to the 4th Amendment's protection against unwarranted search for searches of vehicles, holding in Carroll v. United States that vehicles may be searched without warrants if the officer undertaking the search has probable cause to believe that the vehicle contains contraband. The Court explained that the mobility of vehicles would allow them to be quickly moved from the jurisdiction if time were taken to obtain a warrant. Later the Court developed a reduced privacy rationale to supplement the mobility rationale, explaining that "the configuration, use, and regulation of automobiles often may dilute the reasonable expectation of privacy that exists with respect to differently situated property. . . One has a lesser expectation of privacy in a

motor vehicle because its function is transportation and it seldom serves as one's residence or as the repository of personal effects. . . . It travels public thoroughfares where both its occupants and its contents are in plain view." While motor homes do serve as residences and as repositories for personal effects, and while their contents are often shielded from public view, in California v. Carney, 471 U.S. 386, 393 (1985) the Court extended the automobile exception to them as well, holding that there is a diminished expectation of privacy in a mobile home parked in a parking lot and licensed for vehicular travel, hence "readily mobile." See the FindLaw entry on the 4th Amendment at http://caselaw.lp.findlaw.com/data/constitution/amendment04.

[4] Plato, *The Apology*, tr. Hugh Tredennick, in *Plato: The Collected Dialogues,* eds. Edith Hamilton and Huntington Cairns (Princeton: Princeton University Press, Bollingen Series, 1963), p. 20.

[5] Victor Lasky, "It Didn't Start With Watergate," *Book Digest* (November 1977), p. 47.

[6] Galileo Galilei, *Dialogues Concerning Two New Sciences,* tr. Henry Crew and Alfonso de Salvio (Evanston, IL: Northwestern University Press, 1939).

[7] Rush Limbaugh, *The Way Things Ought to Be* (New York: Simon and Schuster, 1992), p. 302.

[8] Letter to the Editor, *Los Angeles Times,* July 24, 1981, part 2, p. 6.

[9] Letter to the Editor, *Sonoma County Independent,* February 12, 1998.

[10] Editorial, *National Review,* August, 1992.

[11] Aristotle, *Nicomachean Ethics,* trans. Martin Ostwald (Indianapolis: Bobbs-Merrill, 1962), p. 16.

[12] Shana Alexander, "Loew's Common Denominator," *Newsweek*, April 14, 1975, p. 96.

[13] Jose Silva, *The Silva Mind Control Method* (New York: Pocket Books, 1978), p. 116.

[14] Werner Erhard, *The End of Starvation: Creating an Idea Whose Time Has Come* (San Francisco: The Hunger Project, 1982), pp. 10–11.

[15] *The Weekly Standard,* February 10, 1997.

[16] Matthieu Ricard, *The Monk and the Philosopher* (New York: Schocken, 1998), p. 156.

CHAPTER 12

Informal Fallacies II: Assumptions and Induction

Will you forget about logic and give me the benefit of the doubt?!?   WOODY ALLEN[1]

FALLACIOUS ASSUMPTIONS

In Chapter 1 we discussed the role of assumptions in reasoning and proposed the first of our series of Critical Thinking Tips: Be Aware of Assumptions. Assumptions become more dangerous to reasoning to the extent that they remain hidden. Thus, we should be generally on the alert for hidden assumptions wherever inferences are being made from one or more claims to another, and also for hidden assumptions underlying any of the claims explicitly being made. In a general sense, this sort of vigilance and awareness constitutes a tool of informal fallacy criticism. Whenever we become aware of the presence of a hidden assumption in

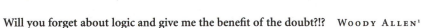

IRREFUTABLE EVIDENCE

fragments of UFO that crash-landed last week near Lambert's Corner, Saskatchewan

Soil taken from site

Some photos taken just prior to landing of craft

A.   B.   C.

Enlarged photo (B.)

Drawings done by Mrs. Kitty Nederson, witness, while under hypnosis

Tape recording of nearby dog barking uncontrollably at time of visitation

an argument and that assumption is questionable or dubious, we may say that the argument commits the *informal fallacy of questionable assumptions.*

FALSE DILEMMA

Of course, the label is not what is important. What is important is the critical activity of carefully pointing out where the assumption is hidden and calling that assumption into question, making clear precisely what is questionable about it. For example, sometimes an argument depends upon the presentation of what is assumed to be an exhaustive range of alternatives. Dilemma is the logical strategy of proving a point by showing that it is implied by each of two alternatives, at least one of which must be true (see Chapter 6). Such an argument depends on the assumption that there aren't any *other* alternatives. If this assumption is false or doubtful, we may say that the argument commits the *informal fallacy of false dilemma*. Have you ever heard people argue in favor of some course of action by saying something like, "Well, we've gotta do *something*, don't we?" The unstated inferential assumption being made here is that we either follow the proposed course of action or we don't do anything at all. The strategy best suited to exposing instances of this fallacy is to articulate a specific alternative left out of consideration in the premises. False dilemma is one of the most powerfully persuasive of the common informal fallacies. This is because its structure is deductively valid, conforming to either the disjunctive syllogism or the dilemma argument forms (see Chapter 7). False dilemma is also appealing psychologically due to the natural human tendency to prefer simplicity, to see things in terms of pairs of mutually exclusive alternatives, or as it is sometimes said, in black and white.

LOADED QUESTIONS

Sometimes a question is so worded that you can't answer it without also granting a particular answer to some *other* question. Such a construction is called a *complex question*, or sometimes simply a *loaded question*. A well-known example is the old vaudeville line "Have you stopped beating your wife (or husband)?" Such a question boxes you in because, first, it demands either "yes" or "no" as an answer, and second, because either of those answers *presupposes* that you are or were beating your spouse.

INNUENDO

Innuendo is Latin for "by hinting." The *informal fallacy of innuendo* consists of implying a judgment, usually derogatory, by hinting. No argument is offered. Instead, the audience is invited by suggestion, by a nod and a wink, to make the assumption. Someone asks, "Where is Jones? Did he get fired or something?" Someone answers, "Not yet." By innuendo, the response numbers Jones's days. The political candidate who distributes a brochure promising to restore honesty and integrity to an office has suggested, but not thereby argued, that the incumbent is crooked.

CIRCULAR REASONING

Three thieves have stolen seven bags of gold. The thief in the middle hands two bags of gold to the thief on the left and two bags of gold to the thief on the right and says, "I'm keeping three for myself." The thief on the left asks, "Why do you get to keep three, when we each only get two?" The thief in the middle says, "Because I'm the leader of this outfit." The thief on the right asks, "What makes you the leader?", to which the thief in the middle responds, "I've got the most gold."[2]

EXERCISE 12.1 | **Topic for Class Discussion**

Perhaps the moral of this little fable is that there's no honor among thieves. In any case, it should be readily apparent that the thief in the middle is pulling a fast one on his two partners in crime. Can you explain the trick?

The *informal fallacy of begging the question,* or *circular reasoning,* occurs when the conclusion of the argument—or some other claim that presupposes it—is assumed as a premise. Such arguments are objectionable because the premise is just as questionable as the conclusion it is intended to support (hence the name "begging the question"). What makes this fallacy particularly tricky to deal with is that arguers are rarely so clumsy as to appeal to a premise that is *obviously* the same as the conclusion. More frequently the question-begging premise is a subtle rewording of the conclusion or is presupposed by the conclusion in a way even the arguer may fail to appreciate. The strategy one frequently needs to pursue to effectively diagnose and expose this fallacy therefore involves sensitive use of paraphrase. If the premise and the conclusion can be paraphrased into each other without significant loss of meaning, then we have a plausible case of begging the question.

EXERCISE 12.2 | Fallacious Assumptions

Each of the following examples contains (or points out) at least one major fallacy involving unwarranted assumptions. In each, check all fallacy categories that apply. Most important, explain each fallacy you identify.

"By the time you have wisely purchased this tome (book, for those of you in Rio Linda, California) most critics will have undoubtedly savaged it. In many cases, their reviews will have been written before the book was published. How do I know this? Because I do." (Rush Limbaugh, *The Way Things Ought to Be* [New York: Simon and Schuster, 1992].)

	False dilemma	Explain your answer:
	Loaded question	
	Innuendo	
	Begging the question	

We must believe in the existence of God because it is written in the Holy scriptures, and conversely we must believe in the Holy scriptures because they come from God." (Rene Descartes, "Letter of Dedication," *Meditations on First Philosophy*)

	False dilemma	Explain your answer:
	Loaded question	
	Innuendo	
	Begging the question	

Captain L had a first mate who was at times addicted to the use of strong drink, and occasionally, as the slang has it, "got full." The ship was lying in port in China, and the mate had been on shore and had there indulged rather freely in some of the vile compounds common in Chinese ports. He came on board, "drunk as a lord," and thought he had a mortgage on the whole world. The captain, who rarely ever touched liquor himself, was greatly disturbed by the disgraceful conduct of his officer, particularly as the crew had all observed his condition. One of the duties of the first mate is to write up the log each day, but as that worthy was not able to do it, the captain made the proper entry, but added: "The mate was drunk all day." The ship left port the next day and the mate got "sobered off." He attended to his writing at the proper time, but was appalled when he saw what the captain had done. He went back on deck, and soon after the following colloquy took place:

"Cap'n, why did you write in the log yesterday that I was drunk all day?"

"It was true, wasn't it?"

"Yes, but what will the ship owners say if they see it? It will hurt me with them."

But the mate could get nothing more from the Captain than, "It was true, wasn't it?"

The next day, when the Captain was examining the book, he found at the bottom of the mate's entry of observation, course, winds, and tides: "The captain was sober all day." (Charles E. Trow, *The Old Shipmasters of Salem* [New York: Macmillan, 1905], pp. 14–15.)

	False dilemma	Explain your answer: .
	Loaded question	
	Innuendo	
	Begging the question	

Topic for Class Discussion: Below you will find a nicely matched pair of examples from the 1984 presidential campaign. The first is from the challenger, Democrat Walter Mondale. The second is from the incumbent and election winner, Republican President Ronald Reagan. Each passage commits the same informal fallacy of questionable assumption. Can you explain how the fallacy works?

- *Walter Mondale:* Our choice is between two futures, between a Reagan future and a better future. It is a choice between expediency and excellence. It is a choice between social Darwinism and social decency. It is a choice between salesmanship and leadership.

- *President Ronald Reagan:* The truth is, Americans must choose between two drastically different points of view. One puts its faith in the pipe-dreamers and margin scribblers of Washington; the other believes in the collective wisdom of the American people. Our opponents believe the solutions to our nation's problems lie in the psychiatrist's notes or in a social worker's file or in a bureaucrat's budget. We believe in the working man's toil, the businessman's enterprise, and the clergyman's counsel.

FALLACIES OF INDUCTION

In Chapters 8 and 9 we explained in a general way how to evaluate inductive reasoning. Inductive strength is essentially a matter of degree—the degree to which the conclusion remains open to doubt, assuming the premises are true. And this—the degree to which the conclusion remains open to doubt—depends on the *type* of inductive reasoning involved. Looking at the various types of inductive reasoning we discussed in Chapters 8 and 9, we can now highlight some of the more common *informal fallacies of induction*. These will consist in overestimating the strength of some particular type of inductive inference.

GENERALIZATIONS

In Chapter 8 we explained that the strength of an inductive generalization depends most heavily on two factors: the size and representativeness of the sample. So this highlights two areas of possible overestimation of inductive strength. The *informal fallacy of small sample* consists in overestimating the statistical significance of evidence drawn from a small number of cases. Sometimes what appears to be a significant pattern in a small number of cases disappears altogether when we investigate a larger number of cases. Suppose we are taking a poll to determine political preferences and of the first 10 responses, 7 favor the challenger over the incumbent. But by the time we have interviewed a hundred people we may find the incumbent ahead 75 to 21 (with 4 undecided). But one must be careful in applying this as a criticism. The size of the sample relative to the target population is not the only factor involved in determining the reliability of the inductive inference. Even a relatively small sample can be used to reliably project trends on a massive scale if the study is carefully controlled and based on a representative sample. Thus, it would be insufficient basis for criticism merely to point out, for example, that a national political preference poll had been conducted on the basis of 5,000 responses. In fact, a poll of just 1,500, adhering to all the criteria of a scientifically respectable sample, can yield accurate information about the nation as a whole with a margin of error of only ± 3 percent. And doubling the sample would reduce the margin of error only by about 1 percent.

But suppose the aforementioned 5,000 responses were all taken from one geographical region. This regional bias would greatly increase liability to error. Fundamentally, the representativeness of a sample is even more important than sample size, since what we are trying to do is to project conclusions affected by many variables. If we can control all of the relevant variables in a relatively small sample, so much the better for the economy of the study. The important thing is to control all of the variables. But this can be very difficult to accomplish in an area such as political preference, since it is affected by such a wide variety of variable factors. The problem is made greater by the fact that not all of the relevant variables may be known. The *informal fallacy of unrepresentative sample* consists in overestimating the statistical significance of evidence drawn from a sample of a particular kind.

To see just how tricky this can be, consider the famous case of the 1936 *Reader's Digest* presidential preference poll, which incorrectly predicted that Alf Landon would defeat Franklin Delano Roosevelt. The poll was based on *2 million* respondents selected *at random* from phone books and motor vehicle registration lists. *Random* means that each member of the target population has a roughly equal chance of appearing among the sample. For example, if pollsters wish to find out what the American Catholic laity thinks about the sexual abuse scandal, they must ensure that every American lay Catholic is *equally likely* to be among those polled. Notice that this doesn't mean that every American lay Catholic needs to *be polled*—only that every American lay Catholic has an equal chance of *being asked*. If pollsters ask only *California* Catholics or *New York* Catholics, that's not random, and so not representative. In its 1936 presidential preference poll *Reader's Digest* picked the names *at random* from the phone book and the motor vehicle registration lists. What did it miss?

EXERCISE 12.3 | **Unrepresented Sample?**

In its 1936 presidential preference poll *Reader's Digest* picked the names *at random* from the phone book and the motor vehicle registration lists. What did it miss? Can you guess?

The relevant variable the poll overlooked was that in 1936 (during the Great Depression) a large part of the electorate couldn't afford a car or even a phone (and they tended to be angry about it). So, even though the pollsters *tried* to take a random sample, the sample they got was far from random and failed rather spectacularly to reflect the political mood of the electorate as a whole.

Besides the sample size and the degree to which the sample represents the target, other aspects of methodology can affect the strength of an inductive generalization. The reliability of inductive generalizations can depend in part upon whether other informal fallacies, such as informal fallacies of language or fallacious assumptions, are involved. For example, if a public-opinion poll is conducted using loaded or leading questions, or questions that restrict the range of available responses, or questions that contain questionable presuppositions, the results are not to be trusted.

EXERCISE 12.4 | **Fallacious Assumptions in Public Opinion Polling**

Topic for Class Discussion: Critique the following hypothetical public-opinion poll. Suppose that you live in a community where rapid growth has stretched existing waste-management resources to the breaking point, resulting in environmental pollution serious enough to have raised public concern. Now suppose the local newspaper conducts a readers' poll asking readers to rank-order the following three policy options:

- A municipal bond issue to construct new sewage treatment facilities.

- A regional bond issue to construct a pipeline to transport excess sewage to the ocean.

- An increase in property tax to pay for improvement and expansion of existing facilities.

Now the newspaper reports that public opinion favors a municipal bond measure to construct new sewage treatment facilities 48 percent to 35 percent over the next most popular option.

So far we have focused on how inductive evidence is gathered and generalizations are reached. We should also look critically at the way the results are presented and interpreted. Sometimes relevant evidence is deliberately kept from view because it conflicts with the arguer's intended interpretation of the evidence that is presented. This constitutes the *informal fallacy of suppressed evidence*. A common political foible and a particular favorite in the field of advertising, particularly where statistical data are used, this is an obviously disreputable argumentative strategy. For example, advertisers are forever referring to "scientific" studies that "demonstrate" the superiority of their products but strategically neglecting to mention that they have commissioned the studies themselves, a crucial piece of information relevant to assessing the objectivity of the studies. It's worth noting that the fallacy of suppressed evidence is not confined to statistical generalizations. It occurs anytime significant information or evidence—information or evidence that makes a difference to the conclusion—is omitted. For example, in 1996 opponents of California's Proposition 215, the ballot initiative measure that made marijuana legally available as a prescription drug, argued correctly that marijuana's safety and effectiveness compared to the already legal synthetic substitute Marinol had not been scientifically established. What they conveniently neglected to mention was that this scientific evidence was lacking because the Food and Drug Administration had up to that point refused to investigate the matter.

Statistics often invite misinterpretation, particularly in the direction of overestimating the significance of some trend. One way that this can happen is by assuming an inappropriate basis of comparison. For example, suppose that that you live in a small town and the local weekly newspaper reports a 33 percent rise in the rate of car theft. This sounds rather alarming. But the alarm diminishes when we read past the headline and learn that the number of car thefts rose from three in the previous year to four. And now suppose that over the same period the town's population has doubled. In this case, the incidence of car theft *per capita* (relative to population) has significantly dropped. We may call this technique of distorting the implications of statistical data the *informal fallacy of bad baseline.* Be on the lookout for this sort of misrepresentation in political speeches about trends in crime, unemployment, balance of trade, welfare dependency, and other social trends. Bear in mind that changing the eligibility requirements for unemployment insurance benefits can make it *look statistically like* the number of unemployed people is dropping.

ANALOGIES

In Chapter 8 we gave a detailed explanation of the standards and procedures for the evaluation of arguments based on analogies. The examples we used there to illustrate these standards and procedures are quite strong inductive arguments. Using these same standards, the identification and critique of a weak analogy is a matter of adding up relevant similarities and differences. If we find that the argument is based on similarities that are *irrelevant* to the conclusion or that it glosses over relevant differences, then we may object that the argument is based on a questionable, false, or misleading analogy. Note that this is a two-step process. First, it has to be established that there is a difference between the items compared in the analogy. Second, and more important, the relevance of the difference to the point of the analogy needs to be established. Overlooking this second step will result in a misapplication of this criticism. One often hears by way of objection, "Your argument is like comparing apples and oranges." Notice that this is also an analogy, the point of which is that the analogy being critiqued is misleading. Bear in mind that no two items in the universe are so different from each other that they cannot be compared in *some* useful way relevant to *some* purpose. Is a comparison between apples and oranges necessarily misleading? Not if you're trying to sort the fruit out from the vegetables. So, we must keep the point of the analogy we are critiquing clearly in mind as we look for differences. And we must show that the differences are relevant to that point. When we have done both of these things, we may say that we have identified an instance of the *informal fallacy of faulty analogy.*

EXERCISE 12.5 | Faulty Analogy?

Topic for Class Discussion: Critique the argument in the cartoon on page 318. Do you think there's anything fallacious about the pig's argument? Explain any criticisms you would offer in detail. What about the fact that the cartoonist has put the argument into the mouth of a pig?

BURDEN OF PROOF

The *informal fallacy of arguing ad ignorantiam* (from Latin for "arguing from ignorance") consists in treating the absence of evidence for (or against) a claim as proof of its falsity (or truth). The fallacy is a perversion of the concept of "burden of proof" and legitimate presumption discussed in Chapter 9. Essentially, it consists in misplacing the burden of proof. Understandably, many examples of this fallacy have to do with the unknown and the "supernatural." For example, there is an argument for the existence of extraterrestrial intelligent life that goes like this: Because the universe is infinitely large, it is impossible to prove conclusively that the only intelligent life that exists is on the planet Earth, and so we should assume that extraterrestrial intelligent life exists.

A related fallacy, which we'll call *arguing from invincible ignorance*, consists in refusing to accept one's own burden of proof. For example, in the *Peanuts* episode Snoopy commits this fallacy twice. In the first instance Snoopy dismisses Lucy's expression of doubt as ignorant; later he dismisses the evidence of her research on the basis of the far-fetched assumption of a massive coverup. In each case there appears to be no reason for dismissing the information other than that it conflicts with the hypothesis he is initially, and as it seems inflexibly, committed to. In what might be called a definitive case of "sleeping dogmatism," Snoopy has simply closed his mind on this subject.

HYPOTHETICAL AND CAUSAL REASONING

A closely related fallacy, in this case a perversion of the concept of explanatory power as discussed in Chapter 9, consists in concluding that some explanation or solution holds simply because no one can think of a better one. There are many things we don't adequately understand. For example, as of this writing, the origin of the AIDS virus remains a mystery. Filmmaker Spike Lee once argued that AIDS originated as part of a genocidal attack on gays and black people. His argument seems to rest largely on the idea that there are some peculiarities about the course of the AIDS epidemic for which there is no better explanation. "All of sudden, a disease appears out of nowhere that nobody has a cure for, and it's specifically targeted at gays and minorities. . . . So now it's a national priority. Exactly like drugs became when they escaped the urban centers into white suburbia. . . . The mystery disease, yeah, about as mysterious as 'genocide'. . . ." To call this an *interesting* hypothesis and one worth investigating would be fair enough. But as it stands it is only an empirical hypothesis. This means there should be some hard evidence out there somewhere to confirm it, if it's true. But one thing that does *not* count as confirming evidence is the absence of any better explanation. Philosopher Elliott Sober calls this informal fallacy the *Only Game in Town Fallacy.*[3]

Reasoning about causality is tricky because causal relationships are never directly observable and the things whose causes we most urgently want to understand—our health, the behavior of the physical world, the economy, and so on—are *so* complicated. For these reasons, we recommend that when confronted by any argument about causal relationships, you remind yourself of Mill's Methods of reasoning about causality. Stretch your imagination. Consider as many possible causal factors as you can think of. Try to imagine the kind of experiment you would design to test these as causal hypotheses. From the discussion of causal reasoning in Chapter 9 we can derive a number of fallacies that can be understood as failing to meet one or more of the standards and criteria of good inductive reasoning. Superstitions provide the most obvious cases of this kind of fallacious thinking, as, for example, when a basketball coach refuses to change his "lucky" socks in an attempt to influence the outcome of the game. But there are a number of more subtle pitfalls of causal reasoning to be aware of.

CRITICAL THINKING TIP 12.1

- Remember Mill's Methods of reasoning about causality.
- Stretch your imagination.
- Consider as many possible causal factors as you can think of.
- Try to imagine the kind of experiment you would design in order to test these as causal hypotheses.

One of the most common kinds of evidence for a causal connection is a statistical correlation between two phenomena. For example, medical scientists knew for some time of a statistical correlation between cigarette smoking and lung cancer. The incidence of lung cancer in the smoking population was higher than in the nonsmoking population. Such a correlation is genuinely relevant inductive evidence for a causal connection between lung cancer and smoking. The problem is that by itself it is inconclusive. It suggests, but does not establish, the causal link. For several decades the tobacco industry was successful in eluding the implications —and liabilities—of the causal connection between smoking and cancer on the basis of this distinction between statistical correlation and causality. That's how real and significant a distinction it is. Some people may find this hard to accept and may even be inclined to wonder why we should not, as a society, have been able to move earlier and more decisively against the tobacco industry to establish antismoking policies. Notice, however, that there is also a strong statistical correlation between the incidence of lung cancer and age. Yet it would be misleading to suggest that age causes lung cancer, or that lung cancer causes aging. So, isolating the causal factor does indeed require further scientific evidence. The *informal fallacy of jumping from correlation to cause* occurs whenever someone interprets an observed statistical correlation as showing a causal connection without first having made a reasonable attempt to isolate the cause by controlling the relevant variables experimentally as described in Chapter 9.

A similar fallacy consists in inferring a causal connection from temporal contiguity. In other words, it is a fallacy to infer that one thing is the cause of another simply because it is preceded by it in time. For example, someone observes that crime among youth has increased in the United States since the arrival of punk rock from England and concludes, therefore, that punk rock is causing an increase in juvenile crime. Or someone observes that every war in this century has followed the election of a Democratic president, concluding therefore that the Democrats caused those wars. This kind of reasoning came to be known in Latin as *post hoc ergo propter hoc,* which means literally, "after this, therefore because of this."

Two phenomena may be so closely connected that one of them seems to be the cause of the other, though both are really results of some additional, less obvious factor. Suppose a person suffers from both depression and alcoholism. Does the drinking cause the depression or the depression cause the drinking? Or could it be that the depression and the drinking sustain each other causally? Perhaps so. But one shouldn't overlook the further possibility that there is some additional underlying cause of both the depression and the drinking—for example, a biochemical imbalance or a profound emotional disturbance. The *informal fallacy of overlooking a common cause,* then, consists of failing to recognize that two seemingly related events may not be causally related at all but rather effects of a common cause.

The *informal fallacy of causal oversimplification* consists in assuming that what merely contributes causally to a phenomenon fully explains it. For example, intense debates are waged regularly over the wisdom of increased taxation as a means of balancing the federal budget. Opponents of such measures frequently point to the predictable negative effects that taxation will have on the vitality of the consumer economy, while proponents of such measures stress the effects on real disposable income of the increasing debt burden on the economy as a whole. It is likely that both sides have a point, but it is at least as likely that both sides are in effect oversimplifying the economic equation in a number of ways. Clearly tax policy is not the only causal factor that affects the consumer economy. But neither is public indebtedness the only such causal factor. Both factors, and numerous others, are involved and influence each other in a great many ways.

SLIPPERY SLOPE

A specific kind of causal fallacy consists of objecting to something on the grounds of the unwarranted assumption that it will inevitably lead to some evil consequence that will lead to some even more evil consequence that in turn will lead "on down the slippery slope" to some ultimately disastrous consequence. For example, it is commonly argued that marijuana is a dangerous drug that inevitably leads to experimentation with harder drugs and eventually to hard drug abuse and addiction. Frequently, the alleged slippery slope is supported by further fallacious causal inferences such as pointing out that a high percentage of admitted heroin addicts testify to having tried marijuana early in their drug experience. But there is in fact no slippery slope here, as can easily be established by pointing out that numerous people, who at one time or another have tried or used marijuana, have never experimented with harder drugs, much less become addicted to them, and have moderated or given up their use of marijuana. A variation on slippery slope reasoning takes the form of posing the rhetorical question, "Where do you draw the line?" This of course has the effect of suggesting that there is no location for the line to be drawn. For example, some people are moved by the arguments like this one:

EXERCISE 12.6 | **Slippery Slope?**

Topic for Class Discussion: Evaluate the following argument against a form of euthanasia:

"If you permit the withdrawal of life support from terminally ill patients, where do you draw the line between this form of 'mercy killing' and the convenient disposal of one's sick and burdensome elders, or the 'euthanasia' of the mentally or physically or racially 'defective'?"

We think the argument in Exercise 12.6 is an example of slippery slope reasoning. Here it is merely assumed that we can't clearly distinguish between cases of "passive euthanasia" (withholding extraordinary life-prolonging measures) and "active euthanasia" (taking steps to hasten death or bring death about). Or between euthanasia done to alleviate pointless suffering of a terminal patient and euthanasia done for selfish reasons or with deliberate disregard for the interests of the patient. Now it is easy to see that such distinctions *are* possible, since they have just been made. It is not much harder to see that they are relevant distinctions. Indeed the argument presumes the relevance of such distinctions; otherwise, why assume or suggest that they can't be made? Thus, an effective strategy for exposing this sort of slippery slope reasoning is to simply draw the relevant distinctions. It is, however, important to recognize that in some contexts the question "Where do you draw the line?", rhetorical question though it is, makes a good point. There are contexts—and there *are* some very important ones—in which some fundamental principle is at stake that would be irreparably compromised if a certain exception to it were allowed to pass.

GAMBLER'S FALLACY

The so-called *gambler's fallacy* consists in thinking that past outcomes of chance events have any influence on the probability of future outcomes. For example, suppose we are gambling on coin flips and the last 10 flips have come up heads. Many people are tempted to think that tails are therefore *more* likely to come up than heads on the next flip. The problem here is failure to recognize that the chances of heads or tails coming up are the same for each flip (50-50), because each flip is an independent chance event. The chances of a run of 11 heads in a row are of course much lower than 50-50, but the odds against such a run have no bearing whatsoever on the outcome of the next flip. And yet people persist in the belief to the contrary. Watch people play the slots in Nevada. Again and again you will see people pumping coins into a machine that hasn't paid off for hours, thinking that this fact alone makes it more likely that the machine will pay off soon. Just as unreliable is the inference to continue playing because one has been winning. The idea of "riding a streak" involves the same mistake as thinking that the odds against you eventually have to "even out." If chance determines the outcome of the next play, past outcomes have no bearing whatsoever. Gamblers also tend to be (sometimes pathologically) attracted to "systems" designed to "beat the odds," most of which are completely fallacious products of wishful thinking and don't work at all. (The occasional exception, such as card counting in blackjack, is very quickly found out and one gets escorted from the premises of gaming establishments.) One such system consists in "doubling the bet." Suppose you put $2 on red at even money and lose. Following this system you would put $4 on red on the next play. If you win, you're up $2. If you lose, you're down $6, but you bet $8 on the next play. If you win, you're up $10. The idea is that eventually you win, and when you do, you're ahead of the game. The main trouble with this system is that the odds remain uniformly stacked against you throughout the game as you continue to raise your stake, which has the effect primarily of digging you more deeply and quickly into a hole. In other words, if you follow this "system," the only probability you raise is the probability that you will run out of money before you win.

EXERCISE 12.7 | Fallacies of Induction

In each of the following examples, check all fallacy categories that apply. Most important, explain each fallacy you identify.

> In spite of the objections of the Associated Students and the Faculty Senate, we are moving ahead to implement the new tuition fees recommended by the committee. We have to do something and we have to do it immediately to restore our reputation as a leading undergraduate educational institution. No one has come forward with a better alternative.

		Explain your answer:
	Ad ignorantium	
	Invincible ignorance	
	Only game in town	
	Correlation to cause	
	Post hoc ergo propter hoc	
	Overlooking a common cause	
	Causal oversimplification	
	Slippery slope	
	Gamblers' fallacy	

> A real miracle is something that demonstrably does occur but that cannot be scientifically explained. Now we formed a prayer circle over sister Sadie and her T-cell count has returned to normal and she no longer tests positive for HIV. The doctors have confirmed what the lab work shows but they can't seem to agree on an explanation. We believe God has sent the virus from her body.

		Explain your answer:
	Ad ignorantium	
	Invincible ignorance	
	Only game in town	
	Correlation to cause	
	Post hoc ergo propter hoc	
	Overlooking a common cause	
	Causal oversimplification	
	Slippery slope	
	Gamblers' fallacy	

> "Everything in this book is right and you must be prepared to confront that reality. You can no longer be an honest liberal after reading this entire masterpiece. Throughout the book you will be

challenged, because you will actually be persuaded to the conservative point of view. Whether you can admit this in the end will be a true test of your mettle as a human being." (Rush Limbaugh, *The Way Things Ought to Be* [New York: Simon and Schuster, 1992].)

Ad ignorantium	Explain your answer:
Invincible ignorance	
Only game in town	
Correlation to cause	
Post hoc ergo propter hoc	
Overlooking a common cause	
Causal oversimplification	
Slippery slope	
Gamblers' fallacy	

"I've always reckoned that looking at the new moon over your left shoulder is one of the carelessest and foolishest things a body can do. Old Hank Bunker done it once and bragged about it and in less than two years he got drunk and fell off of the shot-tower, and spread himself out so that he was just a kind of layer, as you may say; and they slid him edgeways between two barn doors for a coffin, and buried him so, so they say, but I didn't see it. Pap told me. But anyway it all come of looking at the moon that way like a fool." (Mark Twain, *The Adventures of Huckleberry Finn*)

Ad ignorantium	Explain your answer:
Invincible ignorance	
Only game in town	
Correlation to cause	
Post hoc ergo propter hoc	
Overlooking a common cause	
Causal oversimplification	
Slippery slope	
Gamblers' fallacy	

A FINAL WORD OF CAUTION

By now it should be pretty clear that evaluating arguments, particularly in informal terms, can be a pretty messy business. You can expect to encounter a fair number of arguments that can quite clearly be faulted in one way or another, and occasionally you'll find an argument that is pretty clearly impeccable. But a great many arguments are neither clearly fallacious nor clearly not. In such cases, you should consider your criticisms to be essentially contestable, and therefore you should also recognize the need to supply arguments in support of them, to deal with arguments against them, and perhaps to change your mind. In other words, assessing arguments, like verifying value judgments, takes you into areas where knowing how to construct and evaluate arguments becomes more and more important.

Bear in mind Critical Thinking Tip 11.1 (see page 277). The point of all of this activity is not to vanquish one's opponent, not to humiliate anyone, not to experience the thrill of victory, not to score points. The point of this activity is to *improve understanding*—to shed light, not generate heat. Moreover, this is not an idle intellectual exercise—not some arcane variety of Trivial Pursuit. Fallacy labels have no *intrinsic* importance at all. Their value is entirely instrumental. Above all, remember that a *fair and accurate understanding* of the argument is an absolute prerequisite to a well-reasoned judgment of its merits. Make sure your criticisms are based on thorough and careful argument analysis.

CRITICAL THINKING HALL OF SHAME

Few things are more embarrassing to a discipline like Critical Thinking than the kind of inept instruction that provoked the late Jack Smith to publish the following column.

Critique of an Ironic Writer's Critical Thought
By Jack Smith
Syndicated Columnist

In writing these pieces, it never occurs to me that I am going to be accused of critical thinking, either good or bad.

However, I have received a letter from Howard Holter, professor of history at California State University Dominguez Hills, enclosing an analysis of my critical thinking by one of his students.

Holter explains, "I assigned my students the task of evaluating a piece of newspaper copy in terms of the formal evaluation of critical thinking. They were to use 'fallacies of critical thinking' listed in the textbook to apply to the piece in question."

A student named Melanie Martinez chose to evaluate one of my columns, and Holter says her paper was one of the best. I do not come off too well.

Her paper criticizes a column I wrote about transcendental meditation as taught at Maharishi International University, Fairfield, Iowa. These folks believe, as you may remember, that if enough people meditate together, achieving a state of pure consciousness and connecting with the Unified Field, the basis of all life, they can actually alter events—lowering crime rates, quelling riots, easing international tension and even causing the Dow Jones average to rise.

The theme of my essay was that I did not believe this. However, my tone was irony, which, as we have often seen, is a risky tone to effect.

Martinez aims right at the heart.

"This article," she begins, "contains many vague and ambiguous words and statements, as well as fallacies of presumption."

I am reeling already.

Pinpointing my first fallacy of presumption, she quotes a paragraph: "The meditators held a mass meditation . . . thereby raising the temperature and saving the Florida orange crop, lowering drunken driving arrests is Des Moines, influencing Fidel Castro to give up cigars, and causing the stock market to rally."

Obviously, I hope, I am being ironic. I do not for a moment believe that the meditation had any effect whatever on the events cited.

But Martinez comments:

"This is the fallacy of False Cause, or thinking that because someone did one thing, something else happened as a result. The meditators may have believed that they were the reason for the temperature rise in Florida, but were probably wrongly justified . . . "

My thought exactly.

Later, Martinez observes, while I question the validity of the meditations, I claim that I was the one who meditated the success of Corazon Aquino in her bid for the presidency of the Philippines.

"Not only is this also a Fallacy of False Cause, but this is also a Fallacy of Special Pleading. After denouncing meditation, he does that exact thing."

Obviously, again, I was being ironic when I took credit for meditating Mrs. Aquino into the presidency. I was merely showing how easy it is for anyone to claim the Maharishi Effect for himself.

Martinez also accuses me of the Fallacy of Bifurcation. Bifurcation does not seem the sort of fallacy I might fall into, but let's see.

She quotes me: "I do believe that if we could get millions of people all around the world to sit down and meditate, instead of shooting and bombing one another, conditions would improve."

She says, "Here the author is saying, 'If we do one thing, this will happen.' Actually the opposite could happen: While the majority of people are meditating, a few of the people who aren't participating in the meditation could take advantage and cause destruction."

Alas, Martinez is all too close to the mark on that point. If we had thousands of people sitting around meditating, the barbarians might well say, "Hey, look at those crackpots meditating! Let's kill 'em!"

Or am I bifurcating?

She writes, "The author also included the phrase 'I am out on a limb,' which according to critical thinking, means either he is standing on someone's arm or leg, or he is standing on a tree branch. This is an ambiguous statement."

Nothing ambiguous about "out on a limb." It is an ancient metaphor, much honored in the use, which means, according to A Dictionary of American Idioms, "with your beliefs and opinions openly stated; in a dangerous position that can't be changed."

I am always out on a limb.

ADDITIONAL EXERCISES

■ **EXERCISE 12.8**   In our experience, the best way to study the material in this and the previous chapter is in conversation with other people—in a facilitated discussion section, or in a small autonomous study group, or with a study partner. Take turns critically examining the following examples, using the tools and terminology covered in this chapter. Listen to each other's critical assessments and weigh them for their clarity, their explanatory power, and their fairness. As you work your way through the following examples, alternately play the role of finding and explaining the flaw in the argument, and the complementary role of trying to defend the argument against the proposed criticism. Don't forget, sometimes the difference between a fallacy and a reasonable argument is a matter of considerable subtlety and delicacy. An argument may look a lot like a fallacy of some kind and yet be deeply defensible.

And on the other hand a given argument can have more than one thing wrong with it. The discussion of these examples may well prove to be of greater importance than the "answer" to the question which fallacy if any has been committed. If you arrive at a consensus criticism, move on to the next example.

- The Ayatollah Khomeini speaking in defense of state executions of those convicted of adultery, prostitution, or homosexuality: "If your finger suffers from gangrene, what do you do? Let the whole hand and then the body become filled with gangrene, or cut the finger off? . . . Corruption, corruption. We have to eliminate corruption."[4]

- Suppose a survey shows that more than half of all college students with below-average grades smoke pot, while, by contrast, only 20 percent of non-smokers have below-average grades. On the basis of these data, one person concludes that pot smoking causes students to get lower grades. Another person concludes that getting lower grades causes students to smoke pot. What do you make of this disagreement?

- Argument against raising cigarette taxes: "Taxing cigarettes encourages interstate traffickers in stolen cigarettes by opening up a whole new and very profitable market for them. A vote for this measure is a vote for increased crime. Vote 'NO.' Vote against the smugglers and traffickers and black marketeers."

- Adding a health tax to tobacco products is unfair to the tobacco industry. We're like any other legitimate business in this country. We sell a legal product to willing buyers in a free market, and we pay a fair share into the public purse through various forms of taxation. If tax revenue is to be raised to support Medicare, let the burden be shared across the board.

- It's a bit mysterious, because Smith's numbers are less than spectacular. He scores fewer points than any of his teammates. We don't let him handle the ball, because he's sure to turn it over. And he's slow and clumsy on defense. But he's a starter and he plays the first few minutes of each game simply because, when he's in the starting lineup, we win 70 percent of our games. When he's not, we only win 50 percent of the time.

- "Is adultery bad for your health? The chances of having a heart attack while making love are infinitesimal, but if you do have one, the chances are you'll have it with your mistress and not your wife. A study of 34 cardiac patients who died during intercourse revealed that 29 of the 34 were having an extramarital affair." — *Playboy* magazine

- I knew a guy who was so influenced by statistics, numbers ruled his entire life! One time he found out that over 80 percent of all automobile accidents happen to people within five miles of where they live. So he moved!

- "Whatever you do, DO NOT DESTROY THIS LETTER! Send it out to five of your friends. Mildred Wimplebush of Detroit destroyed her copy of this letter and a week later she died of a stroke. Henry Hinklefrump of El Segundo lost his copy of the letter and was fired within a month. Marlena Gorwangle of Missoula broke her ankle in a freak accident while tossing a salad only days after throwing her copy away."

- "My last three blind dates have been bombs. This one's bound to be better!"

- A poll is being conducted to find out what students think of their college newspaper. A sample is taken in the cafeteria on a Tuesday between 8:00 A.M. and noon. Every fifth person who enters the cafeteria is asked his or her opinion. The results find that 72 percent of the students are highly critical of the newspaper. The student government decides to use these results to re-vamp the editorial board.

- Professor Smith, wishing to improve his teaching, decides to poll his physics class. He commissions a questionnaire from one of his colleagues in statis-tics that satisfies all the criteria of a sound polling instrument. He calls each member of his class individually into his office and asks them to complete the questionnaire. What is wrong with his polling methods?

- Survey question: "Whom do you think the U.S. should support in the Middle East: Israel or the Palestinians?"

- In 1997 the small town of Sulphur Springs experienced a 200 percent in-crease in felony auto theft, according to the Sulphur Springs *Weekly Standard*. This report was based on the fact that three cars were stolen by joy-riding teenagers, compared to 1996, when only one car was stolen.

- At the 1992 National Religious Broadcasters convention in Washington, D.C., an Israel Solidarity Rally was sponsored by the Christians' Israel Public Ac-tion Campaign (Cipac), whose director, Richard Hellman, suggested that the poor state of the U.S. economy, President Bush's attack of nausea during his state dinner with the Japanese prime minister, and storm damage to his house in Kennebunkport, Maine, were all signs from God. According to Hellman, "I did point out certain interesting coincidences. One day the President said there were a thousand lobbyists up on the Hill speaking out on behalf of loan guarantees for Israel (as if those of us who were up there were somehow do-ing something that was illegal) and it was very shortly after that that his house was blown in. And the fact that one day the U.S. strongly condemned Israel in the U.N. (in language more harsh than was used against Iraq), and the very next day we witness the quite literally terrifying view of our President stricken, many of us thought almost as though dead, before our very eyes in the paper and on television. One might say these are just coincidences. But I think that if it were I, and I were leading a nation that had gone through the worst quarter economically in 30 years, I would start to wonder if there was something more I could do. What more might I do for my nation, including what more might I do to bless Israel, so that my nation in turn would be blessed?"

- Rush Limbaugh on abortion: ". . . [R]ight to choose what? Can a woman choose to steal using her own body? Of course not. Can she choose to do drugs? No. Not according to the law. Can she legally choose to be a prosti-tute? Again, no, which establishes, as does the drug example, that there is precedent for society determining what a woman can and can't do with her body. Look at it in another, and admittedly provocative, way: What if a man claimed the right to rape using the same principle found in the theory that it is his body and he has the right to choose? Well it's nonsense, and it is non-sense for a woman, or any citizen to assert such a right as well."

- "For three decades ('60s, 70s, 80s) the environmentalists, Greens, tree huggers—choose any epithet that suits your fancy but mainly descriptions of those who've ranted and railed against growth—have managed to defeat every attempt to modernize Sonoma County transportation to handle the growing load. I would like to point out that sticking your head in the sand and saying you're against growth simply won't cut the mustard. You cannot pass a law (urban growth boundaries) against growth; stupid even to think of it. If you can manage to come up with an elixir that can be delivered in the water system a la Big Brother, which will prevent human sexuality, then you can slow growth."[5]

EXERCISE 12.9 *Essay Assignment:* At the beginning of this chapter there is a cartoon in which a bunch of dubious "irrefutable" evidence of a UFO landing is presented. Which particular fallacies are illustrated in the cartoon?

EXERCISE 12.10 *Essay Assignment:* In frame 11 of the *Peanuts* episode (p. 320) used to illustrate the fallacy of invincible ignorance, Lucy makes reference to medical history. See if you can explain why her argument is not (repeat: NOT) an instance of the informal fallacy of arguing from ignorance.

EXERCISE 12.11 *Essay Assignment:* Read the following commentary from the magazine *The Nation* in which several distinct criticisms are made of the general interpretation and reception of a published sociological/psychological study. Explain and evaluate each of these criticisms, using the concepts and terminology presented in this chapter.

"In 1989 [Judith] Wallerstein published a [longitudinal] study [of 131 children whose parents had divorced in 1971] claiming that almost half had experienced serious long-term psychological problems that interfered with their love and work lives. This summer she released an update based on twenty-six of these young adults, all of whom had been 2–6 years old when their parents separated. They had been extremely vulnerable to drug and alcohol abuse as teens, she reported, and were still plagued in their 20s and 30s by unstable relationships with their fathers, low educational achievement and severe anxieties about commitment.

But there is good reason to worry about the massive publicity accorded Wallerstein's work. Her estimates of the risks of divorce are more than twice as high as those of any other reputable researcher in the field. Her insistence that the problems she finds were caused by the divorce itself, rather than by pre-existing problems in the marriage, represents an oversimplified notion of cause and effect repudiated by most social scientists and contradicted by her own evidence. Wallerstein studied 60 Marin County couples, mostly white and affluent, who divorced in 1971. Her sample was drawn from families referred to her clinic because they were already experiencing adjustment problems. Indeed, participants were recruited by the offer of counseling in exchange for commitment to a long-term study. This in itself casts serious doubt on the applicability of Wallerstein's findings. The people most likely to be attracted to an offer of long-term counseling and most likely to stick with it over many years are obviously those most likely to feel they need it. And after twenty-five years in a study about the effects of divorce, the children are unlikely to consider any alternative explanations of the difficulties they have had in their lives.

Wallerstein admits that only one-third of the families she worked with were assessed as having "adequate psychological functioning" prior to divorce. Half the parents had chronic depression, severe neurotic difficulties or "long-standing problems controlling their rage or sexual impulses." Nearly a quarter of the couples reported that there had been violence in their marriages. It is thus likely that many of the problems since experienced by their children stemmed from the parents' bad marriages rather than their divorces, and would not have been averted had the couples stayed together. Other researchers studying children who do poorly after divorce have found that behavior problems were often already evident eight to twelve years before the divorce took place, suggesting that both the maladjustment and divorce were symptoms of more deep-rooted family and parenting issues."[6]

EXERCISE 12.12   *Essay Assignment:* Read the following report from the magazine *Consumer Reports* in which the editors effectively *explain* several distinct informal fallacies involved in a particular advertising campaign. Can you explain each of these fallacies, using the concepts and terminology presented in this chapter?

"Dodge dealers in the New York City area recently aired a series of TV commercials boasting that more than 70% of the owners of Toyota Corollas, Honda Civics, Ford Escorts and Chevrolet Cavaliers actually preferred the new Dodge Shadow, according to '100 [people] surveyed.' Since our own surveys of subscribers have shown that owners of Civics and Corollas are more satisfied with their cars than are owners of Dodge Shadows, the commercial piqued our interest. The reasons for the difference between our survey results and those reported in the Dodge commercial became clear after Chrysler described the survey's methodology to us.

A survey firm retained by Chrysler chose owners of 1988 to 1991 Civics, Corollas, Cavaliers, and Escorts to participate in an experiment. The willing respondents—about 25 for each competitor—were given an opportunity to inspect a '92 Dodge Shadow and a '92 version of the car they already owned. They were also allowed to take the Dodge—but not the other car—out for a spin. After the look-see, the 100 people were asked if they thought the Dodge was better or worse than their current car. 73% reportedly said the Dodge was better.

Does this mean that most Civic and Corolla owners would prefer a new Dodge Shadow to a new Civic or Corolla, as the commercial implied? Probably not. Here's why.

First, of course, since the respondents were allowed to test-drive only the Dodge, not a new version of the model they owned, they were actually comparing a new car with a used one. For balance, we would like to have seen what owners of a older Dodge Shadow thought of their car after driving a new Corolla, Civic, Escort, and Cavalier.

Second, combining the opinions of owners of four different cars hides any distinctions among them. Civic and Corolla owners, for example, might have preferred their own car to the Dodge Shadow, while Escort and Cavalier owners might have strongly opted for the Dodge. One can't know from the reported result.

Finally, it's hard to believe that the respondents couldn't have guessed what the test was all about (and perhaps have wanted to please the sponsor), since they'd been promised $60 apiece to do a test that involved driving just one manufacturer's car."

■ **EXERCISE 12.13**   At the end of Chapter 11 you were challenged to critique the argument in your original 100-word "Position Statement" (Exercise 10.18). Has your position changed at all as a result of this process? If so, your argument will need revisions. So, when those have been accomplished, reanalyze your own argument. Then ask, "Is my argument open to any of the kinds of criticisms (Does it commit any of the fallacies?) we have just studied in Chapter 12?"

GLOSSARY

ad ignorantium   fallacy of inferring a statement from the absence of evidence or lack of proof of its opposite

bad base line   fallacy of statistical inference based on an inappropriate basis of comparison

begging the question   fallacy of assuming or presupposing one's conclusion as a premise

biased methodology   any methodology, such as a loaded question, that distorts a statistical study

causal oversimplification   variety of causal fallacy in which significant causal factors or variables are overlooked

circular reasoning   another name for "begging the question"

common cause   variety of causal fallacy in which one of two effects of some common cause is taken to cause the other

correlation   an observed or established statistical regularity, often fallaciously thought to establish a causal connection

false dilemma   fallacy of underestimating or underrepresenting the number of possible alternative positions on a given issue

gambler's fallacy   any of a variety of fallacies of inductive reasoning having to do with estimating or beating the odds, often based on the use of past outcomes to predict the future outcome of chance events

innuendo   implying a judgment, usually derogatory, by hinting

invincible ignorance   fallacy of refusing to give due consideration to evidence that conflicts with what one is already committed to believing

post hoc   variety of causal fallacy in which order of events in time is taken to establish a cause and effect relationship

slippery slope   fallacy consisting of objecting to something on the grounds that it will lead, by dubious causal reasoning, to some unacceptable set of consequences

small sample   fallacy of statistical inference consisting of overestimating the statistical significance of evidence drawn from a small number of cases

suppressed evidence   persuasive strategy consisting of covering up available evidence that conflicts with an intended conclusion

unrepresentative sample   fallacy of statistical inference in which the sample underrepresents the range of relevant variables in the population

ENDNOTES

[1] Woody Allen, *The Curse of the Jade Scorpion,* Allen's character, C.W. Briggs protesting his innocence after being caught in possession of the stolen jewels.

[2] Cf. W. Fearnside and W. Holther, *Fallacy: The Counterfeit of Argument* (Englewood Cliffs, NJ: Prentice Hall, 1959), p. 167.

[3] Elliott Sober, *Core Questions in Philosophy* (Englewood Cliffs, NJ: Prentice Hall).

[4] *Time,* October 22, 1979, p. 57.

[5] Letter to the Editor, *Sonoma County Independent,* February 12, 1998.

[6] Stephanie Coontz, "Divorcing Reality," *The Nation,* November 17, 1997.

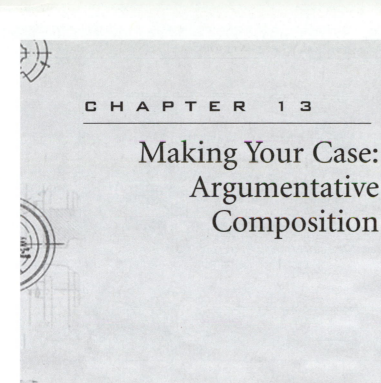

CHAPTER 13

Making Your Case: Argumentative Composition

I write because I don't know what I think until I read what I say.   FLANNERY O'CONNOR

At the beginning of this book we discussed the importance of Critical Thinking for both personal autonomy and democratic citizenship. At the culmination of our course of study in Critical Thinking it is appropriate to reflect again on these crucial and connected ideas. Let us now focus on the important connection between personal autonomy—the ability to use one's reasoning capacity to govern and regulate oneself, to make up one's own mind rationally—and democratic citizenship. The good functioning—and hence the health and very survival—of a democracy depends on an intellectually autonomous citizenry. If individual citizens are unprepared to make up their own minds on a rational basis, the collective decision-making processes of the society will be disabled and misguided as a consequence—and

"It's plotted out. I just have to write it."

will therefore become vulnerable to corruption. The citizenry of a democratic society that loses its grounding in the "art of reasoning," as Jefferson worded it, may expect one day to find their democratic institutions (like the Congress) and processes (like elections) corrupted and no longer reliable or effective in serving the public interest. The citizens of California, for example, now find that while they weren't paying attention, their own state legislature dismantled the people's ability to regulate the energy industry, and did so at the bidding and according to plans dictated by energy traders and speculators. And now, as they learn that these very same energy speculators dictated these arrangements, manipulated the energy markets, took and hid millions of dollars in profits, cooked their books, and defrauded *even their own shareholders (!!)*, it would be readily understandable if the citizenry of a democracy in such a state of corruption and decay started to feel rather powerless. And this might lead some citizens into apathy, others to commit acts of desperation and even violence.[1] Neither of these directions offers any hope of improving the situation. Better to regain some command of the art of reasoning and get busy cleaning up the mess.

OK. So, let's suppose that you have taken this message to heart and are now ready to engage as a citizen in the political processes of your community. Suppose you care enough about some local issue to actually go to a city council meeting and witness the process of public deliberation. Suppose there's a period for public comment. Now suppose you care enough about the issue that you would like to take a turn at the microphone and address the city council members and your fellow citizens. What are you prepared to say?

EXERCISE 13.1 | **Field Trip**

In fact, let's move this out of the realm of the purely hypothetical. Pick some local organization or civic body that holds open public meetings in your community. It could be a city or town council, a local school board, a county board of supervisors, the board of trustees at your college or university, a state legislature. Go to a meeting (or two). Witness the process of deliberation. Pay close attention to how decisions are actually made. How is discussion handled? Is there opportunity afforded for direct public input into the discussion? What role is assigned to argumentation in the discussion? Find out what issues are coming up on the agenda. See if somewhere in your community you can find an issue that matters to you and is scheduled to come up for discussion and deliberate resolution.

We try to get our students to think along these lines to help them understand and appreciate the value of what they are learning in Critical Thinking. In the context of democratic citizenship, what Critical Thinking provides can be understood and appreciated as follows: Suppose you are about to take your turn at the microphone at a public meeting where an issue you care about is under discussion. Naturally, you want your contribution to the discussion to be attended to with respect. Critical Thinking is what makes it possible for you to make the kind of contribution *that commands the respectful attention of others* who are interested in the issue, whether or not they share your views. What kind of contribution will command respectful attention in an open and democratic discussion of an issue of common interest and concern? Answer: a good argument. An argument, as we defined it in Chapter 3 and understood it throughout this book, is a composition intended to persuade one's audience by appeal to reason. A *good* argument, whether it is presented as a written composition, as a prepared speech, or "extemporaneously,"[2] will be one that is well suited to the function of persuasion by appeal to reason. It will be a composition that is well informed, well designed as an argument, and well presented.

As much as we might wish it to be otherwise, there are no reliable shortcuts here. A *good* argument is almost always the result of a sustained investment of effort in which all of the general areas and many of the specific concepts and skills covered in our study of Critical Thinking can be usefully applied. For this reason, a standing assignment in the Critical Thinking classes of the authors of this book is to carry out a sustained project focused on some significant issue. The work of the project involves research, argument identification, argument analysis, argument evaluation, argument design, and written composition. The finished "work product" is an argumentative essay—or, to put it more plainly, a good argument presented in writing. In this final chapter, we will discuss the composition of an argumentative essay in the context of the sort of project we assign in our Critical Thinking classes.

THE ISSUE STATEMENT

The project begins, of course, with the selection of an issue. In our classes we as instructors sometimes select an issue as the common focus for the class; sometimes we allow the class to select the issue; and sometimes we allow the students to each select an issue individually. We try in any case to focus on issues that would score high on both media visibility (how likely the issue is to come under public discussion in the media) and public importance (how much does—or *should*—the issue matter to the general public).

Similarly, an argumentative essay will ordinarily begin with a statement of the issue to which it will be addressed. The introduction to an argumentative essay should orient the reader to and attract the reader's interest in the topic. At the end of Chapter 1 (Exercise 1.28) you were encouraged to draft a one-page issue statement. Let us now return to that assignment and process it more deeply.

EXERCISE 13.2 | Issues and Disputes: Review

Review the section in Chapter 1 entitled "Looking Ahead: Issues and Disputes," pp. 27–35.

We propose to evaluate issue statements according to three criteria: articulation, balance, and clarity. We will comment on each of these criteria in turn, but in reverse order.

CLARITY

Clarity is in one sense the easiest of the three criteria to explain and understand. It refers to the overall mastery of the language used in the composition. Clarity applies as a criterion of evaluation not just to the issue statement but to the entire composition. When we evaluate a piece of writing for clarity, we ask, "Is the language being used effectively to get the ideas across without confusion?" To the extent that it is, the composition is clear. To the extent that it is not, the clarity can be improved. Grammar, vocabulary, idiom, spelling—all play a role in this. To check for clarity, we recommend having someone (preferably someone whose writing you respect or admire) read your draft. We will say a bit more about clarity shortly.

BALANCE

Since you're writing about an issue, a topic about which reasonable people may disagree, your initial statement of the issue should be "balanced." This means not prejudiced either in favor of or against any of the positions a reasonable person might be inclined to hold about the topic. You don't want to alienate any of your potential readers before they have a chance to consider your argument in its totality. One of the best ways to achieve this is to make a relatively clear distinction between your *issue* statement, in which you bring your topic into focus for your reader, and your *thesis* statement, in which you tell your reader where you stand on the issue. If you can present the issue in a balanced way, this tells your reader that you understand that there is room for reasonable disagreement on the matter and that you are capable of respectfully understanding positions that may differ from your own. This will encourage your reader to pay respectful attention to *your* argument.

ARTICULATION

Articulation, as we explained in Chapter 1, relates to the inherent complexity of issues. For any given issue there will be many different ways to frame, focus, and organize the inquiry. What do we mean by "framing," "focusing," and "organizing" the inquiry? "Framing" the issue means situating it within a larger context and determining what will be considered within and what will be considered outside the scope of the discussion. "Focusing" means determining what will be considered central and what will be considered peripheral within the scope of the discussion. And "organizing" refers to the order in which things will be considered. When you enter into a complex area of controversy, you need to make decisions about all of these things in order to develop what we might call an *orderly agenda of inquiry.* This is what we mean by "articulation." An "articulate" issue statement is one that has carefully considered how to frame, focus, and organize the discussion of the issue in its inherent complexity and has arrived at and clearly communicated an orderly agenda of inquiry. This is a challenging aspect of the process, but facing this challenge squarely at this early stage will greatly enhance your ability to maintain your own bearings as you work your way through the complexity of the issue. And it will make your argument much easier to follow for your reader.

EXERCISE 13.3 | **Issue Statement: Revision**

Revise the issue statement you drafted in Exercise 1.28, paying special attention to the clarity, balance, and articulation of the statement.

Drafting the issue statement is a good way to begin the kind of project we are discussing here, as well as a good way to begin the argumentative essay that comes out of the project as the final "work product." Before we return to a discussion of other elements in the argumentative essay, let's explore the second of the preliminary stages of the project: research. Remember that in the end a good argument will be a composition that is well informed. Thus, even from the earliest stages of articulating the issue, one of the most important ingredients of a good argument will be the quality of the information that goes into it.

RESEARCH AND THE MEDIA

Once an appropriate issue has been selected, an early stage of the project involves research. *Research* essentially means finding out something we don't already know. In researching an issue, we need to gain access to reliable information relevant to our topic, and more importantly, since our topic is the subject of debate and disagreement among reasonable people, we need to gain access to arguments of a reasonably high standard representing the range of opinion on our topic. We live in what has come to be known as the Age of Information. Among the many meanings this label carries with it is that we have unprecedented access to information. Individually and collectively we presently can gather, collect, store, sort, process, transmit, and receive more information more quickly than at any previous time in human history. This is both a blessing and a curse for research. Obviously, the fact that information is so readily available is useful to research. But in an information-rich environment like ours, it's easy to get lost, distracted, and overwhelmed by the sheer volume of information available. Equally important, perhaps even more so, we need practical means of assessing the reliability of the information available to us.

Over the last several decades we have seen profound changes in the way research is conducted. A generation ago (when the authors of this book were in college) to do research you went to the card catalog in the college library. The information and the arguments were in books (or periodicals) that were in the library and listed in the card catalog. And you just went there, looked them up by subject, found them in the stacks, and took them home and read them. Today the library is still the first and best place to go to do research. But now the information and the arguments are in all kinds of media—not just print—and all over the place—not necessarily housed in the actual library building. Today you can "go to the library" via the Internet. The Age of Information has made do-it-yourself research an easy undertaking, undoubtedly a good thing in and of itself. Yet at the

Used by permission of David Suter.

"Selectovision"

same time the Age of Information has raised some "quality-control issues" for the do-it-yourself researcher. With so much information so readily available, how can we be sure that the information we're getting is reliable? How do we determine which of the many and often conflicting factual claims we may encounter in our research are accurate? How do we find among the arguments in wide circulation those that represent the broadest spectrum of opinion with the highest standard of reasoning? The best piece of general research advice we have to offer is to consult your college reference librarians. Make sure you have your issue well and clearly defined. Today librarians are even more crucial as assistants to research than they were a generation ago. They are the college's experts in using new and increasingly powerful information technologies (such as InfoTrac College Edition) to sift through the mountains of information available on nearly any issue. Beyond this piece of general advice, it may be worth saying just a little bit about media, sources of information, reliability, and skepticism.

TELEVISION

In the woodcut on page 340, "Selectovision" by David Sutor, a video cameraman is recording a man fleeing from an attacker with a knife, but the identities of attacker and victim are reversed in the video image. Thus, the artist makes the point that television is capable and often guilty of completely misrepresenting reality. This sort of skepticism of television is much deeper today and more commonplace than it has been throughout most of the medium's short history. It is well worth considering the reasons for this sort of skepticism not only about television but about other sources of information as well.

Though the technology was already emerging in the 1920s, television really came into its own after World War II. During the 1950s television quickly became a dominant communications medium in American society and throughout the industrialized world. Throughout much of this period television was widely accepted as a generally reliable source of information. This may be partly attributable to the technology's ability to record and transmit audiovisual imagery of events taking place in real time. It may also be partly attributable to the "realism" of television programming. ("The camera does not lie.") Viewed as a technology and an information medium, television has always had immense functional potential for human society. It is a highly flexible medium, able to accommodate information in a wide range of forms, from spoken word, to music, to moving visual imagery, to graphic text, simultaneously in all manner of combinations. Once programmed, its messages engage the human perceiving subject simultaneously through multiple sense modalities, thus giving television unusually high power to attract and hold attention. With the enhancement of satellite transmission and reception technology, fiber optics, and cable, television makes possible the instantaneous transmission and reception of huge quantities of audiovisual information on a global basis. Now an international audience of almost any size can witness a significant event—for example, the second hijacked airliner crashing into the North Tower of the World Trade Center—as it is occurring (as well as over and over again after the fact).

However, even as television technology has become more elaborate and powerful, television audiences have become more sophisticated and are coming to understand television not only as a technology and an information medium but also as a business, indeed an industry. Through this process of growth and maturation, television audiences have seen through certain naïve illusions and become more skeptical, perhaps even cynical. For example, we've all heard the expression "brought to you through the courtesy of . . ." many times on television. Here we are encouraged to understand television as a free entertainment and information service. Entertainment and information are delivered to the public free of charge, and this service is paid for by Dr Pepper, or Nike, or ADM (Archer, Daniels, Midland—Supermarket to the World!). From the vantage point of the audience (the vantage point most of us occupy), this is no doubt a comfortable way to understand television's institutional role. But it completely misrepresents the economics of the industry. From within the television industry such a description makes no sense at all. Why in the world would the makers of Dr Pepper want to pour money into providing a free entertainment and information service for millions of people?

What the makers of Dr Pepper are paying for, of course, is public attention. What's really going on is that *we* (the audience) are being brought to *them* (the sponsors) by CBS. Viewed in these terms, television's primary function in our culture has been as a tool for harvesting public attention for sale in the public-attention market. The primary function of television programming is to round up an audience and hold that audience in place in a receptive attitude (what the industry calls a "buying mood") for the sponsor's message. This explains why television programming is nearly 100 percent entertainment and why the boundaries and distinctions between entertainment (showbiz) and public-service programming (journalism) have gotten blurrier and blurrier. And television audiences are more acutely aware of this nowadays. When we see the major network news anchors Dan Rather, Tom Brokaw, and Peter Jennings making regular celebrity guest appearances on the late-night talk shows, after a while we start to realize that television news is as much a part of showbiz as *Wheel of Fortune*.

MASS MEDIA

During the 19th century, industrial expansion created so-called economies of scale in many areas of enterprise, including journalism. This meant that the capital costs of acquiring, maintaining, and operating a large industrialized printing press, and the associated need to reach a more and more massive audience, rose by several orders of magnitude. In such a business climate, large businesses dominate and small businesses get eaten or die. As these trends progress, ownership and control grow increasingly concentrated and further removed from the community. Fewer and fewer larger and larger corporations come to control more and more of the flow of information, while small local independent voices are lost. These trends have been studied and documented by media scholar Ben Bagdikian, a Pulitzer Prize–winning journalist and former dean of the University of California Graduate School of Journalism, who writes:

> A handful of mammoth private organizations have begun to dominate the world's mass media. Most of them confidently announce that by the 1990's they—five to ten corporate giants—will control most of the world's important newspapers, magazines, books, broadcast stations, movies, recordings and videocassettes. Moreover, each of these planetary corporations plans to gather under its control every step in the information process, from creation of "the product" to all the various means by which modern technology delivers media messages to the public. "The product" is news, information, ideas, entertainment and popular culture; the public is the whole world.[3]

The public is also increasingly aware that the major media, because they are big businesses, have interests to advance and protect that may interfere and conflict with the public interest in access to relevant and accurate information. This applies not just to television but to the major media generally. Professional journalists who work in the industry are well aware of this potential for conflict of interest as an issue of professional ethics, and the best of them are indeed capable of "biting the hand that feeds them." But the public is still right to be skeptical.

Another factor contributing to growing public skepticism is an accumulating history of political and corporate scandal. Watergate, the Pentagon Papers, Iran-contra, pedophilia in the priesthood, the Enron-Andersen-WorldCom corporate accounting scandals, each one with its own series of coverups and evasive press conferences, have had the cumulative effect of undermining public trust and confidence in many important social institutions, including the press. The public is now increasingly aware that presidential press conferences and Pentagon briefings are "public-relations events" planned and orchestrated to manage public opinion. In short, we have good reason to be skeptical of information made available through the major media and to wonder what may really be going on behind the scenes. However, there is a danger that we may become so cynical as to suspect the worst at all times and trust no one ever. This, in effect, is a form of intellectual paralysis and something we ought to avoid. We should remember that the events underlying at least some of these scandals (Watergate, the pedophile priests) were brought to light through good old-fashioned hard-nosed investigative journalism. Instead of becoming cynical and refusing to trust or believe anything we hear or read, we should become skeptical consumers of information. This means actively seeking out information (rather than passively receiving it) and questioning and challenging the information as it comes in to us (rather than simply accepting it as reliable).

THE INTERNET

The Internet provides an excellent environment within which to practice and develop good habits of active skepticism in research. One reason for this is the *importance* of active skepticism in researching the World Wide Web. When the first edition of this book was published in the 1980s, the Internet was not much more than an obscure and geeky experiment and the World Wide Web didn't even exist. Now we're talking about the world's largest and fastest growing computer and communications network, a development that has already brought big changes in information access generally and promises more and perhaps even bigger changes to come, especially in the practice of research and education.

Once connected to the Net, you can gain access to information stored on computers literally all over the world. And with a few additional tools and steps you can also publish information to the whole world via the Internet. It's little wonder that there's so much excitement surrounding the Internet. This is Very Impressive Technology. It literally opens up a "World of Information" on any imaginable subject from astronomy to zen. You can get into the world's great libraries, you can get into government files and databases, you can get detailed up-to-the-minute weather information, celebrity gossip, sports scores, and stock quotations from any part of the world, and on and on. So vast and dynamic is this information environment that it has spawned a hugely profitable new industry devoted to maintaining up-to-date Internet databases and constructing computer programs called "search engines" to assist people with Internet research.

Anyone with a computer and an Internet connection can publish on the Internet. Many Internet enthusiasts point to this as an indication of the Internet's democratizing potential. By effectively eliminating barriers to publication, the Internet seems to enhance freedom of speech and expression and freedom of access to information, yet at the same time it raises some of those "quality-control issues" we mentioned earlier. If you look up information about the human genome project in the *New England Journal of Medicine* or the *Journal of the American Medical Association,* you can be confident in the reliability of the information. Why? Because these and other reputable scientific or academic journals are very careful about what they let into their pages, using rigorous peer review processes designed to maintain high standards of accuracy and integrity. There is no editorial board screening Web pages. Anybody—and this includes crackpots and hustlers—can put up a Web page. They don't have to know what they are talking about. They don't need any credentials. They don't have to check their facts. And not only can they put up a Web page, they can make it *look* as "professional" as an official Harvard University Web page. Indeed, this is exactly what members of the Heaven's Gate cult were doing to support themselves and raise money before they committed mass suicide—building Web pages. So, Internet surfers need to beware: Although the Internet is an abundant information resource, the "garbage-to-good-stuff" ratio is way higher on the Internet than in the Expanded Academic Index.

So, we have to do the evaluation. Many institutional or organizational Web sites include statements about the type and source of information provided on their Web pages, as well as the purpose of the organization itself. If this information is *not* offered, be especially careful about evaluating the data you find there. Here are a few commonsense questions to ask:[4]

CRITICAL THINKING TIP 13.1

Be an "Active Skeptic" in research. Ask questions like these:

- *What are the sources of the information?* Where did the information originate? Who put it there?
- *Where to Look:* On a Web page, look near the top of the page. Check the title, the section headings, and the opening paragraphs to see if some person or organization is named as the person(s) responsible for the content of the Web pages. Also look near the bottom of the page for this information. (Keep in mind that the Webmaster, or person who designed the Web page, is not necessarily the one responsible for the content of the page.)

  You can sometimes learn something about the source of a Web page by examining the page's URL. The URL often indicates what type of organization and what country a Web page comes from.

  If you can't find any information about the author(s) on the page you're looking at, try erasing the last part of the URL for that page in your Web browser's location box. Delete from the very end of the URL backwards to the first slash mark("/"), then press the RETURN or ENTER key on your keyboard. If you still don't see any information about the author(s), back up one more directory or slash mark. Keep going until you come to a page that identifies the author(s) of these pages.

- *How authoritative is the source?* What qualifications does this person or organization have to talk on this topic? Does the author have a university degree in the discipline? Or is she or he an amateur or a hobbyist or merely someone with an opinion to air? If an organization is responsible for the pages, is the organization widely recognized as a source of scholarly and reliable information? (For example, the American Cancer Society for information on cancer-related topics.) What other information can you find about the author or organization responsible for the content of this Web page?
- *Where to Look:* On a Web page, look near the top and the bottom of the page. Is there a link to more information about the person or organization?

  For organizations, there's often a link called "About Us" or something similar that leads to a page explaining the organization's mission, when and how it was founded, and so forth. Read it for clues.

  For a single person or author, there might be information about the person's educational background or his/her research or other qualifications for speaking on this topic. There might be a link to his or her faculty or professional Web pages.

  Look for links to articles and publications by the person or organization. Look for an address or a phone number by which you could contact the author(s) if you wanted to.

  If you can't find any information about the author(s) on the page you're looking at, try erasing the last part of the URL for that page in your Web browser's location box as described above. Keep going until you come to a page that has more information about the person or organization responsible for the pages. Remember that a URL that has a ~ in it is almost always someone's personal home page, as opposed to an organization's official page.

  If you can't find any information about the author(s) anywhere on their Web pages, try searching for the person or organization's name using one of the Internet search engines to see if you can find Web pages about them elsewhere. Check some library catalogs and magazine or newspaper databases to see if the person or organization has published books or articles in the field.

If you can find no information at all about the Web page's author(s), be very wary. If you can't verify that the information is authoritative, don't use it in a class paper or project.

- *What is the purpose of the document?* Does the author claim this page to be factual? Is she or he trying to persuade you of something? To whom is the author of this page talking? To scholars and experts? To students? To anyone who will listen? Is he or she trying to sell you a product discussed on the page? Does the page include advertising? If so, can you tell clearly which parts are advertisement and which parts are informational content? Does the page remind you of a television "infomercial," that is, does it look like an informational article but is actually an advertisement?

- *Where to Look:* If the author or organization has provided an "About Us" page, you can probably determine something about the Web page's purpose by reading about the mission of the organization.

- *How "straightforward" is the source?* Does the author or the organization she or he represents have an identifiable vested interest or an obvious bias concerning the topic? Does the author or the organization represent a particular point of view? (The Catholic Church, the National Organization for Women, the R. J. Reynolds Tobacco Company, the Republican or Democratic Party, etc.) If you don't know the answer to this question, be sure to read the "About Us" page. If the author does have a vested interest, or particular point of view, is this made clear or is there an attempt to obscure it?

- *Where to Look:* Does the page use inflammatory language, images, or graphic styles (for example, huge red letters or lots of boldface type) to try and persuade you of the author's point of view?

  Examine the URL to see where the Web page comes from. Is it a commercial site (.com)? A nonprofit organization (.org)? An educational institution (.edu)? Think again about the person or organization's mission or charge as you read about it in the "About Us" link.

  Try some of the same approaches you used to determine the authority of the information source; for example, look for the name of the author(s) using one of the Web search engines to see if you can find other information about them. Is the organization an advocacy group, that is, one that advocates for a particular cause or point of view?

- *How current is the information?* Can you tell when the Web page was originally created? When it was last updated? Is this a topic on which it's important that you have up-to-date information (science, medicine, news, etc.) or one where it is not as important that information be recent (history, literature, etc.)?

- *Where to Look:* Look near the top and the bottom of the page to see if any publication date, copyright date, or "date last modified" is indicated.

Look for other indications that the page is kept current. Is there a "What's New" section? If statistical data or charts are included, be especially careful to notice what dates are represented there and when the data was collected or published.

Good habits of active skepticism should be applied also in researching newspapers and other periodical literature. One can ask similar questions to those in Critical Thinking Tip 13.1 about the authors and editors of these more old-fashioned sources of information. Who are the authors and editors? What are their qualifications? Did the information they are presenting originate with them, or are they just passing it along? Are they acting with integrity in their capacity as authors and editors? Do they have an agenda? Do they have any general political orientation or bias? Are they open and forthright about any such agenda or orientation or bias, or do they try to hide it? Approaching all sources of information in this way will enable you much more effectively to gather reliable information and to weed out the B.S.

THE THESIS STATEMENT

Let us now return to the matter of composing an argumentative essay. By the time you get to this stage, you should have a pretty good idea where you stand on the issue you have been considering. The introduction to your argumentative essay should accomplish two essential goals: (1) orienting and interesting your reader in your topic (your issue statement should get this goal accomplished); and (2) letting your reader know where you stand. Your "thesis statement" should accomplish this second goal. The word *thesis* comes from Greek and means "proposed idea." As it is used in the discipline of writing, the "thesis" is the main idea of an essay or longer composition. If the composition is an argumentative essay, the thesis will be in the position of the conclusion of the argument, supported by other ideas that you will present as premises. The essential difference between the thesis statement and the issue statement is that balance is no longer a relevant criterion of assessment. Your thesis statement should be clear and articulate, but it does not need to be "balanced."

As we just said, by the time you come to write an argumentative essay, you *should* have a reasonably clear idea where you stand. Ideally, your current convictions about the issue will have resulted from the work you have by now invested in researching the issue, finding the arguments both in favor of and against the various positions along the spectrum of opinion, and analyzing and evaluating those arguments. However, even after doing all this work, many people find formulating a thesis quite an intimidating challenge. This may be because they recognize the risks inherent in taking a position in an area of controversy. "People will disagree with me. I will be called upon to defend my position with an argument. I have no idea yet how I shall argue for my position. What if I'm wrong?" Do not let any of this paralyze you. Yes, people will disagree with you. Yes, you will be called upon to defend your position with an argument. But at this stage, even if you have no idea yet how that argument will go, you still have time to figure it out. Remember that you are not required to opt for either one of the two "extreme" or "polar" positions along the spectrum of opinion on your issue (if that's how the public debate on the matter has been structured). Indeed, you are not restricted to choose among positions that have been formulated and articulated by others. You are free to be original and creative and to propose a new "compromise" position if you can think of one. And finally, if you *are* wrong, nothing prevents your changing your mind and correcting your position. So go ahead and be honest with yourself about where you stand on the subject, and write that down. This is a draft of your thesis statement.

EXERCISE 13.4 | Thesis Statement

At the end of Chapter 10 you were challenged to write a 100-word "position statement" (Exercise 10.18), which we expect will contain an argument. Through Chapter 11 and 12 you were prompted to analyze, critique, and revise that argument. Now, draft a thesis statement in 100 words or less. Just the thesis—just what you will go on to support with your argument.

ARGUMENT DESIGN

In general, good argument design flows from a clear and detailed understanding of both the thesis and the issue to which the thesis responds. Depending upon the precise nature of the issue, the subissues involved in it, and the claim one is defending as one's thesis, different argument design strategies will be more or less viable and promising. The kind of argument we might need to design to effectively support and defend a value judgment may not work very well to support and defend a causal hypothesis. One general principle for argument design, therefore, is simply to study your issue closely and analytically, letting your insights into its character and complexities guide you to a deeper awareness of the strengths and vulnerabilities of your position. Make your argument as logical as you can. If you can, build an argument that is deductively valid. If you can't find or devise valid deductive support for your thesis, perhaps one or more of the varieties of inductive reasoning will be applicable. In any case, make full use of what you have learned about argument analysis and evaluation in designing your argument. And of course, be careful not to fall into any fallacious patterns or tendencies.

OUTLINING

As you build your case you will want to ensure that your argument hangs together and that your thesis is convincingly and legitimately supported. An excellent device for testing the web of logical relationships in your essay— as well as for guiding and controlling the work of composition— is an outline of your argument. Many student writers (and nonstudent writers, for that matter) fail to fully exploit the outline as an argument design tool. We've seen quite a few outlines that go no further than this:

I. Introduction

    A. My issue statement

    B. My thesis statement

II. Body

    A. Reasons in favor of my position

III. Conclusion

This is *not* what we mean by an outline of your argument. You can do way better than this. To get the most out of your outline you will want to go into much greater depth and detail. Concentrate on the argument you are building. Break item II down further. What *are* the reasons in favor of your position? Be specific. And how are those reasons related to each other? What evidence supports those reasons? What positions are you opposed to? What are your objections to those opposing positions? Be specific. And what objections can you anticipate coming from those opposing positions? How will you respond to such objections? Be specific. Make sure to define key terms and concepts. Be conscious of the need to support your claims with facts and to illustrate your points with examples. All of this material needs to be placed in some order so that your reader can follow your train of thought through your composition. One the most basic functions of outlining is to allow you to think through these details of your argument and get them organized, without at the same time having to work out all of the subtleties of wording and presentation that will eventually go into the finished composition. Outlining is a flexible tool. You can use it before *or* after you have written a draft—better yet, use outlining both before *and* after. Use outlining as a tool in *revising* what you've written.

APPRECIATE YOUR OPPONENT'S POSITION

Because your thesis responds to an issue, and because issues are by definition topics about which reasonable people may disagree, your thesis will tend to be relatively controversial. A second general principle for argument design flows from this and from the fact that in arguing for your thesis, you are essentially trying to be persuasive, to win your audience over. Try to identify premises that are less controversial, less subject to debate, than your thesis. In other words, try to find "common ground" on which to base your argument for your thesis.

This second general principle of argument design suggests some further ideas about argument design and construction. The medieval philosopher and theologian Thomas Aquinas once remarked that when you want to convert someone to your view, you go over to where he is standing, take him by the hand (mentally speaking), and guide him to where you want him to go. You don't stand across the room and shout at him. You don't call him nasty names. You don't order him to come over to where you are. You start where he is and work from that position. To put it another way: When you think that someone is wrong and you disagree with her, you should first try to figure out in what way(s) she is right. This is not as paradoxical as it sounds. Suppose you're firmly convinced of some particular position on a complex and controversial subject like the death penalty. Are you absolutely certain that you're 100 percent correct? Can you be absolutely certain that those who disagree with you are entirely wrong in everything they might have to say? Wouldn't it be wiser to thoughtfully consider what your opponent might have to say and concede as much as you honestly can? Then when you go on to offer criticisms of your opponent's position, you can reasonably expect them to be given thoughtful consideration as well. After all, think how you would react as a reader to a criticism of your position. If the criticism starts out by identifying your position as out to lunch, you're not likely to be very receptive, are you? You'd be much more open to a criticism that began by stating your position in a way that you would yourself state it, recognizing its intuitive plausibility, its explanatory power, the weight of evidence in its favor, or whatever strengths it may have. If you are going to criticize someone else's argument or position, make sure you state it so that *they* know that you have fairly and accurately understood it.

OBJECTIONS AND REPLIES

Just as you should be aware of the possibility that your opponent's position may embody certain strengths, you should be aware of the possibility that your own position may have certain weaknesses—weaknesses that very likely will be more apparent to your opponent than to you. Thus, an additional strategic advantage for the writer of an argumentative essay flows from making a genuine attempt to appreciate the opponent's position. Your opponent's position affords you a much better vantage point from which to troubleshoot your own position and argument—to make yourself aware of where your argument needs additional support or where the thesis itself needs to be qualified or refined.

EXERCISE 13.5 | Outline Your Argument

Based on your issue statement as revised in Exercise 13.3 and your thesis statement in Exercise 13.4, now outline your argument.

THE PRESENTATION

So much good advice is already available about writing and how to get better at it that for us to offer any such advice of our own here would seem to be either a redundant waste of time, arrogant, or both.[5] Do we have anything new and distinctive to add to what the many courses, tutorials, books, tapes, Web sites, and consultants on becoming a better writer have to offer? Probably not. But we're not going to let that stop us. We will, however, try to keep this brief and to the point.

Back in Chapter 1 we made a very quick comparison, almost in passing, between thinking and writing (p. 11). We were talking about discipline. Our point there was that even though learning a discipline (like writing, or Critical Thinking, or music—our other example) involves the mastery of rules and regularities through extensive practice, you still have room to develop your own distinctive individual style. This is important because writing is a means of self-expression. It would be very disappointing if in order to learn how to express ourselves effectively in words we each had to wind up sounding exactly like everybody else. At the same time, just as you can keep on developing and refining your thinking throughout your life by disciplined study, so too can you continue to improve your writing, getting better and better with more and more disciplined practice even as you get more and more distinctive in your individual style as a writer. (So, it's really a good thing that there is so much good advice out there for the developing writer.)

In Chapter 2 we began our exploration of language by remarking on its amazing flexibility and power as a tool kit for communication. There are *so many* different things one can accomplish, so many different tasks one can undertake, through the use of language. There are, accordingly, many different kinds of writing. And what makes for a good piece of writing of one kind (poetry, or a sermon) may not serve the purposes of some other kind of writing (say, a software user manual) at all well. We do better as writers generally when we are guided by an understanding of the specific goals of the kind of writing we are working on. Composing an argumentative essay is a rather specialized application of writing. It requires and also helps to build language skills of certain special kinds in certain special ways. Some of these should come as no surprise, since they have occupied center stage throughout this course of study. They all derive from the function of an argument: to persuade by appeal to reason.

RELEVANCE

We have a friend who tells endless stream-of-consciousness stories. She might start out by saying, "Do you remember Sally so and so from junior high school? Well I ran into her the other day in the parking lot outside the supermarket, and she had just been to the deli. You know they have this new deli in the supermarket and they make the greatest pasta salad. They use pine nuts. That's the secret ingredient. And smoothies! You know, since they started making smoothies, I seem to have to go in there every single day! Smoothies have changed my life! But you know I think they've started using less frozen yogurt and more ice. Don't you just hate when they do that? Take some good thing, and just when people start to catch on, raise the price or something. Like my cell phone company. . . " And on and on she goes. We got to the point of taking bets as to whether the story would ever wander back around to Sally so and so from junior high school. Try not to write like this. This kind of improvised discourse is OK for around the campfire, although even there it can be exasperating. But not when you are composing an argumentative essay. Know where you are headed, and go there. Don't wander. Don't interrupt yourself. Don't go off on tangents. If all of a sudden something occurs to you as an important point that should not be left out, try to find the place in the argument where it is most relevant and insert it there so that the orderly flow of the reasoning is preserved. This is one of the most important applications of outlining. You don't want to leave anything important out, but you do want to present it all in good order.

CARE AND PRECISION IN CHOOSING AND DEFINING TERMS

This applies throughout the entire composition. Suppose your issue is "Terrorism." Naturally, you will want to define the term *terrorism*. But it is not enough just to define the word if in so doing you don't *choose the terms in the definition with great care and precision.* Many students seem unaware of this, or at least that's how it looks when you read their essays and notice the general carelessness with which words and phrases get thrown around. If you don't know the difference in meaning between the words *credible* and *credulous,* you shouldn't use either one. If you don't know the difference between *affect* and *effect,* or between *principal* and *principle,* don't just fake it by alternating between them. If you aren't *absolutely certain* what the word you're thinking of using means, LOOK IT UP! Otherwise, how can you really know if you have made a good vocabulary choice? How can you really know if the word is going to work the way you need it to work in its context? How will you improve your vocabulary? The same goes for idiomatic phrases. People often seem to be shuffling these together like some kind of refrigerator-door-poetry-kit, ending up with accidental comedy like, "We need to grab the bull by the tail and look the facts squarely in the eye." This is not the effect you want to have on your reader.

CRITICAL THINKING TIP 13.2

How to use your spell checker: The spell checker we have in our word processor highlights <u>mispelled</u> words in red or by underlining them. This is supposed to prompt us to revise the spelling. Instead of just tinkering with the spelling until the highlighting disappears, go to the dictionary and look the word up. Use this as an opportunity to learn more about the word.

ECONOMY OF EXPRESSION

Don't waste words. Don't pad your paper. Don't embellish. Many writing instructors advise their students to avoid repetitive use of the same terminology throughout a single composition. You may have received such advice. The idea is to spice up the composition by using a variety of synonymous or roughly synonymous terms instead of consistently using the same ones. This may well be good advice if what you are writing is a short story or a travelogue or a biographical essay for a scholarship competition. But when you are writing an argumentative essay, you're trying to enlighten, not entertain. So, you should be more concerned about confusing than about boring your reader.

Also, avoid affectation. Don't try to sound like you think an academic scholar should sound. Academic scholarship, you might as well know, often presents a model of how *not* to write. Here, for example, is the winner of last year's "Bad Writing Contest" sponsored by the academic journal *Philosophy & Literature.*

> Indeed dialectical critical realism may be seen under the aspect of Foucauldian strategic reversal—of the unholy trinity of Parmenidean/Platonic/Aristotelean provenance; of the Cartesian-Lockean-Humean-Kantian paradigm, of foundationalisms (in practice, fideistic foundationalisms) and irrationalisms (in practice, capricious exercises of the will-to-power or some other ideologically and/or psycho-somatically buried source) new and old alike; of the primordial failing of western philosophy, ontological monovalence, and its close ally, the epistemic fallacy with its ontic dual; of the analytic problematic laid down by Plato, which Hegel served only to replicate in his actualist monovalent analytic reinstatement in transfigurative reconciling dialectical connection, while in his hubristic claims for absolute idealism he inaugurated the Comtean, Kierkegaardian and Nietzschean eclipses of reason, replicating the fundaments of positivism through its transmutation route to the superidealism of a Baudrillard.[6]

Is this what you want to sound like? God help us! Keep it simple. Be direct. Get straight to your point.

CRITICAL THINKING TIP 13.3

As you write, and especially as you revise, ask yourself: "What exactly is my point in this sentence (or paragraph)?" Then ask yourself, "Can I make my point clear in half the words?" Cut out anything that is not absolutely necessary to making the point clear.

RHETORIC

Rhetoric is the classical discipline devoted to the general study of expressive discourse. Indeed, the word *rhetoric* derives ultimately from the Greek for "I say." Classical rhetoric classifies all kinds of writing into four categories: narrative (storytelling), descriptive (using words to create mental imagery), expository (the presentation or explication of information), and finally, persuasive (using words to change other people's minds). Arguments and argumentative essays fall into this last category, which as it turns out has gotten the most attention among the four categories. The main traditional concern of rhetoric as an academic discipline has been the development and systematic refinement of skills, techniques, and strategies of persuasion—strategies like rhythmic repetition, alliteration, presenting ideas and examples in groups of three, and so on.

Historically, rhetoric's traditional emphasis on persuasion arose in ancient Greece. In the developing political context of the city-states, citizens found it increasingly important to learn how to make effective and persuasive presentations in the assemblies and law courts, the principal institutions of self-government, where the laws were made and interpreted. So there is a deep historical connection between rhetoric and argument. Argument design is part of rhetoric understood as the general art of persuasion. And argumentative essays, though they may employ narrative, descriptive, and expository discourse as well, fall into the persuasive category. However, rhetoric is broader than argument and encompasses more than argument design because persuasion is a broader category than *rational* persuasion. There are other ways to be persuasive than by appeal to reason. So the question arises when we come to the presentation of the argument, "Should we (and if so, *how* should we) use persuasive strategies and rhetorical devices other than the argument itself in our composition?" Answer: By all means sweeten the presentation as best you can. But remember that the main persuasive tool in the composition should be the argument itself. Don't let the rhetorical sweeteners be a substitute for a good argument. In the absence of a good argument, all rhetoric is "empty."

EXAMPLES

Well-placed and well-chosen examples will do more to enhance your presentation and strengthen your argument than just about anything else we can think of. Examples assist the reader to grasp difficult and unfamiliar material. Examples also lend support to points that the reader may be inclined to question. In addition, many of the ingredients of a good argument—for example, precisely defined terms and concepts and rigorous logic—tend to make the argument "abstract." Examples help keep it "real." Examples can also be colorful, juicy, spicy, entertaining. They provide an excellent opportunity to liven up a composition. So, make good use of examples, but just as with the rhetorical sweeteners, make sure the examples *serve*—rather than distract from—the argument.

REVISIONS

Real writers revise, and revise, and revise again. Real writers are constantly reviewing and revising—taking the composition apart and reorganizing it, inserting and deleting, making small improvements here and there—because they *care* how the composition comes out. Some of us can't even stop revising after we're finished. So, take a cue from the best writers, and revise your work. Start early, so you have time to revise. Writing is at least as much a process of *discovering what one thinks* as it is a matter of composing the results of prior thinking. The essay is not merely a format for the presentation of the results of your deliberations, a sort of literary Jell-O mold into which you pour your thoughts when they're finished and ready to go to market. The activity of organizing and composing the essay is—or can and should be—an integral part of those very deliberations, an integral part of the process of rationally making up your mind.[7] Sometimes in the course of outlining (or drafting or revising) you may find your argument taking you in unplanned and unanticipated directions, suggesting maybe a different approach or even a different thesis than the one you originally undertook to defend. If this happens, it is not necessary to resist. Perhaps what is happening is that you are discovering things about the argument and the issue that are important. Let your reasoning take you where it wants to go. There's nothing wrong with adjusting your thesis in accordance with the best reasoning you find yourself able to develop. Use the insights you gain through this process of working out your argument to revise your thesis statement. We recommend working with a partner or in a small study group. Have someone else read your draft and offer criticisms. Have someone else read your draft aloud to you. This may help you to detach from your draft enough to hear areas where there may be room or a need for improvement.

We could go on, we suppose, but what is most essential to your learning now is practice. So, we think it is time to wish you the best of luck and let you get to work.

EXERCISE 13.6 | Your Argumentative Essay

Based on your issue statement as revised in Exercise 13.3, your thesis statement in Exercise 13.4, and your outline from Exercise 13.5, now draft an argumentative essay. Try to make your case in (say) 1,500 words (5–6 pages).

ADDITIONAL EXERCISES

■ **EXERCISE 13.7**   When you have worked out your position and your argument for it at the length prescribed in Exercise 13.6 or by your instructor, try condensing it. Try to compose it as a letter to the editor. Consult the "opinion pages" of your local newspaper for guidance as to length and format.

■ **EXERCISE 13.8**   When you have worked out your position and your argument for it at the length prescribed in Exercise 13.6 or by your instructor, try condensing it for oral presentation. Reduce it to a set of notes from which to speak publicly. Try your speech before a mirror, or better yet, a video camera.

GLOSSARY

articulation   as applied to the analysis of complex issues, refers to framing, focusing, and organizing the inquiry
balance   as applied to an issue statement, not prejudiced either in favor of or against any of the positions that a reasonable person might be inclined to hold about the issue

framing   as applied to the analysis of complex issues, determining what will be considered within and outside the scope of discussion

focusing   as applied to the analysis of complex issues, determining what will be considered central and/or peripheral within the scope of discussion

rhetoric   classical discipline devoted to the general study of expressive discourse; currently, the art or science of persuasion by stylistic and expressive means

thesis   from Greek, proposed idea; in the discipline of writing, the main idea of an essay or longer composition; the conclusion of an argument

ENDNOTES

[1] On January 16, 2001, during the first wave of "rolling blackouts," while the State Assembly was in session, 37-year-old parolee Mike Bowers drove his 18-wheeler at 70 mph smack into the south entry to the State Capitol Building in Sacramento, where it burst into flames. In the post–September 11th environment, this might have looked an awful lot like a suicide bombing and an act of terrorism. No one knows what Bowers's motives were. He died in the fiery crash.

[2] It is most impressive to see someone present a good argument without any apparent "script" to follow. But we should be clear that in nearly every case, this ability to think critically "on one's feet," so to speak, results from the same sort of sustained investment of effort that goes into a well-developed argumentative essay.

[3] Ben Bagdikian, "Lords of the Global Village," *The Nation*, June 12, 1989.

[4] This list is derived from a Web page developed by our reference librarians at Santa Rosa Junior College.

[5] We recommend Michael Harvey's *The Nuts and Bolts of College Writing* (Chicago: Hackett Publishing, 2003); and the associated Web site: http://www.nutsandboltsguide.com

[6] From Roy Bhaskar's *Plato etc: The Problems of Philosophy and Their Resolution* (London: Verso, 1994).

[7] See V. A. Howard and J. H. Barton, *Thinking on Paper* (New York: Wm. Morrow, 1986).

INDEX